THE GALLANT HOOD

The Gallant Hood

By JOHN P. DYER

SMITHMARK

This edition published in 1995 by SMITHMARK Publishers,
a division of U.S. Media Holdings, Inc., 16 East 32nd Street,
New York, NY 10016.

SMITHMARK books are available for bulk purchase for sales
promotion and premium use. For details write or call the
manager of special sales, SMITHMARK Publishers, Inc.,
16 East 32nd Street, New York, NY 10016; (212) 532-6600.

This edition published by special arrangement
with W. S. Konecky Associates, Inc., 156 Fifth Avenue,
New York, NY 10016.

ISBN: 0-8317-3285-7

Printed in the United States of America

10 9 8 7 6 5 4 3 2

To FRANK LAWRENCE OWSLEY

CONTENTS

LIST OF MAPS

THE GALLANT HOOD

CHAPTER I

But Not from Texas

On a dreary, cold, rainy night in late December 1864, a gaunt emaciated figure in the uniform of a full Confederate general slumped wearily on the camp chair in his tent pitched for the night by the side of a road near Nashville. His left arm dangled almost useless at his side. It had been that way since Gettysburg. His right leg was hardly a stump. The rest of it had been buried on the field at Chickamauga. His head was bowed in grief and despair, and great tears ran down his long face into his flowing beard.[1] John Bell Hood was drinking his bitter agonizing cup of defeat and humiliation. This was the end for him and his army.

That afternoon one of his officers had seen him make pitiful efforts to control the mob of men stumbling over each other in their efforts to make more speed. But no one paid any attention to the tall crippled man who was having such difficulty handling his crutches and the reins of his horse at the same time.[2] The troops flowed on past him. Many of the men were barefoot. The rain turned the roads into slushy, freezing quagmires. Wagon trains, caissons, cavalry and infantry were all blended in inextricable confusion.[3] This mob which had once been a valiant army was now obsessed with only one thought—to get out of Tennessee as fast as it could.

But it had not always been so with Hood. Under Lee he was a "blond young giant of fine military mien."[4] At Gaines's Mill he had been superb, leading his Texas brigade in relentless charges that opened a gaping hole through which the rest of Lee's army rushed to victory—Lee's first important victory. This brought Hood's name to everyone's lips. And then there were Sharpsburg and Gettysburg and more fame as a brilliant and fearless combat officer. Between campaigns and battles he had been the toast of Richmond where hostesses considered their parties successful if the tall handsome cavalier attended. Choice food in the midst of increasing scarcity in Richmond was his, and charming women found him fascinating. After Chickamauga he had returned to Richmond to recuperate from the loss of his leg and now even more he was the idol of capital society. He became a confidant of the President that winter of 1863, attending his receptions, calling on the family and on fine winter days driving with Mr. Davis in his carriage.

But all that was before he took over, in July 1864, the army commanded by General Joseph E. Johnston at Atlanta, thus setting into motion a series of events which led up to the abortive Tennessee campaign. As he sat in his tent on this December night and listened to the drumming of the rain on his canvas roof he must have remembered those halcyon days in Richmond. He must also have remembered that there were many who questioned President Davis' wisdom in replacing Joe Johnston with the impetuous crippled young lieutenant general. Even General Lee, who so greatly admired Hood, had been doubtful, and Hardee and other officers had been emphatic in their opposition. But Davis had appointed him anyway—and now this disaster was the result.

Nor had this army always been the shambles it was now. The mob retreating from Nashville was the ghost of the butternut-clad army that swarmed up out of the mists at Shiloh that April morning in 1862 and struck with such ferocity that it drove the Yankees cowering to the protective banks of the Tennessee. It bathed its wounds at Bloody Pond and then saw night and death snatch victory from its perch on her banners. This was the army whose dried blood starched Kentucky's earth at Perryville and which again slaked its thirst with gall as it retreated from another defeat in victory. It had followed the inept leadership of Braxton Bragg through Stone's River to Chattanooga and beyond; and there on the banks of Chickamauga Creek it turned like a wounded animal and struck the pursuer an almost fatal blow. Like a tired fighter it had sparred and feinted and backpedaled from Chickamauga to Atlanta under Joe Johnston. Then under Hood it had found the strength for one vicious but ineffective counterpunch. This was the army of which a Northern general is reported to have said: "I doubt if any soldiers in the world ever needed so much cumulative evidence to convince them that they were beaten."[5] This was the Army of Tennessee.

And now just before Christmas in 1864 it was retreating again— its last retreat. A few weeks earlier, led by Hood, it had pushed ahead from Georgia over these same Tennessee roads and turn- pikes to strike Sherman's base at Nashville and perhaps push on to the Ohio. But the really decisive action had come at Franklin before the army even reached the main objective. Strapped in the saddle astride his favorite roan "Jeff Davis," Hood led his Army of Tennessee into battle, and when the smoke cleared away on that fateful November 30, 1864, the Confederates counted their losses. On the Franklin battlefield burial details counted nearly 6,000 bodies of men, roughly 20 per cent of the army, dead or seriously wounded. On the porch of the McGavock House near the battlefield five Confederate generals were lying dead. Six other Southern generals were wounded and one was captured.

But the aggressive, indomitable and, by many standards, reck- less Hood had pushed on toward Nashville where on December 15 and 16 the Confederates dashed themselves to pieces against "The Rock of Chickamauga" on the thawing slopes around the city. General Thomas, Hood's instructor at West Point, had taught his pupil a costly lesson in tactics. And as Hood's men splashed their way southward through the freezing sucking mud they were treading the death march of the Confederacy which had been, like Hood, lusty and full of the certainty of victory in its youth. Now it could only await the end—wait until Grant's constrictor finished the job in the wilderness.

But Hood's men were not completely dispirited, for as they marched they were able to raise a tune. The tune was "The Yellow Rose of Texas," but the words were a parody:

> And now I'm going southward
> For my heart is full of woe,
> I'm going back to Georgia
> To find my Uncle Joe.
> You may sing about your dearest maid
> And sing of Rosalie,
> But the gallant Hood of Texas
> Played hell in Tennessee.[6]

Hood, indeed, had played hell in Tennessee, but the song was incorrect in one respect: Hood was not a Texan. He commanded Texas troops in the Civil War, he served in the 2nd U. S. Cavalry in Texas, he loved the pioneer spirit of Texas and, in turn, was greatly loved by Texans.[7] In his whole life, however, he never spent more than a comparatively brief period in the state, and that as a soldier. Hood was a Kentuckian, the descendant of forebears whose roots were as firmly set in Kentucky's soil as were those of the bluegrass. The formative years of his life were spent in Kentucky, where reports indicate that he courted Bluegrass beauties, drank occasionally of Bourbon County's famous product, gambled a little now and then and in company with other gay young blades raced his horse up and down the rolling hills and country roads of Montgomery County. The story of his family is almost the story of the founding of Kentucky. It is a chapter in the history of the westward movement of land-hungry pioneers from Virginia who during and just after the Revolution moved to the frontier, took up land, fought the Indians and fanned out from Boonesborough to create a state.

This family history is a part of that story:

On the thirtieth day of November in the year of our Lord 1770 Lucas "Luke" Hood of Frederick County, Virginia, "being sick and weak in body," made a will. The next May he was dead, leaving to his wife and seven children his meager estate. To his son Luke Hood he gave the sum of "four pounds Pennsylvania money."[8]

Just what happened to Luke Hood and his four pounds during the next few years is not completely clear. He apparently served in the Revolution, as did his two brothers Andrew and Thomas.[9] It is recorded that he had moved to Pennsylvania in 1774 and that ten years later he and his wife, Frances, moved to Kentucky along with other families who were traveling the Wilderness Road through Cumberland Gap.[10] In 1783 there were 12,000 of these pioneers in Kentucky. By the spring of 1784 when Luke Hood and his wife arrived their number was 30,000.[11]

Luke and his wife settled in what was then Lincoln County, Kentucky.[12] But it would be a mistake to assume that he "settled down" on the frontier. He took up no land as did his brother Thomas, who received 400 acres for his three years of service as a sergeant in the Virginia Line.[13] Luke apparently was a restless adventuresome individual who preferred fighting Indians to cultivating the soil and amassing land, although the latter was an easy matter on the frontier. So, it appears, he became a sort of lesser known Simon Kenton. Peace with the British Government had not meant peace with the Indians nor with British agents in America. If anything the savages were, after Yorktown, more seriously alarmed than ever, and British agents missed no opportunity to incite them against the border settlements. They were in a state of almost constant warfare, and wherever there was Indian fighting Luke Hood was apt to show up. He was among the Kentucky militia which accompanied General Harmar on his ill-fated expedition against the Indians under Little Turtle on the upper reaches of the Miami River in 1790. Three years later he was serving as a spy and scout for Mad Anthony Wayne and participated in the battle of August 21, 1794, commonly known as "Fallen Timbers."[14] It is recorded that he was scalped on one of these expeditions and left for dead.[15] Perhaps this scalping is responsible for the fact that in his old age he had "spells," and when one came on he was likely to line up the children in the neighborhood and march and countermarch them while he shouted orders at the top of his voice.[16]

But Luke Hood did come home between scouting expeditions and Indian battles each year long enough to plant and harvest a small crop and beget three sons—Andrew, William and finally John, born on January 1, 1798.[17] Three sons and not a soldier among them! It would be interesting to know what the old Indian fighter thought of all his sons becoming doctors and rolling pills instead of molding bullets. He could not know that his own wild free nature would skip a generation and then reappear in his grandson, John Bell Hood, and that this grandson would also fight Indians but on a new frontier far to the west of Kentucky.

Before Luke Hood had migrated to Virginia, Daniel Boone had started work on a fort called Boonesborough on the banks of the Kentucky River. Associated with him in the endeavor was Richard Callaway, a Virginian almost as well known as Boone himself. Callaway had fought under young Colonel George Washington in the French and Indian War in which both men caught a vision of the great west and its vast wealth in land. Pursuing this vision, Callaway became a land promoter, colonel of Virginia Militia, and finally in 1779 joined with Boone in building the fort and town of Boonesborough.[18] Here Colonel Callaway and his family experienced the traditional dangers and hardships of frontier life. Two of his daughters and a daughter of Daniel Boone were captured by the Indians and held for three days before a rescue party from the fort headed by Boone saved them. One of his sons was stolen from a watermelon patch and held by the Indians for several years. Finally in 1780 the Colonel himself met his fate. While he was supervising the construction of a ferryboat about a mile from the fort the working party was ambushed, Colonel Callaway was scalped and his body horribly mutilated.[19]

Colonel Callaway's daughters did not return to Virginia after their father's death, however. There were too many unmarried young frontiersmen about for that; and in the wilderness even more than in civilization a man needed a woman to make him a home, sew his clothes, cook his victuals and bear him children. All the Callaway girls married in the fort, the ceremonies being performed by Squire Boone, Daniel's younger brother, who was, among other things, an itinerant Baptist minister. The youngest of the Callaway daughters was Keziah, who in 1782 married a young soldier, James French, who had fought in the Revolution and who brought with him to Kentucky references from William and Mary College declaring him to be a surveyor. Soon he was appointed surveyor of Madison County by Patrick Henry.[20] In addition to surveying other people's land he managed to secure for himself a grant of 225,000 acres of mountain land for which he paid $40.16 and three mills. Later he bought in at a tax sale the 600-acre Bluegrass farm of famed Indian fighter Simon Kenton for $2.46.[21] When the Kenton place was purchased James and Keziah French moved to it and built a home.

It was here in Clark County that the Hood and French lines converged, for John W. Hood, the young medical-student son of old Luke Hood, fell in love with and married Theodosia French, granddaughter of Colonel Callaway and daughter of James and Keziah French. And with the marriage there apparently was a decision made by the Hood brothers. Evidently they felt that three doctors by the name of Hood were too many for the little town of Winchester, Kentucky, so in 1823 John W. Hood and his bride moved to Owingsville in Bath County some twenty-five miles away.[22] In February 1825, he and his wife purchased a home on main street and in August of the same year they bought four adjoining lots. In May of 1827 another lot was acquired.[23]

It would be natural to assume that the purchase of a home meant permanency for the budding young doctor and his wife, but such was not the case. In 1828 he sold his home and prepared to go to medical school in Philadelphia to pursue the ruling passion of his life, the study, practice and teaching of medicine.[24] This was to be the first of many long and difficult trips across the mountains to the City of Brotherly Love. Leaving his wife and children—James, Olivia and William—behind, he entered the University of Pennsylvania's School of Medicine for the year 1829-1830.[25] After that year he apparently returned to Owingsville to build up a practice and to save enough money so that he might finish his medical education.

On June 29, 1831, there was another mouth to feed in the home of the struggling and sickly young doctor, for a baby boy was born that day and they named him John Bell. Perhaps the arrival of another baby at this particular time delayed the young doctor's return to medical school, or perhaps it was the state of his health or lack of funds or a combination of all three. At all events he did not return to Pennsylvania until 1834 when he again enrolled in the School of Medicine.[26] This time he registered as "John W. Hood, M.D.," although it is not clear just how he merited the title unless like so many doctors of his day he merely assumed it after a certain amount of study under other doctors and after a certain amount of experience. During this same year of 1834-1835

Hood also enrolled in Jefferson Medical College as a "visitor."[27]

It appears that shortly after his return from this year of study he and his family moved from Owingsville to Montgomery County near Mt. Sterling, which place was to be their home until his death.[28] Mrs. Hood's father died in 1835 leaving the Bluegrass farm to his son Richard. Before his death, however, he had deeded the 225,000 acres of mountain land to Theodosia Hood.[29] In his will he left her an additional bequest of $700 in cash.[30] Apparently this money went for the purchase of the Hood home immediately adjacent to the Kenton-French farm. It was, and with minor modifications still is today, a substantial but not pretentious thick-walled square brick house with fine old random-width floors, high ceilings, gracefully paneled doors and cavernous fireplaces. Situated as it is on a knoll it looks away in every direction to rolling acres of bluegrass as fine as Kentucky affords. The great sugar trees in front and the orchard in the rear during the years when the Hoods lived there added greatly to the quiet beauty of the place.[31]

In the Kentucky tradition Dr. Hood acquired land. Beginning in 1841 and continuing for almost as long as he lived he bought land on Somerset Creek which meandered over limestone rocks down the valley between the Hood home and the French farm. Along with the land he bought slaves to work it.[32] His largest single land purchase and perhaps the one which afforded him the greatest satisfaction was in 1844 when he bought 210 acres of the old French home place from his brother-in-law. Other purchases recorded indicate that he finally came to own well over 600 acres.[33]

This then was young John Bell Hood's heritage and environment: a background of hardy pioneers who fought Redcoats and Indians, bought land and slaves, raised crops and families, prospered and worshiped God in the Baptist manner at old Lulbegrud Church. There was no insecurity in the Hood home, for there was always the rich Kentucky soil which at harvesttime yielded most of the things necessary for a good life. Young Hood as a boy never knew poverty. As a matter of fact it seems quite probable that he had too much money and too much freedom for his own good. He acquired in his home a taste for good living which followed him all the days of his life. Even on the battle-field he carried a silver cup presented to him by the ladies of Rich-mond, and when his tent was pitched it was his own fine china and silver which was laid out on the camp table.[34]

Although Dr. Hood apparently was never in the best of health his portraits show him to have been tall and well built. His clean-shaved face showed clearly the features so evident in all the male Hoods—long oval faces, high foreheads and prominent eyes. John Bell Hood inherited to a remarkable degree his father's physical features and his grandfather Hood's temperament. Theodosia Hood apparently was a plump little woman of great vitality much given to piety and good works. Although Dr. Hood was a Presbyterian, she brought up her children in the Baptist faith.[35] That is, all except John Bell. He was a nonconformist.[36]

Although the Hood home was not one of great wealth, it is obvious that Dr. Hood was in a position to give his children many advantages; but it must have been a disappointment for him to see how his sons responded. William evidently was an amiable and unambitious fellow who shuffled through life making a lot of friends and little money. James "Jeems" apparently spent most of his life looking for the legendary Swift Silver Mine and doing a little preaching on the side.[37] John, the youngest son, was considered a wild youngster who would come to no good end. Just what his wildness consisted of is not completely clear except that like many other young men of the Bluegrass he gambled and drank a little and courted the girls incessantly and assidu-ously. There is evidence that many of his escapades consisted more of exhibitionism than wickedness. Having acquired a reputation as a bad boy, he apparently felt compelled to live up to it. "Other boys don't lead me into trouble," he reportedly boasted to an elderly aunt. "I lead them."[38]

Stories of young Hood's prowess with the girls float around through the somber Kentucky hills like the ghosts of chuckling satyrs, and as far as the historian is concerned are just as evasive. There is one story about Hood's love for the vivacious Sally Blythe. Then there is the recently revived story of his tragic affair with Anne Mitchell, a story partly fact, mostly legend, with as many versions as there are storytellers in the hills. The beautiful and wistful Anne and young Hood were in love when he went away to West Point, the story goes. When he returned on his first furlough from the academy in the summer of 1851 they found their love still strong. Quietly they made their plans to elope, but when the evening appointed for the elopement came Anne's father intervened, broke it up and later persuaded her to marry an older and more settled man.[39]

Most of the alleged details of the Anne Mitchell story probably are the products of vivid imaginations which over the years have distorted a youthful love affair out of all proportion to its real importance, but whether it be truth or legend it does fit in with Hood's characteristics. Even as an adolescent he apparently loved the pursuit of women, and this pastime he never forsook until his marriage after the Civil War. It appears that charming women were as necessary to him as food and drink. And obviously women found him fascinating. They admired him because he was a splendid physical specimen—six feet two inches tall, broad shoulders, narrow hips, blondish auburn hair with a provocative off-color cowlick. They liked his shy deferential manner, his long lean face and his great sad eyes which made him resemble nothing so much as a dejected and melancholy young blood-hound. But, perhaps, most of all, women were drawn to him because they sensed his admiration for women and his love of their companionship.[40]

Perhaps young Hood might have been a different boy if he had had the constant companionship and supervision of his father. But he didn't. The children were left alone with their mother about eight months each year during the middle and late 1840's while Dr. Hood was away teaching his own special formula for curing ailments. Each fall he rode away to Philadelphia and each spring he returned to resume his local practice and to supervise planting. About all the supervision he could give the boys was to see to it that a careful record of their spending was kept and to get them out of debt annually.[41]

In his memoirs General Hood states that his father was teaching in a medical college in Philadelphia, but the facts considerably alter the meaning of the term "medical college." The records show that he was not a member of the faculty of any of the organized medical schools of that day in Philadelphia.[42] But he was in Philadelphia teaching his own theory of medicine and quarreling with the medical profession there. In 1848 he climaxed his teaching career by publishing *Principles and Practice of Medicine,* a book which advocated certain principles his associates could not accept. Briefly the theory which he advocated was that many, if not most, of the ailments of humanity were due to an "error loci of the abdominal viscera." Their being forced from their natural positions, Dr. Hood wrote, brought on fevers, constipation, uterine disturbances, biliousness and many other aches and pains. Obviously, then, if these visceral organs could be put back into their proper places and kept there, much illness and suffering could be alleviated. With this in mind he devised, patented and offered for sale a series of abdominal supporters to hold the various organs in their natural positions.[43]

Almost immediately he was attacked by Dr. Arthur V. Meigs in his book *Females and Their Diseases* on the grounds that Dr. Hood's anatomical observations were faulty.[44] Hood replied with a scathing pamphlet entitled *A Review of Females and*

Their Diseases with an Essay on Displacement of the Uterus.[45]
In it he pulled no punches in declaring Dr. Meigs frightfully out
of date and in error on his anatomy. Then *The American Journal
of the Medical Sciences* joined in the fight by openly stating what
obviously many of the doctors felt. There were many, it was
said, who thought that "the essays of Dr. Hood have been written,
and his theory of disease invented, solely for the purpose of recommending certain mechanical instruments of support which he has
invented, and of which he would fain dispose."[46]

But apparently Dr. Hood had gathered about him a considerable body of disciples, and every year new ones came to attend
his lectures on his new theory and on how to fit his trusses and
supporters properly.[47] This apparently was the "medical college"
referred to in his son's memoirs. But the project appears to have
been profitable, for this was the period when he was buying land
on every side of him in Kentucky. And when he finished his
work in Philadelphia or poor health prevented the annual treks
across the mountains he established a small medical school of his
own in his Kentucky home and there no doubt continued to
advocate the use of his trusses to the young men who came to
study under him and to dissect cadavers in the orchard behind
the house.[48]

Meantime young John B. Hood was growing up. He was seventeen the year his father was jousting with the medical profession
in Philadelphia, an age when preparation for the future had to
be considered. He had attended a "subscription" school just across
the line in Clark County and had finished what might be considered the rudiments of a high-school education.[49] He was ready
for the next step. But what?

According to his own statement his father wished him to study
medicine and even offered the inducement of study in Europe.[50]
But young Hood apparently had other ideas. He wanted to be a
soldier and to seek adventure. He had heard too many stories of

Daniel Boone and Luke Hood and Colonel Callaway and of James French at Valley Forge to settle down to the life of a country doctor. He had inherited too much of Luke Hood's temperament for this. Besides, young Hood probably argued, an appointment to the military academy would be easy since his uncle, Judge Richard French, was then a member of the National House of Representatives from the Ninth District of Kentucky.

The young man won. The appointment was made on February 27, 1849, to be effective July 1, 1849. Hood signed his acceptance of the appointment with a great flourish of curves and curlicues and then dated it March 9, *1848,* instead of March 9, 1849.[51] But this was characteristic of Hood. As Lee and Longstreet and, above all, his fellow officers in the Army of Tennessee could testify in later years, Hood was a master of dramatic flourish but often was careless about details.

As the prospective young cadet left home to report to the academy his father's parting injunction is reported as: "If you can't behave, don't come home. Go to the nearest gatepost and butt your brains out."[52]

Ahead were days when men would curse him and wish he had done the latter.

CHAPTER II

The Making of a Soldier

WHEN Hood entered the military academy in the Fourth Class on July 1, 1849, he found out what the upperclassmen already knew: From the standpoint of the physical plant West Point left much to be desired. The scattered stone buildings on the plain overlooking the Hudson were austere and forbidding, almost prisonlike. The barracks were drafty and uncomfortable. The mess hall was condemned as unfit for occupation, and the food served there was considered very bad by the cadets. The small hospital was inadequate, and in the library the books had never been catalogued. The riding hall was dilapidated and most of the horses were ready for a glue factory.[1] Only the chapel, the academy and the ordnance and artillery laboratories were adequate.

Spartan simplicity was the keynote of cadet life. No cadet could receive money or supplies from his parents or anyone else on the outside. There could be no cooking in the barracks; and no tobacco or playing cards were permitted. Church attendance was compulsory. No visiting from room to room was allowed during study hours or between tattoo and reveille.[2] Life was circumscribed by the constant monotony of close confinement to the post and by incessant drilling and daily inspections. Student recreational activities were limited. Organized sports in anything like their present form were unknown. There were, however, band concerts, debating societies, the lyceum, ice skating in the winter and, above all, bull sessions after tattoo and visits to Benny Havens' Tavern.[3]

Both the nocturnal visiting and the trips to Benny Havens' were, of course, strictly forbidden. However, the records of demerits, courts-martial and other disciplinary measures invoked against cadets show how many violations there were. In reading Post Orders for the period 1849-1853 while Hood was there it seems that almost all the serious punishment was dealt out either for absence from rooms after tattoo or for being absent without leave at Benny Havens'. In fact this purveyor of forbidden food and liquor became almost a legend among graduates, and inspired at least one drinking song. In after years when there were reunions someone was likely to start a song to the tune of "The Wearing of the Green" which started thus:

> Come, fill your glasses, fellows, and stand
>   up in a row,
> To singing sentimentally we're going
>   for to go;
> In the Army there's sobriety, promotion's
>   very slow,
> So we'll sing our reminiscences of
>   Benny Havens, oh!
> Oh! Benny Havens, oh! Oh! Benny
>   Havens, oh!
> We'll sing our reminiscences of
>   Benny Havens, oh![4]

But if student life was simple and severe the uniform assuredly wasn't. Regulations prescribed a gray single-breasted coat with tails, gilt buttons and standing collar trimmed with black silk lace. The gray single-breasted vest likewise was trimmed with black lace while the gray trousers carried an inch-wide black stripe up the sides. Gloves were white and the overcoat ankle length with a cape reaching two-thirds of the way to the waist.

But the crowning glory was the cap which is described as "black cap, round crown, seven inches high, or more in proportion to the size of the cadet, with a circular visor in front, a diamond shaped yellow plate, black plume eight inches long, leather cockade with a small yellow eagle." For summer the cadet exchanged his gray trousers and vest for white ones.[5]

It is not difficult to imagine how the six-feet-two-inch, 200-pound Hood looked in a uniform which accentuated height even without the cap. With a seven-inch cap plus an eight-inch plume he must have appeared a veritable giant. Perhaps it was the uniform and the austerity of cadet life which somewhat sobered the gay young man from Kentucky. Something certainly did, and one suspects it was this plus the course of study which he encountered. Plebes studied and worked out on the drill field a course in duties of a private soldier, which term was merely a circumlocution. What it really meant was that they drilled till their tongues hung out. In addition, they studied French and mathematics.[6] At the end of Hood's plebe year he had only eighteen demerits which gave him a conduct rank of forty-seventh out of a total of 221 cadets in all classes. However, low grades in his studies pulled his general merit rank down to fifty-second out of his own class of seventy-four.[7]

During his second year he really found out how tough the curriculum could be on boys from the South like himself who had received poor high-school training.[8] Military studies this second year were courses in school of the company and artillery tactics. Academic subjects were French, mathematics, drawing, English, geography and history.[9] When the grades for his class were all in at the end of the year he found he was still in the lower quartile, in a lower position than he had been at the end of his first year. So far as his conduct was concerned, he ranked 109th out of 229 in the corps.[10] He had received sixty-six demerits during the year, but this was not serious since for each year after the first that a cadet was a member of the corps his offenses were made to count more. During this second year he got very casually acquainted with the meager and poorly organized library. On November 16, 1850, he checked out Jane Porter's *Scottish Chiefs*.[11] Apparently this almost satisfied his thirst for reading, for he checked out only one other book during the four years. In the spring of his senior year he took Scott's *Rob Roy* to his room.[12]

His third year showed little change. His military subjects were school of the battalion and artillery. His academic subjects were drawing, natural and experimental philosophy and chemistry. This year he had ninety-four demerits which gave him a rank of 116 out of 224. His academic grades were still low and his general merit rank was forty-first out of fifty-seven in his own class.[13] One looks in vain, however, for evidence to support his reputation as a wild youth. About the worst which can be said is that he was "a jolly good fellow a little discouraged at first by unexpected hard work."[14] * The fact that he was promoted to color sergeant in April 1852 attests his general good behavior.[15] As a matter of fact, Hood's delinquency record shows him to be just what he was: a careless and thoughtless young man whose early training did not prepare him for the minutiae of military regulations. This is clearly shown in the type of offenses recorded against him. There were, for example, demerits for "laughing in ranks," "chewing tobacco," "smoking," "hair not cut," "trifling conduct in the philosophical academy" and "making unnecessary noise and dancing on a piazza." Other offenses included numerous instances of a disorderly room in the barracks, and many descriptions such as the following: "inattentive and talking in the philosophical academy," "late at church," "laughing and inattentive in the ethical academy," "clothes not neat" and "breaking

---

* Lieutenant General John M. Schofield, *Forty-Six Years in the Army,* 14. Copyright, 1897, by The Century Company and quoted by permission of Appleton-Century-Crofts, Inc.

ranks prematurely." But one offense stands out above them all. He was guilty of lese majesty. He "visited the commandant's tent with a segar in his hat."[16]

In his senior year, however, the blow fell. Academically there was little change in his position, near the foot of his class, but he earned 196 demerits, four less than the number required for expulsion.[17] His final year had started auspiciously. On September 1, 1852, Brevet Colonel Robert E. Lee assumed his position as Superintendent of the Academy, and three weeks later Hood was made a lieutenant of cadets.[18] But it was not long before the new lieutenant was to receive the full force of the new superintendent's determination to tighten up things at the academy and to enforce stricter discipline.[19] On December 21, 1852, orders were posted to the effect that "Cadet Lt. Hood and Cadet Rich [Lucius L. Rich of Missouri] are hereby placed under arrest and confined within Qrs—charge—absent from their quarters on the evening of the 15th inst."[20] On December 28 sentence was pronounced by the superintendent without the formality of a court-martial. "Cadet Hood for absenting himself from his quarters without authority on the evening of the 15th instant, is deprived of his appointment of Lieutenant in the Corps of Cadets."[21] But the cadets had a less polite term for it. Hood had been "busted"— and in addition had been given enough demerits to run his total to 196. One infraction of the rules between Christmas and June would mean expulsion.

Just where the two cadets went is not a matter of record. Colonel Lee was always inclined to forgive and forget anything which might unnecessarily reflect on a cadet. Thus not even his report to the Secretary of War gives any details of the crime.[22] It is almost certain that Cadets Hood and Rich slipped away to Benny Havens' for the evening, but whatever the reason for the absence was, Lee considered it important enough to give Hood a public reprimand in addition to his other punishment. "It is a source of much regret to the Superintendent," he wrote, "that Cadets of long standing and high soldiership, especially those occupying posts of honor in the corps, who are called on to be examples to others, in the discharge of their duty, should themselves be guilty of conduct destructive of that discipline it should be their just pride to uphold."[23]

Hood apparently was greatly depressed over the turn affairs had taken. His grades, particularly in mathematics, were very poor; he had 196 demerits which placed him on very thin ice with respect to expulsion; he had been publicly reprimanded by the superintendent and had been busted to the ranks. Suddenly the pleasures of Kentucky farm life became most attractive to him, and he discussed with Schofield, who also had 196 demerits, whether he should go back to the farm or keep on trying to be an officer.[24] Schofield takes the credit for persuading Hood to remain at the academy, but one wonders if his father's admonition, "If you can't behave yourself, don't come home," didn't have something to do with his decision to stick it out at the academy. At least he did remain and "fought his way manfully to the end."[25] *

This probably was Hood's first personal contact with Lee, but far from the last. Before long they would be riding stirrup to stirrup across the plains of Texas as fellow officers in the 2nd U. S. Cavalry. And not far away were Gaines's Mill and Sharpsburg and Gettysburg where Hood would superbly lead his Texas brigade in Lee's army. In the corps were other cadets destined for distinction in the impending conflict. In Hood's own class of 1853 were, among others, James B. McPherson, John M. Schofield and Philip H. Sheridan, who had been set back a year for fighting at the academy. In the class ahead of Hood were Oliver O.

---

* Lieutenant General John M. Schofield, *Forty-Six Years in the Army*, 14. Copyright, 1897, by The Century Company and quoted by permission of Appleton-Century-Crofts, Inc.

Howard, J. E. B. Stuart, John Pegram and Stephen D. Lee. One year behind Hood were Henry W. Slocum, Alexander McD. McCook and George Crook. A dour Virginian named George H. Thomas was instructor of artillery and cavalry. In the not too distant future he would prove himself Hood's nemesis at Nashville. Fitz John Porter was another instructor destined to receive the cold steel of Hood's men. There were, too, cadets who didn't make the grade—among them James McNeill Whistler.

And the possibility, even probability, of war was not lost on the cadets, for the academy did not exist in a vacuum. Sectionalism and threats of disunion were strong. From outside the post, newspapers brought reports of many events connected with slavery and expansion. These years from 1849 to 1853 were critical. By 1850 Calhoun was openly stating that disunion was the only course left to the South. In Mississippi Jefferson Davis was working during the same year for a convention at Nashville to adopt some mode of resistance. In Georgia Alexander H. Stephens gloomily saw no prospect of the Union long continuing, and in New York William H. Seward spoke for a law higher than the Constitution. The compromise of 1850 proved to be but a feeble sectional truce. In 1852 Clay and Webster, its authors, died, and soon there were cries of "Bleeding Kansas" as the truce was undone. In these matters the cadets were vitally interested, and in their debating societies the arguments were vigorous and at times so violent that the societies were discontinued for a time.[26]

It is quite probable that Hood had little time during his senior year to take an active part in any extracurricular activities such as debating societies, for he was having a terrific struggle with his studies. When he graduated in July, 1853, he had an order of general merit of forty-fourth out of fifty-five. The 196 demerits he had acquired gave him a conduct rank of 204th out of 225 in the entire corps. His grades were the worst of his cadet career. In engineering he was forty-fifth out of fifty-five; in ethics his position was fifty-second out of fifty-five; in geology he was forty-sixth; in infantry tactics forty-second; in artillery forty-fifth.[27] As to his proficiency in written English, no better example could be cited than his letter accepting his commission:[28]

MT. STERLING, KENTUCKY
July 18, 1853

SIR:

I received your letter enclosing me a certificate of appointment to the position of Bvt 2nd Lieut U S Army, my age is twenty two years, residence Mount Sterling Kentucky, appointed a cadet July 1st 1849 & born in the State of Kentucky & hereby accept the appointment of the President and have the oath prescribed by law & enclose you the certificate.

I am sir very Respet'ly
your obt servant
JOHN B HOOD
Bvt 2nd Lt 4th Regt Inf

S. Cooper
Adj Genl U S Army
D C (Washington)

But it was signed with a simple plain signature minus all curves and curlicues. Perhaps West Point had knocked some of the flourish out of the young officer. But the academy had not made a docile man of Hood, for cockiness was always one of his greatest assets as a soldier—and, one might add, one of his greatest liabilities.

In August of the same year Hood received his first orders. At the conclusion of his leave he was to report to the commanding officer of the 4th Regiment of Infantry then stationed in California. In November he sailed from New York, going via Panama.[29] It was, of course, a routine peacetime assignment with little probability of much excitement, but to the young officer it undoubtedly was thrilling. He was through learning soldiering out of books. He was realizing his youthful ambition. He was a soldier in the United States Army headed for an army post in fabulous and distant California.

California, however, apparently failed to impress Hood except for two things: the fog and high prices. San Francisco he dismissed as "a small city built upon sand hills and distinguished for its foggy atmosphere." But the high prices of things he found more impressive. When he left his ship in search of a hotel he found the cabman wanted $20.00 in gold for his fare, about one third of a second lieutenant's monthly pay. So, shelving his dignity as an officer and a gentleman, he walked.[30] Doubtless he had other experiences with the effects the gold frenzy and the difficulty of transport were having on prices. If he had cared to rent a room the chances were it could not have been secured for less than a thousand dollars a month. Or if he had been a householder the saleratus for his bread would have cost from $12.00 to $16.00 a pound. Men were spending money recklessly and ostentatiously, or gambling it away at the Bella Union or the El Dorado.[31]

Undoubtedly it was a relief when he reported to his post at Fort Scott in northern California early in February 1854.[32] There was little in the way of excitement at the post, but at least there were congenial fellow officers and, as it developed, a way to beat the high cost of living. Captain U. S. Grant was quartermaster of the post, and among the officers was Lieutenant George Crook, who became Hood's warm friend. Together the officers organized a co-operative mess. Game was plentiful; so was time and ammunition. So the officers hunted, using what game they needed for their mess and selling the balance. "This financial policy worked admirably," Hood wrote in later years. But Hood and Crook went even further. They planted a wheat crop.[33]

Hood had ample opportunity to learn another thing about soldiering in the army in time of peace. In remote posts boredom and inactivity were the real enemies. There was the ceaseless monotonous routine of inspection and guard duty, of patrols, of drill and parade, of tattoo and reveille—and then the next day it was all to do over again. It was the sort of life which drove lonely men like Grant to drink. General Wool had promised Californians to do all he could to protect the frontier settlements from the Indians, and Fort Scott was a partial fulfillment of that promise. There had been outbreaks of hostilities in 1852 and 1853, but 1854 was a quiet year. The Fort Scott detachment of the 4th Infantry did little more than watch the Indians on their recently established reservations.[34] During the entire period of approximately fifteen months which Hood spent here his sole activity outside of routine patrols was commanding a detachment of Dragoons which served as an escort for a surveying expedition in the direction of Salt Lake.[35] Moreover, he was still only a brevet second lieutenant.

But promotion and more active service were just ahead, brought about by conditions in Texas and Wyoming and by the importunity of Jefferson Davis, Secretary of War.

After the Mexican War and the annexation of Texas the United States erected a series of border defenses in the state against the Indians. Soon it was found that there was a close correlation between the number of troops in these forts and the marauding activities of the Comanches, Caddos, Wacos and other tribes. When the forts were adequately garrisoned marauding fell off to almost nothing. When troops were withdrawn and sent to other parts of our far-flung frontier marauding activities greatly increased.[36]

This fact Jefferson Davis had dinned into the ears of a miserly Congress ever since he took office. But it took an incident in far-off Wyoming to drive the lesson home. In the summer of 1854 Indians ambushed a patrol under Lieutenant John L. Grattan near Fort Laramie. Every man in the patrol was killed outright or died later. This gave Davis the ammunition he needed to use on Congress. He pointed out again that an army of 11,000 men and officers could not protect an 8,000-mile frontier, and this time

Congress listened and acted.[37] In March 1855 it authorized two new regiments, one of them being the 2nd Cavalry, "the greatest aggregation of fighting men that ever represented the United States Army in the Old West."[38]

The personnel of the 2nd U. S. Cavalry was hand-picked. Albert Sidney Johnston was colonel. Robert E. Lee was its lieutenant colonel. William J. Hardee and George "Old Slow Trot" Thomas were majors. Earl Van Dorn, George Stoneman and E. Kirby Smith were captains. And at the remote border post of Fort Scott, California, John B. Hood learned that he had been promoted to second lieutenant of cavalry and assigned to duty with the 2nd Regiment.[39]

As soon as he was relieved by his classmate Lieutenant Phil Sheridan, he made preparations to leave. He returned to San Francisco and as soon as passage could be obtained sailed for New York the same way he had come out, via Panama. Just before he sailed he made an acquaintance he would never forget. He dropped in at the corner of Jackson and Montgomery streets and met the manager of the banking firm of Lucas and Turner. His name was William Tecumseh Sherman. He was, Hood recalled in later years, a man possessed of "a piercing eye and nervous impulsive temperament."[40]

In October 1855 Hood reached Jefferson Barracks in St. Louis and reported for duty. Here he received a draft for "about one thousand dollars in gold," his share of the wheat crop he and Crook had planted.[41] So with a thousand dollars in his pocket, no debts and new adventure ahead he probably was in the best of spirits. Certainly he was more solvent than at any other period in his life.

Colonel Albert Sidney Johnston personally led his regiment on the near six-hundred-mile trek southwestward to Texas. From Jefferson Barracks he and his men rode through the Ozarks of Missouri via Springfield into the unorganized Oklahoma Indian territory and thence across the Brazos and Colorado rivers to Fort Mason, passing through, on their way, Fort Belknap and Camp Cooper.[42] Apparently the trip was without incident except for the violent capriciousness of Texas weather which they encountered. Just as they crossed the line a sixty-mile-an-hour "norther" roared out of Oklahoma territory striking down the regiment in its icy fury. The mercury dropped below zero and froze the snow and rain into a six-inch cover of ice. Troopers and horses sought refuge behind a skirt of timber, but there just isn't any defense against a norther. One simply rides it out or succumbs.[43]

This was Hood's introduction to Texas, the state he came to love and adopt as his own. It was the frontier where violence was the order of nature and of man. The weak seldom got to Texas and even if they did the primitive selective processes of the plains winnowed them out and left them to perish. Only the fit survived, and they did because they had great physical stamina and a peculiar ability to bend with the storm but never to break. They withstood the broiling heat of summer and the incredibly fierce "blue northers" of winter. They could prove that Texas had the worst dust and heat, the bitingest fleas and ticks, the coldest winters, the most stubborn and cantankerous longhorns, the most beautiful women, the most fluent cussers, the biggest liars and rattlesnakes and the best men in the whole damn world. As Hood shivered behind the fringe of trees riding out his first norther he was learning the first of many lessons about the Lone Star State, lessons which came back to him a very few years later when he molded his Texas brigade into one of the finest units of the Confederate Army.

The norther having blown itself out, Colonel Johnston moved on into Texas. At the site of Camp Cooper he left Major Hardee and Companies A, E, F and K to lay out the camp and prepare for the arrival of its commander, Lieutenant Colonel Robert E. Lee. With the balance of the regiment Johnston marched a hundred and seventy miles farther south to Fort Mason. Hood, being an officer of Company H, accompanied Johnston to the latter post. Hardly had he time to orient himself, however, before he went on leave back to Kentucky. On March 14, 1856, he left Fort Mason, almost exactly a month before Lee arrived on his way to Camp Cooper.[44]

Hood's return to Kentucky was made necessary by the illness of his father. Dr. Hood had suffered a stroke which incapacitated him and made it impossible for him to look after the farm and continue his practice.[45] Although Hood's brothers, William and James, were near by, it seems that Dr. Hood had come to hold John in greater esteem and to rely more on him, for, after all, he was the only one of the three boys who had really amounted to much. Apparently a family conference was held and a decision made how the estate should be divided and how Dr. and Mrs. Hood were to be cared for. Judge Kenaz Farrow, Dr. Hood's brother-in-law, drew up the document which gave Lieutenant Hood sole power of attorney to sell everything his father owned. The proceeds were to be used to set up a fund which would take care of Dr. and Mrs. Hood as long as they lived, and at their death the balance was to be divided among their heirs, "having a due regard in the division of such estate to the charge book kept against my children."[46]

But Dr. Hood made certain that James, who was still looking for the Swift Silver Mine, should not share in the estate. Three days before he made the disposition given above he secured from his son a document in which he renounced all claim to the estate. In consideration of the fact that his father had made numerous advances and assumed numerous debts "the said J. F. Hood and his wife do hereby sell and convey . . . all the right, title and interest which they have now or may hereafter have to the estate of Theodosia Hood and John W. Hood," the document read.[47]

Hood did not report back to Fort Mason until December 9,

1856.[48] Apparently he never saw his father again, for Dr. Hood died November 30, 1857, and at that time his favorite son was on patrol duty somewhere on the plains.

His assignment on his return to duty was the first of a series which made him a sort of utility man for the 2nd Regiment. Although still carried on the muster rolls as a second lieutenant of Company H, he served only briefly in this capacity. Most of his service was detached duty with other companies. He served with Company E and with Company G and finally came out a first lieutenant commanding Company K. And his posts were as varied as his companies. He served at Fort Mason, Camp Cooper, Camp Colorado, Camp Alamo, Camp Wood and points between.[49]

In January 1857 he reported to Lee at Camp Cooper, an assignment which apparently pleased him very much. He and Lee had not seen each other since their West Point days, and since Hood held Lee in such esteem the "relation and duties were therefore most pleasant. . . ."[50] It was a pleasant relationship rather than an intimate friendship, but apparently they found some things outside the field of soldiering to discuss. Hood is described by a traveler who encountered him on the plains as "a splendid man . . . to look upon, every inch a soldier, and withal most courteous and genial."[51] With Hood's good looks and his known fondness for women, Lee apparently was fearful he might form an attachment for someone unworthy of him, and thus gave him some fatherly advice on marriage in the characteristic Lee manner. "Never marry," he advised, "unless you can do so in a family which will enable your children to feel proud of both sides of the house." On this Hood commented that it was an aristocratic view, but at the same time a correct one and that he was inclined to follow it.[52] As a matter of fact, he did follow it when he finally came to get married in New Orleans after the Civil War was over.

This little sermon of Lee's had been delivered while the two of them were riding across the plains looking for a suitable location for a permanent fort to replace the temporary affair at Camp Cooper. The government at Washington was trying out an olive-branch-and-sword experiment in controlling the Indians—an olive branch for those tribes which would settle on reservations and accept the white man's peace and the sword for those who persisted in their warlike ways. Two reservations had been established in 1855. Surviving members of the Caddo, Anadarko, Ioni, Waco and other smaller tribes were assigned to a reservation at the junction of the Brazos and the Clear Fork of the Brazos. The reservation for the Comanches was on the Clear Fork of the Brazos not far away.[53] In between the two reservations was Camp Cooper which the government planned to convert into a permanent fort.

But it was not the reservation Indians who gave trouble. Hood and his fellow officers spent many dull hours on patrol watching the reservations but never encountered any trouble. It was the marauding bands of nonreservation Indians which terrorized the frontier from the Brazos to the Pecos and Rio Grande. For these there was only one treatment: go out, hunt them down and kill them. This was a matter more easily said than done, however, as Lee soon discovered. On the thirteenth of June, 1856, he left his headquarters with four squadrons to hunt down whatever marauders might be encountered. After spending forty grueling days covering some 1,600 miles of territory he returned to Camp Cooper. The result of the expedition was that he had encountered four Indians. Two had been killed, one had escaped and the fourth, a woman, had been captured.[54]

Hood, however, had better luck in locating the enemy. In June he was transferred back to Fort Mason for duty with Company G. A few weeks later, tiring of the monotony and inactivity, he requested of Major Thomas, then commanding in Johnston's absence, permission to conduct a scouting expedition and raid against the Indians. The request was approved, and on July 5, 1857, Hood

with twenty-five men of Company G, an Indian guide and provisions for thirty days moved out from the fort on a course southwest toward the Staked Plain and the Pecos River. Each man was
armed with a rifle and six-shooter; a few had sabers and two revolvers. Hood himself carried a double-barreled shotgun loaded
with buckshot and two Navy six-shooters. Attached to each saddle
was a canteen, blanket roll and waterproof coat. Pack horses
brought up the rear.[55]

For ten days they rode through the shriveling heat and choking
alkaline dust without encountering a single Indian. Then on the
eleventh day they struck a trail indicating that a party with fifteen
or twenty ponies had recently passed moving toward the Rio
Grande via the headwaters of Devil's River. Like hounds on
the scent Hood and his men quickened their pace, and it was
soon discovered that the trail led across a corner of the Staked
Plain, a desolate desert country whose monotonous shimmering
surface was broken only here and there by giant cacti. On
July 17 they marched forty miles and camped for the night in the
eerie stifling stillness where not even the sound of a bird could be
heard. At dawn they were again in the saddle pushing toward
the border, and that evening they bivouacked in the same heat
and silence. On July 18, fourteen days after leaving Fort Mason,
they resumed the march and raised a deer. As it bounded away
the men cheered, for the presence of animal life meant there was
fresh water somewhere near. They found the pool in midafternoon. It stank so that the men had to hold their breath while
drinking; but it was water, and the men drank long and deep
and then filled their canteens and even the sleeves of their waterproof coats.

Next day several of the horses began to show leg weariness and
general fatigue just as the troop came in sight of the mountains
paralleling Devil's River, the ranges on either side leading like a
bowling alley to the Rio Grande. At the point where the San

Antonio-El Paso stage road crossed Devils River Hood and his Indian guide discovered that another Indian party had joined the original one. From the camp remains they estimated the number at fifty, which taken together with the other group meant that a formidable war party was not far away. Now action seemed imminent and Hood had every man check his guns before bivouac.

But as the march continued the next morning it became apparent that several of the horses could not make it. They were exhausted from the heat and the rough terrain. Their condition and the thirst of the men were such that Hood decided to abandon the pursuit, locate a water hole and give the entire outfit some rest. As he swung away from the trail, however, he saw on a parallel ridge some two miles away Indians waving a large white flag. Raising his arm he halted the troop and pondered the matter. Orders from Washington had been issued before he left Fort Mason notifying all troops in the area that a party of Tonkawas was expected to join the reservation near Camp Cooper, and that they would, in the event they met United States troops, raise a white flag and be allowed to pass unmolested. Were these Indians waving the white flag peaceful Tonkawas or warlike Comanches who had prepared a trap?

There was only one way to find out and Hood took it. Deploying seventeen of his men in line and leaving the other eight with their crippled horses, Hood moved cautiously across the cactus-infested valley toward the waving white flag. When he was within twenty or thirty steps of the Indian holding the white sheet suddenly the whole earth became an inferno of fire and yelling Indians. In the immediate front a sheet of flame thirty feet high shot skyward from heaps of dry grass and weeds. On the right Indians charged down the slope shooting as they ran. On the left a mounted party rode in close enough to hurl their spears with considerable accuracy. It was sudden and devastating hand-to-hand conflict. Hood's men met the charge with a volley from their rifles, and then it was every man for himself with saber and six-shooter. Indians grasped bridles and beat the horses over the head with shields and then went down, screaming when slugs from the six-shooters tore gaping holes in them. They would retire, pass their guns to the squaws for reloading, then re-form and charge again. Hood discharged his shotgun and then rode into the center of the fight, spurring his horse and blazing away with his revolver. From the left an arrow pierced his left hand, pinning it and the bridle rein to his saddle. He broke the shaft and pulled his hand away while he continued the fight.

But such a fight had to be of comparatively short duration. Hood himself could fire but fourteen rounds—those with two revolvers and a rifle a maximum of thirteen rounds. And reloading was out of the question while they were mounted on their frightened rearing horses. So Hood shouted to his men to retire and reload. Falling back about fifty yards, they dismounted and began to reload. As they did so what must have been to them sweet music drifted across the valley. It was the doleful chant of the Comanches mourning their dead, and it meant they had given up the fight. They gathered up their dead and wounded and moved off toward the Rio Grande. Hood and his men breathed a great sigh of relief. They all recognized that they had narrowly escaped annihilation. They had had all the Indian fighting they wanted for one day, so they, too, left the field. That night they bivouacked on Devil's River and sent a messenger to near-by Camp Hudson for supplies and medical aid. Two of Hood's troopers had been left on the field dead and four others besides himself were severely wounded.

Almost exactly eight years previously Hood had entered West Point to learn soldiering, and on this twentieth of July, 1857, he had been in his first fight. He had not won a victory. He had not even succeeded in driving the Indians away permanently, for a few days later they attacked the California mailguard near the spot where they fought him.[56] Nevertheless this fight showed clearly some of the characteristics of Hood the soldier. He was willing to take a chance against overwhelming odds. In combat he was in the forefront leading his men with no regard for his own safety. He was a superb combat officer whom battle transformed from a shy young dandy into a fierce, almost terrible, fighter. Nothing revealed this metamorphosis more than his eyes. Normally sad and faunlike, they blazed in battle with a light that almost frightened his own men.[57] The time was not far away when at Gaines's Mill he would lead his men across a valley and into the murderous fire of another enemy. And this he would repeat at Gettysburg and Franklin and Nashville. His great failure as an officer would come when he was taken from combat duty and given command of an entire army.

Wounds never bothered Hood for long, and in August he was back at Fort Mason engaged in the dull routine of camp life again. On November 17, 1858, he was promoted to first lieutenant of Company K, commanded by Captain Charles J. Whiting, West Pointer, Seminole War veteran and former assistant engineer of the American-Mexican boundary survey of 1849. Company K had its headquarters at Camp Cooper, but Hood did not return there immediately for service. Instead he was assigned to command Camp Colorado located almost exactly halfway between Cooper and Mason. For a brief period he was acting regimental adjutant at Camp Cooper, but for the most part he spent the rest of his period of service in Texas on detached duty. He was at Camp Colorado from June 30, 1859, to August 30, 1859, and at Camp Alamo from August 31, 1859, to October 31, 1859. Meantime Captain Whiting had gone on leave and Hood was called to Camp Cooper in temporary command of Company K. On December 31, 1859, however, he was assigned to the command of Camp Wood and served here until September 1860.[58]

On September 29, 1860, Hood went on leave. He had not been home since his father's death and apparently his presence was much needed on matters pertaining to the estate. When he reached Indianola, Texas, to begin the journey, however, he found orders awaiting him directing him to report to West Point as Chief of Cavalry. Immediately he proceeded to Washington and personally requested Adjutant General Samuel Cooper to rescind the order. In great surprise the bluff old soldier turned to the bronzed young lieutenant and said, "Lieutenant, you surprise me. This is a post and position sought by almost every soldier."

"That is true, sir," Hood replied, "but I fear war will soon be declared between the states, in which event I prefer to be in a situation to act with entire freedom."[59]

Hood's reason was good enough to get the order rescinded, but it hardly seems to be the whole story. Staff duty at West Point would have placed no more restrictions on his choice than would line duty. Hood's full reason probably grew out of his personal dislike for staff duties plus the mounting sentiment among line officers of that day that assignment to staff duty meant burial. Staff promotions were slow and the duties were routine and unexciting. Certainly they never appealed to Hood. Even after he had lost the use of an arm at Gettysburg and had a leg shot away at Chickamauga he refused staff duty. He was a combat officer first, last and always.

As for Hood's belief that war was imminent, great insight was not needed to demonstrate it. During his years of border service the country had been moving frightfully fast toward disunion and war. On October 16, 1859, while Hood was patrolling the area around Camp Alamo, the fanatic John Brown had led his men across the river and seized the Federal arsenal at Harpers Ferry. Colonel Robert E. Lee on leave at Arlington from Camp Cooper had been pressed into service to command a detachment of militia to capture him. John Brown was executed, but throughout the North he became a martyr and a symbol of the avenging hand that must sooner or later wreak justice on the South. The Congress which met in the winter of 1859 was marked by an ominous tone of bitterness which was not unlike the Greeks at the opening of the Peloponnesian War whom Thucydides described as being people who "did not understand each other even though they spoke the same language. Words received a different meaning in different parts." During the summer of 1860 a bitter sectional Presidential campaign engulfed the country and in November 1860 Abraham Lincoln, whose mother and father were born a few miles from Hood's home in Kentucky, was elected. Secession, of course, followed in short order, so when Hood returned to Texas in the early spring of 1861 two rival governments were glaring at each other across the Potomac.

Hood's return to Camp Wood was purely perfunctory, almost a casual visit. He had come to bid his fellow officers good-by and to straighten up his accounts. He found $385.20 charged to him on the company books. Of this amount $116.40 was personal, and two items of $85.20 and $183.60 respectively were amounts paid him in the customary army routine for double rations while he commanded Camp Wood. However, some clerk in the War Department had discovered a rule which stated that in order for a post to be a double-rations post at least two companies must be stationed there. Since Hood had had only a portion of one company at Camp Wood it was ruled that the extra pay must be charged back against him. Hood protested, but the War Department was adamant. Finally he paid the $85.20 item, but the $183.60 was left outstanding. Some effort was made to collect it, but eventually it was dropped.[60] After all there wasn't much point in trying to collect a debt from a man who was now a Confederate officer.

CHAPTER III

The Texas Brigade

Hood tendered his resignation from the United States Army on April 16, 1861. His letter was terse and to the point. "I have the honor to tender the resignation of my commission as 1st Lieutenant 2nd Cavalry U. S. Army—to take effect on this date."[1] That was all. There apparently had been no soul searching as with Lee. Hood's mind obviously had been made up for some time, perhaps as far back as his West Point days when the cadets were fighting out sectional issues in their debating societies. His native state of Kentucky was, of course, officially a loyal state but one sending her sons to both armies. The Bluegrass area around Winchester was, however, more closely identified with the plantation system of Virginia, or even of the lower South, than has been popularly recognized. It was a slaveholding section with a social structure closely resembling that of most of the seceding states. It made a great deal of difference where one lived in Kentucky when it came to taking sides in the war.

The transition from an officer in the United States Army to an officer in the Confederate Army was not entirely uncomplicated. The very day he submitted his resignation from the old army he was in Louisville. The next few days he spent conferring with the Governor and other state officials. What would Kentucky do? Would she secede or remain loyal? Those were the questions to which he could not get a satisfactory answer.[2] A few days later he was in the temporary capital city of Montgomery offering his services not from Kentucky but from Texas which he had decided to adopt.[3] He was commissioned a lieutenant in the Confederate regular army and ordered to report to his old commander, Major General Robert E. Lee, commanding Virginia's troops at Richmond.[4]

All over the South other officers were making the same kind of transition. Sorrowfully Lee had resigned on the twentieth of April. On April 23 a slight bearded young man on duty with the Mounted Rifles in New Mexico sent in his resignation. He was Lieutenant Joseph Wheeler destined to become Chief of Cavalry in the Army of Tennessee. Soon the resignations of other officers were in: Joseph E. Johnston, Albert Sidney Johnston, William J. Hardee, Earl Van Dorn, Kirby Smith, Jeb Stuart, Samuel Cooper, A. P. Hill, James Longstreet, G. T. Beauregard and many others. Three hundred and two graduates of the military academy joined the Southern cause. Of these, eight became full generals, fifty-two major generals and eighty-six brigadier generals.[5] Troops, too, were flocking to the Stars and Bars. The early process was pretty much the same in all the states. A leading citizen would receive a colonel's commission from the governor of his state, and then with the assistance of those who expected to be officers under him would raise a regiment. Uniforms often were improvised and arms were likely to be shotguns, squirrel rifles or any other firearm the citizen soldier might have about the house. As troops they were very warlike but undisciplined and unmilitary during the early months of the war until these West Pointers got through with them. Then they became soldiers—perhaps as good as any the world has ever known.

As Hood was soon to find out, the task of converting these raw troops and political officers into effective military units was no easy task. When he reported to Lee at his office in the Mechanics Institute Building he found that officer busy with a roomful of cobblers getting their instructions on how to make cartridge boxes, haversacks and bayonet scabbards. But he was not too busy to give his former general utility officer of the 2nd Cavalry a warm welcome.

"I am glad to see you," he said, grasping Hood's hand. "I want you to help me."

"I came to Richmond with that object," Hood replied. "What duties do you wish me to perform?"

"Go to Yorktown," was the answer, "and report to Colonel Magruder."

"And when shall I leave?" Hood queried.

Lee turned his head, looked at the clock and with a smile replied, "Before you dine."

It was then eleven o'clock in the morning, and that afternoon Hood was on the train to Yorktown and his first military assignment for the Confederacy.[6]

What he found at Yorktown was almost enough to provoke amusement in a trained officer. Left and right as far as the eye could see were new infantry regiments in line of battle, and in their front "officers delivering stirring warlike appeals to the men." Twenty-five miles away at Fort Monroe were Federal troops under General Benjamin F. Butler, and a report had been circulated that the Yankees were about to attack, though where and how no one seemed to have the foggiest notion. Colonel J. B. Magruder, Hood found on the line of works and immediately he pressed the new lieutenant into service in charge of several batteries then in position. He hadn't even assigned quarters to Hood, so on his first night of active duty with the Confederate Army he sat on his trunk under the stars peering into the darkness looking for the Yankees. Excitement subsided the next day when it was discovered that the enemy was no closer than Fort Monroe.[7] It was a case of the jitters which Hood would learn characterized these new troops and their nonmilitary officers.

Hood had been sent to Magruder "for the purpose of instructing the Cavalry troops."[8] Immediately he got down to his duties as an instructor and as officer in charge of the picket outposts between the Confederate lines and the Federal position at Fort Monroe. But in the midst of his work questions of rank arose. Hood was only a lieutenant and the cavalry companies were commanded by captains. It was an awkward situation which Magruder forthrightly remedied by making Hood a captain. Then the question of the dates of the various captains' commissions arose; and Magruder solved this in the same direct manner. He made Hood a major and left the matter of confirmation up to Richmond.[9] He could now proceed unembarrassed with his instruction and his picketing.

This peaceful picketing, however, came to an abrupt end. On June 10 General Butler sent General Ebenezer W. Peirce with about 4,400 men against the Confederate outpost at Big Bethel Church in the center of the Yorktown Peninsula midway between the Confederate and Federal positions. It was the first battle of the war on the peninsula and ended badly for the Northern troops. It was a case of raw troops attacking raw troops with the defending troops having the advantage of intrenched positions and artillery. The first wave of Federals attacked, but as they did so the 7th New York in the rear became confused and its units began firing on each other. The attacking unit, hearing the firing, concluded the Confederates were in their rear and withdrew. Another attack was planned and then called off when it was discovered that the Federal troops could not be re-formed.[10]

It wasn't much of a battle as battles came to be, but it was the first of the war in Virginia and it was the South's first victory. Thus it was magnified in the South out of all proportion to its real significance.[11] However, it did mark the beginning of more activity, especially for the cavalry.

Hood had not taken part in the affair at Big Bethel, but soon afterward he stirred up a little fight of his own. He determined to capture one of the patrols being sent out almost daily by Butler. Hiding a small body of his cavalry in a swamp between the James and York River roads, he quietly awaited a patrol. For several nights he was disappointed, but finally a scouting party of some seventy-five showed up on the James River Road. Hood held his men in check until the patrol passed and then dashed out for a surprise attack from the rear. He was discovered, however, and the Federals ran into the near-by woods, from which they opened fire. Hood and two of his captains dismounted and, with shot-guns and Sharp's carbines blazing, led their men into the woods. It was like quail shooting in a dense thicket, except in this instance the quail were shooting back. For an hour and a quarter Hood and his men cautiously flushed the enemy one by one until finally the Yankees gave up and rode away to the far side of the woods. The Federals lost two men dead, and one wounded; but, best of all, eleven prisoners were taken and brought back to Yorktown, where they were put on display for the bug-eyed recruits who had never seen a Yankee.[12]

It was a typical Hood attack: he went in with guns blazing and shot it out. On the other hand, it was, of course, an insignificant skirmish; but from the praise heaped on Hood one might think he had won a major engagement. Regarding the affair, Magruder wrote Lee:

I have the pleasure of sending a report from Major Hood, the efficient Commander of the Cavalry of my department, of a brilliant little affair with the enemy. . . . Too much praise cannot be bestowed on Major Hood and the Cavalry generally for their untiring industry in efforts to meet the enemy, and for the energy with which they have discharged their harassing and unusually laborious duties.[13]

Lee obviously was pleased at the conduct of his erstwhile lieutenant and wrote Magruder in reply:

I have the gratification of receiving your letter of the 13th instant, containing Major Hood's report of his brilliant skirmish with the enemy on the 12th instant, and of submitting it to the President. Will you express to Major Hood and the gallant men who were engaged in the affair the pleasure which their conduct has given both myself and the President.[14]

And again Hood was promoted, this time to lieutenant colonel!

The tall, rawboned, brown-haired young officer with the kindly blue eyes, the booming musical voice and the ill-fitting uniform was doing all right.[15] In three months he had been promoted from lieutenant to lieutenant colonel, had received the praise of Magruder and Lee and his work had been called to the attention of the President.

Meantime all sorts of troops had been pouring into Richmond with various equipment, all intent on taking part in the big battle which would destroy the Yankees and end the war. Among them were the Texans.

Most of the Texas troops stayed at home to guard the Rio Grande, afford protection against the Indians and repel an invasion should it come.[16] But not all of them. Some 1,500 young, adventuresome Texas youths went to Virginia in the summer of 1861 looking for a fight with the Yankees. Traveling by twos and threes, they reached Richmond the best way they could. By June twelve companies composing the 1st Regiment had arrived. Their colonel was the bombastic former United States Senator from Texas, the Honorable Louis T. Wigfall. They were not organized in time to participate in First Manassas and were assigned to outpost duty at Dumfries near Cockpit Point on the Potomac about twenty miles south of Alexandria.[17]

Meantime two other regiments had been recruited; but, to the disgust of officers and men alike, the Confederate Government informed them they were not needed, since sufficient troops could be raised in the vicinity of Virginia. This position was abandoned in the summer of 1861, however, and twenty more companies comprising the 4th and 5th regiments began the long journey from the Texas plains to Richmond.[18] One of the conditions laid down by President Davis in accepting the troops was that the Confederate Government would name the officers.[19] When the Texans arrived they were billeted near Richmond, and Davis named two capable young officers to command them. Hood was recalled from Magruder on the peninsula and made colonel of the 4th regiment. The 5th was assigned to Colonel James J. Archer.[20]

However, selecting a colonel for the 4th Texas was one thing and getting this regiment of rambunctious plainsmen to accept him was another. The men had never seen Hood, and doubts were pretty generally entertained that any officer would please them. They were problem soldiers in every sense of the term. One previous attempt had been made to organize them under Colonel Francis T. Allen of Texas, but in consequence of a protest from some of the captains the appointment was withdrawn. This produced a feeling that these troops might as well be sent back home; that they would not be satisfied to subject themselves to discipline. But Hood did the job. "In a few days the feeling was gone and everyone seemed to be perfectly contented. His commanding appearance, manly deportment, quick perception, courteous manners and decision of character readily impressed the officers and men that he was the man to govern them in the camp and command them on the field; and his thorough acquaintance with every department of the service satisfied everyone with his competency for the position."[21]

This rapport which Hood was able to achieve with his men enabled him eventually to develop these recalcitrant individualists into a brigade renowned throughout the army for its morale and its fighting qualities. Hood developed in them a feeling of pride and a fierce joy in doing the impossible. If everyone else had tried to take a position and had failed, call on Hood and his Texans.

If a brigade was needed for a long arduous march, call on Hood's Texans. "The enemy never see the backs of my Texans," Lee boasted. The methods used by Hood in creating this superlative morale of "the most renowned brigade of the entire army"[22] are worth study.

The Texas regiments were a cross section of Texas in the 1860's—farmers, ranchers, adventurers, politicians, ruffians and here and there a trigger-happy gunman. Most of the men bore names such as Marshall and Davis and Henderson and Robertson—good American names from Alabama, Mississippi or Tennessee. But then there was a liberal sprinkling of such names as Elmendorrf and Fralick and Von Hutton and Poupot and Sebastian Domino. There were names, too, right out of a western thriller, names like Dock Cantrell, Jesse Benton, John Ford, Ike Noble and Sim Mathews.[23] They had learned in the rough experience of the frontier to defend themselves. Their confidence, often mistaken for braggadocio, gave them strength of arm and will. In a frontier society which required strength and self-reliance these Texans had developed into men who were self-assertive, individualistic and restless under any sort of restraint. Indeed, Texas "worked a curious alchemy with its citizenry, educated and untutored alike. It took the sons and daughters of Tennessee, the Carolinas, Georgia, Mississippi, New York, France and Germany and set its own ineffaceable stamp on their souls."[24]

These Texans Hood understood, and they, in turn, understood him. Save for the almost fanatical response of Forrest's brigade to the leadership of "Old Bedford" there appears to have been no brigade in the Confederacy in which there were greater *esprit* and more mutual understanding between men and their leader than in Hood's Texas brigade. Part of this respect on the part of the men doubtless arose out of the fact that their tall powerful colonel could whip any one of them in a fist fight and would not hesitate to do so if it became necessary. But more important than this seems to have been the fact that Hood treated his men as men and not as automatons whose only duty was to do and die. The Texan proved on many a Virginia battlefield that he could do and would die if necessary, but he was individualist enough to want to know why. Hood never commanded his men. He led them. The command was never "Go take that position." It was always "Come on, men, let's take it. I'll lead you."

These things Hood had abundant time to work out with his men during the long cold winter of 1861-1862. He and Archer remained with their regiments in camp near Richmond until the latter part of November, when they were ordered to Dumfries to be brigaded with the 1st Texas and the 18th Georgia already on picket duty there.[25] Simultaneously Colonel Wigfall was promoted to brigadier and put in command of the entire brigade.

Here at Dumfries Hood had an opportunity to see what a really colorful and nondescript outfit this Texas brigade was. Nothing better illustrated this than its officers. Its brigadier was the fiery politician Louis T. Wigfall, who in 1857 had helped defeat Sam Houston for the U. S. Senate and later had succeeded to Houston's seat. Lieutenant colonel of the 1st was Hugh McLeod, a veteran of the Texas War of Independence and erstwhile commander of the Santa Fe expedition of 1841. A. T. Rainey, major of the 1st, was a lawyer. Archer's regiment, the 5th, had as its lieutenant colonel Jerome B. Robertson, a physician and veteran of the Battle of San Jacinto. Its major was Paul J. Quattlebaum, a West Pointer, class of 1857. In Hood's own regiment, the 4th, John Marshall, a newspaperman, was lieutenant colonel. Other than Hood, perhaps the most colorful officer in the regiment was its major, Bradfute Warwick. Warwick was a wealthy and adventurous Virginia physician, a globe-trotter who had served as a captain in Garibaldi's army of liberation. Now he sought—and found—new adventures right at home in his native state. The 18th Georgia was made up of middle Georgia companies under the command of Colonel William T. Wofford.[26]

Mix a salmagundi of officers such as these in with 2,500 home-sick farm and ranch boys from Texas and Georgia, sick with colds and diarrhea, pranksters, gamblers, bullies, rowdies, a few foreigners, rebellious privates and deserters and one has the rough makings of the brigade Hood was to command. However, during this winter of 1861-1862 he was not thinking in terms of a brigade but only about making his the best regiment in the brigade. How he went about this is vividly related in his memoirs. His purpose was twofold: to arouse in them that indispensable quality called pride or *esprit,* and to bring them to an understanding of the necessity for discipline, irksome as it might be.

"I lost no opportunity," Hood wrote, "whenever the officers or men came to my quarters, or whenever I chanced to be in con-versation with them, to arouse their pride, to impress upon them that no regiment in that Army should ever be allowed to go forth upon the battle-field and return with more trophies of war than the Fourth Texas; that the number of colors and guns captured, and prisoners taken, constituted the true test of the work done by any command in an engagement. . . . Moreover," Hood continued, "their conduct in camp should be such as not to require punish-ment, and, when thrown near or within towns, should one of their comrades be led to commit some breach of military discipline, they should themselves take him in charge, and not allow his misconduct to bring discredit upon the regiment; proper deport-ment was obligatory upon them at home, and, consequently, I should exact the same of them whilst in the army."[27]

Hood knew from his own experience how monotonous and destructive of discipline the routine of outpost duty could be, so he took pains to explain to his men why it was necessary that the daily chores of policing the camp, drilling and dousing the lights at tattoo be performed. All this, he explained to them, became of the greatest importance in combat. "For example," he wrote, "the usual and important regulation, prohibiting lights or noise in quarters after ten o'clock at night, would be regarded by young recruits as unnecessary, and even arbitrary, unless the officer in command illustrated to them the necessity thereof, and made them understand that an army in time of active operations must have sleep at night in order to march and fight the following day; and that for this reason no soldier should be allowed to keep awake, say, six of his comrades in the same tent, be permitted to create a disturbance which would deprive his neighbours of rest, and render them unfit for duty the ensuing morning."[28]

To this sort of approach Hood's men responded. By contrast, however, Colonel Wigfall had had the devil's own time with the 1st Texas before Hood and Archer arrived. His regiment had almost driven him crazy and certainly had driven him to drink, if, indeed, he needed much driving to the latter. In his pompous manner he set out to make soldiers of these Texans and to hell with the reasons. This was the army and by God they would obey orders! Although he was a Texan, he didn't know these Texans. They tormented him by false alarms in the night just to see what he would do. On one occasion, even, a group of them crossed the Potomac to the Maryland side, awakened General Sickles and the Union troops under his command and proclaimed themselves the advance guard of the Confederate Army. The general is reported to have ordered up reinforcements, formed a line of battle and alerted Washington. When morning came, however, not a Confederate was to be seen and both Wigfall and Sickles were left wondering about all this rumpus in the night.[29]

Although the doughty Wigfall did not know what had happened, he was determined that he would not be taken by surprise. The colder the night and the more the wind whistled through the tree tops, the more his imagination was likely to play him tricks. After what Polley delicately refers to as "deep potations" he was likely to hear the rattling of oars as the Federals rowed across the Potomac to attack. Then the brigade would be ordered out on the double-quick to repel the invasion only to find the Potomac flowing silently by in the darkness and Federal campfires dying on the opposite shore.[30]

It was a tough winter for everyone. It was unusually cold for Virginia. Measles broke out in camp. Those who escaped the measles came down with diarrhea, colds or pneumonia. At one time not more than twenty-five men out of 800 in the 5th Texas were fit for duty. Time hung heavily on the hands of all despite Hood's and Archer's daily guard mountings and dress parades and the amusement offered by cards and chess. Perhaps worst of all, there were no leaves, no women. Sometimes the men created diversions of their own. Across the river on the Maryland side the 5th New York Zouaves in their fancy jackets and baggy pants were likewise wintering. When the Potomac would partially freeze over, Texans and Zouaves would walk out on the ice as far as they dared and there hurl good-natured taunts at each other. "We'll wipe your regiment off the face of the earth," shouted the Zouaves.

"We'll cover the ground with your ring-streaked striped bodies," the Texans would hurl back.[31]

And, having exhausted their repertory of imprecations, each side would retire to its own camp, doubtless feeling much better for the exchange.

This winter of 1861-1862 was a time of preparation for both North and South. Each nation girded its loins and made ready for the struggle which everyone now knew must come with the spring. Down on the sandy plains near Pensacola, Braxton Bragg was drilling an army. In Kentucky Albert Sidney Johnston had occupied a line from Cumberland Gap westward through Barboursville, Monticello, Bowling Green, Hopkinsville, Fort Donelson, Fort Henry and Union City to the Mississippi. In August of 1861 U. S. Grant had received a brigadier's commission and in the late autumn was assigned to Halleck's department and stationed at Cairo. During the winter he moved against Albert Sidney

Johnston's right at Forts Henry and Donelson, took them and
forced Johnston to retreat to the Memphis and Chattanooga Railway. Pushing farther south, Grant had been caught napping at
Pittsburg Landing by the combined forces of Bragg and Johnston,
now called the Army of Tennessee. At Shiloh Church on April 6
and 7, 1862, the armies of Grant and Johnston met and almost
slashed each other to death. It was a fearful battle symbolic of
things to come.

In the North feverish preparations were being made after
Beauregard had set it back on its heels at Manassas in July of
1861. On July 24, three days after the battle, Lincoln called thirty-
five-year-old George B. McClellan to Washington and gave him
command of the army in that department. The Northern states
provided him with an abundance of three-year recruits, and Congress was generous with money and supplies. His task during the
fall and winter of 1861-1862 was to organize all this into an army.
And organize he did—but slowly. Weeks stretched into months,
and all the newspapers could report was drilling and reviewing on
the Potomac. The North became impatient and the politicians
howled. November came and no offensive was ready. December
passed and still McClellan had not struck the blow which was to
end the rebellion. Finally on February 13, 1862, he spoke of a
move which he confidently boasted would put him in Richmond
within ten days. He planned to outflank General Joseph E. Johnston, then at Manassas, via the Rappahannock and then beat him
to Richmond. But Lincoln himself had tired of his general's
slowness and offered him the choice of two routes. Either he
could march overland and deliver a direct frontal assault on Richmond or he could undertake a flanking movement via the York
Peninsula. McClellan advocated the latter. In April the campaign
began from Fort Monroe.[32]

McClellan's force of 90,000 at Fort Monroe, however, was not the
only threat. The Confederate high command[33] was forced to

reckon with the fact that McDowell's corps of 40,000 men confronted them at Fredericksburg, that Banks with 20,000 troops was near Winchester and Frémont was moving into the upper part of the Shenandoah Valley with 15,000. Against this total force of 165,000 men the Confederates were able to muster approximately 80,000. Clearly, superb strategy was demanded on the part of the Confederacy if it was to resist and overcome such tremendous odds—and superb strategy was forthcoming. On Lee's advice and against Joseph E. Johnston's wishes President Davis adopted the strategy of delaying McClellan on the peninsula until Jackson could sweep up the valley and threaten Washington, thereby neutralizing McDowell, Frémont and Banks. With them neutralized a favorable moment could be seized and battle given to McClellan. How these audacious plans were developed can be told by Hood's movements from March to June 1862.

In March, General Johnston began drawing in his forces from the Manassas line to a position south of the Rappahannock. On the morning of March 8, the Texas brigade left winter quarters at Dumfries and moved twenty-five miles southward across the Rappahannock to Fredericksburg. General Wigfall had decided earlier in the year that he could best serve his country on the rostrum rather than on the battlefield and had resigned his commission to accept from the people of Texas a seat in the Confederate Senate. To succeed him President Davis appointed Hood as brigadier.[34] It was an appointment, Hood wrote in later years, which was somewhat embarrassing, because of the fact that Archer outranked him by seniority. However, he states that Archer came to his tent, warmly congratulated him and made known his satisfaction at serving under him.[35] The Texans were now all Hood's. He had helped train them. Now he must take them into battle.

Hood and his men remained at Fredericksburg just a month

before they moved to the peninsula. During this month he was engaged in the same old activities—drilling, reviewing and instructing his brigade. There were, however, some changes in the organization of the brigade. Archer remained as colonel of the 5th. John Marshall, the journalist, became colonel of Hood's own regiment, the 4th, and A. T. Rainey became colonel of the 1st. The 18th Georgia and Hampton's Legion remained the same. William H. C. Whiting, the senior brigadier of the Occoquan area, was made a major general and Hood's brigade became one of the two brigades in Whiting's new division. The other brigade was Whiting's old one now commanded by Colonel E. McIver Law. Whiting's brigade was 2,398 strong and Hood had 1,922, making a total of 4,320 in the division.[36] It was a division ultimately to be known as Hood's Division—a roving wrecking crew assigned first to Magruder on the peninsula, then to Jackson in the valley and finally to Longstreet.

The division moved by train from Fredericksburg to Richmond early in April and then marched to Yorktown. It was the first long march Hood's men had ever made, and it took them seven days to cover the sixty miles from Richmond to Yorktown. Shifty sandy roads tired the men and blistered their feet, and when they arrived they were almost exhausted. They were not immediately assigned to duty, however, and thus had a chance to rest and get in a little rifle practice.[37] As for Hood himself he was right back in the same familiar territory he had left a few months earlier when he reported to Richmond to assume the colonelcy of the 4th Texas. He had left the peninsula a lieutenant colonel, and now a few months later he was back as a brigadier general, age thirty.

The Confederate fortifications on the peninsula were much stronger and more formidable now than when Hood left in the fall of 1861. The first line of defense extended from Yorktown on the York River directly across the peninsula to the James River, a distance of some fifteen miles. Farther up the peninsula toward

Richmond the second line centered on Williamsburg, but extended left and right from the York to the James. These lines were composed of a series of trenches, rifle pits and artillery redoubts protected by abatis.[38] Longstreet was in command at Williamsburg with Magruder remaining near Yorktown. They did not occupy impregnable positions but were strong enough to play their part in Lee's strategy of delaying McClellan on the peninsula while Jackson created a diversion in the valley.

McClellan's plans contemplated both a direct assault on the Yorktown line and a flanking movement by McDowell's army, which would move from its position near Washington by water to Fort Monroe and thence up the York River to a point near Eltham's Landing or West Point. If a point midway between the Yorktown and Williamsburg lines could be seized he could divide the Confederate forces and fight them separately. The Fourth Corps under Brigadier General Erasmus D. Keyes was to attack the Yorktown line at Lee's Mills on the Warwick River near where it flowed into the James. At the other end of the line the Third Army Corps under Brigadier General Samuel P. Heintzelman, assisted by the Navy, was to attack Yorktown itself. With McDowell moving into the right and across the peninsula, the Confederate Army would not only be divided but caught in a pincers as well.[39]

It was beautiful strategy, but it had one important difficulty: It didn't work. The Fourth Corps approached Lee's Mills and decided it was too strong to be taken. The Third Corps was stopped cold by the Confederate guns at Yorktown. Commander J. S. Missroon found that the 10-inch guns at Yorktown kept his gunboats out of range and thus he was immobilized.[40] As if all this wasn't enough, McClellan received a telegram from the War Department notifying him that McDowell's army (the First Corps) was withdrawn from his command. Lincoln and Stanton had decided the safety of Washington demanded the presence of

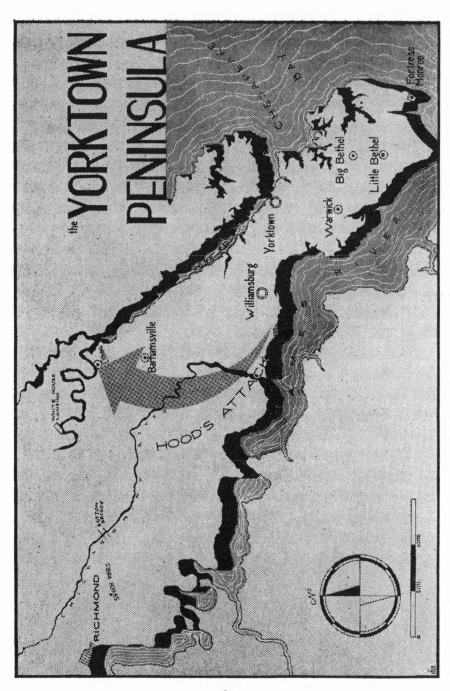

the YORKTOWN PENINSULA

both McDowell and Banks. Consequently McClellan's forces were broken up. The Department of the Shenandoah was given to Banks and the Department of the Rappahannock was put under McDowell. Lee's strategy was working superbly. The enemy was being delayed on the peninsula, and two armies were watching for Jackson's anticipated attack on Washington.

McClellan accepted the new order of things, but he earnestly sought to retain at least a part of McDowell's army. On April 5 he wrote Lincoln: "I am now of the opinion that I shall have to fight all the available force of the rebels not far from here. Do not force me to do so with diminished numbers. But whatever your decision may be, I will leave nothing undone to obtain success. If you cannot leave me the whole of the First Corps, I urgently ask that I may not lose Franklin [Brigadier General William B.] and his division."[41] The next day he repeated his request for Franklin's division.[42] Four days later he again asked for Franklin,[43] and this request was honored. On April 11 he was advised that Franklin's division was marching to Alexandria to embark.[44] On the thirteenth of April, Franklin and his division sailed for Fort Monroe via Baltimore and on May 4 went up the York to West Point.[45]

The arrival of Franklin's division obviously cheered McClellan. The Fourth Corps had failed at Lee's Mills, the Third Corps had failed before Yorktown, the Navy could not co-operate effectively and Lincoln and Stanton had disrupted his entire organization. But at last Franklin was ready for action. He, at least, could move from West Point to that long-desired position midway between the Confederate lines, thus isolating the two armies and preventing a union of them in case the Yorktown line should be abandoned and all troops concentrated at Williamsburg. But this, too, failed, for Franklin was immobilized by Hood long enough for the retreat from Yorktown to be accomplished.

Almost every letter and telegram sent by McClellan from the

peninsula indicates his lack of knowledge of Confederate strategy. Obviously McClellan felt that a major battle would be joined somewhere between Yorktown and Williamsburg, and made his plans accordingly. By the first of May, however, the Confederates had achieved their purpose on the peninsula. They had delayed McClellan for a month and were now ready to withdraw to pre-viously prepared positions closer to Richmond where the final portion of the grand strategy would unfold: Catch McClellan with his army divided and strike each unit separately. Thus on May 3 and 4 Magruder evacuated the Yorktown positions and fell back toward Williamsburg and Richmond. At Williamsburg the with-drawal became general. The four divisions of what later became the Army of Northern Virginia on the peninsula were commanded by Major Generals James Longstreet, D. H. Hill, John B. Magruder and Gustavus W. Smith. In the retirement the divisions of Long-street and Magruder moved on the Lee's Mills Road on the James side of the peninsula. Hill and Smith moved up the Yorktown-Williamsburg Road on the York side of the peninsula. Whiting's division, which included Hood's brigade, moved with Smith.

Although it was a voluntary strategic retirement, it was not ac-complished without great difficulty. Torrential rains turned the roads into quagmires through which the wagon trains crawled and creaked; and the army could move no faster than its wagon trains. Thus it became necessary for Longstreet to halt at Wil-liamsburg and fight off the pursuing Federals until the wagons were safely on their way. The result was a severe rear-guard action known as the Battle of Williamsburg. Stoneman's cavalry led the advancing Federals followed by infantry divisions under Generals Hooker, W. F. Smith, Silas Casey, Darius N. Couch, Philip Kearny and Winfield S. Hancock. At a point where the two lower-peninsula roads converge Longstreet took his stand and there soon developed the makings of a first-class battle. Had it not been for the torrential rains and the condition of the surrounding country McClellan's army might have prevailed. But the weather was more against the attacker than the attacked, and on the night of May 5 after sharp fighting the attack was washed out and the Confederates continued their crawling retirement.[46]

During the action at Williamsburg, Longstreet had called D. H. Hill's division from the Yorktown Road, leaving Smith's division alone with the wagon trains of both divisions. Near Eltham's Landing the newly arrived Federal division under Franklin was disembarking. This posed a threat to the wagon trains of both Hill and Smith. If Franklin should attack at this juncture it might be a serious threat to a successful Confederate retirement. Franklin had to be neutralized and Whiting's division was given the task. His orders were "to prevent the enemy from advancing upon Barhamsville until all the trains had passed."[47] Whiting obviously understood the phrase "to prevent the enemy from advancing" to mean attacking him and this he did, turning over the job to Hood's Texans. Now Hood would know whether they could fight or not.

On the morning of May 7, while Longstreet was still laboriously crawling along the roads leading from Williamsburg to Richmond, Hood at the head of his brigade advanced on Eltham's Landing. His men had not been allowed to march with loaded guns and were thus unprepared for what happened before they had really unlimbered their legs for the march.[48] Upon reaching a small cabin on the brow of the hill overlooking the slope which led down to the landing, Hood ran unexpectedly into the Federal outposts. The slope toward the York was abrupt and thus he had not seen the enemy until he was "almost close enough to shake hands." He leaped from his horse and ran to the head of his column then about fifteen paces to the rear, shouting orders to "load your guns" and "forward into line." As he did so the enemy fired a volley and retired toward their main lines. One corporal, however, could not resist a shot at Hood, who was so conspicuous in front of his men. As he drew a bead, however, Private John Deal of Hood's old 4th Regiment beat the Yankee to the draw and shot him dead. Private Deal apparently felt that fighting a war with unloaded rifles was a lot of damned foolishness. He had disobeyed orders and carried his gun ready for use—and had saved his general's life.[49]

Very quickly the affair assumed the appearances of a real battle. Leaving one battery of artillery and the 19th Georgia at the cabin, Hood led his favorite regiment, the 4th, into the wooded slope. Supporting him on his left was the 1st Texas and on his right was Hampton's Legion personally commanded by Wade Hampton. Anderson's brigade was left in reserve.

Leading in his 4th, Hood received a brisk fire from the enemy, but it was the 1st Texas on his left which received the brunt of the enemy's fire. The advanced skirmish lines of the Federals had been reinforced from the landing, and a flanking movement against Hood's left was attempted. Seeing his 1st Regiment in a difficult spot, he gave the only command he knew to give when in trouble: "Charge!" The 1st Texas responded magnificently and his left was saved—but Anderson's brigade was moved up in support just in case the enemy renewed its attack. In the meantime Archer with the 5th Texas had joined Hampton on the right. Then the entire line surged forward, driving the enemy back to the protection of his gunboats.[50]

General Whiting, who had witnessed the fight from the rear, now ordered up the battery of artillery to shell the enemy landing, but the range was too great and the battery was withdrawn. The Federals responded with a few salvos from their gunboats and the action was over.[51] Hood had accomplished his purpose. He had neutralized Franklin's corps while the Confederate wagon trains were getting beyond reach.

Undoubtedly the fight meant a great deal to Hood. He had trained these Texans, and now he saw them react like veterans in their first fight. It also greatly enhanced Hood's own reputation. It set him apart as a fighting officer to be watched. Whiting commended Hood and his brigade for "conspicuous gallantry." General Smith, commanding the division, referred to the affair as "one of the most brilliant of its many battles." D. H. Hill resorted to less formal language. "Franklin troubled us no more," he wrote. "His experience gained with the Texans had been ample. He desired no more of it."[52] It is even reported that Joseph E. Johnston himself called Hood to his headquarters regarding the fight. Apparently Johnston, fearful of provoking a real battle, had expected Whiting and Hood merely to feel out the enemy and keep them under observation.

"General Hood," Johnston inquired, "have you given an illustration of the Texas idea of feeling an enemy gently and then falling back? What would your Texans have done, sir, if I had ordered them to charge and drive back the enemy?"

"General," Hood replied gravely, "I suppose they would have driven them into the river, and tried to swim out and capture the gunboats."[53]

CHAPTER IV

Seven Days of Battle

BEFORE dawn on the day after the fight at Eltham's Landing, Hood and his men were on the move. Already their wagon trains were far ahead, safe by now, and so were Longstreet's. Silently, almost like ghost men, they moved in the direction of Richmond, being careful not to awaken enemy patrols. By noon they had overtaken the rest of the army and that afternoon passed within Confederate picket lines near Long Bridge on the Chickahominy. Here the brigade rested in a laurel grove until about ten o'clock the next night (May 9) when a torrential rainstorm drove them to higher ground. Struggling through the mud, rain and impenetrable darkness, they crossed Long Bridge and dropped one by one to resume their interrupted sleep.[1]

While Hood's brigade was drying out from the effects of the rainstorm another storm was brewing in Richmond—a storm the effects of which could be measured in rivers of blood. Stirring up the elements were Jefferson Davis and Joseph E. Johnston. In the middle was Lee, calm, dispassionate, polite and urbane. The points of controversy as Richmond prepared for the fight of its life were numerous. Both Johnston and Davis agreed on fundamentals of the strategy to be pursued, but they quarreled over details. Davis agreed with Johnston that all available forces should be concentrated to defend Richmond, but he insisted that other theaters such as Georgia and the Carolinas must be considered. The President also agreed with Johnston that a single unified command was necessary in Virginia, but he felt that the commander should keep the President informed on developments in the field. This Johnston steadfastly and arrogantly refused to do. The two men were in agreement that Johnston should have trained general officers, but Davis felt strongly that it was unwise to reach down and draw up these officers from well-trained individual units. Johnston insisted this was the only way he could get a competent group of brigadier and major generals. There was no serious variation from the original strategy agreed on: keep all units flexible, regard no positions as permanent, retreat and maneuver as necessary and finally strike the enemy at the most advantageous moment. But the clash of personalities of the two suspicious, obstinate men came near to wrecking the plans.[2]

Examples by the dozen might be cited of the almost childish conduct of the President and his commander in the field. However, two must suffice.

Johnston's withdrawal from the peninsula to within three miles of Richmond and the subsequent deployment of troops had been accomplished without the President having the foggiest notion of what Johnston proposed to do. Finally Davis sent Custis Lee, General Lee's son, to Johnston's headquarters with a letter. Would the General be kind enough to let the President know what was going on? But young Lee returned without any information. No, the General would not let the President know what was going on.[3]

The other incident involved Brigadier General William H. C. Whiting, Hood's division commander. "Billy" Whiting, a native of Mississippi, had graduated first in his class of 1845 at West Point. By 1858 he had risen in the old army to the rank of Captain of Engineers. At the beginning of the war he resigned his commission to serve with Beauregard at Charleston. In July 1861 he transferred to Virginia, where he arranged for the transportation of Johnston's army to Manassas, serving on Johnston's staff. In that same year he was made a brigadier general.[4] Despite his

snobbishness and mild arrogance he was a capable officer and
would have served Johnston well. However, Davis turned down
Johnston's recommendation of Whiting. The reason was "his
offensive rejection of a Mississippi brigade in an insubordinate
letter . . ."[5] earlier in the war. Thus because of the President's
petulance Johnston was deprived of what was then a good major
general.

Events were now shaping up, however, which were calculated
to take everyone's mind off quarrels and concentrate it on the
defense of Richmond, for ominous news came from the Chickahominy and the Rappahannock. McDowell from Fredericksburg on
the Rappahannock was marching to join McClellan on the Chickahominy. McClellan had cautiously advanced up the Chickahominy, deploying his troops along both banks. South of the river he
stationed Hooker, Kearny, Couch and Casey. On the north bank
almost directly opposite Richmond were Porter's and Franklin's
corps with Sedgwick and Richardson on the same bank but south
of these. (See map.)

Obviously the time had come for the Confederates to attack
before McDowell's forces reached McClellan. Accordingly a
council of war was held on the afternoon of May 27. McClellan's
troops north of the Chickahominy would be the first to unite with
McDowell. Therefore the logical move was to strike these Federal forces across the river. G. W. Smith's division was selected
to lead the attack, and on the evening of May 28 he reported he
was ready. But at this conference Johnston had a sensational announcement to make. Jeb Stuart, he announced, had reported
that McDowell had halted his advance. Not only had he halted,
but he had returned to Fredericksburg and showed signs of marching even farther north.[6]

What had happened? Had Jackson been successful in the Shenandoah Valley? Was it a ruse? Should they, in view of the circumstances, continue plans for the attack across the Chickahominy?

The council of war did not have all the answers to these questions. They did not know that Jackson on May 25 had disastrously defeated Banks at Winchester and that Washington was again in the grip of paralyzing fear.[7] But the members of the council did know that the wisdom of attacking the Federals north of the river was now open to question. G. W. Smith felt it would be better to abandon the original plans and instead attack that portion of the enemy's forces south of the river. To this Longstreet objected heartily and suggested an attack immediately according to the previous plan. When this was overruled he then suggested an attack the next morning on the Union center at Seven Pines and Fair Oaks.[8] Johnston partially concurred in Longstreet's second suggestion, but he felt he could now wait a day or two since McDowell was no longer an imminent threat.

But battle could not long be delayed. On the morning of May 30, D. H. Hill made a reconnaissance on the Williamsburg Road and found the Federals advancing. He also reported that the whole of Keyes's corps had crossed to the south side of the Chickahominy.[9] Johnston, therefore, decided to attack the Federal center at Seven Pines on the morning of May 31.[10]

Orders were issued, some verbal, some written. Longstreet with his own and the brigades of D. H. Hill would attack the Federal center supported by Huger's division. On the left Whiting's division would move down the Nine Mile Road and strike in flank and rear.[11] Longstreet moved to the right, but confusion soon became rampant. Longstreet's and Hill's brigades became an almost inextricable mass of bewildered men and officers. Johnston's secretive verbal orders were bearing fruit. There was no firing and no report from Longstreet as the hours slipped by. Johnston and Lee, who had come to the field, were apprehensive. Johnston was holding Whiting in readiness, but still there was no indication that Longstreet was in action. Lee and Johnston could not know it at the time, but a part of this lost time was being spent by

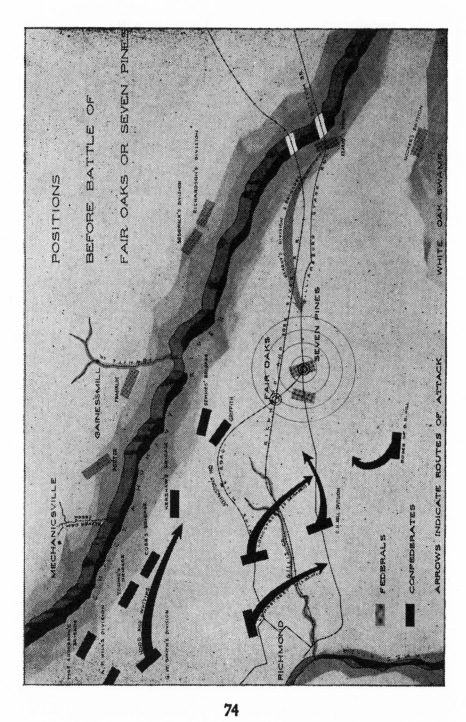

POSITIONS

BEFORE BATTLE OF

FAIR OAKS OR SEVEN PINES

FEDERALS

CONFEDERATES

ARROWS INDICATE ROUTES OF ATTACK

74

Longstreet and Huger arguing who was the senior officer of the two. Finally near four o'clock Lee and Johnston heard the ominous undertone of artillery and the sharper rattle of musketry. D. H. Hill had gone into action followed by Longstreet. They were hurling themselves directly at old Silas Casey's redoubt at Seven Pines.[12]

Hearing the firing from Hill's guns Johnston ordered Whiting to move into the fight. Whiting's, Hood's and Pettigrew's brigades had been stationed on the Nine Mile Road one and one-half miles east of Fair Oaks with Hatton's and Hampton's brigades in reserve. These positions were maintained all day until the sound of battle at Seven Pines came to them. Now the advance brigades moved forward to Longstreet's relief. Hood moved on the right of the road, Whiting on the road and Pettigrew to the left. Moving on the double-quick through the mud, the three brigades rushed eastward, racing with the sunset. Hood's Texans moved ahead and had already crossed the Richmond and York Railroad when the other brigades ran into trouble. The Federals opened on Hampton's and Hatton's brigades in the rear with artillery supported by infantry. Whiting and Pettigrew turned about to assist the other two brigades, and Hood, not knowing what was happening, kept on pushing his men toward Longstreet.[13]

Although Smith reported that Hood had maintained his "well-earned reputation for skill and gallantry,"[14] the truth of the matter is that he had, through unfortunate circumstances, been cheated out of a fight. He had spent the morning and early afternoon waiting and the late afternoon marching toward Longstreet's guns, which he did not reach before sunset.

Meantime the other four brigades had run into stiff resistance at Fair Oaks. The Federals had been reinforced from across the Chickahominy, and Whiting was barely able to hold his own under the withering enemy fire. Neither side could advance through the dense tangled wood which lay between them. They simply stood and shot it out, and when night came Whiting found his losses heavy. General Robert Hatton was dead, General J. J. Pettigrew was seriously wounded and taken prisoner. General Wade Hampton was shot in the foot but refused to leave the field. A total of 1,283 Confederates were killed, wounded or missing.[15]

Thus two battles were fought May 31, 1862—one at Fair Oaks and one at Seven Pines. And when night came both sides could claim a victory. The Confederates could say they won at Seven Pines, and the Federals could boast of winning at Fair Oaks. But the losses had been heavy. Out of 41,797 effectives the Federals had lost 790 killed, 3,594 wounded, 647 missing—a total of 5,031. Out of 41,816 effectives the Confederates lost 980 killed, 4,749 wounded and 405 missing—a total of 6,134.[16] Fortunately for the Confederacy General Johnston was seriously wounded and left the field, yielding up his command.

That night Lee and Jefferson Davis mounted their horses and turned toward Richmond. Johnston was seriously wounded, and neither the President nor his chief military adviser knew what the stricken general's plans for the battle really were. All they could determine was that it had been badly mismanaged and that the hoarse moans of the wounded underlined that fact. As they rode, Davis turned to Lee and in a simple statement changed the whole course of the war. "General Lee," he said, "I shall assign you to the command of this army. . . . I shall send you the order when we get to Richmond."[17] On June 1, 1862, Robert E. Lee assumed command of the Army of Northern Virginia.

The new commander lost no time in fully acquainting himself with the situation on the field at Fair Oaks and Seven Pines. After conferring with Generals Smith and Longstreet it was decided not to renew the battle on the second day, but to leave the troops where they were. Lee believed McClellan would do likewise, and events proved him correct. Thus the situation stood as Lee's horse struggled through the deep mud carrying his master over the battlefield to get his bearings. A battle had been fought. Neither side really could claim a victory. The Federals were as far away from Richmond as they were before the battle, and the Confederates were still as close. Moreover, Lee was faced with the awesome fact that a powerful army still confronted him.

After a quick but thorough analysis Lee came up with his strategy. Obviously Richmond could not long withstand the slow steam-roller attack of such a powerful force as McClellan's. The only way the city could be defended was to attack McClellan and drive him back. Throw up fortifications about Richmond, Lee reasoned, so the city could be held with a minimum fórce; then strike with the rest of his army. In all of this, however, he took one great chance. Suppose McClellan should strike while preparations were under way? Well, it was a chance which had to be risked. But at the same time Lee felt it was not too risky because he had done what every great general since Hannibal had found necessary. He had correctly estimated the character of his opponent. He reasoned McClellan would be timid in attacking precipitately, but instead would cautiously move forward, intrenching as he moved.[18] And all this came to pass.

During the early days of June 1862 Lee earned for himself the sobriquet of "King of Spades." Every man who could be spared and who could use a pick and shovel was put to work digging and constructing earthworks around Richmond. At the same time Lee was working out his plans for the attack. He arrived at these conclusions: (1) The attack would be directed against McClellan's forces north of the Chickahominy rather than striking at the center again as Johnston had at Fair Oaks and Seven Pines. (2) He would move his own army directly across the Chickahominy and strike the Federal right under Fitz John Porter. (3) Simultaneously Jackson would move rapidly from the valley and strike Porter's exposed right flank and roll it back.

To answer Jackson's request for reinforcements before the

campaign should begin, Lee sent him Whiting and Hood, the two brigades now constituting Whiting's division.[19] On June 11 the division marched into Richmond with colors flying and drums beating. They were, they proclaimed, on their way to join Stonewall Jackson and then they would attack Washington. Federal spies, of course, picked up the information as anticipated and forwarded it to Stanton.[20] At the same time Jackson, resting his men after the battles of Cross Keys and Port Republic, was furthering the ruse. A mysterious cloak of secrecy was suddenly thrown over the army. The cavalry demonstrated and the engineers were put to work on mysterious maps of the valley. It was allowed to leak out in strictest confidence that Jackson intended to pursue Frémont and perhaps attack Washington. Friend told friend, always in strictest confidence, and finally it became general knowledge that Jackson was cooking up a new valley campaign.[21]

With jaunty swinging steps and much good-natured banter the Texas brigade marched through Richmond to the station where they took the cars for Lynchburg. This was the first chance Richmond onlookers had to see the famous Texans, but assuredly not the last. There would be many times in the near future when their noise and antics would enliven things in the city. The Texans never failed to draw a crowd when they marched and Richmond always knew it when they were in town.[22] Arriving at Lynchburg, the men were allowed two days rest and then boarded the cars again for the trip to Charlottesville. Here they transferred to the cars of the Virginia Central Railroad for the final leg of the journey to Staunton in the heart of the Shenandoah Valley.

Upon reaching Staunton, Whiting reported to Jackson and in his usual rather condescending manner asked Jackson to reveal the plans of the campaign to him. But all he got was a curt "Hold yourself and command, sir, in readiness to march at six o'clock on Monday morning."

Somewhat taken aback at Jackson's manner, he inquired: "In what direction will we march, General?"

"That will be made known to you, sir, at the proper time," Jackson replied archly. And with that Whiting had to content himself.[23]

Jackson intended no rudeness, but he was determined that his plans would not leak out. He had taken elaborate precautions to prevent such a leak. His own mail from Richmond was addressed to him at "Somewhere." A long line of cavalry covered every road and prevented straggling and communicating with civilians. The men were even forbidden to ask the name of villages through which they marched, and if they were asked any questions by anyone they were to answer "I don't know." And the men responded to the extent of making a joke of it all. This Jackson found out when he accosted one of Hood's Texans who was climbing a fence preparatory to robbing a cherry tree.

"Where are you going?" demanded Jackson.

"I don't know," replied the Texan.

"To what command do you belong?"

"I don't know."

"What state are you from?"

"I don't know."

"What is the meaning of this?" Jackson asked of another Texan near by.

"Well," he said, "Old Stonewall and General Hood gave orders yesterday that we were not to know anything until after the next fight."

Jackson laughed and went his way.[24]

When Monday morning came and marching orders were issued Hood found that he was to make an about-face and march right back to Charlottesville. As they marched, a Texas private sidled up to his captain and inquired, "Where we goin', Cap'n?"

"Damned if I know," he replied, "but I'll ask the colonel."

Moving up to the head of the column he questioned his colonel. "Where the mischief and Tom Walker we goin'?" he inquired.

"I'll be durned if I know," answered the colonel. "I'll ask General Hood."

But when the colonel approached Hood all he got was, "I don't know."

So furious did the questioning become that Hood called a halt and explained the matter to his regiments. Going to each regiment separately he made his speech. "Men," he said in essence, "we are now subject to the orders of General Jackson and he alone knows our destination. It was General Jackson who issued the orders to say you didn't know. But, men, while I myself don't know where we are going I can assure you that such of you that keep up with your command will witness and take part in stirring and glorious events."[25]

Apparently this satisfied the Texans and the march was resumed.

The country through which this army was passing is one of great beauty. Traveling east from Staunton, one soon sees ahead the misty ranges of the Blue Ridge. On every side are cool green coves and rich valley farms with their stone-chimneyed white farmhouses. Fruit, particularly apples, grows well in this soil, and in the 1860's quantities of these apples were made into brandy. Almost any cove was likely to have its still, and this fact Hood's men soon discovered. To prevent straggling and drunkenness among his men Hood authorized the circulation of the story that smallpox was raging in these mountains and any man who left his column and wandered off into any of these coves was likely to come down with the dread disease.

Riding at the rear of his brigade to pick up stragglers Hood soon discovered one lying in the middle of the road drunk.

"What is the matter with you, sir? Why are you not with your company?" Hood demanded.

The voice of his general brought the culprit to a weaving and uncertain sitting position and with drunken gravity he replied, "Nussin' much, I reckon, General, I jus' sorter feel weak an' no account."

"So I see, sir," Hood rejoined. "Get up and rejoin your company."

The soldier made several ineffective attempts to rise, but to no avail. Looking about him, Hood directed a passing group to take charge of him. But as they approached to carry out the order the drunk suddenly decided what his trouble was. Holding up his arm in a warning gesture, he mumbled, "Don't you fellers that ain't been vaccinated come near me. I've got smallpox. Tha's whassa matter with me—I've got the smallpox."

"Leave him alone," Hood laughed. "Some of the teamsters will pick him up."[26]

When the brigade reached Charlottesville it was believed by many of the troops that they were on their way northward to fight Banks again. At Gordonsville they were sure Washington was their objective. On Monday, June 23, Jackson himself mysteriously disappeared. Securing a pass from Whiting allowing him to leave the lines for the purpose of procuring horses, he rode incognito into Richmond for a conference with Lee. By three in the afternoon he was at Lee's headquarters where he found Longstreet, A. P. Hill and D. H. Hill. No record of this historic conference was kept, but it is known that Lee outlined his plans in detail. Jackson was to move his army, now arrived at Hanover Junction, to Ashland, some sixteen miles due north of Richmond. On the night of June 25 he was to halt six miles east of Ashland. At three o'clock on the morning of June 26 he was to leave this position and march southeastward to turn the Federal right at Beaver Dam Creek. A brigade under General L. O'Brien Branch would move up the south side of the Chickahominy, cross to the north side above Meadow Bridge and meet Jackson in front of the Federal positions on Beaver Dam Creek. Together Jackson and Branch were to drive in the Federal outposts and force the Federals to retire. This would uncover the Meadow and Mechanicsville bridges. When this was accomplished A. P. Hill would cross at Meadow Bridge, and D. H. Hill and Longstreet would cross at Mechanicsville Bridge.[27]

On the morning of June 26, Lee rode out on the Mechanicsville Road along which Longstreet's and D. H. Hill's men were moving toward the Mechanicsville Bridge. Before he left headquarters after breakfast he had received news which was ominous—Jackson was three hours late. Immediately he sent a message to Branch. "Wait for Jackson's notification before you move unless I send other orders."[28] Thus Branch joined the distinguished group of Hill, Hill, Longstreet and Lee who were biting their nails and waiting for Jackson. The hours ticked away. Across the Chickahominy Lee could see through his binoculars the enemy troops in the village of Mechanicsville. Just to the east of the village they were firmly set behind Beaver Dam Creek. A few minutes after ten, Branch received a note from Jackson informing him that he was then crossing the Central Railroad—seven hours late. Immediately Branch marched down the north bank of the Chickahominy, skirmishing as he marched. But he was late because Jackson was late.[29]

Meantime A. P. Hill was patiently waiting at Meadow Bridge for Branch to clear it by driving in the Federal advanced positions across the river. By three o'clock, however, Branch had failed to put in an appearance, and Hill decided to push across Meadow Bridge without his assistance. This he accomplished with little opposition, and his troops began skirmishing with the enemy in front of Mechanicsville.[30]

Crouched in the woods near Mechanicsville Bridge, D. H. Hill heard A. P. Hill's firing across the river. A. P. Hill was expected to join Branch and clear the way for him, but now the firing indicated something had gone wrong. So D. H. Hill poured his men across the rickety Mechanicsville Bridge shortly after three o'clock.[31] Three hours later Longstreet marched his men across the same bridge.[32]

Lee now had all his troops across the river or in the process of crossing—and still no Jackson. Where was Jackson?

On the morning of June 26 Jackson had taken up the march from Ashland, Whiting's division in front. Marching down the Ashcake Road he crossed the Central Railroad seven hours late. To quote Jackson's own words: "Approaching the Totopotomy Creek, the Federal picket crossed to the south side of the stream and partially destroyed the bridge and by felling trees across the road farther on attempted to delay our advance. After the Texas skirmishers had gallantly crossed over and Reilly shelled the woods for the purpose of driving the enemy from it, in order that we might effect a lodgment beyond the creek, Whiting rapidly repaired the bridge and the march was resumed. That night the three divisions bivouacked near Hundley's corner."[33]

That was all. No excuses for his tardiness. His men were in bivouac while Lee was fighting desperately at near-by Mechanicsville.[34]

Meantime Lee continued to watch and listen. Between three and four o'clock a volley of musketry rolled in across the river—then another and another. Out of the woods swept A. P. Hill's men in formation, loading and firing as they advanced. Before them the Federal skirmishers fired a return volley and then retreated behind Beaver Dam Creek. Then from the area around Mechanicsville Bridge D. H. Hill's men moved in. For a brief period the enemy formed a line in front of Mechanicsville, fired a few volleys into the advancing Confederates and then retired behind the same creek. Was the enemy going to make a stand behind Beaver Dam Creek? This Lee had not anticipated.[35]

Lee's answer was the roar of Federal artillery from behind the

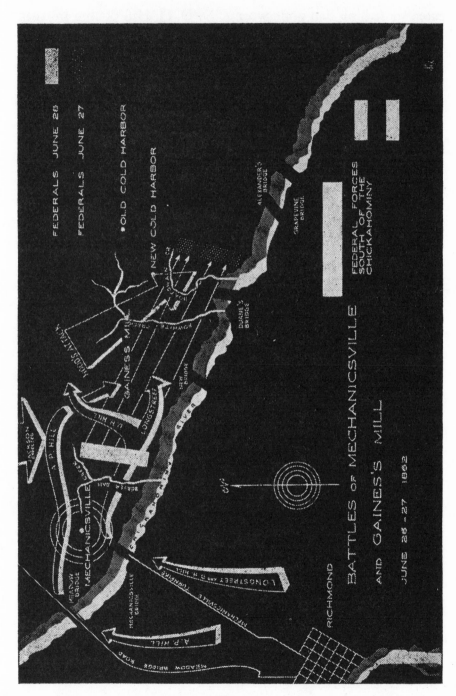

BATTLES OF MECHANICSVILLE
AND GAINES'S MILL
JUNE 26 - 27 1862

FEDERALS JUNE 26
FEDERALS JUNE 27
*OLD COLD HARBOR
NEW COLD HARBOR

FEDERAL FORCES
SOUTH OF THE
CHICKAHOMINY

creek. Yes, they would stand here and fight. It was a strong position, the banks of the creek in front being high and almost perpendicular, and the approaches to it over open fields commanded artillery and infantry fire.[36] In front of these positions the rapidly developing battle increased in intensity. By four o'clock A. P. Hill was in Mechanicsville and D. H. Hill could cross and go to join Jackson, if Jackson got there. But Jackson wasn't there, and Hill went ahead without him. He moved in on A. P. Hill's right and went into action—but still there were the open fields, Beaver Dam Creek and the Federal artillery on the elevations beyond. An outright assault on the Federal positions was suicide. The enemy's right flank must be turned without Jackson. But this flanking movement failed with terrific slaughter. By nightfall Lee was forced to the painful realization that he had failed. All the results from the more than four hours of intense fighting were the sight of his dead and the moaning of his wounded. He had lost 1,484 men killed and wounded while the Federal losses were only 256.[37] And the Federals were still firmly ensconced behind the creek while Jackson's men were sleeping at Hundley's Corner.

At nightfall the rifle fire died to an occasional burst here and there along the front. By ten o'clock the defiant roar of Federal artillery had quieted to a whimper and Lee's weary men slept on their arms. This Battle of Mechanicsville or Beaver Dam Creek was Lee's first major battle and he had been defeated—but this was only the first of seven days of fighting, and Hood was sleeping with his men at Hundley's Corner.

On the morning of June 27 Lee snatched a hasty breakfast and then rode toward Mechanicsville where the battle had been renewed in a desultory manner. Jackson still had not come up, but Lee knew just where he was and how fast he was moving. Consequently this early-morning fighting was merely to enable the Confederates to hold their positions while waiting for Jackson's attack. Finally about 11:00 A.M. Jackson's advance columns led by the renowned Ewell appeared on the Confederate left and united with D. H. Hill's division, a position Lee had hoped for about twenty-four hours earlier. And now it was that the enemy's movements of the previous night were revealed. This force now in position behind Beaver Dam Creek was hardly more than a brigade left to cover the Federal withdrawal behind Powhite Creek and Boatswain Swamp two miles to the east. Before Jackson had time to go into action this brigade retreated to join the others who had moved during the night.[38]

The day before, Lee's men had fought and died in the attempt to cross Beaver Dam Creek to get at the enemy. Now they repaired the bridges and crossed with no opposition, moving eastward to attack the enemy behind another creek, behind Powhite Creek, Lee thought.

Powhite Creek runs north and south, roughly parallel with Beaver Dam Creek. It is a small sluggish stream with marshy banks which in rainy weather became virtually impassable. Behind this natural defense Lee had expected to find the Federal lines running north and south. Instead, he soon found that the enemy was behind Boatswain Swamp a half mile farther east and that his lines were almost directly east and west instead of north and south as expected. McClellan's engineering ability was clearly demonstrated. He had selected the strongest possible defensive position. As one approached he found the topography ideal for the Federals. There was an almost impenetrable growth of trees, then the swamp and the creek, more swamp on the opposite bank and then an incline which lead to the top of a low hill. The slope was bristling with two lines of infantry behind log and earth works protected by abatis. On the hill were other lines of infantry and batteries of artillery.[39]

Against this strong position Lee moved about eleven o'clock on the twenty-seventh. D. H. Hill moved to his left from Mechanicsville to meet Jackson. A. P. Hill and Longstreet moved to their right and down the Chickahominy, then swung to their left to come up on the enemy's left and center. By 2:00 P.M. A. P. Hill had made contact with the Federal center. Assaulting with savage fury, Hill threw his brigades time and time again at the center and each time was repelled with terrible losses. At one time he reached the crest of the hill, but Federal artillery snuffed out the success. For more than two hours the carnage continued. It was the artillery on the hill, not the infantry on the slopes, which Hill's men could not withstand.

Seeing A. P. Hill's plight on the center, Lee ordered Longstreet on the right to create a diversion in Hill's favor. But Longstreet soon discovered that a mere feint was not enough—it had to be a real attack. But as he prepared to charge the heights, Whiting's division moved in between him and A. P. Hill. Jackson was in action! Here was a division of fresh troops to replace A. P. Hill's decimated regiments. And here was Lee's opportunity for an all-out frontal assault which would bring victory or death.[40]

Jackson had come on the field skirmishing, the element of surprise completely gone. The enemy had felled logs in the road, and behind the logs lay sharpshooters sniping at the advancing columns. Because of the delay thus engendered, Jackson shifted his line of march and thus came on the field in D. H. Hill's rear. Soon Hill became engaged with the enemy, a bitter seesaw battle similar to A. P. Hill's fighting in the Federal center, and with no more results.[41] Again and again, as A. P. Hill had done, D. H. Hill threw his men at the infantry and artillery nests behind the creek—and each time they were thrown back with staggering losses. If the day was to be won it had to be won quickly, for it was now five o'clock. Longstreet was getting ready for an assault on the Federal left, A. P. Hill was hardly holding his own on the center and D. H. Hill was hard pressed on the right. The job of winning was up to Jackson's troops.

In deploying his brigades for action Jackson had not held all of them on the right. Ewell and Lawton filled the space between D. H. Hill's right and A. P. Hill's left. Hood and Law were moved in on A. P. Hill's right, next to Longstreet.[42] Thus Hood's and Law's brigades were in an extremely strategic position. In their immediate front was the section of the Federal defenses doing the most damage. It was the area against which A. P. Hill had almost dashed himself to pieces and from which his weary soldiers were now streaming back toward the rear. Dazed with battle shock, they had had all they could stand.

At this point Lee made a decision which won the battle. He would use Hood's and Law's brigades as shock troops in one final desperate effort to break the enemy's center. If they succeeded he would call up fresh reserves from Longstreet and pour them through the gap.[43]

Lee rode out looking for Whiting's division, and when he found it he inquired for Hood. Within a matter of moments Hood rode up, saluted and asked for orders. Briefly Lee told him what was needed. The enemy was holding out and pouring a murderous fire into A. P. Hill's men. They were shocked, dispirited and almost ready to give up the fight. In fact, some of them were already slipping out of the fight toward the rear. Unless the enemy's line could be broken the battle was lost. "This must be done," Lee said quietly. "Can you break his line?"

"I will try," Hood replied gravely.[44]

As Lee turned to ride away he lifted his hat and said almost like a benediction, "May God be with you."[45] Perhaps at this moment there flickered through his mind that this was his boy. He had punished him at West Point and counseled him in Texas.

Hood rode back to his brigade and explained to his officers what was expected of them. Have the men put their haversacks, canteens and blanket rolls in piles. Then line up the men and on signal march as on parade across the open space in front of the enemy's lines. No one was to break ranks and no one was to fire a shot until the order was given. When men were shot down close up the ranks and keep going. Give the first line the bayonet and, when it falls back on the second line, fire and make every shot count. Then the battle line was formed—from right to left, the 18th Georgia, the 1st Texas, the 5th Texas and on the extreme left Hampton's Legion. In reserve was the 4th Texas, Hood's regiment when he was a colonel.[46] When he was promoted to brigadier he had promised the men to lead them personally in their first battle. Now he proposed to carry out that promise.

Away to Hood's left in communication with the Legion was Whiting's other brigade, Law's, composed of the 6th North Carolina, the 4th Alabama, the 11th Mississippi and the 2nd Mississippi. Law was likewise instructing his officers and men, for they were to advance in the same manner as Hood's men.

Now Hood checked his lines. On the left Colonel M. W. Gary with the Legion was ready. In front of the 5th Texas the remnants of a Georgia regiment fell back in disorder over the same ground the Texans were now ready to cross. "Don't go any further, men—you'll all be killed if you do," they shouted. Far out in no man's land a lone Georgian, crazed from a shot in the head, gyrated and gesticulated wildly. Someone from the 5th ran out and brought him in. Sergeant Onderdonk of Company A raised the colors. The 5th was ready.[47] Colonel Rainey reported his 1st Regiment ready, as did Colonel Ruff of the 18th Georgia. Riding back to his own 4th, he found Captain T. M. Owens waving his sword and reciting the dying lines from "Marmion." The eager tense faces told Hood the 4th was ready.[48]

In front of Law as he readied his men for the charge, weary men were leaving the field in every direction and in disorder. Two regiments had actually made an about-face and were marching to the rear. Over on the right the fragments of a brigade were lying flat. On the left men were slinking into the woods. These

SECTION of FEDERAL DEFENSES at GAINES'S MILL

federal artillery & infantry

federal entrenched infantry
PROTECTED BY LOG AND EARTH WORKS AND ABATIS

federal sharpshooters
PROTECTED BY LOG AND EARTH WORKS AND ABATIS

WOODS

MEADOW ACROSS WHICH HOOD CHARGED

90

men had suffered all they could endure. Their eyes were glazed with fright and shock. This murderous fire from the Federal artillery on the hill was beyond human endurance.[49]

Tension along the line was relieved by the command "Forward," and with guns at right shoulder lift the men sprang forward at quick-time march. Hood had boasted that he could double-quick his men to the gates of Hell and never break the line. Now everyone would know whether this was an idle boast or not.

It was almost sundown when the brigade advanced. As the line moved into the clearing in full view of the enemy, Hood moved his regiment up on the right of the 18th Georgia, and then the entire line swept forward. The men did not run or shout. They moved at quickstep in perfect formation. As they marched they began to step on and over dead bodies of their comrades. These were A. P. Hill's men who had died trying to do what the Texans were now attempting. Still not a shot was fired, but now as they came closer to the creek the Federal artillery found the range and men began to go down like figures in a shooting gallery. Still the men marched in perfect order, closing up the ranks when a man dropped.[50] Bradfute Warwick, the adventure-loving lieutenant colonel of the 4th Texas, paused momentarily to hoist the colors of a defeated regiment which had left the field. Bearing the colors aloft, he went to his greatest adventure, death. If the men had looked to the rear they would have seen the ground covered with their dead and wounded. But the men were looking forward, pressing on silently and relentlessly. Then gallant old Colonel Marshall of the 4th went down, and a moment later a bullet found Major Key of the 4th.

Just before they reached the creek there was a halt while bayonets were fixed and the lines were dressed. Then came the command "Charge." Down into the creek ravine they wallowed under the deadly spittle of the belching artillery on the hill. Up on the other side they came and with a terrific shout gave the first line the bayonet. It fell back on the second line and it broke. As the blue mass retreated up the hill the fire of the Texans was poured into it with terrible effect. The target was large, the range short, and scarcely a shot fired missed its mark.[51] On the crest of the hill the Federals stood by their guns bravely, but nothing could withstand these inspired Texans. At one gun a cannoneer, fatally wounded, pulled himself up by the spokes of his gun's wheel and fired one last defiant charge into the faces of Hood's men[52]—but his comrades were gone. Hood had broken through!

Now the 18th Georgia moved obliquely to the right and poured into the gap; then the 5th Texas; then the 1st Texas and the Legion. Farther down Law pushed his men forward. Back to Lee went the wild cheering and the miraculous news that the lines were broken and the enemy was in retreat. Quickly he ordered Longstreet to send up Anderson's brigade to widen the gap. All along the front now the Confederates took new hope. It was getting dark, but D. H. Hill hit the extreme Federal right and saw it give. Then A. P. Hill and Jackson and Longstreet struck and the entire Federal right was in retreat.

The battle was won. The Federal infantry was in full flight toward the Chickahominy swamps. But Hood's fighting was not over. Several Federal batteries on the far side of the plateau were still firing, covering the Federal retreat. Hood's 4th Texas and 18th Georgia together with Law's 11th Mississippi and 4th Alabama raced across the intervening area to silence them and were met by a thundering cavalry charge. General Fitz John Porter had sent in his cavalry to protect his retreat.[53] It was the old 2nd Cavalry of Hood's Texas days, and at the head of the charge rode Captain Charles J. Whiting, Hood's old commander of Company K. Standing their ground, the Confederates poured a deadly volley into the front of the charging column, and it collapsed as though it had run into an invisible wall. Captain Whiting's horse was shot from under him and he fell dazed almost at Hood's feet and was taken prisoner. Farther to the rear of the column, Captain William P. Chambliss, another of Hood's friends from the Texas days, fell seriously wounded.[54]

And then darkness fell and men began to go about the field with lanterns, giving aid to the wounded. This was the end of the second of seven days of battle. It is called the Battle of Gaines's Mill. "Undying gratitude is due to God for this great victory, by which despondency increased in the North, hope brightened in the South, and the capitol of Virginia and of the Confederacy was saved." Thus wrote Jackson.[55]

It is no wonder this battle gave Hood's Texans a place in Lee's heart which Freeman believes no other command ever won.[56]

But after every battle there comes a lull when bodies must be buried and items entered on the ledger—items such as gains and losses. Hood had broken the line and turned the tide of battle, had captured fourteen pieces of artillery and a regiment of New Jersey infantry. But the price was high. Every officer in the 4th Texas above the rank of captain had been killed. In addition 253 men, half the regiment, were casualties. Colonel Rainey of the 1st Texas was seriously wounded as was Colonel Robertson of the 5th Texas. The 18th Georgia lost 146 men. Hampton's Legion lost only twenty men. In all, Hood's and Law's brigades lost a total of 1,016 men and officers in less than an hour.[57]

After every battle, too, there comes a time for cooking and eating and sleeping and a time for recounting experiences— some heroic, some humorous. And Gaines's Mill was no exception. There is, for example, the story of plain Lieutenant Colonel J. C. Upton of the 5th Texas who, clad only in his shirt and with a frying pan in one hand, received the surrender of the officers of the 6th New Jersey. The officers had insisted on a formal sword-presenting surrender, but Upton was more interested in frying his meat than in the formalities of surrender. But when told he must receive these Federal officers and gentlemen he buckled his sword over his shirt and, standing naked from the hips down, made a cradle of his arms. Into the cradle went the swords of the conquered—and he held on to his frying pan.[58]

The 4th Texas laughed at Lieutenant Hughes's attempts to do a bit of cussin'. While the regiment was catching its breath at the top of the hill some of the men were annoyed by a lone Federal who kept sniping away at them from a log stable. Private Jim Stringfield decided to go in after him. Leaping the fence, he ran with gun in hand toward the stable, and at this juncture mild-mannered, noncussin' Lieutenant L. P. Hughes of the 4th Texas yelled his encouragement: "Go it, Stringfield—go it! Kill him, dod damn it, kill him."[59]

But not all the stories were humorous. At the top of the hill, just as Hood most needed the services of his officers who had been killed in the charge, Lieutenant Langdon C. Haskill, General Wade Hampton's son-in-law, raced up to offer his services to Hood as an aide. But when Hood looked he discovered that the young officer's left arm had been completely shot away. But so persistent was he that Hood had to order him to a hospital.

And that night as Hood rode over the field looking for his dead and wounded he heard a voice calling his name over and over again. Directing one of his men to locate the voice, he soon had a report. It was Captain Chambliss, shot down in the cavalry charge. He wanted his friend Hood, the soldier stated. And in the gray of the dawn after his own wounded had been removed from the field he went to Chambliss and found him still alive. They greeted each other warmly, and then Hood ordered him taken to a field hospital to receive the same attention his own officers were getting.[60]

It was almost dawn when Hood finished supervising the removal of his dead and wounded from the field. Throwing himself on the ground among his troops, he caught a few hours sleep, but with sunrise he and the rest of Lee's generals were up and stirring. Lee himself took a sandwich and ate it as he rode to the field.[61]

No one knew what the day would bring. No one knew just what yesterday's victory meant or how the Federals would react to it. So Longstreet cautiously pushed forward a brigade in the first light of dawn. Jackson likewise felt out the enemy's positions. Soon it became apparent that McClellan's forces were gone. Yesterday the area was an inferno, filled with the roaring of cannon and the incessant metallic crash of rifle volleys. Today it was calm and quiet except for the creaking of ambulances and the low calls of burial details going about their work.[62]

Riding over from the Confederate left, Jackson examined the area over which Hood had charged the previous day, and as he saw the almost impossible obstacles which had been overcome "his admiration overcame his reserve."[63] "The men who carried this position were soldiers indeed," he exclaimed.[64] And that from Jackson was equal to pages of praise from less taciturn men. Hood now had the respect of both Lee and Jackson—a respect fairly won by soldierly conduct and bravery on the field of battle. In turn, Hood greatly admired Jackson, and his feeling for Lee was almost one of awe and reverence. In spite of "Old Pete's" eccentricities, Hood always got along well with Longstreet, too.

And at this particular time the qualities of co-operation and soldierly conduct were badly needed in Lee's army. In the second echelon of command there was much carping and bickering. Magruder was excitable and emotionally unstable; Huger was slow and uncertain; D. H. Hill was unduly critical and at times downright unco-operative; Robert Toombs was a bombastic troublemaker; Whiting was arrogant, jealous and frustrated.[65] In singular contrast, Hood was well adjusted, physically strong, jealous of no one, had no desires to run the army and when given an assignment he carried it out promptly and effectively. As later events were to show, both Lee and Jackson had in the back of their minds that day after the Battle of Gaines's Mill a promotion for Hood.

Now, however, other matters occupied the attention of Lee. As the situation was surveyed from the slopes above Boatswain Creek certain questions had to be answered and decisions made. In what direction had the enemy moved? Did this move mean that McClellan was giving up the attack on Richmond or was he concentrating his forces for another attack from positions south of the Chickahominy? What should be the next move for the Army of Northern Virginia?

Lee's analysis of the situation, we now know, was correct. He correctly diagnosed what McClellan described at a later date. "On the 24th of June," McClellan wrote, "I received information that appeared entitled to some credit, that General Jackson was at Frederick's Hall with his entire force, consisting of his own division, with those of Ewell and Whiting, and that his intention was to attack our right flank and rear, in order to cut off our communication with the White House and throw the right wing of the army into the Chickahominy. Fortunately I had a few days before provided for this contingency, by ordering a number of transports to the James River, loaded with commissary, quartermaster, and ordnance supplies. I therefore felt free to watch the enemy closely, wait events, and act according to circumstances, feeling sure that if cut off from the Pamonkey I could gain the James River for a new base. . . . During the night after Gaines's Mill the final withdrawal across the Chickahominy was completed without difficulty and without confusion [!] a portion of the regulars remaining on the left bank until the morning of the 28th. Early on that morning the bridges were burned, and the whole army was thus concentrated on the right bank of the Chickahominy."[66]

In the face of defeat north of the Chickahominy he was changing his base and had no idea of an immediate attack on Richmond

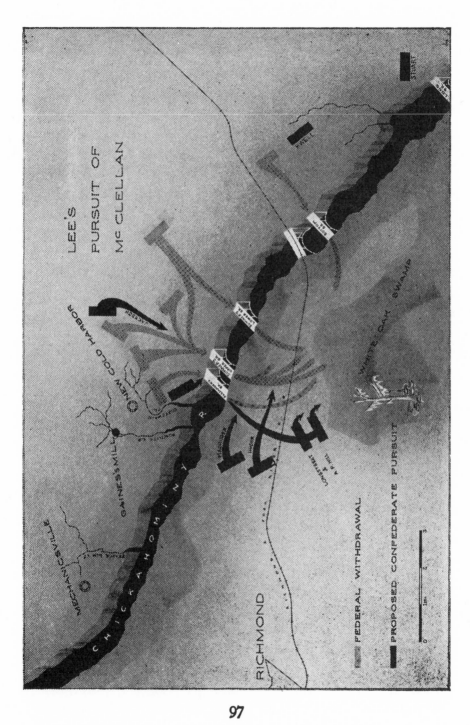

LEE'S
PURSUIT OF
McCLELLAN

MECHANICSVILLE

GAINES'MILL

NEW COLD HARBOR

CHICKAHOMINY R.

JACKSON

MAGRUDER

A P HILL

LONGSTREET

McRIDE

WHITE OAK SWAMP

EWELL

STUART

RICHMOND

FEDERAL WITHDRAWAL

PROPOSED CONFEDERATE PURSUIT

0   1m   2   3

from positions south of the river. This Lee correctly divined and
from it took his cue. What better time could there be to attack
an enemy than when he is in the confusion of a change of base!
Therefore, attack! Pursue and attack! That was Lee's decision.[67]

Lee's plans, if they had been properly executed, were flawless.
The Federal Army undoubtedly would have been surrounded
and trapped in White Oak Swamp if chaos and confusion among
Lee's generals had not intervened. The plans called for Stuart
and Ewell to move south along the left bank of the Chickahominy
to the region of Bottom's Bridge. Jackson and his division were
to repair the Grapevine Bridge, cross over and move south, pressing the enemy toward White Oak Swamp. "Prince John" Magruder, whose division was guarding Richmond, was to move in
support of Jackson; and General Benjamin Huger's division,
which had also been in reserve near Richmond, was ordered to
move on Magruder's right toward the swamp. And, finally, to
administer the *coup de grâce*, Longstreet with his own and A. P.
Hill's divisions was to take a position on Huger's right and be
ready to cut off the enemy's head when he emerged wounded
from the swamp.[68]

But once again poor co-ordination and faulty execution of orders
rose up to plague Lee.

Longstreet to reach his position had to march approximately
sixteen miles from the Chickahominy. Fourteen miles of this he
covered on the twenty-ninth of June, and on the thirtieth he moved
his men up confronting the Federal lines at Frayser's Farm. By
eleven o'clock he was in position, waiting for the signal from his
left that Huger and Jackson were in action. About 2:30 that
afternoon he heard artillery firing on his left and, assuming it to
be Huger in action, he opened with his artillery followed by infantry action. Soon the battle became vicious and sustained. Fresh
troops poured into the Federal lines and Longstreet called up reserves. In a thicket near by, Lee and Jefferson Davis sat on their

horses hoping to be in on the kill. But the kill didn't come off. Longstreet had to be content merely to hold his own.[69] Something had gone wrong, and this stalemate at Frayser's Farm was the result. Again Lee and Longstreet were asking: "Where is Jackson?" And added to their wondering was: "Where is Huger?"

Huger had been slow in coming up. He had marched at daybreak on the twenty-ninth and had not been in motion long before Magruder sent a message that he was in distress after his action at Savage Station and was about to be attacked by superior forces of the enemy. Huger sent two brigades to his relief and then brought them back when it was ascertained that Magruder's fears were baseless. This marching and countermarching in the heat didn't make for vigorous pursuit of the enemy. Moving cautiously onward, he soon found felled trees obstructing the road. Instead of leaving his artillery and pushing on with his infantry he decided to cut a new road instead of moving the felled trees. With poor tools his men began felling trees for a new roadway while the Federals continued felling trees across the old road.[70] Thus a lot of timber was cut and little progress made.

And where was Jackson? Why was he late?

There are many theories and conjectures advanced by those who have attempted to explain his behavior on this second occasion when his delay helped upset Lee's plans: General Jackson was physically exhausted. He knew the condition of his troops was such that a sustained attack was unwise. He thought it was time that Huger's and Magruder's troops did some fighting. He did not like being in a secondary position under Lee. He delayed for religious reasons on the Sabbath (June 29).[71] And all of these may be a part of the explanation, but there appears no reason better than that given by Stonewall himself. June 28 and 29 were spent, he reported, in disposing of the dead and wounded from Gaines's Mill and in repairing Grapevine Bridge. During the night of the twenty-ninth he commenced crossing the Chickahominy and on the morning of the thirtieth arrived at Savage Station. Here he took possession of a large hospital, a large supply of small arms and some thousand Federal stragglers. About noon he reached White Oak Swamp. He found the bridge destroyed and the crossing commanded by Federal artillery and sharpshooters. A battery of guns from D. H. Hill's and Whiting's artillery was brought up and about 2:00 P.M. it opened on the enemy. The Federal artillery was silenced, the sharpshooters were driven to cover and Colonel Thomas T. Munford's regiment of cavalry was sent across the creek. But enemy resistance forced Munford back and Jackson concluded the position was too secure to be taken without a general assault; and for the second time within a week he bivouacked within sound of the battle he was expected to fight.[72] (The other battle, of course, was Mechanicsville when Jackson bivouacked at Hundley's Corner.)

While he was skirmishing at the bridge Jackson heard the sound of Longstreet's guns at Frayser's Farm which made him "eager to press forward; but the marshy character of the soil, the destruction of the bridge over the marsh and creek, and the strong position of the enemy for defending the passage" prevented his advancing until the following morning. During the night the Federals retired. The bridge was rapidly repaired by Whiting's division, which soon after crossed over and continued the pursuit, in which it was followed by the remainder of Jackson's corps.[73]

Led by Hood and Law, Jackson's troops pushed on to join Longstreet but too late to strike the decisive blow expected of them. The Federals had been allowed enough time to concentrate their forces at Malvern Hill and to prepare for a Confederate assault. Whiting, long smoldering with frustration and dislike of Jackson, burst into flame at the way things were going. The attempts of Jackson to repair the White Oak Bridge he described as "sundry ineffectual attempts" and, although the enemy's fire was "distant and random," the "men would not work." They could plainly hear the roar of the battle at Frayser's Farm "scarcely two miles from us." "Our delay at White Oak Bridge was unfortunate." Moreover, Jackson would not permit him to advance with skirmishers deployed and in line, but "caused the troops to press on until the head of the column closed on the advance guard, a regiment of cavalry, in a thick wood. . . ." The enemy opened fire on the cavalry in the wood, and it broke through Whiting's column, further disrupting his advance and adding to his general irritation.[74]

If Hood had any thoughts about the way things were going he kept them to himself. He was only a junior brigadier and in no position to criticize even if he had wished to do so. His admiration for Jackson was a sufficient reason in itself, but, over and above that, Hood was not then of a carping and critical nature. By every act of his he showed clearly that he believed it was his duty to execute his orders and fight when called on—nothing more. He made no official report of this rear-guard action, and his memoirs are completely lacking in criticism of Jackson.

Malvern Hill where McClellan made his last and most successful stand during his change of base was less than two miles from the James River where it curved at Turkey Point, fourteen miles below Richmond. The hill was protected on each flank by small streams and in the rear by a marsh and the James. There was only one way Lee could attack—head on from the direction of Richmond. No turning movement was possible because of the terrain. It was a stronger position than he had faced at Beaver Dam Creek or the one behind Boatswain Swamp. Moreover the entire field was within range of the gunboats on the river under whose incessant fire the Confederate movements had to be executed.

On the morning of July 1, Lee formed his divisions in line of battle in a rough semicircle facing the hill. Jackson formed his line with Whiting's division on his left and D. H. Hill's on his right, one of Ewell's brigades occupying the interval. The rest of Ewell's and Jackson's own divisions were held in reserve. Huger came up on D. H. Hill's (Jackson's corps) right and Magruder formed on Huger's left. Longstreet and A. P. Hill were in reserve and took no part in the battle.[75]

The greater part of the day was spent getting the various brigades into position. Because of inadequate maps, the marshy nature of the soil and the dense growth of trees and underbrush, the whole line was not formed until near 5:30 in the afternoon, and even then the artillery could not be brought up. At a given signal the entire line was to advance, but there was no concert of action. D. H. Hill pressed forward and engaged the enemy, but was driven back with frightful losses by enemy artillery. Then Huger's and Magruder's commands went into action, but they, too, were repulsed with heavy losses.[76] Again as at Gaines's Mill it was the enemy's grape and shrapnel which tore yawning gaps in the attacker's ranks.[77] And as at Gaines's Mill the Confederate attack was piecemeal and sporadic. But there was one important difference—Hood's Texans were not brought up to break the lines. All day his and Hampton's brigades had remained idle in a meadow on the extreme Confederate left. Hood studied the enemy's positions and found what he thought was an unprotected area in their rear through which an attack might be launched. He sent a detachment of scouts to reconnoiter in that direction and their report was favorable. However, when Hood and Hampton requested Whiting to authorize the proposed flank attack he, for reasons best known to him, refused. So Lee's shock troops were held in a meadow under constant enemy artillery fire until night came on and the battle subsided.[78]

That night McClellan continued his retreat to Harrison's Landing on the James. "Under ordinary circumstances the Federal Army should have been destroyed," Lee wrote, ". . . but regret that more was not accomplished gives way to gratitude to the Sovereign Ruler of the Universe for the results achieved. The siege of Richmond was raised, and the object of a campaign, which had been prosecuted after months of preparation at an enormous expenditure of men and money, completely frustrated."[79]

This was the end of the Seven Days Battle. It was a Confederate victory but the cost was high: 19,739 Confederates were killed or wounded against 9,796 for the Federals.[80] In Richmond there was great rejoicing. In the churches divine services were held commemorating the victory and at night throngs of happy people went about the streets shouting and laughing.[81] In Washington there was gloom. "I am in hopes that the enemy is as completely worn out as we are," McClellan wrote Lincoln. ". . . I hope that we shall have enough breathing space to reorganize and rest the men and get them into position before the enemy can attack again. . . . I beg that you will be fully impressed by the magnitude of the crisis in which we are placed."[82]

But Lee was in no position to renew the conflict. McClellan's hopes that his opponent was as worn out as he proved true. Lee was of the opinion "that it may be better to leave a small light force with the cavalry here near Harrison's Landing and retire the army near Richmond, where it can be better refreshed and strengthened and be prepared for a renewal of the contest, which must take place at some quarter soon."[83] Accordingly orders were issued. Longstreet's command was to move to a position on Cornelius Creek; D. H. Hill was to take his men to the Williamsburg Road; McLaws' division was to camp on Gilliss Creek; Jackson to take his men to a position on the Mechanicsville Road north of Richmond.[84]

Here on the Mechanicsville Road three miles above Richmond Whiting's division remained in camp for a month. It was a well-deserved rest, for Hood's and Law's troops had been marching and fighting since the eleventh of June. Now there was time for mail from home; a time when they could cook and eat their food without wondering if a Federal shell would fall in their mess; and a time for trying on the clothes they had captured from the Yankees.[85] And, on top of it all, the officers were liberal with passes to Richmond. Soon the streets of the city were filled with troops looking for entertainment and excitement.[86] Hood himself was often seen in the city. He called at Libby Prison to see his friends Captains Whiting and Chambliss who were taken prisoners at Gaines's Mill.[87] He and Fitzhugh Lee were seen together at the theater[88] and, knowing Hood's nature, one can also conjecture that he found good food and female companionship around the city. The time had not yet come when he was to be a favorite of Richmond society and Mrs. Chesnut's "PMG" (Pet Major General), but the chances are he enjoyed the fleshpots of Richmond during this rest period.

There was, however, one serious problem facing Hood during this period of rest. His brigade of Texans had been whittled down by death and wounds to hardly more than the size of a regiment. On May 21, 1862, his brigade strength is given as 1,922 men and officers.[89] Of this number some 600 were not Texans but were Georgians of the 18th Georgia. From this net of 1,322 Texans one must subtract casualties of some 480 suffered at Gaines's Mill and afterward. This would leave Hood slightly more than 800 Texans. Casualties in the 18th Georgia had also been high. Thus it is doubtful if Hood had more than a thousand men in his brigade.[90] Attaching as he did so much importance to his Texas shock troops, Lee took up the matter with Senator Wigfall. Not only did he urge that Hood's brigade be brought up to full strength but he also urged the creation of a second brigade of Texans for Hood.[91] It is quite probable that Hood himself discussed the matter with Wigfall, for he was on the best of terms with the fiery Senator from Texas and in addition was attracted to the Senator's young daughter, "Louly" (Louise).[92]

This was, of course, only a part of Lee's program of recruitment and reorganization. To Colonel John S. Preston, in charge of conscript service in South Carolina, he sent a request for more South Carolina troops to fill up the ranks.[93] To General Joseph Finegan in Florida, George W. Randolph, Secretary of War, sent a message: "We shall need a considerable accession of force to reap the fruits of our victory. If you can spare any infantry . . . send them on and we will arm them here."[94] And so the calls went—more troops, more ordnance, more commissary stores, more everything. Reorganization, too, was uppermost in Lee's mind. The Seven Days Battle had showed up the defects and dead wood in his organization. Particularly did it turn the spotlight on certain officers who, it appeared, had retarded rather than aided in the fighting. High among these were Huger, Magruder and Whiting. These men Lee dealt with in his customary considerate manner. Magruder was allowed to transfer to the Trans-Mississippi Department; Huger was relieved of duty and assigned as Inspector of Artillery and Ordnance.[95] And Whiting—well, there was a problem Lee obviously didn't know exactly how to handle.

Whiting's case was made more difficult because there had been no overt act of bad faith, insubordination or blundering on his part. His egotism, petulance and dislike for Jackson, however, made it difficult to find an assignment for him where he might serve and be happy. Under existing circumstances Lee apparently felt that it would be best to take no hasty action but rather try to let things work themselves out. General Whiting was on sick leave and no immediate end could be served by haste, so Lee made a sort of temporary independent command of Hood's and Law's brigades under his personal command. When the time came for marching again Hood, though still a brigadier, commanded the division under Longstreet. From that point on it was "Hood's Division." When Whiting was able to return to duty he was assigned to engineering services where his talents could best be utilized.[96]

CHAPTER V

So Near Victory

DURING the ninety-day period following the Seven Days Battle, Southern hopes were at hightide. Never again was the Confederacy to be so near victory and foreign recognition. Not only had Lee been successful in smashing McClellan's campaign against Richmond, but events in the west looked promising. During the latter part of August, Braxton Bragg and his Army of Tennessee marched toward Kentucky with better than an even chance for victory. On the twenty-eighth of July the *Alabama* left Liverpool to play havoc with Yankee shipping and, with the *Florida,* seriously to threaten the blockade. Although New Orleans had fallen, Vicksburg still held out, providing a bridge to the Far West. On the diplomatic front, chances for recognition of the Confederacy by France and England seemed bright. Early in July a motion had been introduced in Commons providing for joint Anglo-French mediation. At the same time, Napoleon III was approaching the English Government on the matter of outright recognition of Southern independence.

At Harrison's Landing, McClellan was adding nothing to Northern comfort. He was explaining away his defeat and loudly calling on Lincoln for reinforcements. After all, he had done pretty well, he thought, in view of the fact that "I had 200,000 enemy to fight. A good deal more than two to one, and they knowing the ground."[1] Actually McClellan had 91,169 effectives and Lee had 95,481[2]; and, as for knowing the ground, lack of proper maps was one of Lee's worst handicaps. In the matter of reinforcements, Lincoln seemed to feel that McClellan might well round up his stragglers. "I am told," Lincoln wrote, "that over 160,000 men have gone into your army on the Peninsula. When I was with you the other day we made out 86,500 remaining, leaving 73,500 to be accounted for. I believe 23,500 will cover all the killed, wounded, and missing in all your battles and skirmishes, leaving 50,000 who have left otherwise. . . . How can they be got to you, and how can they be prevented from getting away in such numbers for the future?"[3]

Instead of reinforcing McClellan, Lincoln did just the opposite. He took away what his general already had. On July 11 he made Major General Henry W. Halleck, then commanding Federal forces in the west, General in Chief, with headquarters in Washington. Halleck's underling, the boastful and pompous Major General John Pope, was given command of a new consolidated unit, the Army of Virginia, composed of the corps of McDowell, Banks and Frémont and located in the area of the Rappahannock around Fredericksburg. On the twenty-fourth of July Halleck visited McClellan at Harrison's Landing and found him still begging for reinforcements. He needed 50,000 more men, he told Halleck, and he could again attack Richmond via the Yorktown Peninsula. That number, said Halleck, was impossible, and, besides, the two Federal armies were separated with Lee between them. That was very unsafe strategy and should be corrected. Despite McClellan's protests Halleck on the third of August ordered the transfer of his troops to the Rappahannock.[4] McClellan was not actually removed from command. He merely had his troops taken away from him.

As far as Lee was concerned, the situation was not far different from what it was when he took command June 1. It will be recalled that at that time McClellan was advancing up the peninsula and McDowell was threatening to march down from Fredericksburg to effect a junction with him. Lee had found it advisable to assail the enemy's right before McDowell could arrive. This he did at Mechanicsville and Gaines's Mill. Now Pope was in the same general area that McDowell had occupied and McClellan was on the peninsula. From what direction would the Federal attack come? Should Lee again assume the initiative and strike first? How could he develop the enemy's intentions? How strong was Pope?

These were the questions Lee had to answer as rapidly as prudence would permit. Jackson was urging an immediate offensive which would by-pass Pope and sweep on into the North. McClellan is beaten, he urged, and there is no need to fear an attack from him. "We are wasting time," he argued.[5] But for the time being Lee continued his policy of watchful waiting. He strengthened the defenses of Richmond and sent Jackson to Gordonsville to watch Pope and to protect the Virginia Central Railroad. Jackson reached Gordonsville on July 16.[6]

Meantime Pope was doing a great deal of boasting, issuing a lot of ridiculous orders and posting his divisions. He was, he assured his troops, accustomed to seeing only the backs of his enemies. He had heard a lot of talk among generals about base of supplies and lines of retreat, he said, but this was utter foolishness. "Let us study the probable lines of retreat of our enemies, and leave our own to take care of themselves."[7] If he had stopped with simply being ridiculous the situation might merely have taken on some aspects of a comic-opera situation, but he went on to issue orders much more serious in their implications. Briefly summarized these orders which made Pope's name anathema to the South were: (1) The army was to subsist off the country in which it operated. "Vouchers will be given to the owners, stating on their face that they will be payable at the conclusion of the war, upon sufficient testimony being furnished that such owners have been loyal citizens of the United States since the date of the vouchers."[8] (2) The people of any given area were made responsible for the acts of any guerrilla bands which might be operating there.[9] (3) All noncombatant males were to be arrested. "Such as are willing to take the oath of allegiance to the United States and will furnish sufficient security for its observance shall be permitted to remain at their homes and pursue in good faith their accustomed avocations. Those who refuse shall be conducted South beyond the extreme pickets of this army, and be notified that if found again anywhere within our lines or at any point in rear they be considered spies and subjected to the extreme rigor of military law."[10]

Having thus delivered himself of orders which make William T. Sherman appear to have worn a glowing halo on his march through Georgia, Pope placed his troops. Brigadier General James B. Ricketts with four brigades was ordered to Warrenton; Major General Franz Sigel with six brigades went to Sperryville; Major General Nathaniel P. Banks, Jackson's old enemy, with six brigades, took position midway between Ricketts and Sigel. Their combined strength was nearly 40,000.[11] As soon as these divisions reached their positions the cavalry and one brigade of infantry pushed south and took Culpeper. From this point the cavalry was directed to patrol all roads leading toward Gordonsville and Richmond. It even had orders to capture Gordonsville and destroy the railroad, but, as stated above, Lee had sent Jackson there on July 13, and thus plans for any further cavalry raids on the town were abandoned.[12]

Lee continued his policy of caution, watching McClellan on the Yorktown Peninsula with one eye and Pope with the other. In late July he sent A. P. Hill's division to reinforce Jackson, and a few days later sent a portion of Stuart's cavalry. He was strengthening Jackson without weakening the Richmond defenses too much. Pope made no new move in response to this one by Lee. He, too, was watching, waiting and trying to ascertain Lee's strength.[13] In Washington, Halleck was pondering Lee's next move. The Confederates might (1) attack McClellan at Harrison's Landing or (2) concentrate against Pope before McClellan's troops arrived.[14] He was of the opinion, however, that the attack on McClellan was the more probable and thus Pope was ordered to make a demonstration on Gordonsville, hoping thereby to cause Lee to rush troops from Richmond and thus be forced to abandon any plans he might have to strike McClellan.[15]

Jackson, having learned of Pope's movement, did not wait to be attacked, but moved out to meet the advancing enemy columns. "I hope you may be able to strike him moving, or at least be able to draw him from his strong positions," Lee wrote. "Relying upon your judgment, courage, and discretion, and trusting to the continued blessings of an ever-kind Providence, I hope for victory."[16] On the next afternoon after this letter was written Jackson clashed with his old enemy, Banks, at Slaughter Mountain. "Banks is in front of me," he had said, "and he is always ready to fight." And then laughingly he had added: "And he generally gets whipped."[17]

And Banks did fight and he did get whipped this afternoon of August 9, 1862. Jackson held his position after the battle for two days and then retired to Gordonsville. "The country owes you and your brave officers and soldiers a deep debt of gratitude," Lee wrote. "I hope your victory is but the precursor of others over our foe in that quarter, which will entirely break up and scatter his army."[18] But it would be impossible for Jackson alone to "break up and scatter" the Federals in his front. Jackson was in an isolated position with McClellan's and Burnside's troops moving from the peninsula to reinforce Pope's army. A large and important battle was shaping up and on August 13 Lee sent Longstreet's command to join Jackson.[19]

On the same day, August 13, Hood received his orders to "march at once with your command to Gordonsville and report to General Longstreet."[20] To Hood and his men this meant that after more than a month of inactivity they were to take up the fight again. During this month they had rested and re-equipped themselves and many of the sick and wounded had regained their health. Efforts to obtain new recruits from Texas had, however, not been very successful. With the return of approximately half the sick and wounded the combined strength of his and Law's brigades was raised to approximately 2,800 men—a "demi-division" Longstreet called it.[21] But it was a division which Hood commanded now instead of a brigade. General Whiting was still on sick leave and thus Hood's command was officially temporary, but Lee had already decided on a change for Whiting and this was made official in the fall.[22] Although small, it was one of the best of Longstreet's divisions. Hood's Texans had proved themselves by breaking the line at Gaines's Mill, but right behind the Texans had come Law's men charging and yelling like demons. Colonel Evard McIver Law, the stouthearted and levelheaded South Carolinian, was considered by Hood "an able and efficient officer,"[23] and he assuredly merited the high opinion held by his superiors.

The two brigades were almost a cross section of the South. Hood's was composed, of course, of his three Texas regiments, the South Carolina Legion and the 18th Georgia. Law's was made up of the 4th Alabama, 2nd Mississippi, 11th Mississippi and the 6th North Carolina. Hood's one battery of artillery had from the beginning been under the command of the swashbuckling, picturesque Irishman, Captain James Reilly. Now two other batteries (South Carolina) were added to Hood's division as it left Richmond to join Longstreet at Gordonsville.[24]

The men were now veterans who had learned what campaigning meant, so they marched light, dispensing with all superfluous equipment. But light as they might march, they could not eliminate rifle, cartridge box, cap box, bayonet, blanket roll, haversack and canteen, which added up to about thirty-six pounds.[25] And if one adds a few more pounds for bowie knives and pistols stuck in the belts of the Texans one comes up with a heavy load for weary legs to carry through the Virginia heat and dust. But hurry they must, for Jackson was doomed if Longstreet did not get there in time. Already Burnside's troops from Fredericksburg were arriving and more were on the way from McClellan on the peninsula.

On August 15 Lee took the train from Richmond to Gordons-ville to establish headquarters and to confer with Longstreet and Jackson.[26] On that same day Longstreet's troops arrived to take position along the Rapidan; and Lee sat down and took counsel with Jackson and Longstreet. On the map they could plot Pope's precarious position. His front was on the Rapidan and his back to the Rappahannock. What better chance was ever presented for a swift stroke. If Lee's infantry could hold on the Rapidan and the cavalry could be sent to Pope's rear to destroy the bridges across the Rappahannock his entire army might be caught in a cul-de-sac and destroyed. Acting with swiftness, Lee sent back to Richmond for the rest of his troops he had left there.[27] He must strike quickly and in full force if his plan was to succeed. But this he was not able to do, for again Lee was thwarted by the inability of his army to move as a co-ordinated unit. This time the chief culprit was Fitz Lee, the loud-laughing, hard-riding, twenty-seven-year-old nephew of the commanding general. On the six-teenth Stuart had ordered young Lee to join him on the evening of the sevententh at Raccoon Ford. Then the combined cavalry force would ride to Pope's rear and complete its part of the gen-eral plan. On the evening of the seventeenth Stuart went to Raccoon Ford for the rendezvous with Fitz Lee, but there was no Lee. Stuart sent his adjutant, Major Norman Fitzhugh, to look for the tardy officer, but he failed to locate him. However, Fitz-hugh did manage to get himself captured and in his pocket was a dispatch which partially revealed Robert E. Lee's plans. Meantime Stuart had spent the night near Raccoon Ford and on the morning of the eighteenth was aroused by the sound of approaching horsemen. Assuming it to be the overdue Lee, he walked out to welcome him. It wasn't Lee, however. It was a body of Federal cavalry and Stuart was forced to flee, leaving behind his hat and coat.[28]

Fitzhugh Lee finally arrived on the evening of the eighteenth, exactly twenty-four hours late, but in the meantime other incidents had occurred to delay his famous uncle's attack until the twentieth. By this time Pope had learned of Lee's plans and was retiring to the east bank of the Rappahannock. On the eighteenth Lee and Longstreet rode to the top of Clark's Mountain and through their glasses watched Pope's army retire. Turning to Longstreet, Lee remarked laconically: "General, we little thought that the enemy would turn his back upon us this early in the campaign."[29] And with that he rode back to headquarters to plan anew for whipping Pope.

Pope's retirement was behind the Rappahannock, where he could command the fords. His hope was that he might hold these passes and fords long enough so that he might be reinforced by McClellan's troops from the Yorktown Peninsula.[30] The Confederate Army thus crossed the Rapidan without opposition. By the twentieth Lee's forces were testing out the passes across the Rappahannock. At Kelly's Ford on the twenty-first Hood and his division came under heavy artillery fire. While the firing was in progress a lone Federal horseman bearing a white flag rode into the river. Swearing that his eyesight had suddenly gone bad Captain Reilly turned a gun on him. The first shot hit the water three feet to the right of the horseman. The next one was to the left and the third a few feet in front of him. Then an aide galloped up and shouted at Reilly, "General Hood says stop your damn foolishness—that man is bearing a flag of truce." His eyesight suddenly improving, Reilly answered with a grin: "And so, be Jasus he is—but why in the name of Saint Patrick and all the ither holy saints, why didn't the spalpeen hold the damned white rag high enough for an Irishman to persaive it?"[31]

The next day things were more serious up the river at Freeman's Ford. In his official report Hood dryly reported: "On August 22, agreeably [*sic*] to orders of the commanding general, I proceeded to Freeman's Ford to relieve General Trimble's brigade. . . . The Texas brigade being placed on the right and Colonel Law's on the left, the attack was made at once, General Trimble leading off in the center. The enemy were driven precipitately over the Rappahannock with considerable loss, not less, I think, than from 200 to 300."[32] What Hood didn't tell was how the battle started, but one of his soldiers related the story in later years. The Texas brigade had formed in line just at the edge of a field of corn in the roasting-ear stage. On the other side of the field were the Yankees just as hungry for fresh corn as the Texans. Two soldiers, one a Yankee and one a Confederate, entered the field from opposite sides and, each unaware of the other, began to gather corn. Eventually they met in the center of the field. Without a word they dropped their armloads of corn and rushed at each other. As they rolled and pummeled each other each let out a lusty yell for help. The Yankees rushed to the rescue. The 5th Texas rushed to the rescue, bearing aloft the Lone Star flag on a tall staff. The Federal artillery opened fire on the flag, and there was a nasty little fight in which Major D. M. Whaley of the 5th Texas was killed.[33]

All up and down the upper stretches of the Rappahannock vicious little skirmishes were going on as Lee's troops tried to move to the east bank. Pope had done a good job of blocking these fords with artillery. The east bank of the Rappahannock was considerably higher than the opposite bank occupied by the Confederates thus favoring Federal artillery. Lee was a caged animal pacing up and down looking for an opening in the bars. On the twenty-second he discovered a chink. The Warrenton Road was open and undefended. Over this he sent Stuart to Pope's rear to investigate. Crossing at Waterloo Bridge near the southern tip of Bull Run Mountains, Stuart pushed on to Warrenton and then turned eastward to Catlett's Station. Here he encountered a friendly Negro who agreed to lead him to General Pope's head-quarters. Advancing cautiously in a blinding rainstorm, Stuart reached Pope's camp and then dashed into it, capturing several officers. But his real prize was Pope's hat and his coat stuffed with dispatches which revealed Federal plans.[34]

The information, however, did not enable Lee to cross the lower fords with any more ease. Federal artillery still contested every attempted crossing, and in view of this Lee decided on his favor-ite device—a flanking movement. Jackson would move around Pope's right and put himself between the Federal Army and Washington. Longstreet would then follow Jackson and, it was hoped, distract and baffle the enemy until he would become dis-organized to the point where individual units could be shipped one by one. The route was left up to Jackson, and he chose to march the long way around—northward behind the protection of Bull Run Mountains, then right face and eastward through Thor-oughfare Gap.

On the evening of August 24 Jackson made preparations for this the most famous of all his marches. Before dawn on the morning of the twenty-fifth his men were in motion. By afternoon they had covered twenty miles and were still marching in good order. By midnight they reached Salem Village and bivouacked. On the morning of the twenty-sixth they were again on the move through Thoroughfare Gap, which was unpicketed and unpro-tected by a single Federal. Through the gap they marched on to Manassas Plain in Pope's rear and still were not attacked or, so far as Jackson knew, even observed. Near sunset the columns reached Bristoe Station on the Orange and Alexandria Railroad, Pope's chief supply line. Here the track was torn up and two trains rolled down an embankment. Then, pushing on through the hot, still night, Jackson struck Manassas Junction near midnight. A vast quantity of stores was appropriated by the Confederates and the rest put to the torch.[35]

Jackson had accomplished an almost incredible feat with foot soldiers. He had marched to the enemy's rear, severed communications, broken and burned the bridges and destroyed vast quantities of supplies. He had accomplished with infantry what any cavalry leader would have considered a brilliant stroke for mounted men. But he was in a highly precarious position. The whole movement would succeed or fail in proportion to the speed of Longstreet in following for the full concentration in Pope's rear.

Meantime Longstreet's divisions were marching, taking the same route as had Jackson. Hood's division was the advance guard. At 2:00 P.M. on the twenty-sixth Hood's men began the arduous and exhausting march. All that night the division marched at route step, taking only the customary five-minute rest each hour. The morning of the twenty-seventh dawned hot and cloudless, and still the men went forward on blistered feet and aching legs. The dust thickened and men drank the water from their canteens in great gurgling gulps only to find that it was almost impossible to refill them. In the villages along the march groups of girls and women gathered and waved, but the soldiers were too tired to care. They were dust-colored robots now pushing on almost as if in a dreamy state of half-consciousness. Many of them never even saw the body of a spy hanging by his neck from the limb of a tree near the line of march.

At nightfall the men of Hood's division dropped to the ground and were asleep almost before they could swallow their cold meat and bread.[36] As the men slept someone on the slope above them kicked over a barrel which had been used as a receptacle for forage, and it came bumping and bounding down the hill, profoundly disturbing as it rolled an old gray mare loaded with regimental pots and pans. As she broke loose and dashed into their midst someone yelled "look out" and "the brave men who had fought so nobly at Cold Harbor sprang to their feet, deserted their colors and guns, and ran down the slope over a well constructed fence, which was soon levelled to the ground, and had continued their flight several hundred yards before they awoke sufficiently to recover their wits, and boldly marched back, convulsed with laughter."[37] The next morning as the march was resumed the brigade had a new marching song. It was "The Old Gray Mare Came a Tearin' Out o' the Wilderness."[38]

On the morning of the twenty-eighth the men awakened rested and ready for another day's marching. As they lighted fires to cook their breakfast they could see ahead of them in the morning mists the break in the mountains called Thoroughfare Gap. Although within sight, however, it was still a good half day's march away. As they approached it shortly after noon they found it occupied by the enemy. Jackson had passed through without opposition, but now Longstreet would have to fight his way through. D. R. Jones's division was ordered to occupy the gap itself while Hood's division was sent to cross the mountain via a cattle trail north of the gap.[39] Jones advanced rapidly with G. T. Anderson's brigade in the lead. As the pass was reached Federal artillery swept the approaches and for a period the Confederates were halted. North of the pass Hood and Law had found a trail which ended abruptly at a small cleft in a rock. Through this cleft their men could pass one at a time. This they did and within a matter of an hour Law had formed his lines overlooking the Federal artillery positions which commanded the gap. Anxiously the brigade pushed forward, but before contact could be made the Federal artillery retired. Jones waited awhile and then marched unopposed through the gap.[40]

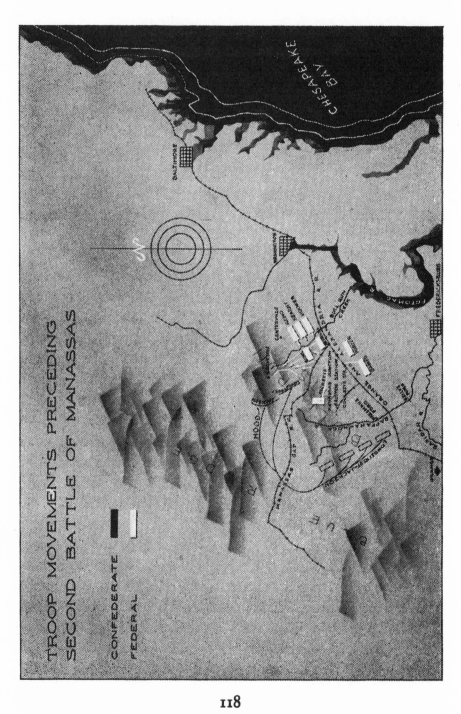

TROOP MOVEMENTS PRECEDING
SECOND BATTLE OF MANASSAS

CONFEDERATE

FEDERAL

118

On the morning of the twenty-ninth Longstreet's divisions began worming their way through the pass. Hood's division, having
crossed the afternoon before via the cattle trail, now led the way
again. The gallant Lieutenant Colonel John C. Upton of the 5th
Texas, now minus his frying pan, was in the lead with a detail
of 150 picked skirmishers. About 10:30 Jackson rode out to meet
Hood on the Groveton Pike and extended hearty greetings.[41] It is
not difficult to imagine how relieved Jackson must have been to
realize that Longstreet's troops were now actually arriving on the
field. Quickly Hood's division fell into line. Law's brigade was
placed on Jackson's immediate right; then the Texas brigade was
deployed; then, to the right of the Texans, Longstreet's other
divisions were formed in line of battle as they arrived.[42]

The impending battle was already under way when Longstreet's troops arrived. Since his raid on Manassas Junction, Jackson had completely baffled the enemy by his tactical legerdemain.
He had crossed Bull Run, had disappeared from the face of the
converging Federals as though the earth had swallowed him and
then reappeared along the unfinished railroad northwest of
Groveton. He had formed his line of battle in an excellent defensive position, his right extended toward Thoroughfare Gap to
receive Longstreet. Here he awaited the Federal attack. But it
was Jackson who attacked. Late in the afternoon of the twenty-
eighth he assaulted King's division as it passed wheeling into position on his right wing. It was a stubborn and vicious fight in
which Jackson lost two of his division commanders, Ewell and
Taliaferro, seriously wounded. On the morning of the twenty-
ninth Jackson had slightly shifted his position and was waiting
for Longstreet, but the artillery of both sides was busy hurling its
grape and canister.[43]

When Longstreet's divisions had all arrived, the Confederate
line of battle was as follows, from left to right: A. P. Hill's division on the extreme left; then Ewell's division commanded by

General A. R. Lawton; Jackson's own division, now commanded by General William E. Starke; and Hood's division, with General N. G. "Shank" Evans' brigade in support, occupying the center of the line. On the right of Hood was D. R. Jones's division with Stuart's cavalry in support here as on the left.[44] Total Confederate strength was approximately 48,000.[45] On the Federal side, Reno's Ninth Corps, Hooker's and Kearny's divisions of Heintzelman's Third Corps faced Jackson, while McDowell's corps was in Longstreet's front. Porter's Fifth Corps was behind the Manassas Gap Railroad some three miles away.[46] Total Federal strength was approximately 75,000.[47]

It was on Jackson's left that the battle first raged. On the twenty-ninth while Longstreet was placing his divisions the Federals had thrown charge after charge at A. P. Hill's men on the left. And each time they had been thrown back with staggering losses. Piles of dead bodies lay thick on the unfinished railroad line and the roar of artillery was deafening. By four o'clock Federal pressure had slackened, but then it burst out afresh. Near five o'clock the fifth and final Federal charge struck Jackson's lines, and they held—precariously, but they held.[48] Five assaults by 30,000 Federal troops had failed to shake Jackson's lines, but there is a limit to what troops can endure and Jackson's had about reached that limit.

Near by, Lee and Longstreet watched Jackson's troops take the deadly assaults. Lee urged Longstreet to attack so that some of the pressure would be taken off Jackson, but Longstreet hesitated and asked for time to make a reconnaissance of the enemy's ground. After an hour he returned and advised against an immediate attack, but did suggest a reconnaissance in force against the Federal center with the idea that if an opening could be found that afternoon it could be utilized the next morning to good advantage. To this Lee assented and Hood's division supported by Evans and Wilcox was assigned the task.[49]

According to Longstreet, Hood's troops found the assignment "an agreeable surprise," and "they jumped . . . to welcome in counter charges the enemy's coming."[50] Within five minutes after Lee gave the order the division was advancing, a strong line of skirmishers leading. On Hood's left, Law encountered a battery of artillery supported by infantry. "Charge them," Hood ordered, and Law's men rushed the guns, firing as they ran. Three guns were limbered up and carried off by the Federals, while a fourth was captured. Then, sweeping forward, Law carried his portion of the field.[51] On Law's right the 1st Texas under Lieutenant Colonel P. A. Work advanced only to be met with a shower of grape and canister; and then when the regiment was within fifteen yards of the battery the firing, for some unknown reason, ceased. Pushing on in the increasing gloom of twilight, they engaged the 79th New York Infantry. After only one volley someone in the ranks of the New Yorkers began to shout "friend," and in the confusion resulting from this false cry in the gathering darkness the Federal regiment retired.[52] On the right of the 1st Texas, Lieutenant Colonel B. F. Carter led Hood's old regiment, the 4th, into the skirmish, but received only token resistance.[53] Colonel William Wofford's 18th Georgia was not heavily engaged and, except for momentary confusion resulting from some unknown person's order to halt, pressed steadily on.[54] The Hampton Legion and the 5th Texas were not engaged sufficiently to merit a report.

This was merely a reconnaissance and losses were light. With the coming of total darkness the men dropped to the ground and in a short while most of them were asleep. As a reconnaissance, however, it had achieved its purpose. As the men slept, Wilcox and Hood examined the enemy positions as best they could in the twilight and then rode back to report to Longstreet. Their views coincided: the enemy's positions were too strong for a successful attack at dawn, and they so informed Longstreet.[55] This confirmed the view held by Longstreet before the reconnaissance; and on the basis of the information Lee determined to avoid a general engagement with Pope and to rely on maneuvering to defeat him. Then, retiring to a cabin in Hood's rear, he caught a few hours' sleep. [56]

When the morning sun awakened the sleeping army there was no immediate resumption of the battle. As the Confederates cooked breakfast there commenced a desultory fire from a few enemy batteries, but it was not of a serious nature. Soon it died away, and almost complete silence prevailed all along the front. Lee and Longstreet were apprehensive that Pope was getting away again.[57] At the same time Pope was quite sure that the Confederates were retreating.[58] As a matter of fact, both Lee and Pope were uncertain of the other's possible plans. Pope's plans apparently went no further than going "forward at once to see."[59] Lee called Jackson and Longstreet for a conference on his plan. If the Federals did not attack before noon he would demonstrate along his present lines during the afternoon and then that night slip around Pope's right near Sudley Springs and interpose himself between the Federals and Washington. Confident the enemy would not attack again, Longstreet rode away from the conference to find Hood and prepare for the demonstration.[60]

But the enemy did renew the attack and it was against Jackson on the left again. Near three o'clock Pope in desperation once more hurled his men against the Confederate lines as if to overcome Jackson through sheer mass force. But again Jackson held, even though his ammunition ran low and many of his men defended themselves by hurling rocks at the enemy.[61] Near by, within sight of the battle, Hood sat with his troops, watching the magnificent charges of the Federals and the equally magnificent stand being made by Jackson. Hood was under orders and could not move his division until told to do so, but he became fidgety and ordered up Reilly's battery to open on the enemy's flank. The battery pulled up, unlimbered and joined Frobel's and S. D. Lee's artillery in ploughing deep furrows in the Federal lines as they moved to the assault.[62]

For nearly an hour Jackson's men took everything the enemy could throw at them—and then it came time for Longstreet's attack to win the day. All along the lines ran the indescribable, tense, sickening and yet thrilling sensation which only men who have gone into battle can know. They were going in to relieve "Old Jack." About four o'clock Hood received his orders to lead the attack and his division moved forward. Through the carnival of death went his Texans and Georgians "at a run, their wild yells rending the dull roar of the fight; their bayonets flashing in a jagged line of light like hungry teeth."[63] "Don't let your men move so rapidly they will get beyond the reach of the supporting troops," Longstreet warned.[64]

As Hood advanced, the whole of Longstreet's command fell in behind in support. Wilcox was on Hood's left. Evans and R. H. Anderson were in support, while Kemper with three brigades flanked him. On Hood's right was D. R. Jones.[65] This was to be no piecemeal assault as at Gaines's Mill. This was the co-ordinated attack of an entire command against the enemy's left and center. Gone now were any thoughts of a demonstration in the afternoon preparatory to slipping around the enemy's right to gain his rear at night.

Hood's division had advanced a scant hundred and fifty yards when they encountered the enemy. Law on Hood's extreme left had watched the heavy attack on Jackson for a full hour. Now Hood ordered him into action in concert with the Texas brigade. Law soon lost contact, however, and was on his own. Moving forward, he clashed with the enemy on his front in heavy force concealed in ravines and pine thickets. They had to be flushed regiment by regiment and finally man by man. However, Law carried his part of the field in a systematic manner. Spectacular charges were conspicuously absent, yet the fighting was vicious,

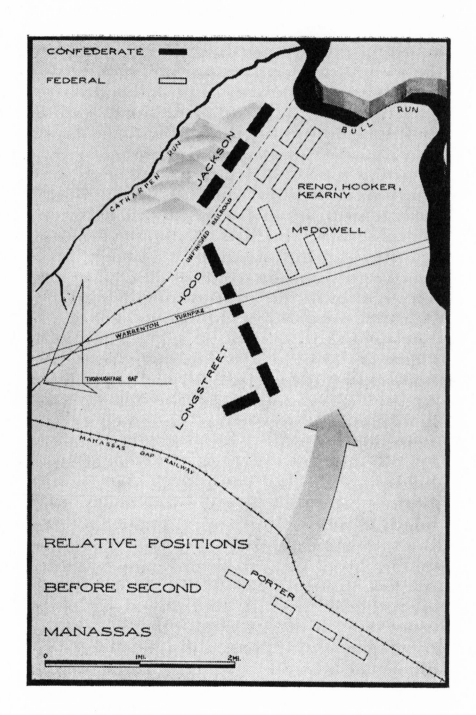

CONFEDERATE

FEDERAL

BULL RUN

CATHARPEN RUN

JACKSON

RENO, HOOKER, KEARNY

UNFINISHED RAILROAD

McDOWELL

HOOD

WARRENTON TURNPIKE

THOROUGHFARE GAP

LONGSTREET

MANASSAS GAP RAILWAY

RELATIVE POSITIONS

BEFORE SECOND

MANASSAS

PORTER

0   1 MI.   2 MI.

as shown by the fact that Law lost 320 men killed and wounded.[66] On Law's right, Colonel Work became a bit confused and the 1st Texas went into battle without him. Running to overtake his regiment he soon became confused again. After crossing two hollows in his front he watched so intently a Federal battery on a ridge ahead that he failed to keep pace with the regiments on his right and left; and when he recovered from his hypnosis he and his regiment were lost. By the time they found themselves and the battle it was almost over. Losses were only ten killed and wounded.[67]

The 4th Texas in Hood's center, led by Lieutenant Colonel B. F. Carter, advanced in double-quick time and soon encountered the same general situation experienced all along the attacking lines—artillery on the ridges and infantry on the slopes. On Work's front the enemy artillery opened with grape and canister, and for a moment the regiment faltered as men will do when they first come under heavy fire. The regiment responded quickly to the order to charge, however, and the infantry was pushed back on the artillery and then both retired to counterattack. Carter, looking to his left for the 1st Texas, could not find it, for the 1st Texas was lost. Then, turning to the 18th Georgia on his right, he asked for assistance; but Wofford could send none, for he was wheeling to his right to assist the 5th Texas and Hampton's Legion, now hard pressed. Carter now found himself in a spot. The enemy was counterattacking on his left where the 1st Texas was supposed to be but wasn't. There was only one thing left other than possible annihilation—retire and go in search of the 1st Texas. This Carter did, but before he located them he had lost sixteen killed and 112 wounded.[68] The Texas brigade was suffering the effects of being poorly led by new and inexperienced officers.

On Hood's right the 18th Georgia, the Legion and the 5th Texas co-operated in a drive which conservatively could be classified as spectacular. They advanced in perfect unison with a shout, carrying the first line of the enemy with hardly a perceptible cessation of their forward movement. Behind the first line, however, was a stouter one composed of the 5th and 10th New York—the Zouaves in their white spats, blue trousers and scarlet jackets. The first line fled to the rear, but the Zouaves stood firm. Re-forming their lines, the three Confederate regiments charged, pouring in a deadly fire from their muskets and then giving them the bayonet.[69] These were the gaily clad troops who had come out on the ice of the half-frozen Potomac at Cockpit Point and half jestingly and half in earnest had taunted the Texas brigade with the threat of annihilation if they should ever meet in battle. Now they had met and the Zouaves were almost destroyed. "The enemy . . . poured upon his little command [Warren's Zouaves] . . . a mass of infantry that enveloped—almost destroyed—him and completely pierced our line," the Federal commander in this sector reported. "It became necessary to retire from the ground we occupied."[70]

The attack having thus been initiated by Hood's division, the battle now became general. Colonel John H. Means, commanding Evans' brigade, came up in support, and as he did so Means dropped with a bullet through him.[71] Now R. H. Anderson moved up;[72] then Jones's division caught up and its commander asked Hood to direct his attack.[73] Like a mighty engine which roars into action after fitful sputtering, Longstreet's entire command joined the attack, sweeping "steadily on, driving the enemy with great carnage from each successive position until 10 P.M. when darkness put an end to the battle and the pursuit."[74] The flight of the enemy was, Hood wrote in later years, "the most beautiful battle scene I have ever beheld."[75] After he had assembled the remnants of his regiments at the close of the pursuit he rode back to Lee's headquarters. He found the general in an open field reading dispatches by the light of a campfire. He was in high spirits and jestingly asked Hood what had become of the enemy. When Hood told him how beautiful it was to see the Confederate battle flags dancing after the retreating enemy Lee changed instantly to a more solemn mood. "God forbid," he said, "I should ever live to see our colors moving in the opposite direction."[76]

The next morning it was discovered that the Federals had escaped to Centreville, four miles beyond Bull Run; but late in the night a torrential rain fell, swelling Bull Run until it was impassable. Further pursuit, therefore, was impossible for Lee on the morning of the thirty-first, and the Second Battle of Bull Run was over. The wounded were collected, the dead were buried and the gains and losses entered as after every battle. Lee had lost 1,481 killed and 7,627 wounded, the heaviest losses being in Jackson's and Hood's divisions.[77] The Texas brigade had lost 628 men killed and wounded, approximately 40 per cent of its strength, including Lieutenant Colonel Upton dead and J. B. Robertson wounded. Law's had suffered 320 casualties, approximately 23 per cent of its strength.[78]

The Confederates had, in turn, inflicted serious losses on the Federals. As Hood rode out over the field on the morning of the thirty-first he saw what his right wing had done to the Zouaves. They had, he noted, literally strewed the ground with their dead and wounded. One of the privates in the 4th Texas wrote about the same scene. The variegated colors of the gaudy uniforms gave the view when looked at from a distance, "the appearance of a Texas hillside when carpeted in the spring by wild flowers of many hues and tints."[79] Federal losses all along the lines had been heavy. In all, Pope lost 1,724 killed and 8,372 wounded.[80] In addition, Lee reported that "more than 7,000 prisoners were taken in addition to about 2,000 wounded left in our hands. Thirty pieces of artillery, upward of 20,000 stands of small arms, numerous colors, and a large amount of stores, besides those taken by General Jackson at Manassas Junction, were captured."[81]

Among the prizes of battle were several new ambulances taken by Hood and promptly divided among his regiments where they were so sorely needed. Brigadier General Nathaniel G. Evans, who by seniority technically commanded Hood's division, ordered the ambulances turned over to his South Carolina brigade and Hood refused. Evans promptly reported Hood's disobedience of orders to Longstreet and Hood was placed under arrest, deprived of his command and ordered to Culpeper Courthouse to await trial by court-martial. When the matter was brought to General Lee's attention he ordered Hood to remain with his command, but did not release him from arrest.[82] Therefore, instead of proudly riding "Jeff Davis" at the head of his division into Maryland, Hood was forced to take a position in the rear where he could give no orders. Ahead of him in the ranks his men restrained their feeling about the matter with difficulty.[83]

Hood previously had avoided any participation in the feuds and quarrels which had been so prevalent in Lee's army.[84] He had been a model colonel and brigadier, fighting vigorously when called on and keeping his mouth shut the rest of the time. His chief virtues were his dependability and dash as a combat officer and his strict regard for the sanctity of orders. Off the battlefield he was congenial, even convivial, but on the battlefield he was likely to be highly emotional. This Evans business came at a time when he was burying his dead and getting his wounded to the rear, always a time of great emotional stress for him, and it was more than he could stomach. He apparently never forgave Evans, and at the risk of losing his command he refused to offer even a hint of an apology.

CHAPTER VI

Maryland—Round Trip

THE decision to seize the initiative and march into Maryland was reached only after the most mature consideration by Lee and his lieutenants. The Federals had been swept from the field of Manassas and were now safe behind the fortifications around Washington, but they would not remain there. Lee was faced with the problem of the direction his next move should take; and after weighing the matter he decided that there was only one way he could go and that was north. Political as well as military advantages were offered in Maryland. The state, it was felt, was fundamentally friendly to the Southern cause and might rally to the Stars and Bars if given the opportunity. (It was the same delusion under which Braxton Bragg was laboring in his invasion of Kentucky now progressing at the very moment Lee was planning the Maryland venture.) From a military point of view the invasion was about all there was left to Lee. If he moved southward he would only draw the enemy closer to Richmond; eastward lay strongly fortified Washington; westward was the Shenandoah Valley, where possible defeat or confinement would lay Richmond bare.

Being reinforced with four brigades under McLaws, two under J. G. Walker from North Carolina, five brigades under D. H. Hill from Richmond and one brigade of cavalry under Wade Hampton, Lee crossed the Potomac near Leesburg on September 4 and concentrated his troops at Frederick, Maryland. The cavalry followed and threw up a screen to the east in the direction of Baltimore and Washington. The strength of his army was approximately 51,000 men.[1]

Meantime in Washington the Federal Army was reorganized. Pope was relieved and assigned to duty in the West and Halleck called on McClellan to resume command. McDowell's corps was assigned to Major General Joseph Hooker and was designated as the First Corps. The corps of Major General Edwin V. Sumner became the Second Corps; Major General Samuel P. Heintzelman commanded the Third Corps; Major General Erasmus D. Keyes took over the Fourth Corps; Major General Fitz John Porter still commanded the Fifth Corps; and Major General William B. Franklin was assigned the Sixth Corps. The troops from North and South Carolina serving in the Union Army were put in the Ninth Corps, commanded by Major General Jesse L. Reno. Major General Franz Sigel was given the Eleventh Corps, and Major General Joseph Mansfield took over Banks's command as the Twelfth Corps. The strength of this new army of McClellan's was 93,000 men and 300 guns. This time McClellan was not so slow and cautious. By September 7 he had taken personal command of the new army and was advancing along the roads running from Washington westward.[2]

Thus the two armies approached each other, one nearly twice as strong as the other. And in the face of these odds Lee did an audacious and dangerous thing: he divided his army in the face of the enemy. After concentrating his dirty footsore troops at Frederick, he found it desirable to protect his communications through the Shenandoah Valley by capturing Harpers Ferry. On the morning of September 10 he sent all of the troops of Jackson, McLaws, R. H. Anderson and John G. Walker to do this job. This left Lee with only the divisions of Hood, D. R. Jones and D. H. Hill. These he moved from Frederick to Hagerstown, Hill being the rear guard. Jackson, McLaws and Walker were to rejoin

Longstreet at Hagerstown after the capture of Harpers Ferry.[3]

Longstreet with Hood's and Jones's troops reached Hagerstown on the eleventh, but hardly had they concluded the march when news came that D. H. Hill, bringing up the rear, was in distress at Boonsboro, midway between Frederick and Hagerstown.[4] McClellan's troops had moved faster than Lee thought and now were threatening him at Boonsboro. Lee sat on his horse Traveler by the side of the road, watching his weary troops countermarch to Hill's relief. Soon the Texas brigade marched past. It was going into battle again, but it had a grudge. Hood was under arrest—and now as the men passed they called out to their commander in chief, "Give us Hood."[5] Lee raised his hat, it is said, and replied, "You shall have him, gentlemen." With this the troops began to cheer.[6]

As Hood rode by at the rear of his troops Colonel R. H. Chilton, Lee's chief of staff, stopped him with the message that Lee wished to see him. Dismounting, Hood approached Lee and saluted.

"General," Lee pleaded, "here I am just on the eve of entering into battle with one of my best officers under arrest. If you will merely say that you regret this occurrence, I will release you and restore you to the command of your division."

To this Hood replied: "I am unable to do so, since I cannot admit or see the justness of General Evans' demand for the ambulances my men have captured. Had I been ordered to turn them over for the general use of the army, I would cheerfully have acquiesced."

Lee repeated his request, but Hood was adamant.

"Well," concluded Lee, "I will suspend your arrest till the impending battle is decided."[7]

With that Hood galloped off to rejoin his division, to receive their cheers and to report to Longstreet for orders.[8]

Hill was indeed hard pressed at South Mountain on this dry hot day of September 14. Since early morning he had, with five small brigades, been engaging portions of the Federal First and Ninth Corps massing in his front. The fight had started near seven o'clock in the morning with an attack by Cox's division (Reno's Corps) on the Confederate right held by Brigadier General Samuel Garland. In the assault Garland was killed, and his brigade broke in confusion.[9] Had Cox known just how serious conditions were at the moment he might have ended the matter of the disputed passage once and for all. Instead of pushing straight ahead, however, Cox turned right oblique and began feeling for an opening. There was one—a gaping unprotected hole in Hill's defense—but Hill hastily brought up two guns and assembled behind them his cooks, teamsters, staff officers and hangers-on to create the appearance of strength. Then G. B. Anderson's brigade plugged the hole.[10] Having thus temporarily strengthened his right against Reno's troops, Hill then turned his attention to the left where Hooker's divisions were massing against Brigadier General R. E. Rodes's brigade. There was severe skirmishing here but no desperate Federal charges.[11]

As a matter of fact, the Federal attack during the morning had been piecemeal, waiting the arrival of all the divisions before a general assault was made. Longstreet arrived just before this full-scale assault and helped hold Hill's position until nightfall. George T. Anderson's, Thomas F. Drayton's and Hood's men were placed on Hill's right. Those of James L. Kemper, Micah Jenkins, Richard G. Garnett and N. G. Evans took position on the left.[12] Longstreet had gone into the battle without conferring with Hill or familiarizing himself with the topography of the position. This, plus the fact that Longstreet's men were exhausted from their long forced march, prevented the most effective use of the troops. In fact, Hill took a rather dim view of Longstreet's efforts. His only word of praise for any of Longstreet's troops was for Hood. "General Hood," he wrote, "who had gone in on the right with his two noble brigades, pushed forward his skirmishers

and drove back the Yankees. We retreated that night to Sharpsburg...."[13] Except for a word of praise for Colquitt's brigade of
his own division that was all. As far as Hill's loquacious report
goes, one would gather that no other troops from Longstreet's
command were engaged.[14]

Other units, of course, were engaged, but it was often difficult
to tell what group was fighting whom. Hood merely states in
his report that as he went into action he met Drayton coming out,
saying the Federals had gained his rear. Hood ordered his two
brigades to fix bayonets and move forward, "which they did with
their usual gallantry, driving the enemy and regaining all of our
lost ground, when night came on and further pursuit ceased."[15]
About all Longstreet could say was: "We succeeded in repulsing
the repeated and powerful attacks of the enemy and in holding
our position until night put an end to the battle."[16] Jones was
equally vague. "While taking position," he wrote, "my troops
were exposed to severe shelling and shortly afterwards to a heavy
infantry attack in overwhelming numbers. Despite the odds they
held their ground till dark...."[17]

The truth is the Confederates were badly confused, and about
all the soldiers knew was to shoot at the Yankees whenever they
saw them. But Ripley's brigade didn't even do this. It became so
confused it did not fire a gun all day.[18] And even after night
covered the battlefield the confusion did not end. About ten
o'clock Hood rode to the rear and found Hill and other officers
gathered on the gallery of a tavern discussing the events of the
day. On approaching the group he called out in an ordinary tone
of voice and was met with a chorus of shushing. In a whisper
they advised him the enemy was in a near-by cornfield. "I there-
upon suggested," wrote Hood, "that we repair without delay to
General Lee's headquarters, and report the situation." This was
done, according to Hood, and later that night it was decided that
the army should fall back toward Sharpsburg.[19]

In addition to the confusion among the Confederate troops it should be borne in mind that apparently Longstreet had not done his best to assist Hill. It is well known that he favored a retirement of Lee's whole army to Sharpsburg and saw no advantage in making a stand at South Mountain. Just what the peculiar advantages of Sharpsburg were is difficult to determine, but on the morning of September 15 Longstreet had his way.[20] Lee withdrew his troops from South Mountain and retired southward seven miles to the village of Sharpsburg. Hood conducted the rear-guard operations with his own division, Ripley's brigade and Frobel's artillery.

There was no enemy pursuit during the night, but Hood was busy keeping the marching men awake and on the move. Just after daylight he advised Hill he was finding it extremely difficult to keep the troops awake and marching.[21] His own troops, he reports, were sorely in need of shoes, clothing and food. They had had no issue of meat in several days and little or no bread. For more than three days his men had been subsisting on roasting ears and green apples.[22] Yet there was no time to rest Hood's or any of the other troops, for the enemy was pressing close on their heels. By noon on September 15 Longstreet's and Hill's troops were being deployed, while Hood held off the enemy's advance guard on the Hagerstown Road.[23] Major Frobel placed Reilly's and Bachman's batteries on a hill to the right of the road, holding Garden's battery in reserve.[24]

A mile directly across the wooded ridges in Hood's front McClellan established his headquarters on the afternoon of the fifteenth. Here, surrounded by a group of his ranking officers, he climbed the slope of a ridge and saw before him the entire field of battle. At his feet Antietam Creek, a narrow fordable stream, flowed toward the Potomac to his left. Almost in direct line of vision to the front was the village of Sharpsburg and behind it coiled the Potomac. To the right of the village was the Dunker

Church, standing out severely white like a monument on the Hagerstown Road. Deployed near the church were Hood's brigades with Frobel's artillery in their front. The cluster of Federal officers was a tempting target, so Frobel sent across a shot just for the hell of it. Immediately Federal artillery replied and for a few minutes Hood's position was under fire.[25] This exchange may be said to have been the opening of the battle of Antietam. No one was killed or wounded, and the Federals continued crossing the creek and taking position.

Hood's division remained in its exposed position until after sunset on the evening of the sixteenth. This made nearly four days (since before South Mountain) that his troops had gone without cooked food except for one issue of beef. Late in the afternoon of the sixteenth, Hooker threw forward Meade's division led by two regiments of skirmishers and a squadron of cavalry. He advanced cautiously, fearing, as he said, that "the rebels will eat me up."[26] Hood did not exactly eat him up, although his men were hungry enough to do so, but he did receive him warmly. Summoning the last ounce of strength from his worn and hungry troopers, he stopped the advance with a deadly fire of musketry and then pushed the advance guard back on the main forces, losing one of his best colonels, P. F. Liddell of the 11th Mississippi, in the action.

Then night closed in swiftly and both sides apparently were glad. Hooker was shaky about the attack to begin with, and now that the resistance had been so "formidable" he was content to let his troops sleep on their arms.[27] In the twilight Hood rode back to Lee's headquarters and begged that his weary men be replaced long enough to cook some food for themselves. Lee, Hood reported, said he would cheerfully do so, but where would the replacements come from? Perhaps from Jackson! Then Hood began his search up and down the lines for "Old Jack." Finally he found him asleep at the foot of a tree. Awakening him, Hood explained the condition of his men and asked for replacements just long enough for his men to have a meal. Jackson assented on condition that Hood make his troops available the moment they were needed; and immediately Lawton's, Hays's and Trimble's brigades moved in to allow Hood's men to retire. Quickly Hood rode off to find his wagons and supplies so the men could eat before they were again called up to resume their position in the battle line.[28]

But Hood's men were not permitted a night's sleep. About six o'clock in the morning Lawton sent word back to Hood that he was hard pressed, was himself wounded and needed assistance badly.[29] The enemy attack had begun in earnest and his plan was being unfolded. He was attacking the Confederate left en masse with the purpose of turning it, gaining the ridge along which ran the Hagerstown Road and then moving toward Sharpsburg.[30] Here on the Confederate left was to be the bloodiest part of this sanguinary day at Sharpsburg. Hood and Jackson (who had arrived on the night of the sixteenth from his capture of Harpers Ferry) were to bear the brunt of the Federal assault by the troops of Sumner, Mansfield, Doubleday and Meade.

A few minutes after six Hood was moving his men into the battle. Even before sunrise Jackson's troops had been under terrific artillery and small-arms fire. As full daylight came the intensity of the Federal attack increased. Wave after wave of fresh troops surged up against Jackson, and with a heroic spirit born of desperation his troops advanced to meet them. They would advance a few hundred yards and then be driven back with staggering losses.[31] A regiment waiting in the cornfield to go into action, their bayonets glistening in the early morning sun, was spotted by Hooker himself. Immediately he gave orders to his artillery to open fire with canister. "In the time I am writing," Hooker reported, "every stalk of corn in the northern and greater part of the field was cut as closely as could have been done with a knife, and the slain lay in rows precisely as they

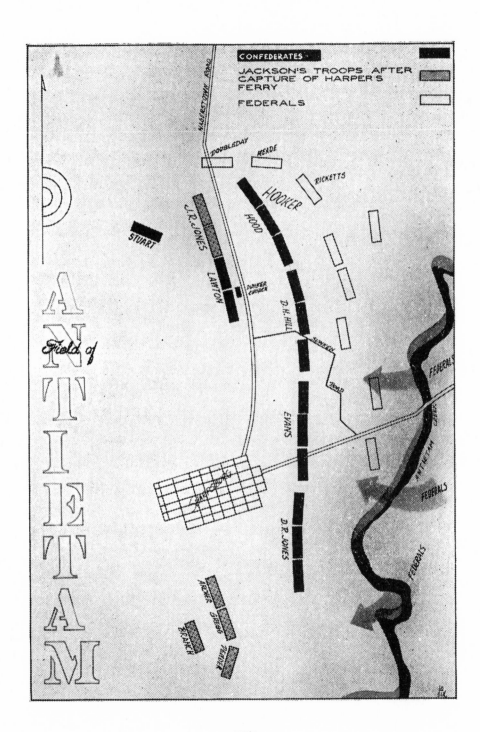

CONFEDERATES

JACKSON'S TROOPS AFTER
CAPTURE OF HARPER'S
FERRY

FEDERALS

HAGERSTOWN ROAD

DOUBLEDAY

MEADE

RICKETTS

HOOKER

HOOD

J. R. JONES

STUART

LAWTON

DUNKER
CHURCH

D. H. HILL

Field of

SUNKEN

ROAD

EVANS

D. R. JONES

ARCHER

GREGG

BRANCH

PENDER

FEDERALS

ANTIETAM CREEK

FEDERALS

FEDERALS

ANTIETAM

137

had stood in their ranks a few moments before. It was never my fortune to witness a more bloody, dismal battlefield."[32]

A shell burst above the head of General J. R. Jones and stunned him so that he had to leave the field.[33] The command fell on General William E. Starke and in a few minutes he was dead, pierced by three bullets.[34] General Lawton was wounded and Colonel James A. Walker of Trimble's brigade was seriously hurt. More than half of the brigades of Lawton and Hays were either killed or wounded, and more than a third of Trimble's, and all the regimental commanders in those brigades, except two, were killed or wounded. "Thinned in their ranks and exhausted of their ammunition, Lawton's division . . . retired to the rear, and Hood . . . again took the position from which he had before been relieved," wrote Jackson.[35] This was something new for Jackson's troops. Never before had they experienced such assaults and such an impenetrable curtain of lead.

Now Hood came on the field with his two brigades just as the battle was reaching its highest peak of intensity. It was a thin line which he formed—some 850 men in the Texas brigade and about 1,000 in Law's. But the men had eaten and had rested a few hours and now they jumped to the fight again. In terms of modern football the line-up was as follows: left end, Hampton's Legion; left tackle, 1st Texas and 18th Georgia alternating; left guard, 4th Texas; center, 5th Texas; right guard, 2nd Mississippi; right tackle, 6th North Carolina and 11th Mississippi, alternating; right end, 4th Alabama.

As the entire line charged it became engaged at varying intervals. On the left the Legion, only seventy-seven strong, encountered the Federals almost immediately. Advancing steadily and firing as they went, they received a galling return fire from the enemy. Herod Wilson of Company F, the color-bearer, was shot down. The colors were raised by James Estes of Company E and he was shot down. Then C. P. Poppenheim of Company A seized the standard and was killed. Major J. H. Dingle raised the colors again and went to his death rallying the men. By the time the regiment reached the fateful cornfield, Colonel M. W. Gary, who was commanding, had only twenty-two men left standing.[36]

At the left-tackle position Colonel P. A. Work led the 1st Texas, 226 strong, into action. Stepping lively, its men cleared the wood in the face of an incessant and deadly shower of canister. When they reached the cornfield it became impossible to restrain the men and they rushed madly into the face of the enemy and broke his advance line. Then on they rushed toward the second line fifty yards to the rear of the first line. Men dropped right and left as the canister tore gaping holes in them. Always that deadly canister! Now the 1st Texas concentrated its fire on the Federal artillery and men and horses went down. But it was hopeless. Always fresh men filled up the enemy ranks and fresh batteries came forward. Colonel Work, realizing he had pushed ahead of the other regiments, stopped momentarily to confer with Major Matt Dale, and while they talked Dale was killed. Work was isolated, his ammunition was exhausted and most of his men were killed or wounded. Then he gave the order which the Texans heard so infrequently—"fall back." When he retired only forty men were on their feet. The rest of them lay in the cornfield with the regimental colors lost in the fight.[37]

The 18th Georgia encountered the same devastating enemy fire in the cornfield. Again the enemy's grape and canister got in its deadly work and always the enemy kept coming at them in fresh waves. Another of Hood's regiments was cut to pieces. One hundred and seventy-six men went into action. Eighty-five of them were killed or wounded.[38] With the 4th Texas it was the same story and the same with Law's brigade—fierce resistance and frightful slaughter, and always the enemy came on and on. The story of the 5th Texas may be told in a few sentences from the report of its commander, Captain Ike N. M. Turner. ". . . General

Hood rode up ordering me . . . to press forward and drive the enemy out of the woods, which we did. . . . Sent four times to Major [Captain] Sellers [Hood's assistant adjutant general] for support, determined to hold my position as long as possible. My men were out of ammunition, the enemy not more than 100 yards in my front, no support, no ammunition; all our troops had fallen back on my left; I deemed it prudent to fall back also." Turner's losses: eighty-six out of 200.[39]

Law's report tells very much the same story of the bitterly unequal contest. He had moved in concert with the Texas brigade on his left. At first he met with success, driving the enemy before him. And then he, too, encountered the fearful curtain of canister and bullet. Expecting reinforcements at any moment, he held his confused troops in action, however, fighting doggedly for every foot. Ammunition ran low and the men began searching the dead bodies of their comrades and of the enemy alike for the precious cartridges which would enable them to hold on. For nearly three hours they held and still no reinforcements came. Then Law permitted his men to fall back to the Dunker Church. Then "reinforcements arrived, and the brigade was relieved for the purpose of obtaining ammunition."[40]

The reinforcements had been sent by Lee. Knowing that Hood could not hold out indefinitely, Lee had as early as 7:30 ordered up reinforcements from the only source he had—his right wing. He ordered Colonel G. T. Anderson's brigade to the support of Hood and General J. G. Walker with two brigades to support Jackson. And then, seeing how pitifully inadequate these brigades were, he sent McLaws, who had just arrived from Harpers Ferry, to Hood's support.[41] Then Lee himself rode to his left flank to see what the situation was. On the way he met Stephen D. Lee, whom Hood had sent with a message. Hood's division, he said, had thrown itself into the breach and by fierce attacks had held the enemy momentarily, but each successive wave of enemy resistance threatened a break-through. Hood was afraid he couldn't hold on much longer without ammunition. As Stephen D. Lee excitedly reported on Hood's plight, General Lee, imperturbable as always on the battlefield, replied: "Don't be excited about it, Colonel; go tell General Hood to hold his ground, reinforcements are now rapidly approaching between Sharpsburg and the ford."[42]

Soon McLaws' men were filing into position, allowing what was left of Hood's division to retire and replenish their cartridge boxes. As Hood rode over the field directing his men to retire he apparently for the first time came to realize how enormous had been the slaughter of his men. So thick were the dead and wounded on the ground that he feared his horse might trample on one of them as he picked his way around.[43] And as he gathered his exhausted survivors together behind Dunker Church the enormity of the loss must have been impressed on him again. Of his own beloved Texas brigade only 318 had survived. Law's brigade had come off a bit better. He had 573 left.[44] Hood's division had virtually been wiped out. But the left had held just as Lee thought it would hold.

And now McLaws had his turn on the left. With magnificent abandon his troops took up where Hood's had left off. Kershaw's and Barksdale's brigades pushed up to the point where Hood had been stopped and where Walker's brigade had met defeat. Again there was the terrible curtain of canister, and fresh troops to replace those who were mowed down. Valiant as the stand was, McLaws could not hold, just as Jackson and Hood had been unable to stand up under the rain of death.

And then suddenly, like a roaring grass fire which veers and changes direction with a changing wind, the battle shifted from the left to the center where D. H. Hill waited. Already the left of his line had been engaged, supporting Jackson, Hood and McLaws. Now he had the massed fury of Franklin's corps hurled at him. Three times they surged up against his thin lines at the "Bloody Lane" in his front, and three times they were repulsed. Then through a mistaken maneuver on the part of General R. E. Rodes's brigade the Federals were made a present of a hole in the Confederate lines.[45] Through it Franklin's men poured. Hood's worn and decimated division was called up again to hold Dunker Church.[46] Hill personally led a small detachment of his men in trying to hold the breach—and then suddenly the Federal attack ceased. General Edwin V. Sumner, Franklin's superior, had come to the field and "directed the attack to be postponed."[47] The gods of war had smiled on Lee again, for the center was ready to break, and it is obvious that Hood could not have held the Dunker Church area.

Hardly had the attack on the center died away when action became heavy on Lee's right. A. P. Hill had not arrived from Harpers Ferry even by two o'clock, and the right had been greatly weakened in order to strengthen the center and the left. If A. P. Hill arrived in time the right might be saved from collapse. Otherwise all the blood and dead bodies on the left and center would be in vain. Heroically the brigade of Robert Toombs, the Georgian, held the enemy, then fell back, then held again. All available artillery was called up and sent into action; and still the enemy pushed its relentless charges over and over again.[48] Then about 2:30 A. P. Hill and 3,000 men arrived and went into action. D. R. Jones's men had grimly held on with Toombs and now A. P. Hill made the difference between complete rout and at least holding on. Precariously the Confederate line held—and then the fight on the left and center broke out again. Hood was moved into the breach again with R. H. Anderson, and again the left and center held as by a miracle.[49]

Then blessed darkness came, none too early for the Confederates. This had been the bitterest and bloodiest battle of them all. On the field lay 11,657 Federals dead or wounded and 11,724

Confederates.[50] What tomorrow morning would bring was anyone's guess. If the Federals renewed the fight Lee was almost certain to be driven into the Potomac and annihilated. As his lieutenants gathered at headquarters after dark he quietly listened to their reports. Just what transpired is a matter of some doubt, although it is certain that he discussed the situation with his generals, probably most informally. As he canvassed them one by one he found them discouraged and advocating retreat. When Hood was questioned about his division he is reported to have shown great emotional stress and to have replied that he had no division.

"Great God, General Hood, where is the splendid division you had this morning?" Lee is reported to have asked.

"They are lying on the field where you sent them, sir; but few have straggled. My division has been almost wiped out," Hood replied.[51]

But Lee was in no hurry to retreat. On the morning of September 18 the Federals did not renew the attack, and it was not until the night of the eighteenth that he finally moved his army south of the Potomac. Hood's division marched to a point near Winchester to rest, re-equip itself and give the wounded a chance to recover.[52] The conduct of the division had been such that Lee again took up with Senator Wigfall the matter of more brigades of Texans. To Wigfall he wrote:[53]

I have not heard from you in regard to the new Texas regiments which you promised to raise for the army. I need them very much. I rely upon those we have in all our tight places, and fear that I have to call upon them too often. They have fought grandly and nobly, and we must have more of them. Please make every possible exertion to get them on for me. You must help us in this matter. With a few more regiments such as Hood now has, as an example of daring and bravery, I could feel more confident of the campaign.

For Hood there was the merited promotion to major general. The matter had first been brought up by Jackson. While Hood was still marching his men from Sharpsburg to Winchester, Jackson had written the Confederate War Department recommending the promotion:

I respectfully recommend that Brig. Gen. J. B. Hood be promoted to the rank of a Major General. He was under my command during the engagements along the Chickahominy, commencing on the 27th of June last, when he rendered distinguished service. Though not of my command in the recently hard fought battle near Sharpsburg, Maryland, yet for a portion of the day I had occasion to give directions respecting his operations, and it gives me pleasure to say that his duties were discharged with such ability and zeal, as to command my admiration. I regard him as one of the most promising officers of the army.[54]

To this preliminary letter of recommendation Lee added his approval a month later.[55] A few days later, November 6, his promotion was officially announced.[56] But another side of Hood, his weaker side, was showing up. He was always greatly concerned about the safety and welfare of his men on the field of battle, but evidence shows that he was careless off the battlefield—careless in the sense that he failed to pay strict attention to the minute details of camp organization and equipment so necessary to the welfare of the foot soldier when he actually went into battle.

In November 1862 an inspection was made of Hood's division which showed up glaring deficiencies that can only be attributed to lack of discipline and supervision on Hood's part. Having read the report of the inspection, Lee found it necessary to address a sharp (for Lee) letter to Hood on the subject.[57] One by one Lee related the condition of each regiment. The 5th Texas was well armed, Enfield rifles in fine order, two thirds of the regiment badly clothed and shod, with forty-five men barefooted, discipline good. The arms of the 4th Texas were in bad order, two thirds of the men were badly clad and shod, with seventy barefooted, camp conditions only tolerable. The 1st Texas was reported in poor condition. Arms were mixed and in bad order, two thirds of the men were poorly clad with sixty barefooted. The camp was in bad order, "showing inexcusable neglect on the part of its officers."[58] In the 18th Georgia arms were mixed and only in "tolerable" order. Clothes and shoes were bad, with 160 men barefooted.

Tiny Hampton's Legion received a good report. Although the men were badly shod and clothed, the appearance of their camp was good and the regiment showed "discipline and attention to duty on the part of its officers."[59] In Law's brigade the 6th North Carolina showed the "high character of its officers in its superior neatness, discipline and drill," despite the fact that, as with the other regiments, most of the men were poorly shod and clad. The 4th Alabama was in "tolerable" condition, although arms were badly mixed. For Reilly's battery there was praise. It was described as being "in a very fine condition, showing intelligence and highly commendable pride in officers and men." The other two batteries (Bachman's German Artillery and Garden's Palmetto Artillery) were in rather poor condition, while the ordnance and supply trains were represented as being in "fine order."[60] "While the commanding general sees much in your management to commend," Lee concluded, "he deems it but necessary to lead to corrections to advise you of deficiencies."[61]

The deficiencies in clothing and shoes could not be charged to Hood, for this deficiency existed throughout the army.[62] His chief fault as a commanding officer appears to have been the fact that he did not exercise close supervision over his subordinate officers and insist that they keep their regiments in good condition. It is clearly shown in Lee's letter that the condition of the regiments varied. If a regiment happened to have officers who insisted on discipline and military neatness then that regiment made a good appearance. If, on the other hand, officers were careless in the discharge of their duties the regiment would show up badly. The mixed arms were, of course, the result of captures on the battlefield. Each regiment, or even each company in a regiment, was likely to leave a battlefield with several types of captured arms. That at least each company should have had its arms standardized is beyond question. That Hood did not insist on this is inexcusable. It obviously was this type of carelessness on Hood's part which caused Lee, in spite of his admiration for the man, to describe him as "a good fighter, very industrious on the battlefield, careless off. . . ."[63]

Carelessness was a fault which Hood possessed from his youth and which he never overcame. From the time he dated incorrectly the acceptance of his appointment to West Point to the end of his military career after the Battle of Nashville in 1864 he never was able to make of himself a capable administrator with a proper regard for details. He had shown as a regimental commander of the 4th Texas at Dumfries that he realized the value of training and discipline at the company and regimental levels. When he became a brigadier and then a major general, however, he seemed to lose sight of these fundamentals.

There are some who hold that the Gettysburg campaign in the summer of 1863 was the crucial one for the Confederacy; that the hope of foreign recognition and intervention died only after Lee lost this battle. However, there is good reason to take Sharpsburg as the turning point in the war. Neither side could claim a clean-cut victory, but it is apparent that Lee was more seriously hurt than his adversary. And as Lee retreated from an inconclusive battle in Maryland, so Braxton Bragg left an equally inconclusive field in Kentucky and retreated into Tennessee. Both Lee and Bragg had aimed at the same objective—bringing border states into the Confederate fold. Both had failed; and, taking advantage of the failures, Lincoln issued his Emancipation Proclamation, thus changing for many the entire concept of the war.

McClellan had shown great improvement in his mastery of offensive tactics in the Sharpsburg campaign, but he had allowed Lee to escape. Because of this he was replaced by the bewhiskered Ambrose E. Burnside, who had not covered himself with any distinction whatever at Sharpsburg. Halleck was retained as commander in chief. Plans for battle went on, North and South.

For Lee there was the perennial problem of reorganization after every campaign. During the Second Manassas and Antietam campaigns losses from wounds, death and straggling among the men had been fearful. Casualties among officers, too, had been high. Food, clothing, blankets, tents, wagons, ammunition—all the enormous stores of war had to be supplied. Men had to be rested and the sick and wounded given a chance to recover. These things rather than the Yankees constituted Lee's problem during the forty-five-day period after Sharpsburg.[64]

The promotion of Hood to major general was a part of Lee's reorganization of his army. Colonel J. B. Robertson of the 5th Texas was promoted to brigadier general and given command of the Texas brigade. Faithful and efficient E. M. Law likewise was raised to brigadier, retaining command of the brigade which had long borne his name.[65] At the same time two other brigades were added to Hood's division, those of D. R. Jones and Toombs. Toombs had been wounded at Sharpsburg and D. R. Jones had been forced into retirement by a heart condition, so the brigades were under new commanders. Colonel H. L. Benning took over Toombs's brigade, while Jones's fell to Colonel G. T. Anderson.[66] The strength of the division on October 10, 1862, is given as 7,064 men and officers,[67] by far the largest body of men Hood had ever commanded.

Other reorganization plans included the promotion of Longstreet and Jackson to the rank of lieutenant general and the designation of their "commands" was changed to "corps." Lee's army, therefore, was thus organized:

I. Longstreet's Corps (First Army Corps)
   McLaws' Division, Major General Lafayette McLaws
   Anderson's Division, Major General Richard H. Anderson
   Pickett's Division, Major General George E. Pickett
   Hood's Division, Major General John B. Hood
   Ransom's Division, Major General Robert Ransom, Jr.
   Artillery (not assigned to divisions)

II. Jackson's Corps (Second Army Corps)
   Hill's Division, Major General Daniel H. Hill
   Light Division, Major General Ambrose P. Hill
   Ewell's Division, Major General Jubal A. Early
   Jackson's Division, Brigadier General William B. Taliaferro

III. Cavalry, Major General James E. B. Stuart

IV. Reserve Artillery, Brigadier General W. N. Pendleton

The total strength of this revamped army is given as 78,204 men and officers on October 10, 1862.[68] By November 10 the size of Hood's division had grown to 7,761, third largest in Longstreet's corps, and the strength of the entire army had climbed to 83,385.[69]

This task of recruiting and rebuilding his army had, of course, been a strenuous one for Lee. At Sharpsburg he had approximately 50,000 men engaged. Of this number he lost 11,724 killed and wounded.[70] Of the remaining 39,000 a large number had straggled—how many it is difficult to judge. "The depredations committed by this army, its daily diminution by straggling, and the loss of arms thrown aside as too burdensome by stragglers, makes it necessary for preservation itself . . . that greater efforts be made by our officers to correct this growing evil," Lee wrote his two corps commanders.[71] The next day he advised the President of the situation. "The subject of recruiting this army," he said "is . . .

one of paramount importance. The usual casualties of battle have diminished its ranks, but its numbers have been greatly decreased by desertion and straggling. *This was the main cause of its retiring from Maryland* as it was unable to cope with advantage with the numerous host of the enemy. . . . We have now abundance of arms, and if the unarmed regiments in Texas and Arkansas could be brought forward, as well as the conscripts from the different states, they would add greatly to our strength." And then he added, one imagines a bit wearily, "Our stragglers are being daily collected. . . . How long they will remain with us, or when they will again disappear, it is impossible for me to say."[72]

But it was not only the straggling private soldier who gave Lee concern. He found all too often that colonels and captains were lax in their duties. Many of them made a practice of being absent without leave and many of those who remained in camp with their companies or regiments were inefficient and careless. "There's great dereliction of duty among the regimental and company officers, particularly the latter," Lee wrote, "and unless something is done the army will melt away."[73] A few days later he wrote President Davis along the same lines. "Strange to say," he reported, "our sick are very numerous, and all the care and attention I can give to the subject do not seem to diminish the number. Until the regimental officers can be made to appreciate the necessity of taking care of their men, keeping them under control, attending to their wants and comforts, and enforcing cleanliness, etc., I fear the sanitary condition of the army will not improve. It is the want of this attention and provision for comfort that causes men so soon to break under hardship."[74]

Undoubtedly it was this condition which prompted Lee to write Hood such a stern letter about the condition of his division. It was encamped near a spring of cold, clear water three miles north of Winchester.[75] Barring guard, fatigue and police duty, the men had little to do except rest, keep themselves and their guns clean;

and yet they had done little to keep themselves and their equipment in good condition. This was the fault of the regimental and company commanders. And it was Hood's fault, for he failed to impress these things on his subordinates. The result was smallpox and other sickness among Hood's troops.[76]

Food, Lee reported, was not a difficult problem. He was able to get flour from near-by mills and he had "an abundance of beef." The greatest needs were horses, forage, artillery, clothes, shoes and blankets.[77] Nowhere was the need of clothing and shoes more apparent than in Hood's division, particularly in the Texas brigade. Even as late as November, 758 men in the division were reported barefooted.[78] Moreover many hundreds of them wore ragged clothes, particularly pants with the seats worn out from sitting on the ground playing cards.[79] So conspicuous was this particular form of raggedness among the Texas troops that Lee is reported to have jestingly suggested to a distinguished British guest: "Never mind their raggedness, Colonel—the enemy never sees the backs of my Texans."[80]

Looked at from the vantage point of today, it seems little less than miraculous that Lee could rebuild a formidable army so quickly after Sharpsburg. His veterans were exhausted after weeks of grueling marching and fighting most of the time on empty stomachs. Thousands had been wounded not once but twice or three times. Their uniforms were nondescript, a combination of anything they might already possess or capture from the Yankees. Commissary supplies were scarce and slow in coming from the limited industrial plants of the South; and the same could be said for ordnance. Southern factories being unable to supply the needs of the army, agents were dispatched to Texas with "large funds" to purchase needed supplies through Mexico.[81] Black marketing became a common practice among the troops and, in general, morale was at about as low ebb as is possible to imagine.[82] And yet out of the confusion, chaos, scarcity and straggling Lee did build a superb fighting army capable of defeating almost twice its number at Fredericksburg.

When General Burnside took command of the Army of the Potomac on November 7, 1862, he, too, did some reorganizing. Unlike Lee's, his problems were not men and supplies and guns. His number-one problem was to so reorganize his command as to come up with a winning combination which could find a way for a vastly superior army to whip a vastly inferior one. As a corollary he must devise a way to get at that army so as to defeat it.

In reorganizing his army, Burnside divided it into three grand divisions.[83] The Right Grand Division was given to Major General Edwin V. Sumner; the Center to Major General Joseph Hooker; the Left to Major General William B. Franklin. The strength of this Army of the Potomac is given as 120,291—abundant men and arms.[84]

As for the second of Burnside's problems—how to get at the enemy—he submitted a simple plan. He would move his army to the south side of the Rappahannock at Fredericksburg and then follow the railroad to Richmond. In the language of football he proposed to resort to "straight football"—center rushes, line bucks through guard, off-tackle smashes and end runs—with no "razzle dazzle." He counted on the superior weight of his lines, the element of surprise and on the strength of his reserves to see him through.[85]

As it developed, nothing worked right for Burnside. The element of surprise was lost, the weight of his superior forces was wasted and his reserve strength was never utilized.

As early as November 17 Sumner's Right Grand Division was near Falmouth opposite Fredericksburg ready to cross the river, but there were no pontoons for bridges. For nearly a month he waited while Lee gathered his army and intrenched himself around the town.[86] His forces had been scattered during the rest period. Jackson was in his beloved Shenandoah Valley; the divisions of McLaws, R. H. Anderson and Pickett, of Longstreet's corps, were at Culpeper; Hood was near Winchester; Ransom was at Madison Courthouse.[87] On the morning of November 19 Longstreet marched with McLaws' and Ransom's divisions for Fredericksburg. There he was soon joined by Hood, Anderson and Pickett. It was almost a leisurely concentration of forces. McLaws' division was placed on the heights in rear of the town. On his left were Ransom and Anderson. On his right were Pickett and Hood, the latter occupying the extreme right of the line.[88] There was plenty of time to dig in and get set while Burnside was laboriously getting his army on the opposite side of the river into position for the attack. Jackson was left temporarily in the Shenandoah Valley in case the opportunity might present itself for him to strike the Federal's flank and rear. However, that opportunity did not appear, and on November 29 Jackson moved his divisions in on the right of Hood below Fredericksburg.[89] Lee was ready.

Then for nearly two weeks Jackson's and Longstreet's men shivered in the prematurely cold weather which descended on them. Snow blanketed the earth as they waited for the Federals to attack. There was enough skirmishing to keep the men alert but not enough to keep the penetrating cold from their bones. As they rode along their lines Hood and Jackson talked of the war and their chance of survival. Jackson, Hood reported, felt with a sort of fatalistic abandon that he would not live to the end. Hood thought he would survive but would be maimed.[90] It was a casual conversation strangely prophetic of the fate of both men.

With a heavy heart Lee was busy in Fredericksburg supervising the evacuation of its civilian population. From the town columns of women, children and the aged crawled over the slopes at the south side and disappeared into space as all refugees have done in war for all time.[91] Longstreet busied himself getting his artillery placed just as he wanted it and in readying his skirmish

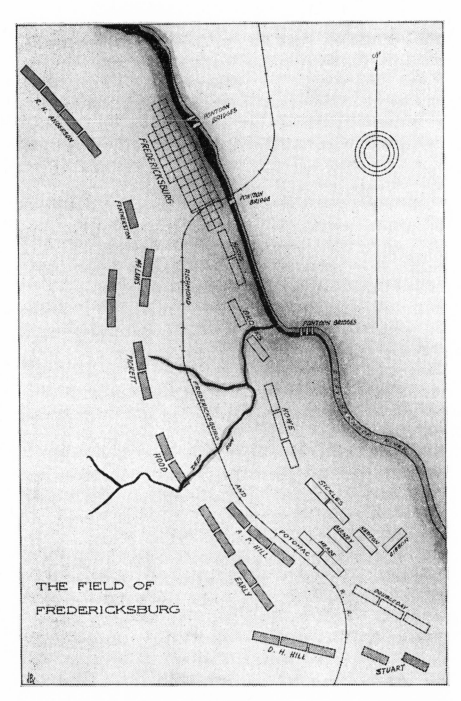

THE FIELD OF
FREDERICKSBURG

153

lines to resist the enemy's crossing.[92] In the woods soldiers constantly labored at the task of cutting wood to feed their campfires, and then as they huddled about these fires they speculated on when the battle would begin. Everywhere there was an atmosphere of confident expectancy—and then near three o'clock on the morning of December 11 Confederate guns gave the signal. Burnside's mighty force was moving. In the cold foggy dawn his troops were laying a pontoon bridge across the Rappahannock directly in front of Fredericksburg.[93]

As a matter of fact, the Federals were attempting to lay three pontoon bridges—two immediately in front of Fredericksburg and a double one below the city at Deep Run immediately in Hood's front. In houses along the river front Longstreet had secreted General William Barksdale's brigade of Mississippians. When the attempt was made by the Federals to get their pontoons in place the Mississippians picked off the engineers and workers as if they were shooting sitting ducks. For nearly six hours Barksdale's men delayed the crossing. By late afternoon, however, men were crossing.[94] Farther downstream in Hood's front the enemy had been noisily getting into position since dawn. Through the impenetrable curtain of fog, Hood could hear the Yankees so plainly it seemed as though they might march directly into his lines. He became apprehensive lest the attack should be launched in his front, but Longstreet reasoned the attack would be delivered against Jackson on the extreme right, as indeed it was.[95] But Hood could not oppose the crossing in the Barksdale manner. The fog was too thick in the morning and when it finally lifted it became clear that his position was too exposed for effective resistance. The first volley from his rifles would have drawn the enemy's artillery fire.[96] Thus Hood was forced to sit on his haunches and watch the enemy cross the river and march left oblique to attack Jackson.

Hood's position in the center of Lee's long line of battle was a strategic one in case there should be an enemy break-through.

He and his shock troops were to take orders from Jackson on the right or from Longstreet on the left. They were to move wherever they were needed. Hood was also instructed to use his own judgment and not wait for orders in case the enemy did crash through.[97] As it developed, Hood's entire division was never called into action, for they were never needed. The battle flared on his right and left, but, except for one sortie, he and his division were little more than tensely alert spectators.

All the night of December 11 was consumed by the Federals in putting men across the river. Daylight on the twelfth again brought the concealing blanket of fog under cover of which the crossing continued unabated. When the fog lifted near noon Lee and Jackson made a personal reconnaissance on the Confederate right. Directly in front of Jackson's lines only a few hundred yards away they saw thousands of blue-coated figures massed and being maneuvered into position. Here on the right, the two generals decided, the main assault would come.[98]

But the attack did not come on the twelfth. Troops were still being prodded into position and any thought that Burnside might surprise anyone was laughable. Darkness brought bitter cold and pickets shivered at their fireless posts. Daylight of the thirteenth revealed a fog so dense the sun could not penetrate it—the third morning of fog and each one worse than its predecessor. But the Confederate battle line was electric. The men guessed this was the day.[99] Near ten o'clock the fog lifted so suddenly it was like turning on the lights in a darkened theater. In Jackson's front was Franklin's corps of some 40,000 men reinforced by two divisions of Hooker's corps. In the sudden sunlight their arms shone brightly and their blue uniforms stood out in bold relief against the drab winter background. It was a splendid army in every sense of the word. And then the lines moved forward, their artillery searing Jackson's defenses with shot. On they pressed steadily, but Jackson held his fire. Then when they were within a few hundred yards of the Confederate works A. P. Hill's gunners pulled their lanyards and hurled a devastating blast of grape and canister at the trim blue lines. They wavered, fell back and re-formed.[100] As they pressed forward again they found an opening. Between the brigades of Archer and Lane there was a gap formed by a wooded promontory which stuck out like a tongue. Into this gap the Federals poured. General Maxcy Gregg's brigade came up from its reserve position and was almost cut to pieces, Gregg himself being mortally wounded. Then Jackson ordered Lawton's, Trimble's and a portion of Taliaferro's and Brocken-brough's into the breach.[101]

Just as the Federals were on the point of being driven back, Hood sent in the 57th and 54th North Carolina regiments of Law's brigade.[102] The men in these regiments were largely non-descript conscripts dressed in homespun and presenting a most unsoldierly appearance, but they showed they could fight.[103] With alacrity they jumped to battle. For most of them it was their first taste of combat and it came at a time when the enemy was being driven backward. Raising the rebel yell, they fired as they ran, and soon Hood discovered they had pushed so far into enemy terri-tory that they were in danger of being surrounded or captured. He recalled them, but as they reluctantly returned they were grumbling. "Durn old Hood! If we had been his Texans he wouldn't have did it," was the way one weather-beaten and pow-der-begrimed North Carolinian is reported to have put it.[104]

On Hood's left Longstreet opened the battle in his sector about eleven o'clock. From its commanding position on Marye's Heights behind Fredericksburg the artillery poured a hail of shot and shrapnel into the Federal lines in and around the town. In front of the artillery was Longstreet's infantry waiting behind breast-works.[105] Against this array of firing power Sumner sent his Right Grand Division, French's and Hancock's divisions leading the way. From the steeple of the courthouse Sumner watched his men mowed down. "I remember that the whole plain was covered with men, prostrate and dropping," an observer wrote in later years.

"As they charged the artillery fire would break their formation and they would get mixed; then they would close up, go forward, receive the withering infantry fire . . . and then the next brigade coming up in succession would do its duty and melt like snow coming down on warm ground."[106]

Back on Jackson's front Franklin's men swarmed to the attack again and again, but each time they were driven back by the murderous artillery and rifle fire of "Old Jack's" men. There was slaughter on the right and left until night mercifully closed in. It was a bitterly cold night and many men on both sides died of exposure. As fast as they died they froze stiff, and on the Federal side the bodies were piled into breastworks to protect those who were living.[107] The next day, Sunday, December 14, Burnside's troops were nervously digging in for fear the Confederates would counterattack. No one had any heart left for a renewal of the fight, for, as General Sumner remarked, "after it is all over and you have been whipped you do not feel very pugnacious."[108] Then about midday Burnside decided to fall back and abandon the fight.

On the Confederate side there was doubt about what the enemy's plans were, however. After firing had ceased on the night of the thirteenth Hood went to Lee's headquarters and discussed with him the prospects of the next day. Hood felt sure Burnside was whipped and would not renew the battle. Lee disagreed with this opinion, and so did his other generals.[109] Consequently, when morning came details were ordered to strengthen the lines for the attack. But it never came. Lee, Jackson and Hood during the morning rode out on a personal reconnaissance.[110] Before them stretched the same valley they had seen on the day before; but it was no longer filled with banners and blue-coated lines wheeling into position. Now not a standard was to be seen, and the only men were the dead and wounded. Ten thousand eight hundred and eighty-four Federals lay in the valley and 4,656 Confederates were on the slopes.[111]

CHAPTER VII

Suffolk Interlude

THE year 1863 opened with Lee's army in temporary winter quarters, but still on the alert, on the heights behind Fredericksburg. The men built makeshift huts and cut firewood for protection against the cold. Officers leisurely did the paper work required of them after each campaign. As Longstreet prepared his report he came to Hood's part in the Federal breach of Jackson's lines. He had given Hood notice, he wrote, "that the enemy would attack General Jackson beyond his right; that he should watch carefully the movements, and when an opportunity offered he should move forward and attack the enemy's flanks." Similar instructions, he continued, were given to Pickett with orders to co-operate with Hood. "The attack was made as had been anticipated. It did not appear to have all the force of a real attack, however, and General Hood did not feel authorized to make more than a partial advance. *When he did move out,* he drove the enemy back in handsome style."[1]

This faint praise apparently went unnoticed at the time, but in later years Longstreet explained that he really meant his report to be a censure of Hood, but that he did not put it in stronger language because Hood was "high in favor with the authorities" and he did not think it prudent to push the matter.[2] During the attack on Jackson, Longstreet related, Pickett rode up to Hood and suggested that the time had come to strike. "Hood did not agree, so the opportunity was allowed to pass. Had Hood sprung to the occasion he would have enveloped Franklin's command, and might possibly have marched it into the Confederate camp."[3]

Actually there appears to have been no neglect of duty on Hood's part, but the fact that he did not attack in full force gave an opportunity for Longstreet to indulge in a bit of petty vindictiveness. He apparently did not greatly dislike Hood, but at the same time he did not share Lee's and Jackson's confidence in him. When Hood was promoted to major general and given command of a division Longstreet had urged that Pickett be selected for that honor.[4] But Lee and Jackson both had recommended Hood, and their judgment was accepted by Richmond. Then there was the matter of "Shank" Evans and the captured ambulances. He had placed Hood under arrest, but Lee had released him and let the matter drop. Both these things apparently rankled in "Old Pete's" sometimes small soul, but he was wise enough not to try again to strike at Lee through Hood. *"Bis peccare in bello non licet,"* he wrote acidly.[5] It is entirely possible that Hood never knew of Longstreet's real feelings, for they were not fully revealed until after Hood's death, when Longstreet was trying so desperately to build himself up in the eyes of the South.[6]

While report writing, hut building and other routine camp activities were going on, Lee was watching Burnside with anxious eyes. By January 20 there were signs of Federal activity, possibly a renewal of the attack, and the army was readied for action. Then days passed and the attack did not come. Burnside's offensive had bogged down in what his men termed "The Mud March."[7] But Lee was not lulled into any state of false security by the failure of the Federals to attack. He busied himself fortifying the entire line of the Rappahannock. He knew that the enemy would be at his throat again when the snows had melted.[8]

Meantime the soldiers made themselves as comfortable as circumstances would permit. There appears to have been a feeling among Hood's troops that their stay in winter quarters would not be long, so they built only temporary shelters for themselves. They did, however, contribute a great deal of time and labor to the building of a log theater where amateur theatricals were staged and where concerts by Collins' brass band were frequent. At times Hood and Lee attended performances to relieve the tedium.[9] Hood even acted as a program arranger, and the performance given by "Hood's Minstrels" on Christmas Eve was pronounced by a young officer as "one of the best performances." A blackface trio which sang "We Are a Band of Brothers" obviously was the hit of the show, since the members were so "supremely ridiculous."[10] * Snowball battles and the interminable card games gave additional amusement and recreation to the men.

One of the sharpest snowball battles was, as one might suspect, started by the Texas brigade. "This morning," the same officer reported, "the 1st, 4th, and 5th Texas Regiments came by our camp, marching in irregular line of battle, with their colors gotten up for the occasion, and with skirmishers thrown out in advance, and passing us, attacked the camp of the 3rd Arkansas, which is immediately on our right. A fierce contest ensued, snow balls being the weapons. The Texans steadily advanced, passing up the right of the camp; the Arkansians stubbornly disputing their progress, and their shouts and cheers as they would make a charge, or as the fight would become unusually desperate, made the welkin ring. A truce was finally declared and all four regiments marched over the creek to attack Anderson's brigade. . . . How that fight terminated I don't know."[11]

While the men thus amused themselves the higher officers, especially Hood, also made themselves comfortable. "I was at Genl. Hood's Head Quarters this morning . . ." the young officer continued; "he has moved into a house and I suppose intends to live in style."[12] For the officers there was a continuous series of

* This and subsequent quotations from Mrs. D. Giraud Wright, *A Southern Girl in '61*, are reprinted by permission of Doubleday & Company, Inc.

such dinners as army fare permitted and many sessions of story-telling in their quarters. On one of these occasions General Lee chided Hood good-naturedly about the alleged petty depredations of his men. Fence rails were disappearing mighty fast from the countryside, he said, and an increasing number of farmers were losing their pigs. Hood, always serious in Lee's presence, stoutly defended his men and denied the charges. To this Lee replied with what for him was an unusual outburst of raillery. "Ah, General Hood," he laughingly rejoined, "when you Texans come about, the chickens have to roost mighty high."[13] It is reported that everyone roared at this,[14] not because it was funny, perhaps, but because it reflected a jovial side the officers had never seen in Lee before. He was joking with everyone during the long cold evenings even to the extent of playing practical jokes. One evening he invited his officers in for a little something out of a jug, and when they stood expectantly smacking their lips he poured each a glass of buttermilk.[15]

But these pleasantries were short-lived. General Joseph Hooker had replaced Burnside, and this meant battle again sooner or later. And Lee was uneasy because of Longstreet's absence. Since December, Richmond had been besieged by prominent North Carolinians for more assistance in protecting the state from the Federals. In February 1863 the Ninth Corps of the Army of the Potomac was sent to Fort Monroe, alarming the North Carolinians even more and giving Lee real concern for fear this might be the opening movement of another peninsular campaign. To meet the possibility of this Lee sent Pickett's division of Longstreet's corps to Richmond and a few days later sent Hood to join Pickett. Then Longstreet and his staff followed.[16]

Pickett's division camped on the Chickahominy and Hood's four miles south of Richmond between that city and Petersburg.[17] So far as Hood and his men were concerned this was ideal. The officers of the Texas brigade had access to their privately rented warehouse where they and their men had stored their private possessions. In addition, Hood was again liberal with passes to the city and soon the men were enjoying the pleasures of Richmond; and when Hood turned his charm on the quartermaster department he was able to secure needed shoes, clothes and food for his men. But there was one article of clothing which simply was not available—hats. However, some inventive genius soon solved this problem. The railroad ran through Hood's camp. A small trestle over a stream forced all trains to slow down in crossing. When the passenger trains slowed down Hood's men would be congregated outside yelling and creating a terrific din. Train windows would go up and hatted heads stuck out to see what it was all about; and they soon found out. The men were armed with pine boughs with which they knocked off what hats they needed. It all went just fine until one day a brigadier general, his staff and several members of Congress were the victims. Then Richmond ordered Hood to put a stop to the outrageous practice.[18]

This hiatus in campaigning also gave Hood an opportunity to visit Richmond. In many respects it was the same city he had known a year before, but there were changes which were more than merely noticeable. The streets were still filled with soldiers, but the soldiers looked different. In the winter of 1861-1862 they had been clean, laughing men and boys in new uniforms pouring into the city ready to fight the Yankees. Now they had fought the Yankees and bore in their bodies the marks of battle. Gaunt men in ragged uniforms hobbled about on crutches or nursed stubs of arms.[19] Women dressed in shabby skirts and coats now wearing thin hurried through the streets with baskets on their arms, carrying delicacies to the men enduring the stench of the hospitals.

It was a city of anxiety, fear, rumors—always rumors: The Federals were whipped and ready to end the war; an alliance with England and France was not far off. Officers and their ladies rode by in carriages or promenaded, trying to laugh away the tenseness. Dirty conscripts fresh from the conscript camps crowded the drinking and gambling places. Scarcity and rising prices plagued everyone.[20] Price control and conscription were debated in the Congress and warring political factions assaulted each other or the President. Politics as usual.[21] Candlelight and gay parties every evening in the fine old houses set back from the streets. Flirting and charades and desperate hurried love-making in the big houses; on the streets brazen prostitutes lured the soldiers to their rooms. The booming of gunboats on the river—more rumors. The churches were crowded on Sundays, and after services the people gathered in little groups and chatted, trying to be natural. A reception at the Executive Mansion with gossip, romance and intrigue in the drawing rooms. More charades and tinkling laughter in the great houses. Handsome officers and drunken vomiting soldiers crowding the streets. Dinners of oysters, turkey, ham, ice cream and champagne in the homes of the well-to-do.[22] J. B. Jones's cat dying from starvation because he could not afford to feed it.[23] Hope and despair; hunger and plenty; beauty and stench; brave soldiers and black marketeers; beautiful ladies and dirty whores; churches and gambling houses both filled; crowded stinking basements and elegant white-pillared mansions—this was Richmond in wartime. "In those days," a resident of the city wrote, "we were sustained by what Cervantes styled the bounding of the soul, the bursting of laughter and the quicksilver of the five senses."[24]

When Richmond was made the capital, officers and civilians from the deep South crowded into the city. Soon two rival "courts" were set up. One was presided over by Mrs. Jefferson Davis and the other by Mrs. Joseph E. Johnston. Mrs. Davis' court was by far the larger of the two and more cosmopolitan. She and Mr. Davis established the custom of fortnightly levees open to all Richmond, and all Richmond responded.[25] Cabinet members and their wives, merchants, officers, visiting foreigners members of Congress and the *hoi polloi* all rubbed elbows; and during the winter of 1862-1863 "the blonde head of Hood . . . towered over the throng of leading editors, senior wranglers from both Houses of Congress, and dancing men wasting their time in the vain effort to talk."[26] Apparently Hood lost no opportunity to be seen with the right people, but this was certainly not the only reason he attended these functions. He was essentially gregarious and convivial; he loved lights and laughter.

The levees and receptions of Mr. and Mrs. Davis were, as stated above, open to everyone who cared to attend. There existed, however, a smaller and much more exclusive coterie centering around Mrs. Davis. This inner group was composed of men and women who had come to Richmond for one reason or another and had been found socially acceptable. These people had been welcomed, but "not without sharp appraisal."[27] Perhaps the position of the "outsiders" who were accepted can best be illustrated by the cases of the Prestons and the Chesnuts, each of whom came to play such an important part in Hood's life as well as in the social life of Richmond.

John S. Preston was from Columbia, South Carolina. He had made a fortune on his sugar plantation in Louisiana and was thus able to indulge his fondness for collecting art objects and for travel. He made frequent trips to Europe, one of them lasting for four years, during which time his daughters were in school. At the outbreak of the war he was a volunteer aide to General Beauregard and in January 1862 was promoted to lieutenant colonel and placed in command of the conscript camp at Columbia.[28] But this assignment as commander of "dirt-eating, lame, blind, lousy conscripts" ran counter to his tastes.[29] He wanted to go back to Richmond where he had first served under Beauregard and where his family was. And above all he wanted to be a general and to see active service if possible.[30] He did not get active service, but in July 1863 he was promoted to colonel and called to Richmond to take charge of the Confederate conscript service.[31]

His wife, the sister of General Wade Hampton, and his two daughters, Mary and Sara, had been in Richmond with Mrs. Chesnut since the summer of 1861, when Mr. Chesnut was also an aide on Beauregard's staff. Like Colonel Preston, James Chesnut had had a distinguished career. He had been United States Senator from South Carolina and an ardent secessionist who helped draft the South Carolina ordinance of secession. When the attack on Fort Sumter came he and Stephen D. Lee bore the surrender note to Major Robert Anderson; and when the war came to Virginia he left Mulberry, his country estate near Camden, South Carolina, and took his family to Richmond. In October 1862 he was made colonel and aide to President Davis.[32]

Mrs. Preston is described by a contemporary as "handsome and aristocratic." Her daughters were "like goddesses upon a heaven-kissing hill, tall and stately, with brilliant fresh complexions, altogether the embodiment of vigorous health." Mrs. Chesnut at forty was seen as "gay and sprightly . . . leading all the fun and nonsense in our talk."[33] Soon the inseparable four of them were lunching with Mrs. Davis, knitting with Mrs. Davis, dining at the Davises' and driving with the Davises.[34] They were "in" along with other ladies who had moved to the capital with their men folk. Mrs. Stephen R. Mallory, Spanish wife of the Secretary of the Navy, was charming and adept at mixing salads. She was "in." So was the beautiful and wealthy Mrs. George Wythe Randolph, wife of the Secretary of War. Mrs. Barton Haxall, famous Richmond hostess, was also in the inner circle, as were Hetty and Constance Cary; Mrs. Clement C. Clay; Mrs. George Pryor and Mrs. George A. Trenholm.[35] Theirs was a daily round of teas, calling, knitting and gossip—and in the evening entertaining for the male contingent of their set and for the scores of unmarried young ladies who fluttered about.

The males of the coterie were the husbands and friends of the ladies plus charming, interesting or successful officers who had achieved a reputation for themselves, or distinguished foreigners.

For them there were tea dances, musicals, dinners, charades and theater parties. A typical evening would show present such men as Colonel Chesnut; Jeb Stuart; Judah P. Benjamin; Secretary Mallory; Wade Hampton; Lieutenant Colonel Heros von Borcke; Francis Lawley, correspondent of the *London Times;* Prince Camille de Polignac; the young English observer, Lord Edward St. Maur; Fitzhugh Lee; Frank Vizitelly of the *London Illustrated News;* John B. Hood; Longstreet; Colonel and later Viscount Garnet Wolseley and Custis Lee.[36] Of Hood's position in all of this Freeman has written: "Successful commanders were received with praise, whatever their lack of social grace, but to those who combined military skill with gracious manners all doors were opened. General John B. Hood, commander of the renowned Texas brigade, was of the company that every hostess, however exacting, rejoiced to have in her drawing room. He not only had the reputation of being a desperate fighter, but he also had magnificent physique, cordial manners, and the suavity of a cavalier."[37]

It undoubtedly would be a mistake, however, to assume that Hood achieved a really high degree of social prominence during the winter of 1862-1863. Rather, it appears he was just on the verge of success when military duties called him away. It is quite likely that he had met the Preston girls, but it seems he had not been formally presented to Mrs. Chesnut.[38] Whatever might have been the status of his social career in March 1863, it was cut short by military orders. On March 18 a portion of Hood's division, the Texas brigade, was called on to move against what appeared to be a possible attack on Richmond via the Rappahannock. Hood marched in haste through Richmond and then a few miles on toward Ashland. When within approximately five miles of the latter point, Hood was ordered to about-face and return to camp. Since it was late in the afternoon when the countermanding orders were received, Hood ordered his men to bivouac for the night. During the night a heavy snow fell and when the brigade began its march back the next morning it was cold and shivering, but full of horseplay. Hood had, over the mild protest of General Jerome B. Robertson, commander of the Texas brigade, given permission for the men to stop over in Richmond. To the men this meant food, drink and women, but to "Aunt Pollie" Robertson it meant the temporary disintegration of his command. "Let 'em go, General, let 'em go," Hood is reported as saying, "they deserve a little indulgence, and you'll get them back in time for the next battle."[39] An observer who saw them arrive reported they were "all morning defiling through Main Street in high spirits and merrily snow-balling each other." "And," he added, "these men slept last night out in the snow without tents. Can such soldiers be vanquished?"[40]

But they did not have long for pleasure themselves, because a campaign was in the making—a barren and fruitless campaign which wasted men and energy and left Lee stranded with inadequate numbers on the Rappahannock facing Pope's great army. This campaign now beginning was Longstreet's. It is usually called the "Suffolk Campaign," but it included much more than a mere effort to take this place. A longer and more adequate name would be "A Series of Poorly Executed and Unco-ordinated Military Maneuvers Carried On by a Motley Collection of Misfits and Malcontents."

It will be recalled that Hood's and Pickett's divisions had been sent to Richmond to meet any contingency which might arise, particularly to meet any thrust which Burnside and the Ninth Corps might make from Fort Monroe. Longstreet's orders were that the divisions were to be placed where "they can be readily moved to resist an advance upon Richmond by the enemy from his new base." Beyond this Longstreet was merely to keep Lee advised of enemy movements and report to the Secretary of War.[41] One sentence, however, apparently raised Longstreet's hopes for the independent command he apparently so intently coveted. That sentence was this: "Should the movement of the enemy from the Potomac render it expedient your other divisions will be ordered to join you."[42] Did this mean that Longstreet would be given independent command of the forces protecting Richmond, while Lee held on the Rappahannock? There was no clarifying answer. On February 26 he assumed command of "The Department of Virginia and North Carolina."[43] Did this mean that he was trying to place Lee in a subordinate position? Longstreet's biographers think so.[44] Whatever may have been his motives, however, Longstreet did take command of the territory in Virginia south of the James and of all North Carolina.

In so doing he took over a rambling, sprawling territory extending from Richmond to South Carolina, the troops therein being commanded largely by officers who, for one reason or another, Lee had transferred from the Army of Northern Virginia. As a matter of fact, it was three departments: the Department of Southern Virginia, commanded by Major General Samuel G. French; the Department of Richmond under Major General Arnold Elzey; and the Department of North Carolina under Major General D. H. Hill. Serving in secondary positions were several officers who had served under Lee. W. H. C. Whiting was at Wilmington; "Shanks" Evans was at Kinston, North Carolina; Brigadier General Beverly Robertson was also in North Carolina along with Major General Robert Ransom. Many of these officers were malcontents.[45] Elzey had a disfiguring face wound, and contemporaries relate he was addicted to the bottle; Whiting was as cantankerous as he was in the Seven Days Battle; D. H. Hill was sick and in ill humor; Beverly Robertson was openly accused of inefficiency by Hill; and smoldering like a threatening volcano was Zebulon Vance, Governor of North Carolina. Truly it was not a group from which one could expect much harmony and concert of effort.

With these and the divisions of Hood and Pickett, Longstreet proposed to drive the enemy out of his department and swell his commissary stores. In his memoirs "Old Pete" devotes only about two pages to the campaign, and one can well imagine why.[46] It was nothing to be proud of. The campaign was inconclusive, but it did seriously raise the question of his fitness for independent command, a question more sharply accented in the Chickamauga campaign still in the future. Jackson was at his best when acting on his own. Hood was soon to demonstrate his unfitness for high command. As for Longstreet, Suffolk and East Tennessee are not positive proof, but they indicate his abilities as an independent commander were probably not much, if any, greater than Hood's.

The ill-fated campaign opened on March 1, 1863, when Longstreet, ill with a sore throat at Petersburg, suggested to D. H. Hill an attack on New Bern on the Neuse River near where it flows into Pamlico Sound.[47] New Bern was important because, occupied as it was by the Federals, it was a threat to Goldsboro and the whole interior of the state. Longstreet felt that the attack might be successful if some 4,000 men could be detached from Whiting's command at Wilmington and along with them a Whitworth gun.[48] But when Whiting was notified of the proposed reinforcement of Hill he exploded. "I perceive you are not acquainted with this territory," he snapped at Longstreet. ". . . So far as considering myself able to spare troops from here I have applied for and earnestly urged that another brigade be sent here immediately."[49] As for the Whitworth gun, he could not possibly spare it, he notified Hill. "What is this expedition of which you speak?" he asked. "General Longstreet wrote me something about it, but wanted me to send off half my force and half my garrisons."[50]

So there was no help from Whiting. Hill, however, went ahead with the attack, if it could be dignified by that term. He did little more than approach the place on March 13 and waste considerable fire through March 15. Then he withdrew, bitter and disappointed.[51]

The next move in the campaign was a proposed attack on Washington, North Carolina, which was, in Longstreet's opinion, a key position. If Washington could be taken he felt that the counties east of that point could be opened to Confederate subsistence and quartermasters' departments.[52] This time Whiting rather reluctantly sent Ransom's brigade to co-operate with Hill, although he complained that this deprived him of his best troops. He had only "Shanks" Evans' brigade left, and in it he placed "but little reliance."[53] Ransom had not been happy serving under Whiting, and was no happier under Hill. He did not desire "service where there has been so little done and where there are poor opportunities to render real good."[54] And Governor Vance was adding nothing to harmony by his attitude. He was, he said in vigorous terms, getting tired of the way Confederate troops were impressing supplies from the good people of North Carolina. "I have no prejudice against the troops from any state engaged in defending the common cause," he wrote, "but I am unwilling to see the bread taken from the mouths of women and children for the use of any troops. . . ."[55] Truly it seemed that no Confederate thought very highly of any other Confederate in this hapless series of sorties.

But Hill went ahead with the attack on Washington. The town was put under siege on March 30—and then Hill bogged down. Alternately he sent encouraging and despondent reports to Longstreet, but by April 7 "he had not been able to make any impression on the fort."[56] While Hill dallied before Washington, Longstreet decided on a movement against Suffolk, employing the troops of Pickett and Hood. On April 9, General French relates, Longstreet "put his command in motion and took from me a division and a number of batteries, and was on his way to Suffolk without informing me of his designs, or of his wishes."[57] But the doughty general was not to be outdone. The next day he and his staff rode to Suffolk and, presenting his compliments to the lieutenant general, he reported for orders.[58] Longstreet countered nicely by assigning French to command of "all the artillery serving with the forces on the Blackwater."[59] Not to be outdone in this exchange, French promptly assigned most of the artillery to Hood's and Pickett's divisions and resumed command of his infantry.[60] Exactly how this left the position of all concerned was anybody's guess—but soon it was determined by a Federal attack on Fort Huger. The answer was that everybody was confused and Confederate officers started fighting duels with each other. One thing is clear, however: French was angry and he seems to have remained that way about Suffolk the rest of his life.

Longstreet had brought Hood's, Pickett's and French's divisions to Suffolk on April 11. So quietly had they moved that they were not discovered until the advance was in open view of the defenses around the town. High up in a pine tree was a lone Federal sentry on the lookout. Some unknown Confederate could not resist the urge to take a shot at him, whereupon he scampered down the tree trunk like a squirrel and gave the alarm.[61] With the Federals aroused, Longstreet could only invest the city, which he promptly did. Pickett's division was on the right, French's in the center and Hood's on the left.[62] The strategy was to hold the Federals in the town while the wagon trains collected bacon in the interior.

The Confederate position on the north and west isolated Suffolk. Pickett's right was firmly anchored on the edge of Dismal Swamp, but the left under Hood was up in the air on the point where the eastern and western branches flow together to form the Nansemond River.[63] Longstreet had tried to get the co-operation of the Confederate Navy to secure Hood's left but had failed.[64] As a second best, he decided to erect a series of earthworks in Hood's sector, one of which was Fort Huger or "Old Fort," as it was sometimes called. It was felt that if properly armed the fort might control the passage of Federal gunboats on the river, as well as more firmly anchor Hood's left. With this in mind

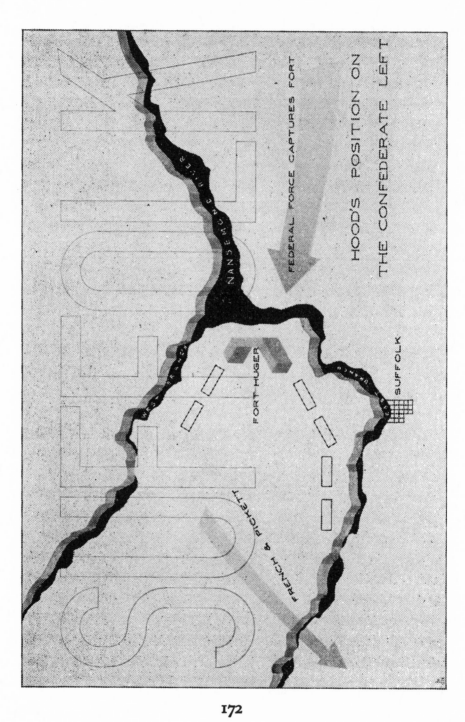

HOOD'S POSITION ON
THE CONFEDERATE LEFT

Longstreet ordered French to put a heavy battery there. French complied by sending in five of Captain Robert M. Stribling's (Farquier Artillery) guns. At the rear of the fort itself pits were dug and two 32-pounders were installed.[65]

These guns were installed on April 16. On the seventeenth French sent three companies from his own division (the 55th North Carolina commanded by Colonel John K. Connally) to take a position in the rear of the fort in general support of the batteries.[66] On the evening of the eighteenth Law sent two companies from the 44th Alabama to garrison the fort itself. These troops, it was understood, were to be relieved by Connally's men on the nineteenth.[67] French, however, was ill on the nineteenth and issued no order for Connally to occupy the fort.[68] Thus Law's men remained in the fort and Connally's to the rear, neither of them clearly understanding their duties.

About six o'clock on the evening of the nineteenth a small party of Federals landed a short distance above the fort and dragged four guns ashore. Neither Hood nor French had placed pickets there, both apparently thinking the other had done so.[69] Finding no pickets, the Federals rushed the fortification and captured it from Law's detachment. Colonel Connally and his detachment from the 55th North Carolina apparently did not know about the capture until it was all over. Shortly after the fort had been taken Connally moved his men forward to within some 600 yards of the captured fortification, formed a line of battle and ordered his men to lie down. He then sent skirmishers forward who were fired on from the fort, and soon the enemy's gunboats began firing on the prone men. Connally then withdrew all his men.[70] About 9:00 P.M. French heard of the affair and went to see Longstreet, who suggested that he go in person and see about it. When he arrived he found Hood and Law already there discussing the matter.[71] In the morning Longstreet arrived and held a conference with his three subordinates, in which it was decided not to counterattack but to let the enemy find out his position was untenable and evacuate it without a fight.[72] This the enemy did. French then confined himself ". . . to the immediate command of [his] division and took no more interest in Hood's line, and ordered Connally's Regiment to join his brigade."[73]

The affair probably should have been allowed to drop with that but it wasn't. Longstreet asked French for a full report, which French turned into a defense of himself.[74] Longstreet studied it and reported "a general lack of vigilance and prompt attention to duties" and exonerated Hood. After mildly censuring French's men, Longstreet tactfully concluded: "I do not know that any of them deserve particular censure. This lesson, it is hoped, will be of service to us all."[75] The men of Connally's and Law's commands took the matter seriously and personally. According to the evidence available the following affair took place: Connally called on Law and asked if it were true that he (Law) had said that the 55th North Carolina had acted cowardly. Law advised Connally that Captains L. R. Terrell and John Cussons of his staff had so advised him. Connally then called on the latter two officers, who repeated their statements earlier made to Law. Connally then rode back to his regiment and a challenge was delivered in the best code duello manner. Major A. H. Belo would fight Captain Cussons while Colonel Connally fought Captain Terrell. The weapons and terms were agreed on. Connally and Terrell would use shotguns at forty yards. Cussons and Belo would use rifles at the same distance.

Surrounded by as many spectators as could arrange to be present, Belo and Cussons took their positions. At the signal they fired. Captain Cussons received a bullet hole in his hat and Major Belo emerged untouched. The rifles were reloaded and again the order to fire was given. This time Cussons was untouched and Belo received a bullet through his coat collar. Then just as the rifles were being loaded for the third round a messenger dashed up with the news that Colonel Connally and Captain Terrell had patched up their differences, so the whole affair was called off.[76]

Just how much Hood knew about the affair is problematical, but it seems reasonable to suppose that he knew all about it. Certainly there is no record of his having done anything to stop it. As a matter of fact, Hood appeared to be pretty well fed up on Suffolk. Day after day there was little happening except minor skirmishing between infantry patrols and the artillerymen popping away at gunboats on the river. Hood apparently was thinking of Lee on the Rappahannock and wishing he were with him. Near the last of April he wrote his chief an almost boyish letter asking to be relieved:[77]

Division Headquarters,
Near Suffolk, Va., April 29, 1863

General R. E. Lee,
Commanding Army of Northern Virginia:

My Dear General: Here we are in front of the enemy again. The Yankees have a very strong position, and of course they increase the strength of their position daily. I presume we will leave here so soon as we gather all the bacon in the country. *When we leave here it is my desire to return to you. If any troops come to the Rappahannock please don't forget me.* I have not lost many men, but I have lost some of my best soldiers. Captain Turner, of the 5th Texas, the leader of my sharpshooters, fell on the 15th instant, in a gun boat fight. A more noble and brave soldier has not fallen during this war. Our line of battle is a very long one. I hope, however, we will accomplish all we came here for.

Please present my kindest regards to all the members of your staff, and believe me, your friend,

J. B. HOOD

That Lee would soon need Hood and Pickett was daily growing more obvious on the Rappahannock. Longstreet's stalemate in southeastern Virginia and North Carolina had not been productive. The enemy had been bottled up while the wagons foraged—but the foraging apparently had been none too successful. Complete figures on the amount collected are lacking but apparently the foragers were confronted with all sorts of difficulties. General Garnett reported to Hill that most of the bacon in the Pungo River region of North Carolina was in the hands of persons loyal to the Union.[78] Secretary of War Seddon felt that the chief difficulty was in getting enough wagons to bring out what supplies had been secured.[79] Longstreet suggested to Seddon that "the reports of bacon and corn are very favorable thus far,"[80] but one searches in vain for any sort of estimate of how much was actually secured.

Meantime Lee was growing apprehensive over the situation on the Rappahannock. Perhaps nothing reveals Lee's fears and Longstreet's almost condescending attitude toward his chief more than the correspondence between the two men from the middle of March to the early part of May.

Lee was patient and tactful as always. "From present indications," he wrote, "it is fair to presume that we shall be called upon to engage him [Hooker] first on the Rappahannock, and I desire you to be prepared for this movement. . . ."[81]

"I have Hood's division on the railroad ready for a movement in any direction," Longstreet replied apparently unperturbed.[82]

But even having Hood in position was unnecessary, Longstreet thought. "I cannot divest myself of the opinion that an obstinate resistance [with Jackson's corps] on the Rappahannock will hold that line," he added.[83]

"If this army is further weakened we must retire," Lee answered.[84]

"I think it utterly impossible for the enemy to move against your position until the roads are sufficiently dry for him to move around you and turn your position," Longstreet defiantly replied.[85]

After more than a month of trying to get Old Pete's co-operation, Lee at length wrote wearily and with a touch of sarcasm: "The emergency that made your presence so desirable has passed for the present, so far as I can see, and I desire that you will not distress your troops by a forced movement to join me."[86]

The "emergency" referred to by Lee was nothing less than the Battle of Chancellorsville where Lee with Jackson's corps had hurled back Hooker's magnificent army and defeated it—but at a terrific loss. Jackson was wounded on the evening of May 2 and died eight days later of pneumonia.[87] Hood states that he was greatly distressed over Jackson's death and one can well imagine he was.[88] He had great admiration for Jackson personally and as a soldier and, in turn, Jackson had on numerous occasions shown his confidence in Hood. The distress he felt, Hood says, prompted him to write Lee a letter expressing his sorrow over Jackson's death and also over his own inability to get to Chancellorsville before the battle.[89] The text of this letter has not been located, but from Lee's reply it seems that Hood suggested a reorganization plan for the army which would have divided Jackson's corps and perhaps Longstreet's as well. Lee's reply is as follows:[90]

My Dear General:—Upon my return from Richmond I found your letter of the 13th awaiting me. Although separated from me, I have always had you in my eye and thoughts. I wished for you much in the last battle, and believe had I had the whole army with me, General Hooker would have been demolished. But God ordered otherwise. I grieve much over the death of General Jackson—for our sakes, not for his. He is happy and at peace. But his spirit lives with us, and I hope it will raise up many Jacksons in our ranks. We must all do more than formerly. We must endeavor to follow the unselfish, devoted, intrepid course he pursued, and we shall be strengthened rather than weakened by his loss. I rely much on you. You must so inspire and lead your brave division, as that it may accomplish the work of a corps. I agree with you as to the size of the corps of this army. They are too large for the country we have to operate in for one man to handle. I saw it all last campaign. I have endeavored to remedy it—this in a measure at least—but do not know whether I shall succeed. I am much obliged to you always for your opinion. I know you give it from pure motives. If I am not always convinced, you must bear with me. I agree with you also in believing that our Army would be invincible if it could be properly organized and officered. There never were such men in an Army before. They will go anywhere and do anything if properly led. But there is the difficulty—proper commanders—where can they be obtained? But they are improving—constantly improving. Rome was not built in a day, nor can we expect miracles in our favor.

Wishing you every health and happiness, and committing you to the care of a kind Providence,

I am now and always your friend,

R. E. LEE.

Was Hood's letter written from "pure motives" as Lee indicated or was it a bid for promotion and command of one of the smaller corps he apparently urged on Lee? Was Lee's letter quoted above a subtle reminder to Hood that he was not ready to command a corps? The answers are not forthcoming; but Lee did, before he received Hood's letter, divide Jackson's corps between newly appointed Lieutenant General Richard S. Ewell, who commanded the Second Corps, and Lieutenant General Ambrose P. Hill, who commanded the Third Corps. Hood was not seriously considered.

Meantime he and his troops were in camp near Richmond awaiting orders. They had arrived in the capital on May 5, while the smoke still hung over the Chancellorsville battlefield.[91] There was no need for haste now, and Hood's division paused while their commander renewed his social contacts in the city. This time he met Mrs. Chesnut and had an opportunity to get better acquainted with the Preston girls. Apparently it was all arranged by Hood's dashing, youthful chief surgeon, Dr. John T. Darby, of Mrs. Chesnut's beloved South Carolina. He brought Hood to call on her and the moment she saw him she apparently was much impressed[92]—an impression that ripened into loyal friendship between the two and eventually led straight to the Executive Mansion.

Hood and Darby came, Mrs. Chesnut relates, to invite her and the Preston girls to a picnic at Drury's Bluff. Dr. Darby was courting Mary Preston and undoubtedly Hood was already greatly attracted to Sally "Buck" Preston; but so were many more officers in Richmond. Apparently she was very popular and much sought after.[93] She has been described as "supremely lovely,"[94] but she was not an ethereal and gossamer beauty. Although she was "tall and fair," she was vigorous, had a healthy complexion, a voluptuous figure and an "abundance of strong common sense."[95] Her features were not delicate and finely chiseled; rather they were inclined to be somewhat plain with a prominent nose, a wide mouth and a firm chin. Her deep-set dark eyes seemed to twinkle with a hidden amusement, perhaps at the antics of her suitors.[96] Apparently Mary was the merrier of the two and much more inclined to display the qualities of an extrovert. She was always ready to take the lead in a social group, while Sally sat in her regal manner and said little, a bit sullen at times and a bit sultry always.

Plans for the picnic included a visit to the camp of Hood's division, music and dancing and a picnic lunch of "turkeys, chickens, and buffalo tongues."[97] The next morning as they were all ready to start, however, Hood was ordered to move his division to join Lee on the Rappahannock. So instead of going on the picnic, Mrs. Chesnut and the Preston girls went down to the turnpike to watch the troops march by. As the ragged regiments marched, Hood and his staff galloped up. The irrepressible Mary gave him a bouquet, whereupon he unwrapped the Bible his mother had given him and deposited between its pages a flower. There was a little joking about how little used the Bible seemed to be, and then Hood galloped away to join his men.[98]

They were on their way to Gettysburg.

CHAPTER VIII

Gettysburg and Chickamauga

AFTER Chancellorsville, Lee had every reason for the pride he displayed in writing Hood that "there never were such men in an Army before." In the wilderness around Chancellor's house a portion of his army only fifty-seven thousand strong had badly defeated Hooker's ninety-seven thousand.[1] But winning the battle only increased the difficulties of Lee's position. As after each of his victories there arose the increasingly perplexing question— what next? He had defeated the Federal Army, but he had not destroyed it. Always, like a sorely wounded giant, the enemy retired after a defeat, licked its wounds and eventually came back for more.

As Lee faced the problem in May 1863, there were three principal alternatives open to him: he could stand on the Rappahannock and develop the enemy's intentions; he could, as Longstreet urged, reinforce Bragg in middle Tennessee; or he could take the offensive again. To stand on the Rappahannock was out of the question, because he could not subsist his men. Longstreet's Suffolk campaign had produced merely a soupçon of supplies and the Fredericksburg area had been eaten barren by the troops. Reinforcing Bragg in middle Tennessee offered definite possibilities for driving the Federals out of that area, but dividing his forces, Lee thought, would lay Richmond wide open. There remained then only one course which he felt he could follow: take the offensive. In this decision he was given the backing of President

Davis and all the cabinet except Postmaster General Reagan.[2]

Having decided on the invasion of Pennsylvania, Lee faced the problem of obtaining men, horses and supplies. Stuart's cavalry was increased by the addition of three brigades, but efforts to increase the strength of the infantry did not go so well.[3] Pickett was at Hanover Junction with three of his four brigades, the fourth one being retained for the defense of Richmond. The three brigades under D. H. Hill in North Carolina could not be counted on at all. Hood's division was marching from Richmond in full force, however. Longstreet's other divisions (McLaws' and Anderson's) were ready. Likewise the Second and Third corps under Ewell and A. P. Hill respectively were, except for losses at Chancellorsville, intact. Lee's total strength is placed at between seventy and seventy-five thousand men of all arms.[4] The numbers hardly met Lee's minimum needs, but with them he had to content himself as he carefully worked out his plans during May and early June.

Hood's division, after marching orders broke up the picnic, marched straight for the upper Rappahannock and reached Verdiersville in the wilderness near Chancellorsville on May 31.[5] Near by at Fredericksburg were A. P. Hill with his corps and McLaws with his division of Longstreet's corps. Stuart with the cavalry was near Culpeper Courthouse. Across the Rappahannock from Fredericksburg was Hooker with his army. By the third of June the Confederates, except for A. P. Hill left at Fredericksburg to observe the enemy, were converging on Culpeper where Stuart waited to lead the invasion.[6]

Here at Culpeper on June 8, Stuart put on a show for the army in the form of a giant review of his cavalry. General Lee was present by invitation and so was Hood. Not only was Hood present but he brought his entire division with him, thereby precipitating a mild crisis. Fitzhugh Lee had invited Hood to "come and see the review, and bring any of his people." Obviously "any of his people" was meant to cover only his staff, but on the second day of the review the gray masses of Hood's entire division emerged with glittering bayonets from the woods in the direction of the Rapidan.

"You invited me and my people," Hood said as he shook hands with Fitz Lee, "and you see I have brought them."

This was a crisis. If Hood's infantry should yell the fighting words "Where's your mule?" at the cavalry the review might wind up in a free-for-all.

"Don't let them yell that," Fitz Lee warned. "If they do we'll charge you," Wade Hampton laughed.

But Hood's troops kept reasonably quiet as they watched squadron after squadron of Stuart's horsemen thunder by the reviewing stand where General Lee sat on his horse and took the salute. But one of Hood's men could not restrain himself. Turning to a comrade he was heard to mumble: "Wouldn't we clean them out, if old Hood would only let us loose on 'em."[7]

The next day these proud troopers of Stuart were fighting the opening battle of the Gettysburg campaign. When Hooker discovered that Lee had drawn off part of his forces from Fredericksburg he began to throw out feelers to see what had happened. He first put a bridge across the Rappahannock below Fredericksburg and sent across a detachment of infantry and artillery. A. P. Hill, however, soon drove these forces back across the river and Hooker learned little. On the ninth, however, he sent General Alfred Pleasonton with a force of some 6,000 cavalry and nearly 5,000 infantry which attacked Stuart in a reconnaissance in force near Culpeper. It was a surprise attack and a bitterly fought battle. But Hooker got the information he wanted this time. Pleasonton captured Stuart's camp, and from letters and orders found there it was not difficult to figure out Lee's plans.[8] Acting on this information, Hooker left his position on the Rappahannock on June 13 and marched toward the upper reaches of the Potomac.

"If the enemy should be making for Maryland, I will make the best dispositions in my power to come up with him," Hooker promised.[9]

Thus began the race for Pennsylvania, though neither side knew where the finish line was. On the Confederate side Longstreet's corps marched north along the eastern edge of the Blue Ridge. To the east of his columns rode Stuart, his cavalry screening the movement of the infantry. Ewell moved northward through the Shenandoah Valley while A. P. Hill tarried momentarily at Fredericksburg and then followed Ewell up the valley. Thirty miles to the east Hooker followed, his march roughly paralleling that of the Confederates.[10] Lee was drawing Hooker out of Virginia. Where would the two armies clash?

On the nineteenth of June Longstreet's corps was distributed as follows: McLaws was at Ashley's Gap, Hood was at Snicker's Gap and Pickett was midway between them.[11] On the twentieth the entire division, except for a part of McLaws' division which was forced to go to Stuart's relief when Pleasonton attacked again, moved through Snicker's Gap, waded the Shenandoah River and camped on the left bank.[12] His corps was now west of the mountains and in a position to effect a juncture with Ewell and A. P. Hill moving up the valley. On the twenty-third and twenty-fourth Lee's three corps were approaching the Potomac ready to cross and debouch into Maryland.[13]

Hood's division crossed the Potomac at Williamsport, Maryland, pausing long enough to draw rations of Maryland whisky. The rations apparently were generous and those who did not drink gave their share to comrades who did. When the march toward Chambersburg was resumed many of the men couldn't find the road, much less hit it with their hats. The colonel of the 3rd Arkansas, however, found a way to sober up his men. There were many small cold streams along the route, and it was found that an immersion worked wonders for wobbly legs.[14] On the twenty-seventh, hangovers and all, the division reached Chambersburg, hungry and tired.

Confederate soldiers were always hungry, especially Hood's Texans. Now they found themselves in a soldier's paradise. All around them were rich farms with lush vegetable gardens, chicken runs and well-filled smokehouses. Although Lee had warned his troops against depredations, he himself was buying with Confederate money and "impressing only when necessary."[15] And if Lee could spend Confederate money for food so could Hood's men. What methods they used in convincing Pennsylvania farmers that Confederate currency was a highly acceptable token of exchange can only be guessed at. Too, hungry soldiers were not likely to molest farmhouses where they were well fed, and owners were not slow in realizing this; so by subtle coercion Hood's men fed themselves.[16] And, according to a contemporary account, they were highly successful. On awakening one morning, a spectator reported, he found "every square foot of an acre of ground covered with choice food for the hungry. Chickens, turkeys, ducks, and geese squawked, gobbled, quacked, cackled and hissed in harmonious unison as deft and energetic hands seized them for slaughter, and scarcely waiting for them to die, sent their feathers flying in all directions; and scattered around in bewildering confusion and gratifying profusion appeared immense loaves of bread and chunks of corned beef, hams, and sides of bacon, cheeses, crocks of apple butter, jelly, jams, pickles and preserves, bowls of yellow butter, demijohns of buttermilk and other eatables too numerous to mention." Sprawled here and there were sleeping foragers who had been out all night. One man's head rested on a loaf of bread and one arm was wound caressingly about a country ham. Another, fearful that his prize would escape or be stolen, had tied the string that bound a half-dozen chickens to his great toe. A third lay flat on his back snoring, but in his right hand he held the legs of three chickens and a duck, while his left clasped the leg of a turkey.[17]

So they gorged themselves that day, and in the afternoon came marching orders. Sluggishly they took up the last lap of the long road to Gettysburg; but they had one consolation. This was one battle they would fight with their bellies full.

And battle was not far away. Hooker had cautiously followed, making his own movements conform to those of the Confederates, crossing the Potomac at Edwards' Ferry on June 25 and 26. On June 27 three corps under Reynolds occupied Middletown and the mountain passes. The Twelfth Corps was near Harpers Ferry and the three other corps were near Frederick, Maryland.[18] On the twenty-eighth Hooker ordered the Twelfth Corps to Harpers Ferry, there to be joined by the garrison occupying Maryland Heights on the Maryland side of the Potomac. But General Halleck disapproved the abandonment of the Heights, and Hooker promptly resigned his command.[19] When General George G. Meade was appointed to take Hooker's place he was the fifth commander of the Army of the Potomac in a year, but the last change did not seriously interfere with Federal operations. Spending one day getting acquainted with the position of his troops (June 28) he put them in motion in the general direction of Lee's army.

Both Lee and Meade lacked adequate information on each other's movements. On the night of June 24 Stuart, availing himself of the discretion allowed him by Lee, took all his cavalry except two brigades and went on a raid in the Federal rear. He was on this wild ride from the night of June 24 through July 1 at the very time he was needed to bring Lee information of the enemy's movements.[20] The two armies, therefore, blundered into each other at Gettysburg. Lee had no word from Stuart while the raid was in progress and hourly grew more apprehensive.[21] Although he joked with Hood about having to go in search of the enemy,[22] he plainly was worried. It was not until late in the night of June 28 that he knew the Federals were across the Potomac and that Meade had replaced Hooker. One of Longstreet's spies had brought the information on which Lee based his decision to concentrate his army at Cashtown, near Gettysburg, and await developments.[23]

Brigade by brigade and division by division the army gathered. It was Lee's purpose to avoid a general conflict until all had arrived, but circumstances which precipitated battle intervened. Ewell's and A. P. Hill's corps arrived in full force at the appointed rendezvous on July 1 and Longstreet's, except for Pickett's division, the next day, but the preliminary stages of the battle were already under way.[24]

On June 29 General Henry Heth commanding a division of Hill's Third Corps arrived at Cashtown. The next morning he ordered General J. Johnston Pettigrew to take his brigade to Gettysburg, search the city for shoes and other supplies and return the same day. When Pettigrew reached the suburbs of the town he found a large force of cavalry and infantry. In the circumstances he did not deem it advisable to enter, so he returned to Cashtown. The next morning, however, Heth moved his entire division with Pegram's artillery toward Gettysburg, where he found the enemy again in considerable force in the hills and ridges just west of Gettysburg. Without the slightest idea of how strong the enemy was Heth decided to find out. Pulling up on a ridge a mile west of Gettysburg, Pegram opened his guns on the cavalry vedettes, one salvo mortally wounding Major General John F. Reynolds, then in command of the Federals in Gettysburg. Then Heth threw forward the brigades of James J. Archer and Joseph R. Davis in a forced reconnaissance to determine the enemy's strength; and very promptly he found it. Every field officer except two in Davis' brigade was shot down and the brigade cut to pieces. Archer's brigade was forced back with heavy losses and Archer himself was captured.[25] Not until Heth brought up his entire division was the enemy dislodged and forced back into Gettysburg.

Lee, on hearing the roar of battle, rode hastily toward Gettysburg, completely ignorant of what was happening.[26] A. P. Hill had ordered up General William D. Pender's division in support of Heth.[27] Rapidly the affair was showing signs of developing into a full-fledged battle. Then from the wood north of Gettysburg another Confederate force appeared out of nowhere. It was General Robert E. Rodes's division of Ewell's corps moving toward the rendezvous at Cashtown. As if it had been deliberately planned he happened to come up at exactly the right time in the right position. Immediately the Federals attacked Rodes and a sharp engagement ensued.[28]

Heth rode out to meet Lee. "Rodes," he is quoted as saying, "is heavily engaged; had I not better attack?"

"No," Lee is reported to have replied. "I am not prepared to bring on a general engagement today July 1—Longstreet is not up."[29]

But Lee had very little control over what happened in the next few crucial hours, for hardly had he finished the conversation with Heth when firing broke out afresh on Rodes's left. General Jubal Early, moving to join the rest of the army at Cashtown, had blundered into the fight at exactly the right time and in exactly the right position.[30] This changed conditions materially. Lee decided now was the time to attack, and the Confederate lines surged forward. Soon the enemy broke in retreat toward Gettysburg. But they didn't stop in the town. Very shortly it was in Early's hands, and the Federals were south of the town securing themselves on the ridges.

Now was the time to finish the enemy before he could fortify himself on the ridges south and southeast of Gettysburg. Early, sensing that victory was within the Confederate grasp, rode to find Ewell or Hill and to urge an immediate advance before the enemy got set. Meeting with one of Pender's staff, Early sent the message to Hill. A short while later he located Ewell personally

and told him of the situation.[31] And from this point on the scene
is blurred by errors and misunderstandings which cost Lee Gettysburg and the South the war. Perhaps these, for the South, tragic
events can best be understood through a rough chronological
summary:

1. Stuart went on his raid in the enemy's rear and left Lee without adequate information for a week preceding the battle.

2. On the afternoon of July 1 when the Federals had fled
through Gettysburg there was an excellent chance to strike while
the enemy was in flight and before he had an opportunity to
secure himself on the ridges south of the town. Lee ordered
Ewell to attack Culp's Hill that afternoon "if he found it practicable."[32] But Ewell did not find it practicable and thus the
Federals were given additional time to dig in on the hill, which
was the Federal right flank.

3. On the afternoon of July 1 Lee and Longstreet were quarreling. Longstreet felt that his policy of an offensive strategy and
defensive tactics should be followed; that Lee's army should not
fight at Gettysburg but should pass around to the south of the
enemy's left flank at Round Top and then swing east, drawing
Meade toward Washington. Somewhere between Gettysburg and
Washington Lee would find ground favorable to him and there
he would await battle and, as at Fredericksburg, slaughter the
attacking Federals.[33] But Lee refused to entertain Longstreet's
plan. "I am going to whip them or they are going to whip me,"
Longstreet quotes Lee as saying.[34] The conversation apparently
left Longstreet very angry,[35] however, and his conduct during
the rest of the battle reflects the attitude that Lee had made his
bed and now he could lie in it.

4. Lee wished to attack as early as possible on the morning of
July 2, but Longstreet's division was not in position until the
afternoon. And where were McLaws and Hood? "Old Pete"
was noncommittal. McLaws was about six miles away, but he

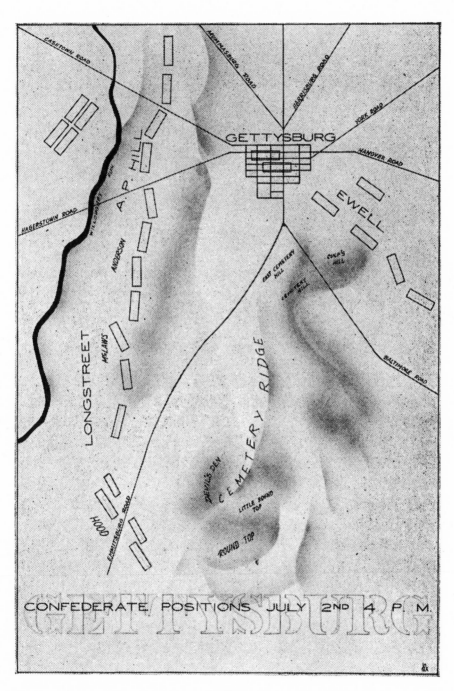

CONFEDERATE POSITIONS JULY 2ND 4 P. M.

wasn't sure about Hood. Well, Lee suggested, they should all be brought up as rapidly as possible.[36]

Hood's division, except for Law's brigade, which was on picket duty near New Guilford, had marched from its camp near Chambersburg at 2:00 P.M. on July 1, about the time that Early was entering Gettysburg. With their bellies full of good Pennsylvania food and their haversacks equally stuffed, Hood's troops, following McLaws' division, picked their way in and out of Ewell's wagon train moving toward Cashtown. For four hours the wagons blocked the road as swearing teamsters urged their critters along. It was 2:00 A.M. on July 2 when the division marched through Cashtown to bivouac near Gettysburg.[37] Although the troops were tired, a few hours sleep would have them ready for battle by seven or eight o'clock in the morning. The same was true of McLaws' division. Missing only were Law's brigade of Hood's corps and Pickett's division.

Hood rode ahead of his division and reported to Lee early on the morning of July 2. He found Lee with coat buttoned to the throat, saber belt buckled around his waist and field glasses at his side pacing up and down under the trees, halting now and then to observe the enemy through his glasses. He seemed to Hood to be full of hope, yet at times buried in thought. "The enemy is here and if we do not whip him he will whip us," he said to Hood and Longstreet. Hood understood this to mean an immediate attack, but Longstreet was unexcited. According to Hood, Longstreet remarked to him in an aside: "The General is a little nervous this morning; he wishes me to attack; I do not wish to do so without Pickett. I never like to go into battle with one boot off."[38]

In the expectation that Longstreet would attack, Lee rode to Ewell's front. Ewell's second corps was to make a demonstration when Longstreet struck, and if the circumstances seemed favorable it was to be converted into a full-scale attack.[39] But as the morning advanced Longstreet did not go into action. Finally near eleven o'clock Lee located his strong-willed lieutenants on the field. McLaws was in position, but Hood's division had not been moved. This time Lee issued no discretionary orders. He directly ordered "Old Pete" to attack with the troops he had in position. Lee even rode nearly a mile with Longstreet to show him just what was desired of him.[40] But still there was no attack. Almost casually Longstreet had moved Hood's division by McLaws' front to the extreme right of the Confederate line opposite Round Top. And then Longstreet decided not only to wait on Pickett but on Law's division as well. Law's division arrived and joined Hood about noon.[41] It was nearly four o'clock in the afternoon before the attack began.[42]

From his position on the Confederate extreme right Hood had a panoramic view of the entire battlefield. It was as if he were a bowler at the head of an alley. On his right was Cemetery Ridge forming one side, and opposite on his left was Seminary Ridge forming the other. Directly in front of him and splitting the alley like a thin strip of carpet was the Emmitsburg Road, leading directly to the pins at Gettysburg. On his left the Confederates were drawn out in lines like spectators on Seminary Ridge, and in front of and along the slopes on his right the Federals, now well set, waited for the bowler to go into action.

It was shortly after four o'clock on the afternoon of July 2 before all of Hood's brigades were up and ready for the attack.[43] To their right rose Round Top like a huge sentinel guarding the Federal left. North of Round Top a few hundred feet was Little Round Top holding hands with its big brother. Farther north were the low-lying wooded ridges of Cemetery Ridge. How strong were the Federals along these wooded slopes and ravines? No one knew the answer, but at intervals puffs of smoke rising from sporadic popping of Federal guns answered part of the question. The Federals were there and in an ideal defensive position. To reach them Hood would have to drive across the valley and then fight his way up these boulder-strewed and densely wooded slopes. In many respects it was a similar situation to Gaines's Mill, except there he could see the enemy. Here on the slopes at Gettysburg the enemy was concealed from view.[44]

Law needed no one to tell him of the carnage to be expected when troops charged well-intrenched positions. He had been at Gaines's Mill when his own men were mercilessly mowed down along with the Texans. He had also been at Fredericksburg, where his brigade had helped turn the tables and where the Federals had been slaughtered as they charged. Was there no way to avoid this bloody advance against the slopes of Little Round Top and Cemetery Ridge? He thought so. While he had been waiting for all the brigades to get into position he had sent scouts around to the right of Round Top and they had found the rear of the mountain virtually unguarded. He could, he believed, quickly move to the rear of Round Top and strike the enemy a surprise blow from which he could not recover. This view Law communicated to Hood, whom he found in accord but who felt that his orders to attack up the Emmitsburg Road must stand until changed. But Law wished to make a formal protest anyway, so Hood called a member of his staff as a witness. Then Law formally repeated his views (1) that the strength of the enemy's position rendered the result of a direct assault extremely uncertain; (2) that even if successful the victory would be at too great a sacrifice of life; (3) that a frontal assault was unnecessary and a movement around the enemy's left flank was not only possible but comparatively easy; and (4) that such a movement would compel the Federals to abandon their position on the ridge and thus reverse the situation, forcing the displaced Federals to attack the Confederates in position.[45]

Although Hood gave Law to understand that he approved his plan, he did not reveal to him just how warmly he approved; but

Longstreet soon found out. Hood's own account of his protests tell the story. Writing to Longstreet he said:[46]

I was in possession of these important facts so shortly after reaching the Emmitsburg Road, that I considered it my duty to report to you, at once, my opinion that it was unwise to attack up the Emmitsburg Road, as ordered, and to urge that you allow me to turn Round Top, and attack the enemy in flank and rear. Accordingly I despatched a staff officer, bearing to you my request to be allowed to make the proposed movement on account of the above stated reasons. Your reply was quickly received. "General Lee's orders are to attack up the Emmitsburg Road." I sent another officer to say that I feared nothing could be accomplished by such an attack, and renewed my request to turn Round Top. Again your answer was, "General Lee's orders are to attack up the Emmitsburg Road." During this interim I had continued the use of the batteries upon the enemy, and had become more and more convinced that the Federal line extended to Round Top, and that I could not reasonably hope to accomplish much by the attack as ordered. In fact, it seemed to me the enemy occupied a position by nature so strong—I may say impregnable—that, independently of their flank fire, they could easily repel our attack by merely throwing and rolling stones down the mountain side as we approached.

A third time I despatched one of my staff to explain fully in regard to the situation, and suggest that you had better come and look for yourself. I selected in this instance, my adjutant-general, Colonel Harry Sellers, whom you know to be not only an officer of great courage, but also of marked ability. Colonel Sellers returned with the same message, "General Lee's orders are to attack up the Emmitsburg Road." Almost simultaneously, Colonel Fairfax, of your staff, rode up and repeated the above orders.

After this urgent protest against entering the battle at Gettysburg, according to instruction—which protest is the first and only one I ever made during my entire military career—I ordered my line to advance and make the assault.

As my troops were moving forward, you rode up in person; a brief conversation passed between us, during which I again expressed the fears above mentioned, and regret at not being allowed to attack in flank around Round Top. You answered to this effect, "we must obey the orders of General Lee. . . ."

This sudden determination on Longstreet's part to obey Lee's orders to the letter was not admirable in the circumstances. Never before had Longstreet had the slightest compunction about advising Lee; but in this instance there is no evidence that he even acquainted him with Hood's and Law's protest. From this distance it appears that Longstreet's attitude was: "Lee has ordered this battle over my protest. Now we will fight it according to his orders. If we are defeated it will be his fault, not mine."[47] There is, of course, no certainty that the flanking movement would have succeeded, but it is obvious that it was preferable to the frontal assault, for in any battle a commander must accept the course which holds the strongest probability of success and then risk the balance.

But the flanking movement was never tried and Hood attacked up the Emmitsburg Road as directed. The time was near five o'clock in the afternoon. Law's brigade on the right led off, followed closely by the Texas brigade. On Law's left Benning and Anderson closed up and the lines swept forward. Confederate batteries ceased their firing lest they hit their own troops. There was an almost eerie silence; and then the slopes ahead exploded with a roar as forty Federal batteries poured canister, grape and shell into the advancing Confederates. Hood was shot from his horse badly wounded in the left arm and borne from the field on a stretcher.[48] Law took command; the lines were re-formed and again surged forward. The enemy was slowly pushed back from the valley toward the slopes and then up the boulder-strewed sides of the ridge. The fighting became almost hand to hand in many places. In Devil's Den the opposing lines stood, with only the boulders between them, breast to breast, and so close that the clothing of many of the enemy was set on fire by the blazing Confederate rifles.

On the right of Devil's Den "Old Rock" Benning strode through the lines of his Georgians shouting, "Give 'em hell, boys."[49] And hell it was on both sides. Officers and men were going down on every hand. In the Texas brigade Colonel J. C. Key of the 4th was wounded and sent to the rear. Colonel R. M. Powell of the 5th was also dangerously wounded, and then Robertson himself was shot through the knee and forced out of the fight.[50] In Benning's brigade a fragment of shrapnel glanced off a boulder and pierced the brain of Colonel John A. Jones of the 20th Georgia. A few minutes earlier Lieutenant Colonel John A. Harris commanding the 2nd Georgia went down.[51] So did Colonel Van Manning of the 3rd Arkansas and General G. T. Anderson.

Brigades and regiments became inextricably mixed and confused as their officers were killed and wounded. Soon it was every man for himself. Loading and firing, the scattered regiments slowly advanced from boulder to boulder in the face of an equally galling fire from the Federals. Will Barbee, one of Hood's young couriers, rode up, dismounted and joined the fight. Springing to the top of a boulder behind which Confederate wounded protected themselves he began firing at the enemy. Standing above the rest of the men like a tower he fired the rifles loaded for him by the wounded below. In a matter of minutes he was shot off the boulder, but he remounted it. Then he was shot down a second time and lay at the base cursing those who would not help him back on the rock again.[52]

Federals and Confederates alike were seized by the wild fury of battle. In a Federal countercharge a handsome young major astride a beautiful gray horse rode straight into the Confederate fire encouraging his men. Right up to the muzzles of the Confederate rifles he rode seeming to bear a charmed life. "Don't shoot him," Hood's men shouted. "He is too brave a man to die.

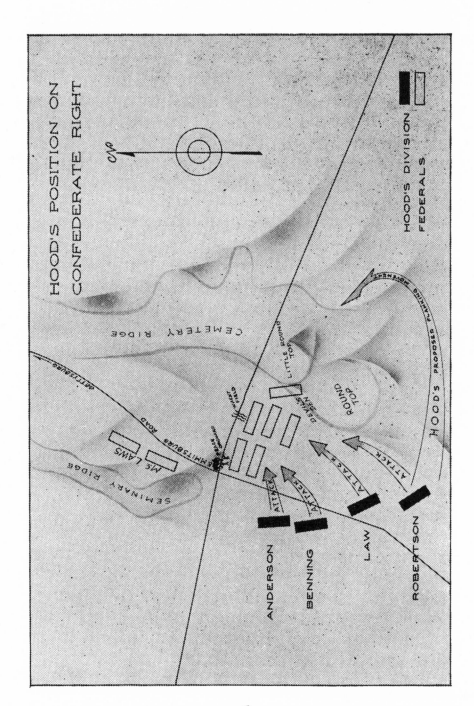

HOOD'S POSITION ON CONFEDERATE RIGHT

196

Shoot his horse and capture him." But no one listened seriously. This was war, and in a matter of moments both rider and horse went down riddled with bullets.[53] Near by a wizened little private from the 3rd Arkansas sat comfortably behind a stump loading and firing as fast as he could, and between biting cartridges and taking aim he was singing at the top of his voice:[54]

> Now, let the wide world wag as it will,
> I'll be gay and happy still.

At the foot of the ridge it was anybody's fight as bodies piled high in Devil's Den and beyond. Perhaps the Confederates had the best of it if there could be any choosing. By night they had taken the hill by Devil's Den, had swept over the northern slope of Round Top, cleared it of the enemy and precariously established themselves on the slopes of Little Round Top.[55]

Meantime McLaws took up the fight on his front, pressing directly forward under the personal direction of Longstreet. Kershaw's and Barksdale's brigades led off, with Semmes's and Wofford's brigades following. Pushing through the peach orchard, they encountered the same type of opposition that Hood's men had on their right. Again Federal artillery and rifle fire cut the gray lines to pieces. Hardly had his brigade swung into action when General Semmes fell mortally wounded.[56] A few minutes later General Barksdale went down. As in Hood's division, regiments became scattered and men were mowed down as they doggedly pushed ahead.[57] But they did push ahead, forcing the enemy back to the slopes of Cemetery Ridge where Hood's men were crawling upward through the boulders.

Ewell, who was to attack the extreme Federal right when he heard Hood's guns, did open fire, but his guns were soon silenced by the Federal artillery on Cemetery and Culp's hills. Two brigades of Early's division attacked Cemetery Hill about 6:00 P.M.

but were soon driven out.[58] General Edward Johnson's division assaulted Culp's Hill about the same time, but was unable to carry it.[59]

Hood's division had partially succeeded on the right; McLaws had partially succeeded on the center; Ewell had failed on the left. This was the news carried back to Hood in his hospital tent in the rear. This is where he would lie during the rest of the battle listening to the roar of the guns and wondering how the battle went. His wound was painful but not serious. He had been shot through the left hand, forearm, elbow and biceps.[60] Dr. Darby, who attended him, found it unnecessary to amputate, however.

The reports which floated back to him on July 3 were underscored by the thunderous storm of artillery and the sharper metallic crashes of rifle fire. General Lee had renewed the battle on this sultry July morning before Independence Day. Leaving Hood's and McLaws' divisions to hold the positions they had won, Lee delivered an attack on the Federal center by the troops of Pickett's division assisted by the divisions of William D. Pender and Henry Heth of A. P. Hill's corps. Proudly these 15,000 men left their positions and marched across the valley into the face of the Federal guns. This was Fredericksburg in reverse. Now it was thousands of graycoats instead of blue advancing against intrenched positions straight into the arms of death. Wave after wave of them rolled against the Federal positions. The fields were strewed with bodies where Pickett's men charged. Likewise the men of Pender's and Heth's divisions were dropping like insects before a spray gun. This was the great American battle, and issues debated since 1789 rode on the outcome. The future of the nation was being hammered out in the Bloody Angle. And when the sun set that hot July day the hopes of the Confederacy sank with it. Lee had failed at Gettysburg.

There was no celebrating this July 4 in the bleeding ranks of the Confederacy. If Meade should counterattack, the battered remnants of the Army of Northern Virginia would be annihilated. Would he attack?

This was the problem Lee faced on the morning of July 4, 1863. But Meade did not attack and soon Lee was on his way back to Virginia. Collecting his wounded, assembling the wagon trains, deciding the route, arranging cavalry protection, feeding the men, guarding prisoners, burying the dead—these and many other details occupied Lee's attention.[61] Finally marching orders were issued. A. P. Hill's corps would start the movement. Longstreet's corps with the prisoners would follow and Ewell's corps would bring up the rear. Guarding the flanks was Stuart's cavalry.[62] This was the *via dolorosa*. The proud army which had entered Pennsylvania had lost—killed, wounded, and missing—nearly thirty thousand men[63]—roughly 40 per cent of Lee's effectives.

Bumping along in the caravan of the wounded was Hood's ambulance which he shared with Wade Hampton, who had been wounded in the head and side on the third day at Gettysburg. Hood suffered acutely from his wounded arm and was unable to lie down. Hampton, suffering severe stabbing pains in his side, was unable to sit up.[64] Thus they covered the 200 miles to Staunton. Along the road after they crossed the Potomac the women of Virginia lined the roads and supplied the wounded with food and care. Defeat made no difference. This was Lee's army coming home.

Hood remained in the peace of the Shenandoah Valley until the early part of August.[65] His recovery was rapid and soon he was thinking of Richmond again—of Louly Wigfall and Sally Preston. "Hood and myself came to Staunton together and he remained there under charge of Darby," Wade Hampton wrote Senator Wigfall. "He is doing well and his arm will be saved. All he needs now is good nursing, together with cheerful company and generous living. He proposes to pay you a visit if he can get rooms at Hiden's, so do drop him a line. . . ."[66] Hood did get rooms at Hiden's, and on August 6 he and his chief surgeon were in Richmond.[67] Darby, of course, was reunited with his beloved Mary Preston. Hood was calling on Sally, but it appears he was not confining his attentions to her alone. He was much attracted to Louly Wigfall. Just how strong his feelings for her were is a matter of some conjecture, but there is no guessing about her feelings for him. "A braver man, a purer patriot, a more gallant soldier never breathed than General Hood," she wrote. ". . . he was a man of singular simplicity of character and charm of manner—boyish in his enthusiasm—superbly handsome, with beautiful blue eyes, golden hair and flowing beard—broad shouldered, tall and erect—a noble man of undaunted courage and blameless life."[68]

"And," she might as well have added, "I cared for him very much."

While Hood was convalescing in Staunton and Richmond his division under Law had moved into Fredericksburg where it lay idle. If any fighting was to be done let Ewell's and A. P. Hill's men up the river do it, the men reasoned. Hood and McLaws and Pickett had done the fighting at Gettysburg—now let these others fight.[69] But there was little serious fighting for anyone from the early part of July until September. The sixty days after Gettysburg were spent by Lee in recruiting and re-equipping his army and in deciding over-all strategy in conference with Richmond officials. And the final denouement of these conferences brought Hood back into action again.

The Confederacy was threatened in two areas during the summer of 1863. The Federal Army was still just north of the Rappahannock; and in the West Rosecrans threatened to occupy all of Tennessee, thus virtually cutting the Confederacy in half so far as communications and railway lines were concerned. In July General William S. Rosecrans had forced Braxton Bragg and his

Army of Tennessee to abandon middle Tennessee and fall back to Chattanooga. In Knoxville, Ambrose E. Burnside and Simon B. Buckner faced each other, and it was conceded that the Confederates had but a slight chance to hold the city. Added to the plight of the West was the fact that Vicksburg had fallen while the smoke still hung over the battlefield at Gettysburg. On the coast, too, the West was threatened. Charleston was under siege and Wilmington was in danger. Strategy conferences very naturally revolved around these questions: What should be done? By whom? Where? When?

Lee felt that the most important choice was between attacking Meade and attacking Rosecrans. From his point of view it was more imperative that he strike at Meade, but on September 2 Burnside occupied Knoxville and this event forced a reconsideration.[70] It was decided to send part of Longstreet's corps to Tennessee to reinforce Bragg, who stood bewildered in the coves and valleys south of Chattanooga near a creek named Chickamauga. On the ninth and tenth of September Longstreet's troops left the Rapidan and marched to Richmond, where they would board trains for north Georgia. But not all his brigades were to make the trip. Pickett's division was to remain in Richmond; "Tige" Anderson's and Henry A. Wise's brigades were sent to Charleston, Micah Jenkins' brigade replacing them in the line-up.[71]

When Hood's men reached the city there was a joyful reunion with their leader.[72] That night his regimental commanders persuaded him that, even though his arm was still in a sling, he should go along and command them; and he consented.[73] Apparently his decision caused great satisfaction all around. Longstreet breathed a sigh of relief, not so much because he was an ardent admirer of Hood as because it meant a postponement of the threatening quarrel between Jenkins and Law over command of Hood's division. Law had been in command during most of Gettysburg and all of the period of Hood's convalescence and had done a good job of it, but Jenkins ranked Law by some two months and would have taken command had Hood not returned.[74]

There was one detail, however, which Hood wished to settle. While his troops boarded the rickety cars at Richmond he rode by carriage with the ubiquitous Mrs. Chesnut and Sally "Buck" Preston to Petersburg. There before he boarded his train he proposed to Sally, and she, as was to be the case so many times in the next few months, left him dangling in uncertainty. She would not say yes and she would not say no. "At any rate," Hood related to Mrs. Chesnut, "I went off saying, 'I am engaged to you,' and she said, 'I am not engaged to you.'"[75] And there the matter rested temporarily.

Hood went on to Chickamauga and Sally returned to Richmond to ponder the matter and to wonder if Hood would suffer the fate of her other lovers. She was so lovely, so full of life, so loved by men, and yet she seemed to cast on her lovers a deadly curse. Ransom Calhoun had been killed in a duel; "Braddy" Warwick had died in the charge at Gaines's Mill; and Claud Gibson, too, was dead on the slopes at Fredericksburg. But, relates Mrs. Chesnut, her grief was "but a summer cloud"; and while she was loyal to all her dead lovers, new ones were never wanting, even though Johnny Chesnut warned everyone that it was safer to face a Federal battery than to fall in love with Sally. Was a man in love with her? Then "Look out! You will see his name next, in the list of killed and wounded."[76]

And Hood was in love with Sally as he rode the cars to Chickamauga!

His troops followed in every conceivable type of railway car—flatcar, boxcar, old passenger coaches and stripped-down improvisations and adaptations of these. Cumberland Gap and Knoxville were in the hands of the Federals, so the troops went the long way 'round—by Wilmington, Charlotte, Augusta to Atlanta. The men slept on the floors and tops of the cars as best they could and lived on hardtack and raw bacon. One of the few stops was at Wilmington, where there was a twenty-four-hour rest period, and then it was back to the jolting, swaying cars bumping over an uncertain roadbed.[77] Benning's brigade, 1,200 strong, reached Atlanta on September 12, the first of Hood's men to arrive.[78] Because the men needed shoes, however, the brigade did not move toward Chickamauga until the evening of the fifteenth when Law with his 2,000 men was ready. Meantime the 1,300 men of the Texas brigade had started northward from Atlanta on the evening of the fourteenth under the command of "Aunt Pollie" Robertson, still a bit lame from his leg wound at Gettysburg.[79] It was not until the afternoon and evening of the eighteenth that Kershaw's and Humphreys' brigades of McLaws' division reached Ringgold.[80]

Hood's division was, therefore, already on the field when he arrived at Ringgold on the afternoon of September 18. Not waiting for an unloading ramp, he had "Jeff Davis" leap from the boxcar door, mounted him and rode toward the sound of skirmish fire seven miles away.[81] A messenger had awaited him at the station with directions and orders from General Bragg, so he quickly located his division. As he rode among his men they suppressed a cheer lest their position be betrayed to the enemy, but up and down the lines every hat was raised in silent salute.[82] at the head of his troops.

The "Great Battle of the West" was taking form when Hood arrived to take charge of his troops. Since the middle of August it had been evident that Bragg and Rosecrans would come to blows in or around Chattanooga. Bragg's army had spent the summer in Chattanooga while the Federals occupied middle Tennessee. In August, Rosecrans had moved eastward across the hill country and by early September was ready to push into the mountain coves south of Chattanooga. It was apparent that he expected to get across Bragg's communications with Atlanta, so Bragg evacuated Chattanooga and fell back behind Missionary Ridge into the same coves Rosecrans expected to occupy.[83] In preparation for the inevitable clash, Bragg had sent out urgent appeals for reinforcements. From Joseph E. Johnston's army had come the divisions of General John C. Breckinridge and General W. H. T. Walker—some 9,000 men. Lee had sent Longstreet with the divisions of Hood and McLaws, numbering approximately 6,000; and from east Tennessee General Simon B. Buckner brought another 5,000. In all Bragg increased the strength of his army to approximately 66,000 effectives. Moving in along the banks of Chickamauga Creek were some 58,000 men in the Army of the Cumberland, divided as follows:[84] Fourteenth Corps, Major General George H. Thomas; Twentieth Corps, Major General Alexander McD. McCook; Twenty-first Corps, Major General Thomas L. Crittenden; Reserve Corps, Major General Gordon Granger. Federal cavalry was commanded by Brigadier General Robert B. Mitchell. Confederate cavalry was under the direction of the two renowned cavalry leaders of the Army of Tennessee, Joseph Wheeler and Nathan Bedford Forrest.

Bragg had evacuated Chattanooga on September 8, and Rosecrans' army began occupying the valleys and coves south of the city on the sixteenth. Neither general knew much about the other's movements. Rosecrans believed Bragg was in disorderly retreat toward Atlanta. Bragg, in turn, knew virtually nothing of his opponent's disposition. The two armies, therefore, unexpectedly came to blows, the opening skirmishes beginning just as Hood reached his troops on the afternoon of September 18.

Chickamauga Creek flows in a northeasterly direction paralleling Missionary Ridge and empties into the Tennessee some four miles above Chattanooga. It was not a wide stream, but it was deep enough to be an obstacle to the Confederates as they moved toward the enemy lining up with his back to Missionary Ridge. Each bridge and ford, therefore, was guarded by Federal cavalry and infantry detachments. At Reed's bridge, where Hood's division was to cross, he encountered the Federals drawn up in line of battle too strong for a detachment of Forrest's cavalry to dislodge. Ordering up artillery, Hood opened fire and sent a line forward to assist the cavalry. The Federals hastily retreated and Hood's men were able to cross, but on the other side the skirmishing continued as they marched the remaining six miles to their bivouac.[85]

On the morning of September 19 the two armies faced each other along a scattered six-mile front. Still Bragg was not ready to force the issue. He had planned to spend the day getting all his divisions across Chickamauga Creek and deploying them for the fight.[86] However, as at Gettysburg, the explosion was accidentally touched off. Some time near nine o'clock Thomas ordered General John M. Brannan's brigade to reconnoiter the Confederate right. Here they ran into Forrest's dismounted cavalry and a sharp fight was soon under way. Forrest was forced to give ground, but he was reinforced by W. H. T. Walker's brigade and Brannan was driven back. Then General Absalom Baird came to Brannan's relief and he, too, took a beating. Now General Richard W. Johnson's division of McCook's corps fell on Walker's brigade, which was saved from disaster by the troops of B. F. Cheatham and the fighting Irishman, Pat Cleburne.[87] For a battle which had not officially begun this bitter fighting must have seemed to the participants a reasonable facsimile of the same.

Hood also became engaged. In addition to the three brigades of his own division Bragg had assigned to him the divisions of Kershaw and Bushrod Johnson. The burden of the fighting on the nineteenth, however, was carried by Hood's three brigades— Benning's, Law's and the Texans. At 3:00 P.M. the three brigades moved forward to feel the enemy. Law's brigade was on the right, Robertson's Texans on the left and Benning in support of both. They had not advanced 200 yards before Robertson discovered the enemy in heavy force on his left. Changing front, he detached himself from contact with Law's brigade and met the enemy. With no artillery support he pushed them back to the crest of a ridge but could not hold it in the face of a raking fire of grape and canister. Recoiling down the hill, Robertson re-formed his men and charged a second time, losing three regimental commanders.[88] When he had gained the crest of the hill again, Benning moved to his assistance only to be met by the same devastating fire. He was able to come up with the Texans on the hill, but his foothold was precarious. He, too, was without artillery to counter the Federal batteries and his losses were heavy.[89] The two brigades managed to hold on until darkness, but they were bloody and exhausted. Hood's "Jeff Davis" was shot from under him and sent to the rear badly wounded. This was meant to be merely a reconnaissance in force. It had turned into a portent of the ghastly battle to take place on the following day, Sunday.

That night Hood, as was his custom in Lee's army, rode to the commanding general's tent to report on the day's fighting. Here for the first time he met a number of the officers of the Army of Tennessee, the army he was destined to command in a few months. He was surprised, he wrote, to find these men discouraged and not very hopeful of victory the next day. To his friend and fellow Kentuckian, John C. Breckinridge, slumped against the root of a tree, Hood voiced the belief that the Federals would be routed the next day. Immediately Breckinridge sprang to his feet. "My dear Hood, I am delighted to hear you say so," he cried. "You give me renewed hope; God grant that it may be so."[90]

Actually there was little basis for Hood's optimism. The afternoon's fighting had been stubborn and indecisive, with his own men barely able to hold their positions. But Hood was always buoyantly hopeful. He had, right or wrong, only one philosophy of battle—attack and fight. He was never clever at maneuvering or deception. His strategy was never brilliant, but he had com-

plete confidence in the ability of the men in his division to fight
and win against any odds; and they usually did. That night Longstreet arrived after Hood had left Bragg's headquarters to share
General Buckner's tent.[91] The next morning, Hood reports he
discussed this apparent lack of morale with "Old Pete" and received from him the assurance that "of course" they "would whip
and drive him [the enemy] from the field." Whereupon, Hood
writes, he rejoiced to find Longstreet in such a frame of mind, "as
he was the first general I had met since my arrival who talked of
victory."[92]

When Longstreet arrived at Bragg's headquarters on the night
of the nineteenth plans were laid for the next day's battle. The
Confederate Army was divided into two commands and assigned
to the two senior lieutenant generals, James Longstreet and Leonidas Polk. Longstreet was to command the left where his troops
were, and Polk was given the right. Plans for the battle called for
Polk to open at dawn. Longstreet was to await Polk's attack on
the right, and take it up promptly. Then the whole line would
surge forward, rolling the Federal left flank back on the right, thus
driving the entire army back into McLemore's cove.[93]

That night Rosecrans also made his dispositions. Thomas commanded the left with the divisions of Absalom Baird, Richard W.
Johnson, John M. Palmer, Joseph J. Reynolds and Milton Brannan. General Alexander McD. McCook commanded the right
with the divisions of Jefferson C. Davis, Phil Sheridan and James S.
Negley. Thomas L. Crittenden with the troops of H. P. Van
Cleve and Thomas J. Wood was in reserve and could move to the
relief of either Thomas or McCook.[94] Four miles away near Ross-
ville was Gordon Granger and his division, not even counted in
line of battle, but destined to play a most important role in the
battle. All night the men were felling timber and building breastworks. Rosecrans would let Bragg attack.

Polk faced Thomas with Forrest's dismounted cavalry, the division of D. H. Hill lately arrived from service in Mississippi and

Polk's own corps commanded by General B. F. Cheatham. Facing McCook was Longstreet with the divisions of T. C. Hindman, Simon B. Buckner, William Preston, Bushrod R. Johnson and five brigades of Longstreet's own corps commanded by Hood. General Joseph Wheeler and his cavalry were on Longstreet's extreme left. W. H. T. Walker was in reserve.[95] These were the men who waited for the sun over their backs when they were to strike through the woods and thickets, first at Thomas and then down the line division by division.

But Bragg's plans to attack at daybreak on Sunday, September 20, ganged agley. There was confusion of orders and formations and, as usual under such conditions, everyone blamed someone else. D. H. Hill maintained he received no orders until after sunrise and even if he had he could not have complied because his men had to have their breakfasts. Moreover, Hill claimed, his brigades were not properly aligned and the position of the enemy had not been reconnoitered.[96] Bragg, on the other hand, was infuriated. He insisted his orders were clearly given and he held both Polk and Hill responsible.[97] Finally by 9:30 Hill was ready for action and the attack was begun on Thomas' left by Breckinridge, Cleburne and Forrest's cavalry fighting dismounted. It was a vicious and slashing attack which caused Thomas to call for help. But the Confederates could not withstand the fire from the breastworks and fell back.[98] Then the fight rolled down the Confederate lines. One by one the divisions took up the fight until it reached Longstreet on the Confederate left about eleven o'clock. And now came the "break" of the battle. Thomas was advised that no troops were in sight supporting his right flank and that there was a gap between Brannan and Wood. Rosecrans hastily dictated an ambiguous order to General Thomas J. Wood ordering him to "close up on Reynolds as fast as possible and support him." Wood interpreted this to mean that he should close up on Reynold's rear, which he did.[99] This left the gap on Reynold's

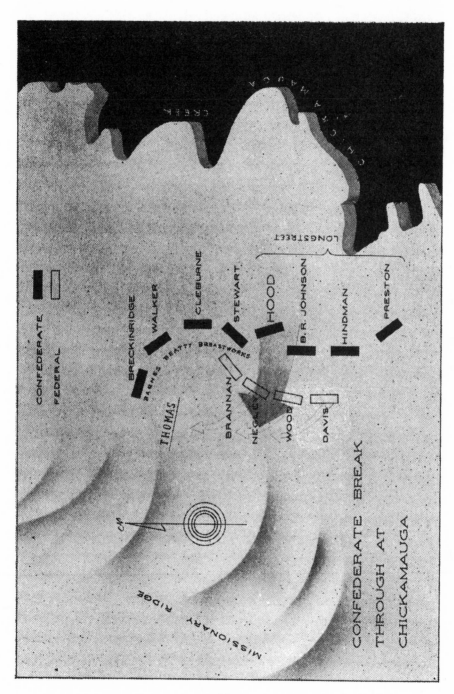

CONFEDERATE BREAK THROUGH AT CHICKAMAUGA

right still open as Longstreet attacked. A. P. Stewart advanced and was thrown back. Then Longstreet threw in Hood with eight brigades and by sheer good fortune they hit the gap. Once through it they wheeled right and took the Federals in reverse. Eight brigades in three lines swept through, screaming the rebel yell and driving everything before them.[100]

General Gates P. Thruston of the Federals describes the charge. "On they came like an angry flood," he writes. "They struck McCook's three remaining brigades, the remnants of the Federal right. Under the daring personal exertions of McCook and Davis, they made a gallant but vain resistance. The massed lines of the enemy swarmed around their flanks. Pouring through the opening made by Wood's withdrawal, they struck his last brigade as it was leaving the line. It was slammed back like a door and shattered. Brannan, on Wood's left, was struck in front and flank. His right was flung back; his left stood fast. Sheridan, hastening to the left with two brigades, was called back and rushed to the rescue. His little force stayed the storm for a time. Wave after wave of Confederates came on; resistance only increased the multitude . . . all became confusion. No order could be heard above the tempest of battle. With a wild yell the Confederates swept on far to their left. They seemed everywhere victorious. Rosecrans was borne back in the retreat. Fugitives, wounded, caissons, escort, ambulances thronged the narrow pathways."[101]

But Hood was not on the field to share the triumph of his men. At the height of the attack when his brigades were wheeling right to strike the enemy in reverse, "Aunt Pollie" Robertson rode up for orders for the Texans. Just as he was about to speak he saw Hood drop his reins and slide out of the saddle.[102] As he lay on the ground he gave his last orders to the Texans. "Go ahead," he shouted, "and keep ahead of everything."[103] Then he was borne from the field on a stretcher.

CHAPTER IX

Hero in Gray

THREE days after the battle Hood's friends in Richmond read in their newspapers that he was dead. "We understand," said the *Enquirer,* "that Major General Hood is dead. If true, the victory, however great and decisive, has been most dearly purchased. . . . His many virtues and gallant conduct won hosts of friends. He was a noble leader of gallant soldiers."[1]

It is quite possible that as Sally Preston read these words it occurred to her that Hood had gone the way of so many of her other lovers; but Hood's men had another explanation for his wounds. They were due to the fact that he was not riding "Jeff Davis," they said. At Gettysburg he had been lame and unable to carry his master into battle. The result: Hood was shot from the saddle of his other mount. Now, at Chickamauga, Jeff had been wounded during the first day's battle and sent to the rear. The result: Hood was shot from the saddle again.[2]

His wound proved serious; he had been shot through the right thigh a few inches below the hip.[3] The ball had shattered the bone and made amputation necessary. Since his friend and chief surgeon, Dr. John T. Darby, had not yet arrived from Richmond, the amputation was performed by Dr. T. G. Richardson of New Orleans, chief medical officer of the Army of Tennessee.[4] The next day he was carried by litter twenty miles south of the battlefield to the home ot one of his officers, Colonel F. H. Little, deep in Armuchee Valley.[5] Here under the friendly care of Colonel

Little's parents and Dr. Darby, Hood spent a month.[6] Here he learned that his Texas brigade had passed the hat and collected nearly $5,000 to buy him an artificial limb.[7] Here also he learned that Longstreet had recommended him for the rank of lieutenant general. On September 24 "Old Pete" had wired Richmond: "I respectfully recommend Major General J. B. Hood for promotion to the rank of Lt. General for distinguished conduct and ability in the battle of the 20th inst. Genl. Hood handled his troops with the coolness and ability that I have rarely known by any officer on any field. . . ."[8] With good food, good nursing and such encouragement it is small wonder that early in October he was sitting up and asking when he would be well enough to get back into the field.[9]

Late in October it was feared that he might be captured by an enemy raiding party and was moved to Atlanta.[10] Soon he was well enough to travel, and late November found him again in Richmond lodging with friends. Mrs. Chesnut sent him a rice pudding, his favorite dessert, but Sally calmly announced that she never had cared much for him but now that he was going with "those people" she wouldn't marry him "if he had a thousand legs, instead of having just lost one."[11] Just who "those people" were is not revealed, but it is clear that this was the beginning of the second act of the hectic romance of "Sam" and Sally. Soon it had all Richmond speculating as to the outcome.

A few days later he called on Mrs. Chesnut just as a group of her female friends were arriving for a luncheon. She and Mary Preston received him "as if nothing was the matter," but they could not control the feminine guests fluttering about him looking "as if it would be a luxury to pull out their handkerchiefs and have a good cry."[12] Someone brought him cut-up oranges and another remarked that the money value of friendship was easily counted since oranges were $5.00 apiece. But in the midst of all the attention being paid him he kept watching the door to the upstairs rooms. Finally he came out with it: "How is Buck?"[12] He had not seen her since his return to the city and she had not seen him as a cripple. Now that she was upstairs ill and he could not see her he quickly made excuses for leaving; but before he left he assured his fluttering admirers that while he was in Richmond he expected to be "as happy a fool as a one-legged man can be."[13]

This promise he carried out. For the next three months he had little to do except get well, and while he was doing it enjoy the social life of Richmond. This time he was "in." Not only was he fully accepted in the top social brackets, but he was the center of attention wherever he went. "Half the youth and beauty in Richmond brooded over his convalescence," one chronicler reports.[14] For a crippled man he got around amazingly well, for there was hardly a drawing room in Richmond which did not resound to the thump of his crutches on the floors. There was the customary round of dinners, card parties, taffy pullings, receptions, teas and charades. There was the same hurried love-making and brittle small talk bandied back and forth across tables set with gleaming silver which threw back the soft light of candles winking in their candelabra. For Hood it was a time when his love for Buck quickened and became, at least temporarily, the overwhelming passion of his existence.

On the day after his call on Mrs. Chesnut he saw her for the first time. He called on the Prestons and she was home, having recovered from her real or simulated illness of the day before. Now they met face to face. When he had left her in Petersburg in September he was a wiry, vigorous six-footer, handsome and full of life and laughter. True he had his left arm in a sling, but that only added glamour. Now he was an emaciated cripple hobbling about uncertainly on crutches, his right trouser leg empty, his face deeply lined. Now as Buck talked with him there were "tears not quite in her eyes but audible in her voice."[15] The shock was considerable, undoubtedly severe enough to cause her to examine her feelings anew; and the evidence indicates she came up with no answer whatever. She apparently never knew whether she loved him or not.

At the same time Hood himself was very naïve or blindly sure of himself, or both. A few days after he and Buck had met he invited Mrs. Chesnut to go driving with him. He and his aide, Colonel H. P. Brewster, called first at the Chesnut apartment on Cary Street and then drove to the Prestons'. Williams, the Prestons' butler, reported that Buck was ill; but she suddenly recovered her health when she found out who was outside, and came down dressed in black velvet and ermine to join the group. As they were returning from a long drive through the bitter cold, Hood put a question to Brewster which must have startled him no little considering the circumstances. What, asked Hood, were the symptoms of a man being in love? At seventeen he had fancied himself in love (with Ann Mitchell?) but now he wasn't sure, he explained.[16]

Recovering his aplomb, Brewster listed the symptoms: "When you see her, your breath is apt to come short. If it amounts to mild strangulation you have it bad. You are stupidly jealous, glowering with jealousy, and with a gloomy, fixed conviction that she likes every fool you meet better than she does you. This is especially true of people that you know she has a thorough contempt for. That is, you knew it before you lost your head. I mean before you fell in love. The last stages of unmitigated spooniness I will spare you."

"Well," Mrs. Chesnut reports Hood as saying, "I have felt none of these things so far, and yet they say I am engaged to four young ladies. That's a liberal allowance, you will admit, for a man who cannot walk without help."

"To whom do they say you are engaged?" asked Buck staring straight ahead.

"Miss Wigfall is one," Hood replied.

"Who else?"

"Miss Sally Preston."

Without batting an eye Sally queried nonchalantly, "Are you annoyed at such a preposterous report?"

"No," Hood shot back emphatically.

"God help us!" Brewster said in an aside to Mrs. Chesnut. "He is going to say everything right out here before our faces."

"Richmond people are very liberal," Buck continued archly. "I never heed these reports. They also say I am engaged to Shirley Carter, and to Phil Robb."

Viciously Hood shot back, "I think I will set a mantrap near your door and break some of those young fellows' legs."[17]

"Young fellows" and "legs"—these seemed to be key words in Hood's thinking. Although only thirty-three years of age, he seemed to realize that being a cripple made him look and act much older. That afternoon after the drive, when Sally had been safely deposited at her home on Franklin Street, Hood almost pathetically gave voice to the fears which were gnawing at him. "Those young soldiers," he remarked as if seeking reassurance from Mrs. Chesnut, "they are men who dare hope for something in this world." But Mrs. Chesnut gave him no reassuring words.[18] A few days later he sought similar reassurance from Brewster. He would not marry, he said, even if he could, any sentimental, silly girl who would throw herself away on such a maimed creature as he was. Instead of encouraging him and saying the sort of things he expected, Brewster reported the conversation to the Preston girls and they agreed Hood was showing good sense. Whereupon he rose in his wrath and threatened to break a crutch over his aide's head.

However, nothing daunted Hood in his love-making. Shortly after the carriage ride Mrs. Chesnut dropped in on the Wigfalls. Mrs. Wigfall was ill, but the Senator insisted that she come in anyway. In the living room she found her "Sam" stretched on a couch with a spread thrown over him, and with him was Louly Wigfall. As Wigfall innocently introduced her to Hood she detected her Sam laughing with his eyes and blushing guiltily like a little boy caught at the cookie jar. Neither of them gave anything away, but Mrs. Chesnut apparently took a little more seriously his previous boast that he was courting four girls. Now she could account for two of them.[19]

In the midst of his convalescence there now came disquieting news from his division. Under Longstreet in east Tennessee it was disintegrating, coming apart at the seams. As a matter of fact, the entire Army of Tennessee was permeated with a malignant discord and internal dissension which threatened its very existence. It had begun while Hood was still recuperating from his wound at the Littles' home in Armuchee Valley. Longstreet and Bragg had quarreled almost from the very moment they met. Early in October several of Bragg's officers came to "Old Pete" and asked him to take up Bragg's deficiencies with President Davis. Longstreet felt he was not in the President's confidence but agreed to take up the matter with the War Department.[20] Not content with this, the officers signed a round-robin letter and sent it to Davis,[21] a message soon followed by a protest from Polk.[22] At these Bragg struck back. Polk was put under charges for failing to open battle early on the morning of September 20. General Thomas C. Hindman was relieved under charges. Finally, after a visit from Davis, Polk was sent to Mississippi to take General William J. Hardee's place there, the latter rejoining Bragg's army. Daniel H. Hill was relieved of his command and sent to North Carolina. Buckner took a leave of absence. Bragg had cleaned house.[23]

Then Longstreet wrecked the morale of his own corps. It will be recalled that Law and Jenkins had been bitter rivals for the command of Hood's division before it boarded the cars for Chickamauga. Hood's decision to accompany his troops shelved the rivalry for the time being. Now that Hood was absent, Longstreet named his favorite, Brigadier General Micah Jenkins, temporary commander of Hood's division. Then the two men, Jenkins and Law, were sent on the night of October 28 to strike at a portion of Hooker's rear guard at Wauhatchie, some six miles south of Chattanooga on the western side of Lookout Mountain. In a night attack everything became confused and Jenkins' brigade suffered a much higher loss than did Law's. The attack failed and Longstreet placed the blame on Law. "As General Law's troops were veterans I can only attribute the want of conduct with his troops to a strong feeling of jealousy among the brigadier generals," he reported.[24] There was, however, insufficient evidence at the time to bring charges. This had to wait developments, but charges were placed against General Jerome B. Robertson, commander of the Texans—charges not of negligence at the Wauhatchie fight (although this was basic in Longstreet's thinking) but charges that he had criticized the campaign and discouraged his troops.[25] In the face of the charges Bragg suggested that Robertson be brought before a board, but before the board could assemble Longstreet began his fantastically unsuccessful invasion of East Tennessee to strike Burnside at Knoxville. Robertson was restored to his command.[26]

On November 6 Longstreet and his demoralized brigades departed from the Confederate positions near Chattanooga and wormed their way toward Knoxville. By the twenty-eighth he was ready for the assault on the city; on the twenty-ninth the attack failed miserably; and for the rest of the winter Longstreet's men sloshed about in the cold and achieved nothing. However, charges against Robertson were renewed, and, to make the job of wrecking his corps complete, Longstreet without warning relieved McLaws for alleged negligence and failure.[27]

All this Hood assuredly was aware of as he sat down to Christmas dinner at the Prestons'. Present for the feast were the Chesnuts, John C. Breckinridge, Simon B. Buckner, Senator James L. Orr of South Carolina and William Porcher Miles. Both the Chesnuts and the Prestons had received boxes of provisions from their plantations, so everyone was able to gorge himself on good food. Soup *à la reine,* boiled mutton, ham, boned turkey, wild duck, partridges and plum pudding made up the courses. The wines were sauterne, burgundy, sherry and madeira.

Buckner was in fine fettle telling jokes at Hood's expense, and polite conversation went 'round the table. But Hood sat morosely having little to say. After dinner Mrs. Chesnut found out why. It was not because of the condition of his division. He had proposed to Buck again, and again had been turned down. "I was routed," he said. "She told me there was no hope." It was, he said, the hardest battle he had ever fought; and, having lost it, he could not sleep.[28] Perhaps his disappointment was somewhat mitigated, however, by tangible evidence of his growing popularity in other circles. On December 28 the House of Representatives of the Confederate Congress unanimously resolved that "in appreciation of the gallant services rendered to the country during the present war by Major General John B. Hood, the speaker be instructed to invite him to a seat on the floor of the House."[29]

Now the east Tennessee quarrel caught up with Hood. Shortly after Christmas, Law came to Richmond and sought out his wounded chief. About a week before Christmas he had tendered his resignation and had asked for a leave of absence while action on the resignation was pending.[30] Then he made an unusual request of Longstreet. He would, he said, like to carry the resignation with him and personally present it to the War Department. When Hood saw the resignation he apparently took it and showed it unofficially to the Secretary of War in the hope that something might be done to save this good officer for the Confederacy. Law assumed that his resignation had been refused and returned to his troops.[31] When he returned, his officers prepared a petition asking that they be allowed to return to Lee or be sent somewhere other than where they were. When this petition was presented to Longstreet he was furious and immediately put Law under charges of "purloining" the resignation. However, the charges were not entertained by the War Department and Law was ordered to resume his command.[32] There matters rested with McLaws awaiting an inquiry and with Robertson and Law in command of their troops, but under the cloud of Longstreet's displeasure.

Meantime January brought a veritable rash of social events to Richmond and Hood, of course, was in the midst of them. He was at President Davis' receptions,[33] at numerous parties and teas, on carriage rides with the ladies and by the middle of the month was able to ride his horse again.[34] Although Buck had turned him down twice he apparently was still hopeful, for when Dr. Darby went through the blockade to Europe to buy medicines Hood sent along a purchase memo: three cork legs and a diamond ring.[35]

Possibly the outstanding social event of January was the party given for "social and official Richmond" by Mrs. George Wythe Randolph, the sultry Oriental-looking wife of the Secretary of War. The entertainment was a series of charades in pantomime in which various words and literary figures were portrayed. Everyone who was anyone in Richmond was there. Hood "looking like the hero of a Wagner opera" sat well to the front with Buck at his side. The President and Mrs. Davis were near by; so were Colonel and Mrs. Chesnut; Colonel and Mrs. Preston; General John C. Breckinridge; General Simon B. Buckner; members of the cabinet; members of both Houses of Congress; assorted beautiful ladies; newspapermen; visiting dignitaries—the top layer socially and officially.[36]

The word *penitent* was posed by Miss Lizzie Giles who was dressed as a novitiate with what seemed real tears on her cheeks.

Glamorous Hetty Cary enlivened things and drew the eyes of all the males in the audience when she illustrated *rye* by appearing in kilts while the piano banged out "Comin' Through the Rye." And then Mary Preston dressed in Grecian robes almost broke up the party. Her word was *knighthood* and she chose to use a poem:

Knight is my first, my second is a name
That's doubly linked unto enduring fame;
The gentle poet of the Bridge of Sighs,
The hero, cynosure of tenderest eyes.
Hood, whose keen sword has never known a stain
Whose valor brightened Chickamauga's plain
Well might he stand in glory's blazing roll
To represent to future times my whole;
For goodlier knighthood surely never shone
Round fair Queen Bess upon her stately throne
Than his, whose lofty deeds we proudly call our own.

Hood, the chronicler reports, was totally unprepared for such a thing and as the applause swelled he was forced to stand and bow "blushing to the roots of his hair, and it was several minutes before the performance could go on."[37] The party did go on, however, to be brought to a resounding finish by Constance Cary, who was soon to become the wife of the President's secretary. Her word was *money* acted out against a backdrop painted by Vizitelly and representing a scene in the English countryside. As she perched on a painted wall supported by a somewhat unstable framework the whole thing gave way and she crashed to the floor. In her embarrassment she could think of only one thing to do—dart back of the curtain and scold the stagehands, Jeb Stuart and Fitz Lee.[38]

Hood and Sally were seen together everywhere as the last gay winter social season Richmond was to know got under way; and Richmond society buzzed with gossip and speculation. Brewster told everyone publicly: "I want him to go back to the army. Those girls are making a fool of him."[39] Major Reid Venable, Jeb

Stuart's inspector general, gave his opinion to the effect that Buck just had to flirt; that her feeling for Hood was just sympathy for a wounded hero.[40] Mrs. Chesnut even went so far as to warn Hood that Sally had never been in love with anyone; that it was doubtful if she knew what love was; and that certainly she was not in love with him.[41]

Yet Hood apparently paid not the slightest attention to these warnings. He was suffering from a disease as old as man himself—acute blindness due to passionate love. He seemed to have no doubt but that this provocative, dark-eyed young woman with the voluptuous ample figure and brains to match would succumb at length. Her tantrums he considered as mere childish peccadilloes—something to be tolerant of, to chuckle over and to forget. He believed the way to whip any situation was to take the offensive and keep on the offensive. He had an incurable belief in his own ability to come out victorious whether the battle be on a distant field or in a Richmond parlor. Some of his enemies were known to have remarked that he had "the heart of a lion and a head of wood."[42] They must have been discussing his love-making.

At Mrs. J. C. Ives's party he and Buck were, as usual, the center of attention. While an orchestra played behind palms between acts *The Rivals* was presented. Mrs. Clement C. Clay was Mrs. Malaprop, and so well was it all presented that Hood, unacquainted with the play, came out during a moment of silence with the naïve remark: "By Jove, I believe that fellow Acres is a coward."[43]

When the party was over Hood stood uncertainly on his crutches in the hall while his gay admirers pressed about him. Seeing his plight, Buck sprang to the rescue and stood in front of him holding off the crowd.[44] "What did it mean?" people asked. Did this indicate she felt she was protecting something which was hers? Or was she merely dramatizing a situation?

Perhaps Hood was as puzzled over the whole thing as everyone else. Certainly he had a right to be confused, for the night before in the carriage en route to a dinner party she had told him that if it weren't for the fact that her parents objected to the match she could care for him. But as they reached the Chesnuts she angrily scolded him for speaking roughly to Cy, his body servant. "I hate a man who speaks angrily to those who dare not resent it."[45] And then after dinner she confessed to Mrs. Chesnut that she was sorry she had told him she might care for him if it weren't for her parents. It wasn't true, she insisted. "Good heavens, how I wish the man was gone."[46]

But there was another matter besides his love affair which occupied a great deal of Hood's attention during the winter. To the accompaniment of considerable head shaking, he appeared to be using his popularity as a stepping stone to the President's confidence. At least he was accused of such.[47] Certainly he did draw very close to Davis, but there was also good reason for the President to draw close to him. Hood was a fighter and a popular hero; and if there was any one thing the President needed just at this time it was public favor and a general who would draw public acclaim for battles won. Davis had seen with his own eyes just how popular Hood was. At the President's reception on January 27 Hood, on the arm of his prospective father-in-law, Colonel Preston, had received a "perfect ovation" from the crowd.[48] If other reasons were needed, there was the fact that the Chesnuts and Prestons, particularly Buck, were warm supporters of the President.

But whatever the exact course of circumstances which brought them together was, the fact remains that the two men found much to admire in each other. Both men loved horseback riding and often they rode together in and around Richmond.[49] Often Hood shared the Presidential carriage or used it alone for his own private affairs.[50] On one occasion he escorted Mrs. Davis in to supper and they remained at a small table prepared for her for more than an hour after the rest had left the room.[51] The next Sunday after services the President took Hood's arm and assisted him slowly down the steps.[52] Definitely Hood had the confidence of the President and his family and "every man Jack who was a general while he was a colonel grumbles and says he is going up too fast."[53]

If we could know what Davis and Hood talked about on their rides about the city we might have a better understanding of the conduct of the war during the fateful last year, particularly in the West. But Davis revealed nothing of the conversations, and Hood only says that "he imparted to me his purpose to largely re-enforce General J. E. Johnston's army at Dalton, for the object of moving in the early spring to the rear of the Federal Army, then concentrating at Chattanooga. He also expressed a desire to send me to command a corps under General Johnston. I was deeply impressed with the importance of this movement, and cheerfully acquiesced in the proposition of the President, *but with the understanding that an aggressive campaign would be initiated.*"[54] We do know, however, that lines were being drawn in Richmond. On one side were Davis, Bragg and Hood. On the other were Joseph E. Johnston and James Longstreet, who opposed the administration.[55]

The fact that Hood was now a lieutenant general[56] and soon was to be off to the war again seems to have brought a change in Buck's attitude. Now she consented, or halfway consented, to an engagement. Many of her friends said openly that she seemed always to care more for her lovers when they were dead or away in the war than when they were alive and with her. It would appear that this was now the case. As usual Buck told Mrs. Chesnut all about it. She and Hood had been riding. As they rode he held out his hand.

"Don't do that," she protested. "Let it rest as it is. You know I like you, but you want to spoil it all."

"Say yes or say no," Hood cried. "I will not be satisfied with less. Yes or no, which is it?"

Well, he kept holding out his hand, Sally related, so what could she do? Cy was riding behind and she didn't want to embarrass the general in front of his servant, so she put her hand in his. "Heavens, what a change came over his face!" she continued. "I pulled my hand away by main strength. The practical wretch said at once: 'Now I will speak to your father. I want his consent to marry you at once.' "[57]

"Do you believe I like him now?" Buck asked Mrs. Chesnut, almost as if she were trying to convince herself.

"No!" Mrs. Chesnut emphatically replied.[58]

And so they were engaged.

Her parents wept in despair and managed to postpone a formal announcement. But Hood was irrepressible, "preposterously sanguine and happy." He could not keep the secret; in fact, he apparently saw no reason for keeping it. "I am so proud, so grateful! The sun never shone on a happier man! Such a noble girl, a queen among women." This to Mrs. Chesnut. Soon the news was published in the Charleston *Mercury* and all Richmond was buzzing again with gossip. Would they marry? Did she really care for him? Everyone in Richmond it seems had the answers except Buck. Apparently she was trying hard to convince herself that she loved him. An evening or two after the engagement Hood drove by the Chesnuts'. He sent word that he could not come up but would Buck please come down and see him. According to Mrs. Chesnut, Buck "flew down and stood ten minutes in that snow, Cy holding the carriage door open while the General kissed her hands and proclaimed his love."

"Now do you believe I care for him?" she asked triumphantly when she returned to the house.[59]

There was much talk about Hood going away, and when he spoke of it his eyes blazed.[60] He was readying himself to travel the glory road as the personal representative of the President. A victorious Confederate offensive in Tennessee and Kentucky, a reunion with Lee in time to defeat the Federals before Richmond, fame and a beautiful wife.[16] This obviously was Hood's dream; and apparently Buck shared it, for she now actually seemed to take pride in her engagement. She stopped by the Chesnuts' while the colonel was in to receive his congratulations. Kissing her tenderly, he extended his best wishes and said he would likewise congratulate Hood. "You know, if I speak of him at all, I must speak handsomely; for he has won his honors like a man." At this Buck was so excited she had to have a glass of water. As she sipped it Hood himself unexpectedly thumped in.

"You look mighty pretty in that hat," he bluntly told Buck. "You wore it at the Turnpike that day when I surrendered at first sight."

Blushing, Buck nodded and then left with Colonel Chesnut. Going to the window, Hood watched "until the last whiteness of her garments was gone." Then turning to Mrs. Chesnut he said: "The President was finding fault with some of his officers in command, and I said, 'Mr. President, why don't you come and lead us yourself? I would follow you to the death.' "[62]

Undoubtedly Hood was sincere in his admiration of the President, but these words are indicative of outright flattery. It appears that fame and popularity had wrought a change in the man. No longer was he the gay, happy-go-lucky combat officer who asked nothing more than orders to lead his men into battle. The virus of ambition was now strong in his veins, and many of his friends feared he was showing the characteristics of a sycophant. Certainly there was no more certain and direct way to Davis' heart than to remind him that he was a soldier before he was anything else, and to have him feel that at the opportune time he might step in and lead the Confederate forces to victory. It was not very clever flattery on Hood's part, but, then, he was never accused of being a brilliant strategist. However, as in the case of his other frontal assaults, it seemed to succeed.

This talk between Davis and Hood about the military situation was a small part of the larger conversations going on between the President and his field commanders. Lee with the corps of Ewell and A. P. Hill together with Stuart's cavalry occupied the area south of the Rapidan with headquarters at Orange Courthouse. Longstreet with two divisions of the First Corps was wandering unhappily through the coves and mountains of east Tennessee. Pickett's division was in the Department of Richmond. In South Carolina, Beauregard was defending Charleston. In Georgia, Joseph E. Johnston was in command of the Army of Tennessee with headquarters at Dalton.[63] How could they all be correlated to bring victory? everyone asked.

On February 9 Hood was ordered to join Johnston's army as a corps commander.[64] But he was unable to tear himself away from Buck, and nine days later Johnston wired the War Department: "Lieutenant General Hood is much needed here."[65] Finally on February 25 he arrived in Dalton and was assigned to command.[66]

As he left Richmond he gave Buck the diamond-studded silver star which he wore on his hat.[67] The days ahead would tell whether it would grow brighter or become tarnished.

CHAPTER X

Joe Johnston and Atlanta

WHEN Hood arrived at Dalton he was assigned command of a corps made up of the divisions of Carter L. Stevenson, Alexander P. Stewart and Thomas C. Hindman, with the artillery under Lieutenant Colonel J. W. Bondurant.[1] Although not noted for brilliance, these division commanders were veterans with long service records. Major General Stevenson was a Virginian and West Pointer, class of 1838. He had served in the Mexican War, under Kirby Smith in Bragg's invasion of Kentucky and in 1863 was sent to reinforce Pemberton at Vicksburg.[2] Alexander P. "Old Straight" Stewart had earned his nickname because of his military bearing. A Tennessean, he was also a West Pointer, class of 1842. He had resigned his commission in 1845 to become professor of mathematics and moral philosophy at Cumberland University and the University of Nashville. His service in the Confederate Army ran from Fort Donelson to Chickamauga, where his division under Hood participated in the break-through.[3] Undoubtedly he was the ablest of Hood's three major generals.

Thomas C. Hindman was a fiery Arkansan who might have called any one of four states home. He was born in Knoxville, Tennessee, lived in Alabama and Mississippi and finally in 1856 moved to Arkansas, where he was elected to the lower House of Congress. He had served in every campaign of the Army of Tennessee from Shiloh to Chickamauga. In this latter battle he had become greatly confused and charges of inefficiency were mentioned, but none doubted his patriotism.[4]

Most of the 17,084 men who composed Hood's corps were veterans, for there had been little recruiting since the preceding summer (and as time went on the task of keeping the army supplied with men became increasingly difficult). The large majority of the troops were from Georgia and near-by Alabama and Mississippi. It became almost impossible to hold them in winter quarters with home so near. Desertions, therefore, were frequent, as is evidenced by the fact that there were on the rolls of Hood's corps the names of 34,658 men.[5] Although the morale of the men appeared good, Johnston reported that their equipment was poor, food supply uncertain and forage for horses almost nonexistent.[6] It was the old, old story of the Confederate soldier. He fought a lot of the war barefoot and with an empty gut.

Hood, however, was not so much concerned at the moment about such details as shoes, blankets, rifles and horses for the artillery. He had come with a burning zeal for the offensive, and the very night of his arrival at Dalton saw him closeted with Johnston explaining the plan Richmond had in mind. "I . . . laid before General Johnston the plan to join Polk's Army and Longstreet's Corps on the march into Tennessee, gave him assurance that the authorities in Richmond would afford him every assistance, and informed him, moreover, that General Lee favored the projected campaign."[7] But Johnston demurred. There were difficulties in the way of such a movement. He felt it would be best if Longstreet's and Polk's armies could be brought to Dalton, and joined with his army. Then he could await developments, and move forward, stand his ground or retreat as the situation seemed to dictate.[8]

Thus the issue between Hood and Johnston was joined. Or perhaps it is more accurate to say that the issue was between Johnston and Davis, for Hood was merely the President's mouthpiece. On March 7 Hood reported to Davis in the first of a series of letters which appear to be a clear violation of military protocol.

He as a corps commander was going over the head of his superior in the field and discussing strategy with the commander in chief and Bragg, his chief adviser. The army, Hood reported, was in good condition, being well supplied with food, clothing and transportation. If Longstreet and Polk were brought in, Johnston would have an army of nearly 70,000 men, which would be sufficient "to defeat and destroy all the Federals on this side of the Ohio River."[9] "We should march to the front as soon as possible," he continued, "so as not to allow the enemy to concentrate and advance upon us. . . . I never before felt that we had it so thoroughly in our power. He is at present weak, and we are strong. His armies are far within our country, and the roads open to his rear, where we can have a vast quantity of supplies. Our position in Virginia can be securely held by our brave troops under General Lee, which will allow us to march in force from our center, the vital point of every nation."[10] The same ideas were expressed to James A. Seddon, Secretary of War, and, three days later, to General Braxton Bragg.[11]

A few days later Davis, through Bragg, made the plan quite specific to Johnston. Federal forces in Knoxville depended in a great measure on their connection with Chattanooga for support, and both were dependent on regular and rapid communication with Nashville, it was pointed out. Therefore a stroke severing the Chattanooga-Nashville line would force the enemy to abandon both Knoxville and Chattanooga. "To accomplish this it is proposed that you move as soon as your means and force can be collected so as to reach the Tennessee River near Kingston, where a crossing can be effected; that Lieutenant General Longstreet move simultaneously by a route east and south of Knoxville, so as to form a junction with you near this crossing. As soon as you come within supporting distance Knoxville is isolated and Chattanooga threatened, with barely a possibility for the enemy to unite. Should he not then offer you battle outside of his entrenched lines, a rapid move across the mountains from Kingston to Sparta (a very practicable and easy route) would place you with a formidable army in a country full of resources, where it is supposed, with a good supply of ammunition, you may be entirely self-sustaining, and it is confidently believed that such a move would necessitate the withdrawal of the enemy to the line of the Cumberland."[12]

He went on to point out that if after crossing the mountains the entire Confederate force could be thrown on Nashville the enemy would indeed be in a precarious position. Ammunition, food, transportation, all could be supplied. Nothing remained except to determine when the movement would begin.[13] But the defense-minded Johnston was not ready for such a campaign and on March 18 he wired Bragg his reasons: Sherman was at Memphis. Grant was at Nashville. They were preparing an advance. When they advanced it would be toward Atlanta. Therefore the thing to do was to stand his ground, defeat them and then take the offensive.[14] But this reply did not please Bragg, and Johnston attempted to clarify his position a day or so later. "In my dispatch of the 19th I expressly accept taking offensive, only differ with you as to details," he wired. "I assume that the enemy will be prepared for advance before we are and will make it to our advantage; therefore, I propose as necessary both for offensive and defensive to assemble our troops here immediately. Other preparations for advance are going on."[15]

To Longstreet he wrote: "I will obey any orders of the President zealously and execute any plan of campaign of his to the best of my ability." However, he added his usual qualifications. He would obey the orders of the President and take the offensive on his own terms: ". . . the only practicable mode of assuming the offensive here seemed to me to wait for the enemy's advance, and if we beat him, follow into middle Tennessee. . . ."[16]

In an effort to prod Johnston into activity, Bragg wrote Hood to see what he could do to help matters along. But Hood was unable to accomplish anything. "I have received your letter," he wrote Bragg, "and am sorry to inform you that I have done all in my power to induce General Johnston to accept the proposition you made to move forward. He will not consent, as he desires the troops to be sent here and it is left to him as to what use should be made of them. . . ."

"I regret this exceedingly," he continued, "as my heart was fixed upon our going to the front and regaining Tennessee and Kentucky. . . . When we are to be in a better condition to drive the enemy from our country I am not able to comprehend. To regain Tennessee would be of more value to us than a half dozen victories in Virginia. I received a letter from General R. E. Lee on yesterday, and he says, 'You can assist me by giving me more troops, or driving the enemy in your front to the Ohio River. If the latter is to be done it should be executed at once.' I still hope we shall yet go forward; it is for the President and yourself to decide."[17]

Had Johnston known about this correspondence he might justifiably have asked who was commanding the army, he or Hood. Hood was writing not only Bragg and Davis but Lee as well; but no amount of pressure could change Johnston. It must have become evident to all concerned that nothing could move him; and shortly the matter was dropped. Polk was left in Mississippi, and Longstreet was recalled to Lee's army. Johnston was left without reinforcements to await the enemy's next move.

When Longstreet moved to join Lee, Hood's old division went with him. Law was still in command of his brigade, but Robertson no longer commanded the Texans. He had resigned under Longstreet's displeasure and gone back to Texas. Youthful Brigadier General John Gregg, another Texan, succeeded him. As the division readied itself for the final campaign in Virginia both Law and Jenkins were eliminated as division commanders and that assignment went to Major General Charles W. Field, a Kentuckian. Hood was never to see his old division in action again nor any of his beloved Texans until after the war. For better or worse, he had surrendered his destiny to the Army of Tennessee.

In Richmond in early March Mrs. Chesnut made an entry in her diary which undoubtedly would have been of interest to Hood: "Annie reports that R. L—— has arrived and that she believes he is the only man Buck really cares for. *Le roi est mort. Vive le roi.* There is hardly a day's interval between the king who goes, and the king who comes."[18]

The grand strategy of the last year of the war now began to unfold.

On March 4, 1864, Lincoln called U. S. Grant from Nashville to receive from him personally the rank of lieutenant general. He was expected, the President told him, to come east and assume supreme command of all the Federal armies, turning over the western command to W. T. Sherman, then floundering in Mississippi. On the eighteenth of March the change was consummated, and Grant and Sherman had a chance to exchange views and plot their strategy. As soon as circumstances and the weather permitted they would put into operation a "bold offensive" by concentric lines and would finish the job in one single campaign. The objectives would be Lee's army behind the Rapidan and Joe Johnston's army at Dalton.[19] Johnston had expressed over and over again his preference for a defensive operation before he should take the offensive. Now he would have an opportunity to vindicate his judgment.

The Federal offensive movements began to roll on May 5. Sherman's army was composed of approximately 100,000 men, abundant artillery and horses and capable leaders. In Major General George H. Thomas' Army of the Cumberland were such veterans as Oliver O. Howard and Joseph Hooker. Two of

Hood's classmates at West Point commanded armies—Major General James B. McPherson the Army of the Tennessee and Major General John M. Schofield the Army of the Ohio. Scattered among their divisions and brigades were such names as Grenville M. Dodge, Frank P. Blair, Peter J. Osterhaus, George Stoneman and Jacob D. Cox. In Thomas' army was an up-and-coming young cavalry officer, Brigadier General Judson Kilpatrick.[20] Johnston's chief of cavalry, Major General Joseph Wheeler, was his classmate at the academy.

Johnston's army numerically was only half the size of Sherman's and the ratio of guns was about the same. Only in cavalry could the Confederates match the enemy. But the morale of Johnston's army was high and it boasted some of the fightingest names in Civil War history—names such as William J. Hardee, Bishop Leonidas Polk, John B. Hood, Pat Cleburne, Joseph Wheeler, A. P. Stewart and Benjamin F. Cheatham. These men held off Sherman for four months and then delayed the end of the war another seven.

The early phases of the Atlanta campaign set the pattern for the whole. It was to be a war of movement with Sherman bobbing, weaving and constantly pressing the attack while his lighter opponent sidestepped and backpedaled, always on the alert for an opening when he might throw a counterpunch, always hoping to catch his opponent with his guard down so he might deliver a knockout blow. By the seventh Sherman's initial tactical movement was under way. Thomas and Schofield demonstrated heavily in front of Dalton while McPherson with his army of approximately 25,000 moved south behind the screen of the mountains to Johnston's left. Snake Creek Gap in Johnston's left rear, it was thought, was unguarded. If McPherson could suddenly pop out of the gap and cut the railroad he could force Johnston to retreat from Dalton. Moreover he would be in a position to strike him as he retreated.

The plan had merit, but it didn't come off as expected. When Johnston was certain the advance was about to begin, he had sent an urgent request to Richmond for Polk's army from Mississippi to be sent to him at Resaca. The vanguard of this reinforcing army was Brigadier General James Cantey's division of 4,000 men. It arrived at Snake Creek Gap just in time to surprise McPherson. Instead of meeting no resistance as had been anticipated he now ran into a small division which fought like a corps. McPherson was stopped cold by these Confederates who popped up out of nowhere, and, furious as Sherman was, there was nothing to be done about it.[21]

As soon as Johnston heard of the affair at Snake Creek Gap he sent Hood south to Resaca with his three divisions to await the arrival of Polk. Two days later the solid old bishop arrived and was welcomed by Hood. Together the two men rode back to Dalton to confer with Johnston, now preparing the rest of his army for the retirement to Resaca. As their horses' hooves kicked up little clouds of early summer dust the two men talked. Of all the things they discussed we cannot be sure, but the bishop always carried his prayer book into battle and we know they must have talked about religion and man's immortal soul, for Hood expressed to him a desire to be baptized. That night after midnight when they had finished their conference with Johnston the two men went to Hood's tent. Laying aside his sword and using a tin wash basin for a font, he administered by the flickering light of a single candle the rite of baptism in the Episcopal manner to the tall bearded Hood who stood with bowed head, leaning on his crutches.[22] A few days later Bishop Polk administered the same rites to Joseph E. Johnston in the presence of Hood and Hardee[23]—but that is as far as Hood and Johnston ever got in the spirit of brotherly fellowship.

Johnston retired to Resaca and on May 13 drew up his lines to meet the enemy. Polk was on the left, Hardee in the center and

Hood on the right. But there was no battle. Again Sherman flanked him and again Johnston was forced to retire to protect his communications. The retirement this time was south to Cassville, where Johnston issued a proclamation to his troops declaring they were now ready to turn on the enemy. Hardee had changed to the left, Polk was in the center and Hood on the right. At the first signs of enemy activity in his front Hood moved to attack what was believed to be the extreme left of the Federal line. As he moved forward, however, he discovered to his astonishment Federal infantry and artillery where they had no right to be—on his right flank and rear. Hindman's division was faced right and skirmishers were thrown out to develop the strength of this unexpected body of troops. There was a brief skirmish, just enough to interrupt Johnston's plans for a concerted attack by Polk and Hood.[24] As a result, both commands were withdrawn to a ridge below Cassville.

That night (May 19) Johnston attended a conference at Polk's headquarters. Polk and Hood were present when the conference began and Hardee came in later. Apparently General Samuel G. French, the stormy petrel of the Suffolk campaign, was also present for at least a part of the meeting,[25] as was also Captain Walter J. Morris, Polk's chief engineer. Just what was said is a matter of some dispute. Hood states in his memoirs that he advised Johnston that the position occupied by his and Polk's corps was enfiladed by Federal artillery and that they should *either attack or abandon it.*[26] Captain Morris testified that he made a personal inspection of the lines and found them untenable and that both Polk and Hood advocated an attack as the best way out of the enfiladed position.[27] Johnston states that both generals urged him "to abandon the ground immediately and cross the Etowah."[28] Thirty years after, French was unable to shed much light on the conference except that he felt sure Hood and Polk were wrong about everything.[29]

At all events Johnston decided to abandon the defenses at Cassville and to fall back behind the Etowah River at Allatoona Pass. When Hardee finally showed up at the meeting and heard the decision he protested and expressed confidence in his ability to hold his ground.[30] But Johnston stuck to his decision. It apparently did not require much persuasion to convince him that a retirement was necessary. After all he could put the blame on Polk and Hood if he ever had to justify his decision.

Allatoona had much to recommend it from the standpoint of defense. It is a narrow gorge or pan in the mountains through which ran the Western and Atlanta Railroad. So strong was the position that Sherman decided on another flanking movement. He abandoned the railroad and struck out due south toward Atlanta. On May 25 Johnston moved southward to intercept him near Dallas and New Hope Church.

In Richmond, Buck was in love with Colonel Rollins Lowndes, handsome young scion of a wealthy and prominent Charleston family. All the ladies were tittering about an incident with his tailor. He chose a fine piece of Confederate gray for a new uniform. But the tailor said: "No, my dear sir, you can't have that. It is laid aside. General Hood asked us to keep that and our best stars for his wedding clothes."[31]

South of the Rapidan the Wilderness grew green again under the warm Virginia sun. In the tangled mass of trees and undergrowth Lee and Grant were shooting it out. On the Orange Plank Road Longstreet's men in the confusion wounded their general and killed Micah Jenkins. A few days later Edward "Allegheny" Johnson was shot from his horse and captured. George H. Steuart was captured. And then in a few more days came the greatest blow since Chancellorsville—Jeb Stuart was killed. Such attrition could not be long endured.

In Camden, South Carolina, John Witherspoon told Mrs. Chesnut: "The President did wrong when he did not arrest Joe Johnston before Seven Pines when Johnston was in full retreat, apparently ready to abandon Richmond. . . . General Lee stopped those retreating tactics, but now every newspaper except a few in Georgia is busy as a bee excusing Joe Johnston's new retreats. He gives up one after another of those mountain passes where one must think he could fight, and is hastening down to the plain. . . . Joe Johnston's disaffection with our President and our policy has acted like a dry rot in our armies."[32]

By his rapid retirement southwest from Allatoona, Johnston had placed his army squarely in Sherman's path to Atlanta; and this time there was sharp fighting. With Wheeler's cavalry guarding the crossings of Pumpkin Vine Creek Johnston posted his three corps to cover the roads leading to Atlanta. Hardee was on the left near Dallas, Polk was in the center and Hood on the right near New Hope Church. Along most of this front the Confederates hastily threw up breastworks behind which lay the infantry protected by artillery.

On May 25 Hooker's Twentieth Corps crossed the creek and assaulted a portion of Hood's corps (Stewart's division). As they moved to the attack the darkly overcast sky emptied itself and for seventeen days thereafter torrential rains flooded the countryside. Driving in Hood's skirmishers, Hooker pushed on until he struck the main lines, only to be thrown back by rifle and artillery fire. In the pelting rain to the accompaniment of crackling lightning and booming thunder Sherman himself rode to the scene. Quickly he called up two divisions and on the twenty-seventh again assaulted Hood's lines, now reinforced by Cleburne, and again the attackers were thrown back with heavy losses. That night the nearest house to the field was filled with wounded. Torchlights and candles lighted up dimly the incoming stretchers and the surgeons' tables with their shining instruments. "The very woods seemed to moan and groan with the voices of sufferers not yet brought in."[33]

Both sides now resorted to extensive engineering operations despite the fact that it was a war of movement. Breastworks were thrown up hastily by both sides, and so adept did the Confederates become at this that they were accused of carrying their breastworks with them. This was indicative of the growing intensity of the campaign as Atlanta loomed ahead. And in Richmond the uneasiness of Bragg and Davis increased. Davis plainly expressed his disappointment,[34] but Johnston promised nothing. He had expected to fight at Cassville, he said, but Hood, the fair-haired boy of the Administration, had been deceived into believing there were Federals on his right and thus had frustrated plans for an attack.[35] (To the end of his life Johnston persisted in saying there were no troops on Hood's right, despite convincing proof to the contrary. The Federals weren't supposed to be there, therefore they weren't there, he reasoned.) Undoubtedly Johnston's strategy was sound and his tactics brilliant, but his unfortunate personality traits almost nullified his effectiveness. He was displaying the same characteristics he had shown before Seven Pines—secretiveness, vindictiveness, stubbornness and near insolence. Had he possessed Lee's tact and humility the story of the Atlanta campaign might have been entirely different.

Hood apparently had settled down to the seriousness of the campaign. Since his last letter to Bragg on April 13, he had made no report and given no advice to Richmond. It is quite probable that his zeal for the offensive was undiminished, but at least he was keeping quiet and in an undistinguished sort of way was carrying out Johnston's orders. John Darby was back from Europe with two artificial limbs. One Hood with great discomfort was learning to wear and the other was always strapped to the saddle of his spare mount.[36] Apparently the artificial limb helped him maintain balance in the saddle, but was of little use to him in walking.

On the twenty-eighth, the day after the bloody attack on Hood's corps and Cleburne's division, the three lieutenant generals met at Johnston's headquarters for a conference. Hood suggested an attack to begin early the next morning with him on the right and to be taken up successively by Polk and Hardee. If it should mark the beginning of the great battle, well and good. It had to begin somewhere. The suggestion was accepted by Johnston, and the three officers left expecting to fight the next morning at the sound of Hood's guns. However, Hood did not attack. When morning came he found the Federals had dropped their left back behind Pumpkin Vine Creek and had securely entrenched themselves behind breastworks. In front of Hood's corps was a swamp, a stream and Federal breastworks, so he decided against an attack. He so notified Johnston and there was no battle.[37]

Johnston himself apparently was not anxious for battle at this point and thus did not blame Hood unduly for his failure to attack, but this incident and the one at Cassville did not help Hood's reputation any. In the army, rumors filter down from the top to the lesser officers and to the men in the ranks—and the rumor about Hood was, one young officer reported, that "he talks about attack and not giving ground, publicly, and quietly urges retreat."[38] Certainly he had done little in this campaign to sustain the reputation he had won under Lee. The fact that there were those who doubted his sincerity and that others disliked him because of his known allegiance to Bragg and Davis did not make for a very promising future.

Sherman now decided to swing back to the railroad he had left at Allatoona. On June 4 Johnston moved with him, both armies floundering in the incessant rain, which made a quagmire of the countryside. Johnston's engineers had hastily thrown up field-works to receive the army, and when Sherman reached Ackworth on the railroad he again found his enemy between him and Atlanta. Hood's corps was on the right behind Noonday Creek with his left extending to Brush Mountain. Hardee was in the center and Polk was on the left, his lines extending to Pine Mountain. The positions were intended to cover both the railroad and wagon-road approaches to Atlanta.[39]

Both Johnston and Sherman spent several days (June 8-21) getting troops into position and strengthening their lines. During this interval Johnston, Polk and Hardee made an inspection of the bishop's lines on Pine Mountain. While engaged in this work the party came under fire of Federal artillery and General Polk was killed.[40] The Pine Mountain sector was now abandoned and a new and consolidated line established. Hardee on the left occupied the level ground just west of Kenesaw Mountain; Polk's corps, temporarily commanded by General William W. Loring, took over the center on Kenesaw and Hood was on the right, his lines pointing toward Marietta. Then because Sherman seemed to be concentrating in Hardee's front, Hood was shifted to the left to meet the anticipated attack. Wheeler's cavalry was assigned the task of holding the position he evacuated.[41]

On the afternoon of June 22 Hooker pushed forward his Twentieth Corps to Hood's front, and a few minutes later Schofield likewise brought up a division from the Twenty-third Corps. Before they had advanced very far they encountered Hood's skirmishers; and then Hood attacked. Acting on his own initiative, he loosed a fierce assault reminiscent of Gaines's Mill and Chickamauga. Wave after wave of Hindman's and Stevenson's divisions rolled up against the Federal position, only to be repulsed with heavy losses. "As often as he made his assaults," Hooker reported, "he was spiritedly repulsed, sometimes with his columns hopelessly broken and demoralized."[42] Johnston reported Hood's losses at "about a thousand men."[43] Little or nothing had been accomplished except to excite Joe Hooker to the point where he hastily dashed off a message to Sherman that he was being attacked by three Confederate corps. Sherman immediately rode to Hooker's position, only to learn that "Fighting Joe" had not utilized all his available men and that actually only one Confederate corps was involved. Now there was dissension in the Federal ranks. When Sherman reproved Hooker for his mistake he sulked and finally resigned his command.[44]

Now Sherman matched Hood's fruitless assault by one equally ill advised but on a larger scale and more deadly. He determined to strike the Confederate center on Kenesaw Mountain, hoping he would find his enemy weak here. On the morning of June 27 the artillery along Sherman's entire line opened with a terrific bombardment and then Logan's corps of McPherson's army struck at Little Kenesaw. Simultaneously Thomas went straight for Kenesaw defended by Cheatham and Cleburne of Hardee's corps. Wave after wave of brave men surged up against the Confederate breastworks, only to be cut to pieces by deadly fire. At length the attack was abandoned, but not until long windrows of blue-clad dead had piled up.[45]

This reverse did not long delay Sherman, however. With re-newed respect for his adversary behind breastworks, he planned his next move. His decision was to put pressure on Johnston's left under Hood and feel his way from there on. If nothing else, he might flank Johnston out of his position on Kenesaw.[46]

The possibility of such a movement was not lost on Hood, who notified his division commanders to be prepared for an assault on their positions on the Confederate left.[47] The attack did not come, however, for Johnston abandoned Kenesaw and Marietta and fell back to previously prepared positions about five miles south of the latter place. Here he deployed his lines again: Hood on the left, Hardee in the center and Loring on the right. It was the old familiar pattern except that something new had been added to Hood's corps. He had received a nondescript division of 3,000 Georgia "home-guard" troops commanded by General Gus-tavus W. Smith. They were old men and boys without uniforms, had never drilled more than a few days at a time and were com-pletely inexperienced in warfare.[48]

Sherman now began pressing Johnston more intensely and

again he fell back to prepared positions, this time on the north bank of the Chattahoochee. This was the crisis! For more than two months these two armies had been sparring. Now on this the eighth of July fateful decisions had to be made.

At usual it was Sherman who moved first. While Thomas and McPherson demonstrated on Hood's left, Schofield moved far off the Confederate right, crossed the Chattahoochee and was in Johnston's rear between him and Atlanta before he knew what had happened. That night Johnston evacuated his position on the north bank and withdrew to the south. "I have always thought Johnston neglected his opportunity here," Sherman wrote, "for he had lain comparatively idle while we got control of both banks of the river above him."[49]

If Sherman thought Johnston had blundered he should have heard what Jefferson Davis thought and said. For weeks he had been trying to ascertain just what Johnston proposed to do. Johnston faithfully answered every request, but revealed nothing. Everything depended on what Sherman did, he said over and over again. On June 27 he had suggested to Bragg that the best thing to do was to throw strong bodies of cavalry on Sherman's communications.[50] Bragg promptly advised that no cavalry was available for this purpose.[51] Then Davis himself wired his fears about the retreat across the Chattahoochee and politely asked what was to be done.[52] "Our falling back was slow," he replied. "Every change of position has been reported to General Bragg. We have been forced back by the operations of a siege, which the enemy's extreme caution and greatly superior numbers have made me unable to prevent. I have found no opportunity for battle except by attacking intrenchments. It is supposed in the army that Sherman's immediate object is the capture of Atlanta. . . ." He concluded by again recommending that cavalry be thrown on the Federal communications, "thus compelling Sherman to withdraw."[53]

In spite of all of Johnston's ability and his brilliant conduct of the retreats, it is not difficult to see how much letters as this would infuriate Davis by their studied vagueness. Johnston's greatest mistakes in the campaign were not of a military nature. They had to do with his relations with Davis. He never seemed to realize that he might have confided in the President at times, even though he thoroughly disliked him. Johnston simply took the bit in his teeth and refused to let Richmond know where he was going—if he knew himself.

In Richmond many leaders, both in and out of official life, joined Davis in condemning Johnston's tactics. Delegations of prominent Georgians went to Richmond to urge the removal of the retreating general. Senator Benjamin H. Hill attended a cabinet meeting to urge the removal.[54] Seddon and Benjamin in the cabinet were outspoken in their views that Johnston must go.[55] Johnston, of course, had his friends in the capital, and they carried to him in the field the rumors that he was to be replaced. But still he was unwilling to express any views which would enable his friends to defend him.[56]

Would Atlanta be defended?

To that question Johnston gave no answer except to wire Bragg a strong recommendation that Federal prisoners at Andersonville, 125 miles south of Atlanta, be removed.[57] Did this mean that the Confederate Army might fall back into south Georgia? No one knew.

But Davis did not act hastily. He apparently fully realized the gravity of changing commanders at this stage of the war, even though an outstanding successor to Johnston might be available. When Senator Hill was demanding that Johnston be replaced Davis calmly asked him: "Whom would you appoint to succeed him?" And there was no answer.[58] Hardee had eliminated himself earlier in the campaign. Polk was dead. A. P. Stewart had not the experience. Lee could spare no one. Almost by default the name of John B. Hood kept bobbing up as the logical man.

On July 12 Davis asked Lee's opinion on Hood as the possible commander of the Army of Tennessee. Lee sent a hasty telegram in reply. "It is a bad time to release the commander of an army situated as that of Tenn. We may lose Atlanta and the army too. Hood is a bold fighter. I am doubtful as to other qualities necessary." Later that night when he had more time he amplified his earlier message: "I am distressed at the intelligence conveyed in your telegram of today. It is a grievous thing to change commanders of an army situated as is that of the Tennessee. Still if necessary it ought to be done. I know nothing of the necessity. I had hoped that Johnston was strong enough to deliver battle. We must risk much to save Alabama, Mobile, and communication. . . . If Johnston abandons Atlanta I suppose he will fall back on Augusta. This loses us Mississippi and communication with Trans Mississippi. We had better therefore hazard that communication to retain the country. Hood is a good fighter, very industrious on the battlefield, careless off and I have had no opportunity of judging of his action when the whole responsibility rested on him. I have a high opinion of his gallantry, earnestness and zeal. Genl Hardee is more experienced in managing an army."[59]

Davis then sent Bragg to visit Johnston in the field. He arrived in Atlanta on July 13 and conferred with "Old Joe," but the conversations were not fruitful. Johnston understood that the visit was purely unofficial and incidental to a conference with Stephen D. Lee in Mississippi and Kirby Smith in Texas.[60] The conference, therefore, never got beyond the stage of polite trivialities. Bragg apparently took the position in his own mind that if Johnston wanted to discuss the situation he would bring up the subject. Since he didn't bring it up Bragg could only report: "He has not sought my advice, and it was not volunteered. I cannot learn that he has any more plan for the future than he has had in the past."[61] He did, however, add that the morale of the army was reported good and that the impression prevailed that Johnston was more inclined to fight.[62]

The day after Bragg's arrival at headquarters Hood broke his silence and handed him a letter. The army, he said, was in a precarious position, having passed up "several chances" to strike the enemy. The sadly depleted ranks of the army, he felt, should be replenished from Kirby Smith's Trans-Mississippi forces. Having reinforced the Army of Tennessee, Hood would then hold Atlanta and then attack the enemy, "even if we should have to cross the river to do it. I have so often urged that we should force the enemy to give us battle as to almost be regarded reckless by the officers high in rank in this army, since their views have been so directly opposite," he continued. "I regard it as a great misfortune to our country that we failed to give battle to the enemy many miles north of our present position. Please say to the President that I shall continue to do my duty cheerfully and faithfully, and strive to do what I think is best for our country, as my constant prayer is for our success."[63]

Just how much influence this letter had on Bragg is problematical. He did, however, a few hours after its receipt make a recommendation to Davis. If any change was to be made he felt that Hood would give "unlimited satisfaction." He had always had a high opinion of him, he said, and this estimate had been raised by his conduct in the Atlanta campaign. But, he added, Hood must not be thought of as "a man of genius" or as "a great general" but merely as "far better in the present emergency than anyone we have available."[64]

Still Davis did not act. On July 16 he again asked Johnston what he proposed to do. "I wish to hear from you as to present situation, and your plan of operation so specifically as will enable me to anticipate events."[65]

To this Johnston replied in the same generalities he had employed all along. "As the enemy has double our number, we must be on the defensive. My plan of operations must, therefore, depend upon that of the enemy. It is mainly to watch for an opportunity to fight to advantage. We are trying to put Atlanta in condition to be held for a day or two by the Georgia Militia, that army movements may be freer and wider."[66]

That did it!

On the night of July 17 at headquarters on the Marietta Road three miles from Atlanta, Johnston received this message:[67]

Richmond, July 17, 1864

General J. E. Johnston:

Lieut. Gen. J. B. Hood has been commissioned to the temporary rank of general under the late law of Congress. I am directed by the Secretary of War to inform you that as you have failed to arrest the advance of the enemy to the vicinity of Atlanta, far in the interior of Georgia, and express no confidence that you can defeat or repel him, you are hereby relieved from the command of the Army and Department of Tennessee, which you will immediately turn over to General Hood.

S. COOPER
Adjutant and Inspector General.

On the same day Seddon, Secretary of War, wired Hood. "You are charged with a great trust," he said. "You will, I know, test to the utmost your capacities to discharge it. Be wary no less than bold. It may yet be practicable to cut the communication of the enemy or find or make an opportunity of equal encounter whether he moves east or west. God be with you."[68]

In Columbia, South Carolina, Buck heard the news with excitement in her eyes, but it was not the excitement of elation. "Things are so bad that they cannot be worse, and so they have saved Johnston from the responsibility of his own blunders, and put Sam in. Poor Sam!" she cried.

"Why, Buck, I thought you would be proud of it!" Mary answered perplexedly.

"No!" she replied gravely. "I have prayed God as I have never prayed Him before, ever since I heard this. And I went to the convent and asked the nuns to pray for him too!"[69]

CHAPTER XI

Hood Fights

Hood received the telegram informing him of his appointment as commander of the Army of Tennessee about eleven o'clock on the night of July 17. The "totally unexpected order," he said, so astounded and overwhelmed him that he remained in deep thought throughout the night.[1] Although he might have been ambitious for the command, it had come at a very awkward time just at the crisis of the campaign. Shortly before dawn he ordered his horse and rode toward Johnston's headquarters. On the way he was joined by A. P. Stewart, who apparently was also much perturbed by the news he had heard. Together the two men reached Johnston's headquarters as dawn was breaking. When Hardee arrived the three of them joined in an earnest plea to Johnston to pocket the order until the impending battle was fought.[2] But Johnston refused their request. Then the three corps commanders made a plea to Davis himself. Leaving Johnston's headquarters, they rode to the adjutant general's office and in Hood's name sent a telegram.[3]

There is now heavy skirmishing and indications of a general advance. I deem it dangerous to change the commanders of this army at this particular time, and to be to the interest of the service that no change should be made until the fate of Atlanta is decided.

To this Davis made the only reply which he could have in the circumstances. To Hood, Hardee and Stewart he sent the same message:[4]

247

A change of commanders under existing circumstances was regarded as so objectionable that I only accepted it as the alternative of continuing in a policy which had proved so disastrous. . . . The order has been executed, and I cannot suspend it without making the case worse than it was before the order was issued.

Johnston began getting his personal effects together, but before he left he sent a curt, almost peevish message to General Cooper in Richmond, a message which reflected his jealousy of Lee. He had, he said, done a better job in Georgia than Lee had in Virginia. Yet, he intimated, Lee was left in command while he was removed. "Confident language by a military commander is not usually regarded as evidence of competency," he concluded acidly.[5] However, he spent most of the day acquainting the distraught Hood with the positions of his divisions and with plans for the battle, and that evening was on his way to Macon.[6]

Now Hood was on his own, caught in a tragic web of circumstances, but a web partly of his own weaving. Upon the abilities of this crippled man and upon the success of Lee in Virginia rested the fate of the Confederacy.

In the army now backed up against Atlanta the change brought disappointment and frustration to officers and men alike. Most of Johnston's generals, taking their cue from him, were critical of the government at Richmond; and as Hood was known to be in favor with this government he became a sort of vicarious object of the dislike they bore Davis and Bragg. Cleburne was outspoken in his dissatisfaction. He felt the death warrant of the Army of Tennessee had been signed.[7] A. P. Stewart is quoted as saying he felt it was the *coup de grâce* to the Confederate cause.[8] General Josiah Gorgas confided to his diary: "The general judgment is that Hood has not capacity for such command."[9] But it was Hardee who was most disturbed and piqued. The new situation was to him "personally humiliating." He was willing, he said, to make any sacrifice for the cause except his self-respect. This now demanded that he be relieved or transferred. He had declined command of the Army of Tennessee when Davis offered it to him at Dalton earlier in the year, but now he made it clear that his refusal of the command did not convey the idea "that the appointment of a junior to command me would be satisfactory."[10] It was only after considerable persuasion from Davis that he reluctantly consented to serve under Hood.

Perhaps Senator Wigfall, implacable foe of Davis but personal friend of Hood, was right when he urged that someone "go at once, get Hood to decline to take this command." It would, he thought, destroy him if he accepted. "He will have to fight under Jeff Davis' orders. That no man can do, now, and not lose caste in the western army."[11]

Undoubtedly this political factor was an important element in the dislike and discrediting of Hood. He became the focal point of the attack on Davis. As time went on, he made serious blunders, but probably no more serious than those made by other Confederate commanders from time to time. (Johnston himself at Seven Pines or Longstreet in east Tennessee, for example.) There was a difference in Hood's mistakes, however. They came at a time when the Confederacy was in its death throes and at a time when the enemies of the President could use them to discredit him and his Administration. When this is considered along with the fact that Hood never had adequate strength at his disposal with which to wage offensive warfare, it emerges clearly that he never had a chance to succeed.

But it was not politics alone which influenced the army. Stewart and Hardee were not little mean men with shriveled souls who would attempt to discredit a commander because they disliked his political affiliations. There were other reasons.

The evidence clearly indicates that the plaudits of Richmond society were still ringing in Hood's ears. Richmond had made him a hero and he felt compelled to sustain this reputation, just as in youth he had felt the necessity to sustain his reputation as a bad boy. This compulsion undoubtedly gave him an exaggerated sense of his own personal worth, which feeling became obvious to his fellow officers. Moreover there was developing in him a pronounced tendency to take credit for successes but to lay the blame for failures on his subordinates. He also let it be known that he felt the officers and men in the Army of Northern Virginia were superior to those in the Army of Tennessee. He could not forget that it was troops from Lee's army which crashed through at Chickamauga. Neither could he forget his impression of the Western army when he arrived for the battle. Both officers and men, he felt, were timid, discouraged and lacking the *élan* and optimism to which he was accustomed.[12] Throughout the Atlanta campaign he insisted the troops were dispirited and lacking in the will to fight. He even found it desirable to apologize to Richmond and promise that the troops under his leadership would fight better.[13]

Over and above all, however, was the fact that his officers felt a deep-seated distrust of his ability to command a large army. They doubted his vision, his administrative ability, his capacity as a strategist and his military maturity. Perhaps no one has better summed up this feeling than General John B. Gordon. "As division or corps commander," he wrote, "there were few men in either army who were superior to Hood; but his most intimate associates and ardent admirers in the army never regarded him as endowed with those rare mental gifts essential in the man who was to displace General Joseph E. Johnston. To say that he was as brave and dashing as any officer of any age would be the merest commonplace tribute to such a man; but courage and dash are not the sole or even the prime requisites of the commander of a great army."[14]

This distrust of Hood quickly filtered down to Johnny Reb in the ranks. Soldiers in any army are likely to grumble when a commander to whom they have become attached is replaced. They grumbled when Lee replaced Johnston after Seven Pines.[15] McClellan's soldiers were disappointed when he was removed. But the army's dislike of Hood appears more deep-seated and virulent than mere griping. The army was not only disappointed—it was angry.[16]

On the other hand, the civilian attitude as revealed through the press was not so explosive. The *Richmond Enquirer* expressed complete confidence in Hood and thought the change simply meant that "we are ready to fight instead of retreat. . . . The appointment has but one meaning and that is to give battle to the foe."[17] The *Whig* went further in its opinion: "Of General Johnston's merits the country is well aware, but his habit of retreating has been so often indulged in that it long since became weary of it to a point bordering on nausea. On the other hand Hood is young, dashing, and lucky. . . . The army [?] and the people all have confidence in his ability and inclination to fight, and will look to him to drive back Sherman and save Atlanta."[18] Other papers took a mildly negative or a wait-and-see attitude, but few of them reflected an attitude as pronounced as that of the army.[19]

The change apparently brought complete satisfaction to the enemy, however. As soon as the change was announced Sherman inquired of Schofield, who was Hood's classmate at West Point, what manner of man he was. Schofield replied that the new commander of the Army of Tennessee was "bold even unto rashness and courageous in the extreme." From this Sherman concluded that Hood would fight and this, he said, was just what he wanted—"to fight in open ground . . . instead of being forced to run up against prepared intrenchments."[20] General O. O. Howard found the change "much to our comfort."[21] In Nashville a group of Federal officers who said they were with Hood in Texas told a reporter what a gambler he was. They had seen him on one occasion when he was broke borrow six hundred dollars, put it on one card in a faro game and win. At another time, they related, he put a thousand dollars on one card and won. "This is the man who now has charge of the rebel Army of Tennessee consisting in all of nearly forty thousand men. His whole character is one of utter recklessness."[22]

Thus charges of rashness and recklessness were leveled at Hood by friend and foe alike; but the cold light of analysis and reason eighty-six years later fails to reveal how he could have at the time he assumed command pursued a course much different from the one he took. With Sherman pushing across Peachtree Creek to within shouting distance of Atlanta, Hood had only three practical alternatives: fight then and there (as Johnston wrote in later years he planned to do) when the enemy divided to cross; fall back within the Atlanta fortifications, thus permitting Sherman to put the city under a siege which could end only in capitulation; or fall back to Atlanta, hold the city temporarily and then swing northward on Sherman's communications, hoping to lure him out of Georgia as Lee had lured his foe out of Virginia in the invasion of Pennsylvania.

Hood chose the first alternative, a decision which appears to have been entirely justified. However, this could not be said of his views on the conduct of the Atlanta campaign up to the time he assumed command. His original approval of the idea of bringing in Polk's and Longstreet's armies and swinging east of Chattanooga and then west into middle Tennessee before the Federals could concentrate a huge army in the city at least had the merit of logic and plausibility, and it might have worked.

Once the plan was dropped, however, and the Georgia campaign substituted there is little in logic or strategy to justify Hood's constant clamor for the offensive. He himself justified his course by declaring himself a disciple of the Lee-Jackson school of maneuver and attack.[23] It is true that he believed in the offensive and was never afraid to take a chance against overwhelming odds. So Lee and Jackson had been. They took ragged, poorly shod, poorly fed troops and defeated numerically superior Federal armies by attacking. Hood's own division had been noted in Virginia for its ability to carry positions by assault, and his belief in the efficacy of this strategy was strengthened by the lucky break he got at Chickamauga.

One of the tragedies of the Atlanta campaign was that he failed to see that this strategy might need to be revised in the light of the inferior strength of the Confederate forces. Lee had seen this in Virginia and had changed from his earlier type of razzle-dazzle attack to a strategy of progressive retirement behind breastworks much as Johnston had done in Georgia. The other tragedy of the Atlanta campaign was Johnston's refusal to make any attempt to explain his strategy or to win over Davis, Bragg and Hood. To the end he remained stubborn, tactless, jealous, disputatious and unable to quench his ancient and burning hatred of the President.

Sherman's general advance had begun on July 17. General Thomas was to cross the Chattahoochee at Powers' and Pace's ferry bridges and then march on Atlanta from the north via Buckhead. To reach the city he also had to cross Peachtree Creek, a small but formidable stream. Schofield was to direct his movement against the Georgia Railroad between Atlanta and Marietta, while McPherson was to strike east of Marietta between that town and Stone Mountain.[24] On the eighteenth McPherson reached and tore up four miles of railroad east of Decatur at about the same time that Schofield reached Marietta. Thomas with great deliberation was moving his men across Peachtree Creek. Then the three corps began to converge on Atlanta. McPherson and Schofield swung toward the city, and Thomas pushed forward to meet them.[25]

On the evening of the eighteenth while Hood was still planning his defenses the Confederate cavalry outposts were driven back over Peachtree Creek by Thomas. The actual advance on the city had begun. To meet it Hood formed his lines north of the city, the left resting on Pace's Ferry Road and the right covering Atlanta. Stewart's corps formed the left, Hardee's the center and Cheatham's (formerly Hood's) the right. General Joseph Wheeler commanding the cavalry watched Schofield and McPherson on the Confederate right near Decatur.[26]

Sherman had done a very dangerous thing. He had divided his army and made it possible for Hood to attack it unit by unit; and that is precisely what he did. He struck Thomas with the expectation of defeating him and then turning on Schofield and McPherson, several miles to the east, before they could effect a junction with Thomas. Calling his three corps commanders together, Hood very carefully explained to them his plans. The attack would begin at 1:00 P.M. on the twentieth, the movement to be by division in echelon from the right at a distance of 150 yards. Cheatham was to hold on his front as a guard against the possible movement of Schofield to Thomas' assistance. Stewart and Hardee were to strike Thomas, push him back to Peachtree Creek and then roll him back into the triangle formed where the creek joined the Chattahoochee.[27]

Before the attack could get under way, however, demonstrations on the enemy's left made it advisable to extend Cheatham a division front to the right. Hardee and Stewart were ordered to extend a half division front to close up the interval. As Hardee moved right to maintain contact with Cheatham, however, he found that this officer had shifted not a division front to the right, but nearly *two miles to the right*. Here Hardee was faced with a decision. Should he carry out the exact wording of his orders and move only the distance of a half division to the right or should he move whatever distance was necessary to close up on Cheatham? Hood was not on the field directing the attack but remained at headquarters in Atlanta. Hardee, therefore, had to use his own

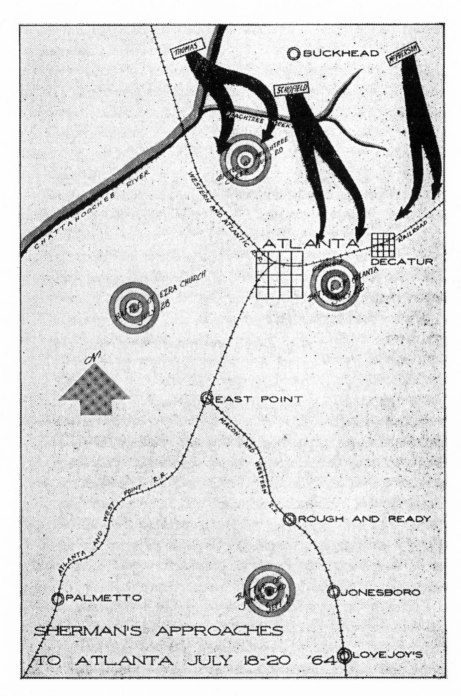

BUCKHEAD

THOMAS

McPHERSON

SCHOFIELD

PEACHTREE CREEK

BATTLE OF PEACHTREE 20

CHATTAHOOCHEE RIVER

WESTERN AND ATLANTIC

ATLANTA

DECATUR

RAILROAD

EZRA CHURCH 28

BATTLE OF ATLANTA 22

N

EAST POINT

MACON AND

ATLANTA AND WEST POINT R.R.

WESTERN R.R.

ROUGH AND READY

PALMETTO

BATTLE OF JONESBORO SEPT 1

JONESBORO

SHERMAN'S APPROACHES
TO ATLANTA JULY 18-20 '64

LOVEJOY'S

judgment and he moved the nearly two miles to the left of Cheat-ham.[28]

This movement resulted in a three-hour delay in the Confeder-ate attack and also brought about a rather strange distribution of Confederate forces. On the left Stewart with one corps came up against four divisions, 16,682 men, of Thomas' army while Hardee with 14,000 men had only General John Newton's division of some 2,700 men in his front.[29] Thus when the attack came it was Stewart's corps which bore the brunt of it.

The Confederate attack was not expected by Thomas. It was fiercely and bravely made, but it accomplished nothing of a permanent nature because it was uneven and poorly co-ordinated.

The Confederate assault was in echelon of division from the right. W. H. T. Walker's division struck first and was hurled back with heavy losses. The uneven distribution was showing up, for as William B. Bate on the right went into action he found no foe in his front. Hardee then ordered him to find and strike the enemy's flank, but he led his division into the thickets and got lost. On the left George Maney's and Cleburne's divisions were ordered in to replace Walker's decimated division, but as they were ready to attack Hardee received orders from Hood to send a division at once to help Wheeler hold the Confederate positions at Decatur. Cleburne was rushed off and Maney's or-ders to attack were countermanded.[30] Out of Hardee's four di-visions only one, Walker's, was thus actually engaged.

Stewart on the Confederate left moved spiritedly to the attack. William W. Loring on the right of Stewart's corps rushed and carried the works in his front but was compelled to fall back with heavy losses. Maney on Hardee's left had not attacked and thus Loring's right was wide open to a murderous enfiladed fire from the enemy's rifles and artillery. Edward C. Walthall's division in Stewart's center also attacked briskly, but was likewise unsuc-cessful. Thus Stewart's attack came to naught because Hardee's attack had been ineffective. "I cannot but think, had the plan of the battle, as I understood it, been carried out fully, we would have achieved a great success," Stewart reported.[31] It seems clear that this remark was directed at Hardee whose conduct of his part of the battle was, to say the least, not in keeping with his usual thoroughness.

Hood thus lost the opening engagement of a series of battles for possession of Atlanta. He had lost approximately 2,500 killed and wounded,[32] but it was by no means a catastrophic defeat. The strategy was sound and the tactical plans adequate for the situation. He had been defeated by circumstances. If a general could always be sure his own army would act just as it was instructed to act and that the enemy would always move as it was supposed to move, then winning battles would be simpler. But things don't always work out as planned and battles are lost. Sherman, however, was concerned with what might have happened. The next morning he, Schofield and McPherson sat on the steps of Howard House and discussed the general situation. "We agreed," he wrote, "that we ought to be unusually cautious and prepared at all times for sallies and hard fighting, because Hood, though not deemed much of a scholar, or of great mental capacity, was undoubtedly a brave, determined, and rash man. . . ."[33]

The flame of battle, having been extinguished on Thomas' front north of Atlanta, now broke out to the east of the city. After being withdrawn late on the afternoon of the twentieth Cleburne's division marched through Atlanta and by midnight was in position with Wheeler on the extreme Confederate right near Decatur. During most of the afternoon while Hardee and Stewart were attacking Thomas, fiery little Joe Wheeler and his dismounted cavalry had been holding the extreme Confederate right. Sherman had sent General Walter Q. Gresham against Wheeler's position on the railroad. Wheeler's skirmish line was in front of the railroad and the rest of his troops were intrenched on Bald Hill two

and a half miles east of Atlanta. Gresham's attack drove back
Wheeler's skirmish line and swept across the tracks toward the
hill. Desperately Wheeler clung to his position until day ended.[34]
That night Cleburne arrived to aid him.

At dawn on July 21 the attack was renewed and was continued
intermittently throughout most of a searing hot morning. It was,
Cleburne said, the bitterest fighting of his life.[35] Line after line of
Federals rolled up against the Confederate positions, only to be
thrown back by the deadly rifle fire. Little artillery was used on
either side. This was a rifle battle and the barrels became so heated
from the sun and from firing that men's sweat sizzled and fried
when it fell on them. Lips were blackened and cracked from
biting cartridges, and here and there in the attacking lines men
dropped from heat exhaustion.[36] But the Confederates could not
hold. General Gresham's brigade had been reinforced by another
from Francis P. Blair's division and the two of them took Bald
Hill. McPherson was now in an excellent position to turn the
Confederate right.

All during this day Hood was laboring to build new inner defenses against Thomas and Schofield north and east of the city.
He had determined on a new movement calculated to befuddle
Sherman and to crush the Federal left under McPherson. He
withdrew his entire army from the outer to these inner defenses
and then sent Hardee's corps on a night march from Atlanta to
the Confederate right, which had been so desperately defended
by Wheeler and Cleburne. Stewart, Cheatham and the Georgia
Militia under G. W. Smith were left in the new defenses.

The movement was admirably if not brilliantly planned.
Hardee was to swing on a wide circle to the right which would put
him in McPherson's rear. Here he, Wheeler and Cleburne would
turn the Federal left flank and drive it back on Schofield toward
the Confederate defenses east of the city. Cheatham, on the right
of this new line of defenses, was to attack as soon as Hardee had

driven the Federals in on him and push them on down Peachtree Creek toward Thomas. Stewart was to watch Thomas and if necessary attack him to prevent his moving to the assistance of Schofield and McPherson. Hardee was expected to move out of Atlanta early in the evening of July 21 and be in position to attack at dawn on the twenty-second.[37]

But plans miscarried and again it was Hardee who was involved. He could not move the last of his troops out of Atlanta until nearly midnight. If he could have moved directly east to the rendezvous he might have made it by daylight, but instead he was forced to take a circuitous route five miles south, three miles east and four miles northeast. This was no easy matter in the dark and over strange terrain; and as a result he was not ready to go into action until past midmorning. It was also found that McPherson's left was not "in air" as had been expected but had been secured by breastworks and abatis.[38] Moreover, almost by accident, McPherson had ordered the corps of Grenville M. Dodge to move to the left in support of Blair's division. It was while Hardee was in the process of striking that Dodge was accomplishing the maneuver.[39] Hardee's was therefore a flank attack rather than a turning movement from the rear.

This battle which Hardee termed "one of the most desperate and bloody of the war" apparently came as a complete surprise to Sherman. McPherson was at Sherman's headquarters discussing plans for the day when they heard Hardee's guns. Taking out his pocket compass, Sherman checked the direction of the sound; like a flash both men realized the firing was too far to their left rear to be explained by known facts. Hastily gathering his maps and letters, McPherson rode to the sound of the firing.[40] That was the last time Sherman saw the brilliant and handsome McPherson alive, for he rode straight to his death from Confederate rifles. The battle was in its full fury when he arrived on the left. Shortly before noon "Hardee's lines came tearing wildly through the woods with the yells of demons."[41] Dodge's troops stood their ground bravely, repulsing wave after wave of the Confederates as they attacked the lines four deep and then counterattacking with their general riding among them. Hardee's men gave their all. "Their assaults were repulsed, only to be fearlessly renewed, until the sight of dead and wounded lying in their way, as they charged again and again to break our lines, must have appalled the stoutest hearts."[42] This tribute to brave men came from a Yankee officer. But their all was not enough.

It was the 11,000 men belonging to the divisions of J. W. Fuller and Thomas W. Sweeny of Dodge's Sixteenth Corps who withstood the sustained impact of Hardee's 16,000.[43] Had it not been for their accidental position it is quite probable that Hood's plan to crush and roll back the Federal left would have been successful. "It was a most fortunate circumstance for the whole army that the Sixteenth Corps occupied the position," General Francis P. Blair noted in his official report.[44] A few years after the war he wrote Colonel J. E. Austin of New Orleans:[45]

The movement of General Hood was a very bold and a very brilliant one, and was very near being successful.

The position taken up accidentally by the Sixteenth Corps prevented the full force of the blow from falling where it was intended to fall. If my command had been driven from its position at the time that the Fifteenth Corps was forced back from its intrenchments, there must have been a general rout of all the troops of the Army of the Tennessee, commanded by General McPherson, and, possibly, the panic might have been communicated to the balance of the army.

General Blair's mention of the attack on the Fifteenth Corps brings out a secondary phase of this so-called "Battle of Atlanta" on July 22. When Hood learned of the fury and partial success of Hardee against McPherson's left he ordered Cheatham to attack the Fifteenth Corps which formed his right and was commanded by Major General John A. Logan.[46] This was Hood's own division now temporarily commanded by Cheatham, and no doubt Hood watched it with particular interest as it moved to the attack to create a diversion in Hardee's favor. The division swept forward, and as Sherman and O. O. Howard watched from headquarters they saw Logan's lines bend and then break with two batteries of artillery falling into Confederate hands. But Sherman had the answer. While Logan regrouped his men the commander in chief brought up artillery and poured a deadly enfiladed fire into Cheatham's ranks. Then Logan counterattacked and the Confederates withdrew.[47]

When night closed in both commanders found what a costly battle it had been. Each side had lost a general—McPherson on the Federal side and W. H. T. Walker on the Confederate. Both deaths were personal blows to Hood. McPherson had been his classmate at West Point, leading his class both in 1852 and 1853.[48] Hood had leaned heavily on him for assistance with his studies and had always found him generous and friendly along with his brilliance. "No soldier fell in the enemy's ranks, whose loss caused me equal regret," Hood wrote.[49] General Walker, who commanded a division of Hardee's corps, had particularly endeared himself to Hood, being one of the few officers who supported him after he assumed command.[50] It is said that when Walker fell General Hardee sent an officer to Hood with the sad news. "Go back," said Hood, "and tell Hardee to press up Peachtree Creek. It's the grandest route of the war." On hearing these orders Hardee could not resist a pun. What concerned him, he remarked dryly, was not the "route" of his army but the "rout."[51]

Both sides had lost heavily in man power and, although absolutely accurate figures are not available, it is estimated that Hood lost approximately 7,000 killed and wounded to approximately 2,000 for Sherman.[52] Although Hood had stopped Sherman cold on two fronts, it is perfectly obvious that he could not go on doing so indefinitely because of the loss of man power with no replacements. There was a limit and Hood was rapidly reaching it. The most critical historian, however, can find no real grounds for serious criticism of his strategy thus far, unless the position is taken that he should not have fought at all.

Hood, however, still felt he could defeat Sherman by attacking, and a demonstration of that belief was soon given at Ezra Church six days after Hardee's fight with McPherson's left. During the interval both sides were adjusting their lines and their personnel and resting their troops. General O. O. Howard was named to command the dead McPherson's corps; and Joe Hooker, who felt that because of seniority he should be named, resigned in a huff and, much to Sherman's satisfaction, went home. General Henry W. Slocum was brought from Vicksburg to command Hooker's Twentieth Corps. On the Confederate side Walker's division was broken up and its three brigades assigned to other divisions. Lieutenant General Stephen D. Lee was brought from Mississippi to relieve Cheatham, who had been in temporary command of Hood's corps.

During this period of respite and cogitation Sherman began a desultory shelling of Atlanta. Elevating his guns so they would carry over the Confederate lines, he began dropping shells in the city's business and residential areas. It was not an intense bombardment, but enough to cause heavy damage to property, especially in the Whitehall district.[53] At night the skies were lighted up from the flames of burning buildings, and long lines of refugees began their toilsome journey southward, fleeing the danger. "I can give you no idea of the excitement in Atlanta," one correspondent wrote. "Everybody seems to be hurrying off, and especially the women. Wagons loaded with household furniture and everything else that can be packed upon them crowd every street, and women old and young and children innumerable are hurrying to and fro. Every train of cars is loaded to its utmost capacity. The excitement beats anything I ever saw, and I hope I may never witness such again."[54]

Sherman's objective now became the railroad to Macon, on which Atlanta depended. As early as July 9 he had sent General Lovell H. Rousseau on a raid to destroy the railroad between Montgomery and Columbus, and he had done a thorough job. Then when McPherson moved in between Decatur and Stone Mountain he had wrecked the railroad connecting Atlanta with Augusta, Charlotte and the East. There remained, therefore, only one railroad intact—the Atlanta and West Point to Macon. Sherman believed that if this road were thoroughly wrecked Hood would be forced to evacuate Atlanta. He therefore decided to send Major General George Stoneman with his own and General Kenner Garrard's cavalry divisions to destroy the rail line between Jonesboro and Griffin. At the same time General Edward McCook was ordered to move his division of cavalry in concert with the other two and to strike at the same objective. This was to be no petty cavalry raid. Nearly 9,000 Federal cavalry participated, and its objectives when the movement began on July 27 included not only breaking the railroad but the capture of Macon and the release of Federal prisoners at Andersonville as well.[55]

But the raid came to disaster due to the frustrating efforts of Joe Wheeler and his cavalry. In the one bright spot of the Atlanta campaign Wheeler cut the Federal cavalry to pieces.

Stoneman started on the twenty-seventh, but instead of carrying out his orders and moving southward from Decatur with his whole force, he sent Garrard to draw off the Confederate cavalry while he with his reduced force rode toward Macon. On the twenty-eighth Garrard was attacked by Wheeler and driven northward. Then, leaving one brigade to watch Garrard, Wheeler rode southward in pursuit of Stoneman and McCook.

Stoneman reached Macon on July 30 and found it protected by

breastworks and the Georgia Militia. This unexpected disclosure caused him to abandon the idea of taking the city but rather to circle around it, cross the Ocmulgee River and ride to the relief of the Federal prisoners at Andersonville. But he never got there. Three brigades of Wheeler's cavalry closed in on him, capturing him and about half his command.[56]

McCook struck the railroad on schedule, and for four hours he tore up track and bent heated rails. But as he started back to Atlanta he encountered portions of Wheeler's cavalry, which forced him to take a circuitous route through Newman. At this town he ran afoul of five brigades of the alert Confederate cavalry. McCook was completely surrounded and each regiment was instructed to fight its way out as best it could. Some of the regiments did get through, but some 500 men were captured and McCook's effectiveness was largely destroyed.[57]

"I now became satisfied that cavalry could not, or would not, make a sufficient lodgment on the railroad below Atlanta, and that nothing would suffice but for us to reach it with the main army," Sherman wrote.[58] He was now more than convinced that his strategy should be to move his entire army south of Atlanta, cut Hood's rail communications and force the city to undergo a siege, which, no one knew better than Sherman, Atlanta could not endure for long.

While his cavalry was still engaged in its ill-fated raid Sherman had shifted McPherson's (Howard's) corps from the left (east) of the city on a wide arc around Thomas to a position west of Atlanta. This was the first movement in a general shift of the positions of the entire army. It was also the beginning of the end of Hood's defense of the city.

The movement began on July 27. Sherman rode with Howard as the Army of the Tennessee marched around Thomas toward Ezra Church, about four miles west of the city. As the men halted and began to throw up hasty breastworks of rails and logs the skirmishing became brisk.

"General Hood will attack me here," Howard suggested to Sherman.

"I guess not," Sherman replied. "He will hardly try it again."

"But he will," Howard insisted. "I knew him at West Point. He is indomitable."[59]

And Hood did attack—his third major sortie since Sherman began closing in on him. Now he planned a stroke which would save his rail communications. Lieutenant General S. D. Lee, commanding Hood's old corps, was to march directly on Howard on the twenty-eighth. The next morning Stewart was to swing south of Ezra Church and come up in Howard's rear. Thus the Federals would be ground to dust between two millstones. It was another ill-fated plan, perfect in concept but poorly executed. Lee's troops attacked "with a terrifying yell," but every attack was stubbornly resisted and thrown back by the Federals, who dug themselves in as they fought.[60]

This stubborn resistance Hood had not expected, and as a result he was forced to modify his plans. Stewart was directed to move to Lee's assistance instead of swinging around to the Federal rear. But this failed to bring Confederate success. As the afternoon wore on each charge became weaker than the previous one. Rows of dead Confederates testified to the effectiveness of Howard's artillery and repeating rifles.[61] Hood remained at headquarters in Atlanta. Whether he could have accomplished anything by his presence on the field is doubtful, but he did lay himself open to censure for not going to the scene of the battle. Instead of going himself, he sent for Hardee and asked him to ride with all haste to direct Lee and Stewart at Ezra Church. But it was too late when he arrived. The battle was lost and evening was closing in. Fate had dealt Hood another numbing blow.[62]

It seems perfectly clear today that after Ezra Church the only question was where and when his army would be destroyed. But there is no indication that Hood even considered such a possibility at the time. It is clear that he was bitterly disappointed, but it was not in his nature to think of defeat as long as he had a division left to fight. In his frustration and bitterness he unjustly blamed the defeats on his officers, particularly Hardee, and on his troops.[63] But it was not their fault that these battles were being lost. Neither can the blame be put wholly on Hood. The real cause is simple: Sherman had a vastly superior army of veterans, and victory eventually lay with the side which possessed the biggest battalions.

Had Sherman known how really depleted the Confederate strength was he might have closed in for the kill with less caution. As it was, he moved slowly. The stinging lashes Hood had delivered had convinced him that his adversary was indeed a reckless man who would fight against any odds whenever the occasion presented itself. As it developed, Hood let down his guard momentarily, thus giving Sherman his chance. Wheeler's victories over McCook and Stoneman had raised in Hood the hope that he might cut off Sherman's supplies by destroying the railroad to Chattanooga and from that town to Nashville. On August 10 he sent Wheeler with approximately 4,000 cavalrymen northward to operate on these lines of communication. He struck near Marietta, Dalton and Resaca and then rode on to Chattanooga, expecting to cross the Tennessee at Cottonport. The river was swollen, however, and he was forced into east Tennessee near Knoxville before he could cross. Then, swinging westward, he cut a wide swath through middle Tennessee to the vicinity of Nashville. Here the Federals took up the pursuit and Wheeler was chased south across the Tennessee River near Florence, Alabama.[64] He had caused a great deal of damage, but he had failed to impair effectively Sherman's communications and his command was scattered and demoralized.

This raid of Wheeler's was Hood's first major blunder. He had sent away his eyes and ears just at the time Sherman was moving. The result was that Hood had insufficient information of his foe's movements.

Cautiously Sherman extended his right southward from Ezra Church toward Hood's vital railroad artery, throwing up breastworks as he moved. At intervals a few shells were thrown into Atlanta, but otherwise there was an ominous quiet over the countryside, broken only by the creaking of wheels, the shouting of teamsters, the thud of marching feet and the ring of axes as breastworks were thrown up. The Federal lines east and north of the city were vacated and their occupants shifted southward by the right flank.

During this movement Hood might have attacked with some hope of success, but he didn't because he was without adequate information. He believed that Wheeler's success in cutting the railroad north of Atlanta was forcing a Federal retreat. The evidence of the retirement, he thought, was the abandoned trenches. Moreover an old woman who lived in the neighborhood was brought to the general's headquarters. She had been within the Federal lines, she related, and when she asked for food she was told they hadn't enough for themselves. She had seen General Jacob Cox himself, and he had replied to her request for food: "I have been living on short rations for seven days, and now your people have torn up our railroad and stolen our beef cattle, we must live a damned sight shorter."[65] On such flimsy evidence Hood was anxious to believe that Sherman had given up the effort to take Atlanta. "No reliable information has been received in regard to the intention of the enemy, but the prevailing impression is that they are falling back across the Chattahoochee River" is the way Hood's chief of staff summed up the matter.[66]

Apparently it was not until August 30 that Hood felt sure Sherman was south of him in full force and aiming at his rail communications.[67] On the evening of the thirtieth Hardee at Rough and Ready had received a telegram from the commanding general asking him to come to Atlanta for a conference. That night Hardee rode a locomotive into the city and soon was closeted with Hood. Hardee was, he found out, to move with S. D. Lee's corps and his own (under Cleburne) to Jonesboro and there attack Sherman once again. And once again tactical errors rose to plague Hood. Hardee was on his way back to his troops before daylight, expecting to find both Lee and Cleburne at Jonesboro in response to telegraphic orders. But Cleburne wasn't there. He had run into unexpected Federal opposition and had been forced to take a circuitous route. Lee, too, was late for the rendezvous, and the attack was not ready until afternoon. Fearing that Sherman had securely intrenched himself, Hardee wired Hood and requested that he come personally and take charge of operations; but, although the railroad was still open, Hood chose not to go.[68] It may be assumed that his physical condition was the reason, but no one can say for sure. "I remained in Atlanta with Stewart and G. W. Smith, anxiously awaiting tidings from Jonesboro," is his only comment.[69]

The tidings he finally received were discouraging. Hardee had used his best judgment and ordered the attack, even though it was midafternoon and afternoon attacks are ordinarily unwise unless the attacker has the benefit of position and vastly superior numbers. Hardee had neither; and in addition his tactical dispositions were bad. Cleburne had orders to turn the enemy's right, and Lee was to attack when he heard Cleburne's guns. Lee, however, mistook the guns of Cleburne's skirmishers for the main attack and began his advance before Cleburne was seriously engaged. The result was a repulse for both these officers and a further deterioration of the general Confederate situation in and around the city. For the first time during the campaign the troops of the Army of Tennessee were not attacking with their customary *élan* and almost reckless bravery. They had learned what it meant for inferior forces in the open to attack greatly superior forces behind breastworks.[70]

Sherman's garrote was tightening about Atlanta's throat. Hardee's repulse had given the Federals control of the Macon Road and made evacuation of the city inevitable. During the night of August 31 Hood ordered Lee's corps back to Atlanta, leaving Hardee to defend Macon alone. It was a move obviously based on Hood's erroneous belief that the major portion of Sherman's army was still north and west of the city. As a matter of fact, the Federal Army was concentrating in force on the south in the direction of Jonesboro. Schofield was moving from the east, Howard from the west and Thomas from the north. That Lee was able to slip through this cordon can only be attributed to the fact that the movements of the three Federal armies were poorly co-ordinated.[71]

But whether Lee got through or not really made little difference now, except for the possible capture of isolated units of his corps. As a matter of fact, it probably would have been better if he had not got through, for as it developed he had to turn around and march right back again. His movement did, however, leave Hardee with only one corps to fight off Sherman's mighty concentration. He could fight only a delaying action and that not for long if Sherman should attack in strength.

Hardee did fight a delaying action on September 1 in front of the railroad west of Jonesboro, but it was Sherman himself who gave the army days of grace. He had it within his power to crush Hood's divided army once and for all—but he didn't. Near midnight he heard the rumble of high explosives borne on the night breezes from Atlanta twenty miles to the north. He had left Slocum north of the city. Had he attacked Hood? There was a lull in the rumbling thunder, then near 4:00 A.M. he again heard the sound of exploding powder kegs and the sharper crack of artillery shells.[72]

But it was not Slocum attacking. It was Hood evacuating the city. He had at last completely comprehended Sherman's plans and was moving to consolidate his army. The movement was under way by 5:00 P.M. Hardee withdrew from Jonesboro to Lovejoy's Station some six miles farther south. Lee was turned about and sent back to Hardee. Stewart and Smith followed close behind.

Commissary stores which could not be moved were distributed among the citizens of Atlanta, but in the confusion eighty-one cars of ordnance stores and five locomotives were blown up.[73] This was the thunder Sherman had heard—the useless destruction of vast quantities of precious ammunition. The fault lay, a court of inquiry decided, in the fact that, although proper orders were given for the safe removal of these stores, no one personally saw to it that the orders were carried out.[74] It was another example of the poor staff work in evidence throughout the Atlanta campaign.

As Hood moved out Slocum moved in unopposed. Hood consolidated his army near Lovejoy's Station and Sherman wired Lincoln the glorious news that Atlanta had fallen. But somehow his dispatches failed to mention the fact that the Confederate Army was still intact.

CHAPTER XII

Hell in Tennessee

ON SEPTEMBER 4 at Lovejoy's Station General Francis A. Shoup, Hood's chief of staff, noted in his diary: "Our army is all united at this point . . . all quiet along the lines. No change in the position."[1]

In his memoirs Sherman wrote: ". . . after due reflection, I resolved not to attempt at that time a further pursuit of Hood's army, but slowly and deliberately to move back, occupy Atlanta, enjoy a short period of rest, and to think well over the next step required in the progress of events."[2]

For a month and a half Sherman had been circling and trying to feint his weaker opponent out of position. Hood had not always been able to fathom the attack and at times had been groggy and confused; but he had thrown stinging counterpunches which dulled the aggressor's zeal and slowed him down. Now the bout was over, and both sides were glad to rest awhile before the return match which must inevitably come. Actually the fight was nearer a draw than an overwhelming victory for Sherman.

Neither army was in an enviable position as the cooler September nights told of the approach of autumn. Sherman commanded an army whose strength he estimated at near 82,000.[3] It was deep in enemy territory, faced by a still dangerous Confederate Army and with a tenuous line of supply over a single railroad to Nashville via Chattanooga. It was not a very comfortable situation. On the other hand, Hood was caught on the horns of a fateful dilemma. If he remained idle for any great length of time his army of some 40,403 would dwindle rapidly through furloughs and desertions.[4] If he moved he was likely to be forced to fight, against overwhelming odds, the great decisive battle which had been so long delayed. Hood simply could not sit quietly by while Sherman dallied in Atlanta; and yet he did not have the strength to launch another series of offensive operations aimed directly at his enemy in the city.

The obvious answer was to move on Sherman's communications. Perhaps he could be forced to evacuate the city and follow the Confederate Army back toward Chattanooga. This, then, became Hood's strategy: to destroy the enemy's communications. And it did not take him long to arrive at this conclusion, for on September 6 he telegraphed President Davis: "The army is much in need of a little rest. After removing the prisoners from Andersonville, I think we should, as soon as practicable, place our army upon the communications of the enemy, drawing our supplies from the West Point and Montgomery Railroad."[5]

Before he could begin offensive operations again, however, there were matters demanding attention. The troops needed shoes, clothes, rest and, not having been paid in ten months, money.[6] Reinforcements were badly needed to build up the army to fighting strength again. It was essential that the approximately 23,000 Federal prisoners at Andersonville be moved, for if Sherman should march to rescue them he probably would succeed, thus swelling the strength of his own army by that number. Above all, harmony and unity of purpose were needed in the Army of Tennessee. In spite of the fact that Hood had done a creditable iob in defending Atlanta, he was still not on good terms with many of his subordinates, notably Hardee.

Hood himself appealed to Richmond for additional troops and in his extremity asked Hardee to do likewise.[7] But the appeals of both men were denied. No resources were available, Davis replied. "It is now requisite that absentees be brought back, the addition required from the surrounding country be promptly made available, and that the means in hand be used with energy proportionate to the country's need."[8] In short, Hood would have to do the best he could with what he had or could bring in from the surrounding countryside. Instead of gaining strength, however, he lost heavily, for on September 10 the volatile and unpredictable Governor Joseph E. Brown of Georgia withdrew all the Georgia state troops under the pretense of giving them an opportunity to gather their crops and look after their private affairs. But this was a sham. The Governor was doing everything in his power to discredit the Administration of Jefferson Davis, even to the extent of secretly favoring a separate peace for his state if he could get a state convention to share the responsibility.[9] Nothing could have upset his plans more than a smashing victory by Hood.

To Hood's problems of supply, recruitment, bickering, political double-crossing and future strategy Sherman now made his contribution by announcing his decision to remove the civilians from Atlanta. On September 7 he advised the Confederate leader that he deemed it best that the civilian population clear out. He would undertake to move these people and their baggage as far south as Rough and Ready and there Hood would have to take over. To carry out the evacuation a truce was suggested.[10]

Two days later Hood sent a stinging reply. He had no alternative but to comply with the request that he assist these unfortunate people, he said. However, he blazed in anger as he closed his letter. "And now, sir, permit me to say that the unprecedented measure you propose transcends, in studied and ingenious cruelty, all acts ever before brought to my attention in the dark history of war. In the name of God and humanity I protest. . . ."

"In the name of common sense, I ask you not to appeal to a just God in such a sacrilegious manner," Sherman shot back. "You who, in the midst of peace and prosperity, have plunged a nation into war—dark and cruel war—who dared and badgered us to battle, insulted our flag. . . ."

Then for two days the generals wrote each other letters ranging in subject matter from who started the war to what a perfect scoundrel the other was.[11] Meantime a steady stream of old men, women and children with as many of their possessions as they could carry on their backs or in improvised carts and wagons flowed southward from the rail terminus.

Meantime Hood was shifting his army from Lovejoy's Station on the Macon Railroad to Palmetto, some twenty miles to the west, on the Montgomery Railroad. From this point he could swing west of Atlanta and strike the enemy's communications at a point or points north of the city. Before the campaign could be undertaken, however, there were certain matters of organization and morale to be settled. To be successful a commander must, of course, have adequate men, guns and supplies. But over and above this he must have the confidence and co-operation of his subordinate officers. This Hood apparently did not possess.[12]

The chief difficulty was with Hardee. Since the day Hood was put in command he had not forgiven his number-one lieutenant general for his loyalty to Johnston and, in turn, Hardee had never changed his opinion that Hood was incapable of high command. The exigencies of the campaign had forced a degree of co-operation between the two men, but Hood had blamed Hardee for the failure to hold Atlanta. Now that there was a lull in the fighting both men were anxious to be rid of the other. This made a particularly difficult situation for Jefferson Davis, since he was friendly with both men and both had his confidence. Hardee was not an anti-Administration man. He was merely pro-Johnston and anti-Hood for military reasons, and Davis understood this.[13] Now with both men demanding a change and with Governor Brown acting up, Davis decided to visit the army.

Accompanied by his confidential aide, Colonel James Chesnut,

Jr., he arrived in Macon at 4:00 A.M. on September 24. No one knew of his visit, so there was no welcoming committee at the station. That night, however, he made a speech of encouragement to the Atlanta refugees and then went on the next day to Hood's army at Palmetto.[14] He arrived about 3:30 on the afternoon of the twenty-fifth. The next morning he and Hood rode out for a review of the troops. There was polite cheering from some of the brigades but, much to Hood's surprise, there were others which shouted in unison: "Give us General Johnston."[15] It was the only sour note in an otherwise happy day which concluded with a serenade by the 20th Louisiana band and speeches by the President, General Howell Cobb, Governor Isham Harris of Tennessee and Hood himself. "Be of good cheer," Davis exhorted the Tennessee troops, "for within a short while your faces will be turned homeward and your feet pressing Tennessee soil."[16]

On the next day Davis held a long conference with Generals Stephen D. Lee and Stewart and a separate one with General Hardee. What was the condition of the army? What should be its next move? By subtle inference he sought information on Hood and his controversy with Hardee. In short, as Davis himself expressed it, his desire was "to learn its [the army's] condition and what might be expected from it in active operations against the enemy."[17] Hood had previously outlined to the President his plan of operations: assume the offensive, cut the enemy's communications, select a favorable position near the Alabama line and there fight the decisive battle. If Sherman should become alarmed at this threat to Tennessee and send a portion of his army there then, Hood felt, he could defeat the portion left in Georgia, "drive it from the country, regain our lost territory, reinspirit the troops, and bring hope again to the hearts of our people." On the other hand, if Sherman should elect to move farther south with his army Hood thought it would be as easy to follow from some point north of Atlanta as from Palmetto.[18]

Thus Davis investigated but kept his counsel. As he mounted his horse to ride away Hood had a final brief conference with him. Hood was, he said, aware of the outcry against him since Johnston's removal, and if the President saw fit to remove him he would serve in any subordinate capacity for which he was fitted. But Davis was noncommittal. He might find it necessary to remove him, he said, but his decision would come later. Meantime he was to continue in command.[19]

There is evidence that Davis himself had come to doubt the wisdom of retaining Hood in command, but he was hardly in a position to remove him now. In addition to his personal loyalty to Hood, there was the matter of his own political enemies. He simply could not afford to admit that he had made a mistake in replacing Johnston with Hood.[20] Instead the President came up with an anomalous solution. On September 28 Hardee was relieved from duty with the Army of Tennessee and assigned to command the Department of South Carolina and Florida. That same day Davis wrote Hood what he further proposed to do: "It seems to me best that I should confer with General Beauregard, and, if quite acceptable to him, place him in command of the department embracing your army and that of General R. [Richard] Taylor, so as to secure the fullest co-operation of the troops, without relieving either of you of the responsibilities and powers of your special commands, except in so far as would be due to the superior rank and the above assignment of General Beauregard. He would necessarily, if present with either army, command in person."

To this plan Hood apparently offered no objection, and yet it presented enough questions to satisfy all the quarreling Confederates. Who actually was in command? If Beauregard was not physically present with the army could he give orders? If he gave an order when he was not in the field was Hood bound to obey it? Was strategy, too, jointly planned? If so, whose views would prevail in case there was a disagreement? Actually these questions never came to a point where they had to be answered, for Beauregard took care of the situation very neatly. When the going got tough he never came to the field. Thus if Hood failed he could be free of any blame for the failure, and if he was successful—well, after all, the commander of the department was entitled to share in the glory.

It was an excellent arrangement so far as Davis and Beauregard were concerned. Although the two men cordially disliked each other, their hatred was not so intense as that between Davis and Johnston. Beauregard at the time was serving in a minor capacity under Lee at Petersburg. This new position as department commander, at least in title, was more in keeping with the prestige and dignity of a full general, albeit a slightly tarnished one. When Davis and Beauregard met in Augusta, therefore, the Great Creole accepted the new assignment gladly.

While in Augusta for the conference with Beauregard, Davis made another of his inept speeches. Undoubtedly his purpose was to rally the people to the support of the waning Confederacy and to his Administration in particular. But in doing so he revealed even more clearly than he had at Macon and Palmetto the plans for Hood's army. Hood was going to attack Sherman's communications, he said, and soon the Federals would find themselves in the position of Napoleon at Moscow. Again there were mysterious references to "treading Tennessee soil" and "pushing on to the Ohio."[21] Immediately northern newspapers took up the speech and the news was spread broadcast. Everyone knew the Confederate plans.[22] For Sherman it was good news. "He promised his Tennessee and Kentucky soldiers that their feet should soon tread their native soil, etc., etc.," he wrote. "He made no concealment of these vainglorious boasts, and thus gave us the full key to his future designs. To be forewarned was to be forearmed. . . ."[23]

Having thus settled affairs in the West, the President returned to Richmond via Columbia, South Carolina. Here he was entertained at the Chesnut home. For him Sally Preston had a big hug and kiss because he had good things to say about "her General." To Sally's display of affection the President responded by "smoothing her down the back from the shoulders as if she were a ruffled dove."[24] In the evening there was a reception where "the President's hand was nearly shaken off" and a dinner with sixty-year-old madeira and boned turkey with truffles.[25]

But life for the Prestons, Hamptons, Chesnuts and all their kind was becoming more overcast with the shadows of impending disaster and defeat. Hood's failure to hold Atlanta had descended on them like a pall, and Lee's inability to do more than hang on in Virginia only deepened their premonitions of doom. There were personal problems and sorrows as well. Mrs. Chesnut was constantly reviling herself for being a "Cassandra" and finding it necessary to resort more and more frequently to the use of morphine. In July Willie Preston, Sally's brother, had been killed at Atlanta, bringing inexpressible sorrow to his family and friends. In Virginia Wade Hampton swung out of his saddle on the battlefield to find both his sons shot down beside each other. Young Wade had a gaping hole in his back and Preston was mortally wounded.[26]

Yet life goes on even in a war, and in September Mary Preston and Dr. John Darby were married in Columbia. "I think it was the handsomest wedding party I ever saw," Mrs. Chesnut recorded. "They certainly are magnificent specimens of humanity at its best."[27] To Hood, news of the wedding must have brought poignant memories and a fierce desire to get the war over with and get back to Sally. But she seemed to be bearing up rather well under the strain of the separation. She had, Mrs. Chesnut reported, rushed into a flirtation "such as never was" with young Johnny Chesnut, the diarist's nephew. "He drives her every day, and those wild, runaway, sorrel colts terrify my soul, rearing, pitching, darting from side to side of the street," she continued. "But my lady enjoys it! When he leaves her, he kisses her hand, bowing so low to do it unseen that we see it all. They seem utterly content with one another. She says she does it to keep him out of mischief. And he answers: 'You are engaged—even if you do say you are sorry it is so.' So there is no deception on either part."[28]

Perhaps she did not realize it at the time, but the closing months of the war were bringing her closer to a problem all her own. Sooner or later this complicated pattern of her suitors was going to be simplified and somebody would get hurt in the process. She was engaged to the crippled Hood. In Virginia Rollins Lowndes rode with Hampton. He was of the stuff from which poets make heroes—a slender aristocrat of such sensitivity that he fainted at the sight of young Wade Hampton's wounds; yet swashbuckling enough to challenge Judson Kilpatrick to a mass duel with sabers between 1,000 of Hampton's men and 1,500 of his Federals.[29] How much she cared for him later events would reveal. And now Johnny Chesnut!

Meantime Hood moved with his army to attack Sherman's communications. On September 28, the day Davis wrote him about his plans for Beauregard, the army began to cross the Chattahoochee. By the close of the next day his three corps of infantry commanded by Lieutenant Generals Stephen D. Lee, Alexander P. Stewart and Benjamin F. Cheatham and two brigades of cavalry under Brigadier General William H. Jackson had crossed. Forrest with approximately 6,000 cavalry was operating in west Tennessee and Wheeler was in north Alabama, having recently returned from his raid through middle Tennessee. Not counting Forrest's and Wheeler's commands Hood had at his disposal some 33,000 infantry and artillery.[30]

By leisurely marches of twelve to eighteen miles a day Hood pushed steadily northward through the rolling wooded country, the cavalry fanned out in front and on the flanks. On the morning of October 4 the Federal garrison at Ackworth surrendered to Loring, and that afternoon Stewart took possession of Big Shanty.[31] Both these posts were lightly garrisoned and offered little opposition, but French had a bad time at Allatoona. On the morning of the fifth he was repulsed with serious losses, and this deep railroad cut remained in Sherman's hands.[32]

As Hood moved, familiar names appeared on his maps: New Hope Church, Lost Mountain, Allatoona, Dalton, Dallas. These were names both armies had cause to remember from their campaigns of the summer as Joe Johnston retired toward Atlanta. Was this to be the Atlanta campaign in reverse? Sherman had followed Joe Johnston into Georgia. Was he now going to follow Hood out again?

With Hood now fairly astride his communications Sherman had little choice in the matter. "Military men believe that Sherman's army will be forced to abandon Atlanta and cut its way out in a very few days," the New York *Times* reported.[33] So Sherman followed, realizing "it was absolutely necessary to keep General Hood's infantry off our main route of communications and supply."[34] So far Hood's strategy was working perfectly.

Shortly after the fall of Atlanta, General Schofield had gone back to Knoxville to take charge of his department. On September 29, as Hood moved, Sherman sent Thomas to Chattanooga and Nashville to reorganize middle Tennessee defenses against Forrest. Accompanying Thomas to Chattanooga was one division of the Fourth Corps and one of the Fourteenth.[35] He reached Nashville on October 4 just at the time Hood struck at Ackworth, Big Shanty and Allatoona. Now Sherman took up the pursuit of Hood, leaving only his Twentieth Corps in Atlanta. As he moved up the railroad Hood swung on a wide arc west of Rome and then turned east again to strike the railroad. On October 12 and 13 Lee and Cheatham captured the entire length of railroad from

Resaca to Tunnel Hill, including the town of Dalton. Then Hood, reassembling his army, moved westward again, halting at Cross Roads about nine miles south of Lafayette near the Alabama line. Here Wheeler, who had recently completed his middle Tennessee raid and been assigned to watch Sherman, reported that Sherman was in full force at Snake Creek Gap only fifteen miles away. What now? Fight or retire again?

"I here determined," Hood wrote, "to advance no further towards the Tennessee River, but to select a position and deliver battle, since Sherman had at an earlier date than anticipated, moved as far north as I had hoped to allure him."[36]

But the long delayed great battle of the West did not take place. When Hood called his officers into conference he found them unanimously opposed to offering battle against such overwhelming odds as were presented by Sherman's vastly superior army. After spending two days "in serious thought and perplexity" he gave his orders. Wagon trains swung into line and went creaking and swaying on their way; the cavalry fanned out in front and on the flanks; the infantry and artillery fell in. Hood was moving again, this time to Gadsden, Alabama, seventy miles farther west. It was a move which baffled Sherman. Hood could "turn and twist like a fox," he said, "and wear out my army in pursuit."[37] "Johnston being a sensible man I could generally divine his movements, but as Hood is not I can tell nothing at all about him," the papers quote him as saying.[38] But he did not give up the pursuit—not yet.

In his dilemma, Hood says, he conceived the plan of marching into Tennessee "with a hope to establish our line eventually in Kentucky." He determined to make the campaign unless restrained by Beauregard or Davis.[39] When Beauregard met him at Gadsden on the twentieth, therefore, this was the number-one topic on their agenda. Far into the night of the twentieth the two generals discussed the plan and finally Beauregard made his decision. The plan was a good one, but success depended on the manner in which it was carried out.[40] In later years Jefferson Davis wrote that he did not approve the plan.[41] However, he did not disapprove and he must, therefore, share with Beauregard and Hood the responsibility for the campaign.[42]

At a time when boldness and speed were of the most importance Hood now became timid and slow. The plan contemplated crossing the Tennessee River at Guntersville, destroying the bridges and supply depots at Stevenson and Bridgeport and then moving on Thomas and Schofield before their armies could unite at Nashville; and with boldness the plan had a good chance of succeeding. But Hood did not cross at Guntersville. Instead he turned left and followed the river toward Decatur and Florence. The reason for the delay seems to have been lack of cavalry. Beauregard had insisted that Wheeler's corps be left in Georgia to watch and harass Sherman.[43] The only other large cavalry force was Forrest's, now engaged in raising hell generally in the vicinity of Jackson, Tennessee. Until Forrest could join him Hood was unwilling to undertake the campaign—an understandable position.

When Hood turned left from Guntersville, Sherman gave up the chase and returned to Atlanta. "Damn him!" he is reported as saying. "If he will go to the Ohio River I'll give him rations! The nearer the rebels come to us the easier it will be to kill them. . . . Thomas will take care of him at Nashville and Schofield will not let him into Chattanooga or Knoxville. The military sky is as bright as the noonday sun."[44] But he did take precautions. The Fourth Corps under Major General D. S. Stanley was ordered to Nashville to reinforce Thomas.

Meantime Hood pushed down the Tennessee River, probing for a favorable crossing. But he had failed to notify Beauregard of his decision not to cross at Guntersville, and as a result the Great Creole was put in the embarrasing position of having lost his army. He caught up at Decatur, however, where Hood was debating whether to attack the garrisoned town or not. It was decided to abandon the idea and to seek a crossing twenty miles farther down at Courtland where Wheeler had crossed at the conclusion of his raid into middle Tennessee. But the engineers rated crossing at Courtland a risky undertaking, so Hood went on to Tuscumbia, arriving there on October 31.[45] There was still time, but precious days had been lost. Convinced of the danger from Hood's movements, Sherman had started Schofield from Chattanooga to join Stanley in reinforcing Thomas. Schofield even now was moving through the rolling hills of middle Tennessee toward Pulaski.[46]

But Hood lost more time at Tuscumbia and Florence. A month earlier a request had been made that the Memphis and Charleston Railroad from Corinth be repaired so that supplies might be brought up. But this had not been done. The bright warm days of October now gave way to chilling persistent November rains which swelled the river and doused the cooking fires of the men. Hood himself had a serious attack of rheumatism which confined him to his bed. Above all, Forrest had not arrived, and Hood could not risk crossing with his wagon trains until he arrived.[47] The whole campaign showed distinct signs of bogging down, and Hood himself seemed to be in doubt as to what he should do. When Beauregard asked him for a written statement of his plans he could only resort to the evasive phrases used by Joe Johnston earlier in the Atlanta campaign: "It is not possible for me to furnish any plan of my operations for the future, as so much must depend upon the movements of the enemy."[48]

On November 13 Hood moved his headquarters across the river to Florence, and the next day General Forrest reported for duty. On the fifteenth Lee's corps crossed and on the sixteenth Cheatham's and Stewart's corps. At 7:00 A.M. of that day, November 16, 1864, Sherman turned his back on a fire-gutted Atlanta and with his troops singing "Glory, glory, hallelujah" began his march to the sea.[49] Thus two great armies which had fought each other for nearly nine months now turned their backs on each other and marched in opposite directions.

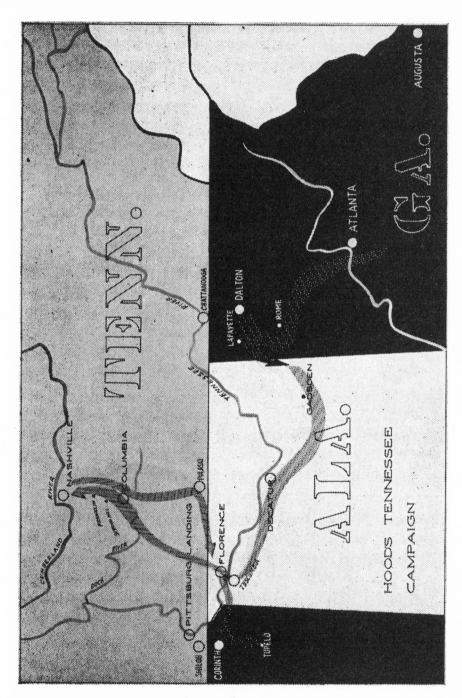

HOODS TENNESSEE
CAMPAIGN

284

But it was five days after the crossing before Hood actually put his army in motion toward Nashville. On the nineteenth Forrest had moved out in front with his cavalry. On the twentieth Stewart's corps moved out several miles on the Lawrenceburg Road, and that day Lee's corps joined them. Then on the morning of the twenty-first the whole army moved north—Lee and Stewart via the Lawrenceburg Road and Cheatham via the Waynesboro Road. Their object: to get in rear of Schofield, then at Pulaski, before he could reach Duck River at or near Columbia. Destiny was in the saddle with Hood as he urged "Jeff Davis" along over the slushy, slippery road. Thomas' army was scattered all over middle Tennessee, the largest units being his own force of some 18,000 in and around Nashville and the forces under Schofield and Stanley at Pulaski, numbering some 25,000. If Hood could prevent Schofield from joining Thomas, complete victory would be in Confederate hands and Hood's dazzling dream of marching to the Ohio and then joining forces with Lee would come true. Such a victory would completely neutralize Sherman in Georgia and compel him to abandon the state. Get in between Schofield and Thomas; whip the former; then turn on the latter and take Nashville! That was Hood's plan.

Once it began moving, the Confederate Army made almost incredible speed, considering the weather and the roads. As the army moved a cold rain began which soon turned into snow and sleet. Wagon trains and artillery dug deep ruts in the muddy earth. Cavalrymen hunched low in their saddles against the icy blasts and the infantry steadily churned the cold slush with the irregular shuffling of their marching feet. On the twenty-second the head of Hood's column reached Lawrenceburg twenty miles west of Schofield's position at Pulaski. In great alarm Schofield moved his army on the double-quick for Columbia on the Duck River thirty miles away. If Forrest should beat him to this point and get control of the bridges and fords he would then be effectively cut off from Thomas. He, therefore, pushed his men in an almost superhuman effort. And he did arrive before Forrest, just in time to throw up temporary breastworks around the town.

When Hood's main forces arrived (on the twenty-seventh) no attempt was made to storm these breastworks. Believing that Schofield would at the earliest possible moment withdraw his army across Duck River, Hood decided on a flanking movement. His surmise was correct and events moved according to plan. Leaving Lee's corps to demonstrate before the town, he moved with the rest of his army across Davis' Ford some five miles above Columbia and marched toward Spring Hill eleven miles away. Almost at the same minute (dawn of the twenty-ninth) when Hood was crossing his men at the ford, Schofield was sending his wagons with 5,000 men under General Stanley to Spring Hill. While Lee's guns thundered before Columbia, creating the illusion that the entire Confederate Army was still there, Hood and Stanley raced for Spring Hill—and from this point the great mystery of Spring Hill begins.

The essential facts are easy to determine, but why things went as they did is a problem which thus far has defied solution. The essential facts are these: When Hood at the head of Cheatham's corps reached Spring Hill about 3:00 P.M. the Federal wagons were parked near the railway station with Stanley's infantry deployed in front of them. Hood made an ineffective and unco-ordinated attack which failed to dislodge the Federals. Inconclusive skirmishing took place during the remaining two hours of daylight and when an early winter dusk closed in both armies were in confusion. That night Schofield with his main forces pushed up the Columbia Pike within a hundred yards of the bivouacked Confederates and escaped the trap.[50]

The author does not claim to have uncovered any new material nor to have a complete explanation for the tragic fiasco, but on the basis of existing evidence it appears that Hood and Cheatham must share the responsibility. As commander, of course, Hood must take the blame for the actions of his subordinates, but it appears that Cheatham unwittingly contributed his full share.

At two crucial points in the affair Cheatham gave orders which were, to say the least, puzzling; and but for these orders Schofield might have been cut off. These are as follows: (1) Cleburne's division of Cheatham's corps was the first to arrive at Spring Hill. Cleburne had been given orders to get in touch with Forrest and to attack at once. This he did about 4:00 P.M. In conjunction with a brigade of Forrest's cavalry he struck the Federals and drove them back on the town under the protection of their artillery. He was re-forming his lines for the second charge when orders came from Cheatham to stop the attack.[51] Considering the situation at the time, it seems almost certain that this second charge would have taken the town and thus have shut off Schofield's retreat. (2) Meantime Major General William B. Bate had come on the field with his division and been assigned by Hood to a position across the pike to the left of Cleburne. About dark as the head of Schofield's main column reached this position, Bate fired into the Federals; and as he prepared for a second round Cheatham, not realizing this was Schofield's entire army, ordered Bate to retire and re-form on Cleburne's left.[52] This movement left no Confederate forces blocking the turnpike.

Other units of Hood's army now reached the field. Stewart's corps moved in near ten o'clock and in a welter of confusing orders went into bivouac on Cleburne's right. Then Major General Edward Johnson of Lee's corps moved in on the extreme left in the area recently evacuated by Bate. Campfires were lighted in the darkness here and there and soon the hills blossomed with thousands of twinkling lights in the darkness. The Confederate Army slept, but not even one regiment stacked its arms in the turnpike.

At headquarters Hood was disappointed over the events of the afternoon but he obviously felt that all was not lost, and in so thinking he made a tragic mistake. That night after he had abandoned the fight on the pike and joined Cleburne's left Bate went to Hood's headquarters to make a personal report of why he had not continued to harass the enemy on the turnpike. After reviewing events Hood said "in substance": "It makes no difference now. General Forrest will hold the turnpike north of Spring Hill and will stop the enemy if he tries to pass toward Franklin. In the morning we will have a surrender without a fight. We can sleep quiet tonight."[53] In short, Hood made the fatal mistake of under-estimating his opponent.

Later that night a barefoot Confederate private excitedly re-ported to Hood after he had gone to bed that the Federals were passing on the turnpike. Wearily he aroused himself and his adju-tant, Colonel A. P. Mason. "Go to General Cheatham," Hood ordered Mason, "and tell him to advance a line of skirmishers and confuse the enemy by firing into his columns." And then Hood went back to sleep. What happened after that is a mystery. Cheatham said he got Hood's order and immediately ordered Gen-eral Johnson (bivouacked nearest the pike) to "cut off anything that might be passing." Johnson apparently made a personal recon-naissance and, seeing no Federals on the pike, returned to his head-quarters.[54] Hood did not check on Cheatham; Cheatham did not check on Johnson; and, to add to the fantastic confusion, Colonel Mason stated afterward that he never sent the order which Cheat-ham says he received.[55] But one thing is sure—the Federal Army slipped by during the night of November 29.

Certainly the situation that night called for a personal investiga-tion by Hood to see that orders were being carried out, but it was not made. It is entirely possible that the state of his health made him loathe to leave the warmth of his bed. He had been ill with rheumatism at Florence, and nearly two weeks in the saddle in cold, wet weather had done nothing to help it. Too, it was gen-erally known that long hours in the saddle irritated the stump of his leg and caused him great discomfort. But his health probably was not the only reason. Hood always left too much to his subordi-nates without giving them adequate supervision.

CHAPTER XIII

Weep for a Fallen Land

Hood was in a towering rage at breakfast the next morning.[1] His officers were touchy and quarrelsome, all denying guilt and each critical of the other.[2] In the ranks the common soldier "felt chagrined and mortified at the occurrence of the preceding day."[3] Everyone, Hood most of all, felt the sting of shame and a consuming desire to wipe out the humiliation by catching up with Schofield and destroying him. "Each man felt a pride in wiping out the stain," one participant wrote.[4] Had a new spirit been generated in the Army of Tennessee? "The weather was clear and beautiful; the cool air was warmed up by the bright sunshine; and our forces were in fine condition," another relates. "Their spirits were animated by encouraging orders from General Hood who held out to them the prospect that at any moment he might call upon them to deal the enemy a decisive blow."[5] General Randall L. Gibson's brigade of Louisianians even brought out its band to play a few numbers as the troops marched by.[6] Hood himself sensed the change. This was what he had said he wanted ever since Atlanta—troops who were spirited and anxious for battle.[7]

This was the spirit in which the Army of Tennessee approached the decisive battle of the campaign. This to a great extent was the feeling which caused Hood to hurl his troops against enemy breastworks with almost maniacal abandon and those troops to respond with a reckless courage unsurpassed in history. The balm of revenge for wounded pride loomed large at Franklin.

289

Hood's pursuit was swift and decisive with Forrest again in the lead. Schofield had driven his men all night, the head of his column arriving at Franklin a little before daylight.[8] Finding no wagon bridges for crossing the Harpeth River and the fords swollen, he immediately set about building a footbridge for his infantry and laying planks on the railroad bridge for his wagons. As the wagons arrived they were sent across, while the infantry dug in as it came on the field. A regiment or a brigade would arrive, throw up breastworks in its front and then fall into exhausted sleep. This was repeated over and over until they had constructed intrenchments and log breastworks from river to river in the bend of the Harpeth.[9] Although only emergency field works, they were formidable when supported by artillery as they were. This then was what confronted Hood as Stewart's corps, leading his advance, marched to the crest of a ridge overlooking the plain which lay before the village some two miles away. Stewart's troops were deployed in line of battle to the right or east of the Columbia Turnpike. As Cheatham's divisions came on the field they were deployed to the left or west of this pike. Lee's corps with the artillery had not yet arrived from Columbia. Forrest's cavalry was divided and placed on the flanks.[10]

By now it was well past three o'clock in the afternoon. Would Hood attack?

Across the river on a high bluff Generals Schofield and Stanley watched through their glasses the Confederates forming in line of battle and ardently hoped he would not. It was not Schofield's idea to fight at Franklin. He merely hoped to get his wagons and troops across the river and safely within the fortifications at Nashville.[11] He had been lucky at Spring Hill the night before, but the gleaming Confederate muskets, the waving signal flags and the scurrying of horsemen here and there along the lines now indicated he might not be so fortunate today. Across the river in front of the town his troops lay behind their breastworks. Out in their front a half mile away was an exterior line lightly held by two brigades under Brigadier General George D. Wagner. It was an army with but one thought: Would Hood attack?

On Winstead Hill, Hood briefly debated that question with his officers. Forrest was opposed to a frontal assault. "Give me one strong division of infantry with my cavalry," he urged Hood, "and within two hours time I can flank the Federals from their works."[12] Cheatham likewise opposed a fight. "I do not like the looks of this fight," he is quoted as saying. "The enemy has an excellent position and is well fortified."[13] Cleburne joined his fellow officers in their views.[14] But Hood was adamant. Without adequate artillery and over the protests of his officers, he ordered the attack against an enemy of approximately his own strength strongly intrenched. He was through with flanking movements and shilly-shallying. Schofield had made him look silly the night before and now, by God, he would pay for it! Hood, of course, did not express it so bluntly. "I knew that it was all important to attack Schofield before he could make himself strong, and if he should escape at Franklin he would gain his works about Nashville," his official report read.[15] "Drive the enemy from his position into the river at all hazards," he ordered Cheatham and Stewart.[16]

It was almost exactly a mile from the point where the Confederate attack began to the Federal lines. The area in between the two armies is a plain between low-lying hills and the Harpeth. It was, in 1864, almost unbroken except for a portion of a low stone wall, two small clumps of bushes and a railroad cut. Straight through the center ran the Columbia Turnpike and a quarter of a mile to the east was the Nashville and Decatur Railroad. Northward along this pike and railroad on the warm, lazy Indian summer afternoon of November 30, 20,000 Confederates marched toward death in what is considered by many to be the most magnificent charge in military annals. Stewart moved along the railroad and Cheatham along the pike. In perfect alignment, with regimental and brigade colors flying in the breeze, they quick-stepped until they reached firing distance and then broke into a slow trot. Ahead of them the enemy lay waiting, rifles cocked and cannoneers standing by their pieces.

Cleburne's and Brown's divisions of Cheatham's corps were the first to become engaged. As they neared Wagner's exterior lines they received a volley from his skirmishers; and then, as if this were the provocation they needed, they charged "with a wild rebel yell, which once heard is never forgotten."[17] Wagner's brigades broke under the assault and ran, but not before the Confederates were on them. Friend and foe became tangled in a seething mass of slugging, cursing men into which the Federal artillery dared not shoot for fear of killing their own men. Those Federals who could ran, but 700 didn't get away and were made prisoners.[18] But the rout of Wagner was only an incident on the way to the main objective. With loud shouts of "Let's go into the works with them," Cheatham's men "now more like a wild, howling mob than an organized army, swept on to the very works, with hardly a check from any quarter. So fierce was the rush that a number of the fleeing soldiers—officers and men—dropped exhausted into the ditch, and lay there while the terrific contest raged over their heads, till, under cover of darkness, they could crawl safely inside the intrenchments."[19]

In the center of the Federal lines where their breastworks crossed the pike was a gap guarded by a raw infantry regiment. When Wagner's men came rushing through followed by hundreds of frenzied Confederates this regiment also broke and ran, thus creating a wider gap which instantly became the focal point of Cheatham's attack. Urged on by Cleburne and Brown, the Confederates poured through, taking possession of both the works and the guns. For a brief period it seemed this might be the "break" of the battle, but the Confederates were too exhausted to hold their ground. From behind near-by Carter's House, Colonel Emerson

Opdyke's brigade was rushed up from reserve. As it moved into the breach there was again the terrible hand-to-hand fighting which had been going on for an hour.

Slowly and with heavy losses the Confederates were beaten back step by step. General Stanley had rushed across the river to steady his troops and was shot down, painfully wounded. General Cleburne was killed as he led his men on foot. So was General Hiram B. Granbury. Then General John Adams of Loring's division was mortally wounded. General John C. Brown was seriously hurt. The toll of Confederate officers was terrific. In Brown's division Generals Otho F. Strahl and States Rights [not a nickname] Gist were killed and General John C. Carter mortally wounded. General George W. Gordon was taken prisoner. In Walthall's division General William A. Quarles was wounded; in French's division General F. M. Cockrell was seriously hurt. In addition to Adams, Loring's division also suffered the loss of General T. M. Scott, who was wounded. General Edward Johnson's division lost one brigadier wounded—General A. M. Manigault. Two major generals commanding divisions and ten brigadiers were lost to Hood that day in a little more than two hours' fighting.[20]

Everything converged on this center of the Federal line. Stewart had moved on Cheatham's right along the railroad, but the configuration of the terrain and the devastating oblique fire of the batteries across the river caused him to veer to the left. Thus as if drawn by an irresistible force his divisions moved left oblique into the seething vortex of death. Again and again they surged up against the Federal breastworks only to be thrown back by the withering rifle volleys and the incredibly vicious spray of canister. Hundreds of his men lay where they fell in the ditches at the base of the breastworks.[21]

After dark General Edward Johnson's division of Lee's corps, which had been in reserve, moved to the support of Cheatham's corps in the bloody gap. Here again it was the same story: gallant charges which carried to the parapets and then recoiled in the searing blasts of fire they received. Neither side could drive the other away, so they stood and slugged it out toe to toe and died. Irresistible Confederates were meeting immovable Federals and the result was the bloodiest impasse in American history.

While this desperate fighting was taking place on the south side of the river, Forrest was engaged with General James H. Wilson's cavalry on the north side. If he could drive off the enemy's cavalry there was a good chance that Franklin might yet be won. If Forrest with 5,000 men could strike Schofield's retreating columns tired and worn out from days of marching and a hellish battle he might literally destroy them. But Forrest didn't have 5,000 men; he had only about 3,000 and this was not enough to cope with Wilson. Hood had weakened Forrest by dividing his corps. Chalmers' brigade was placed on the left flank in support of Bate, where it saw little fighting. Forrest with only Jackson and Buford crossed the river and this was not enough. Wilson drove Forrest back, thus shielding his own army, and another golden opportunity was lost.[22] With Forrest's genius for battle it does not tax the imagination to think what might have happened if he had been given his full force to do the job. But, alas, this entire campaign was rapidly becoming one of "might have beens."

When night closed in at Franklin the firing began to die away fitfully but it was nearly midnight before it ceased. Schofield was hurrying his army across the river toward Nashville, and the exhausted Confederates dropped in their tracks. There were few campfires that night. Most of the men lay sprawled in the field or in the ditches in front of the breastworks. In the morning some of them would awake and yawn and rub their stiffened joints—but the army had lost nearly 6,000 men. Almost 2,000 of these were dead and the rest wounded or prisoners.[23] Included in the casualties, in addition to the twelve generals, were fifty-three regimental commanders.

It was not until the next morning that Hood fully realized how staggering his losses really were. As he left his headquarters and rode toward the enemy's positions of the night before he saw the grotesquely sprawled bodies of the dead and heard the moaning of the wounded. And the closer he came to that acre of hell in front of the gap the more numerous became these bodies. Here and there among the dead men was a dead horse marking the spot where a brigade or regimental commander had been killed. And when he reached the ditch at the base of the front slope of the breastworks he saw there hundreds of prostrate forms with arms stretched up along the slope, showing that their last efforts had been to leap into the ditch and climb up the other side to get at the enemy. Each man had his face powder-burned, while a gaping wound in the forehead or face proved he had fallen at the very muzzle of Federal guns. On the other side of the rifle pits were mingled bodies of the Blue and Gray lying lifeless across one another's bodies.[24] This was Franklin, and these were the men who wouldn't attack breastworks.

And as he rode over the field he undoubtedly was pondering his next move. Should he turn back and march to fight Sherman? On this the first day of December Sherman was halfway between Atlanta and Savannah making Georgia howl, his march uncontested except for an occasional brush with Wheeler's cavalry. Or should Hood push on to Nashville and again take a great risk—the greatest one of all? Thomas was there with 50,000 men behind strong works, while he had not more than half that number left. There seemed little to gain in either course unless he could be reinforced. But where were fresh troops to come from?

From Trans-Mississippi Department under Kirby Smith, Hood thought, and on December 2 he conveyed his thought to Beauregard who, in turn, took up the matter with President Davis. "Cannot I send General E. Kirby Smith to re-enforce General Hood in Middle Tennessee, or take the offensive in Missouri? His assistance is absolutely necessary at this time."[25]

"If General Smith can now act as suggested it would be well that he should do so," Davis replied. "There is no objection to his being called on, but he has failed heretofore to respond to like necessities, and no plans should be based on his compliance."[26]

However, Beauregard's efforts came to naught. Kirby Smith, after a month's delay, referred his request to General Buckner, who commanded the District of West Louisiana.[27] Buckner felt that it would be impossible to move a large force across the Mississippi. A bird if dressed in Confederate gray would find it difficult to fly across the river, he said.[28] After the Tennessee campaign was all over and Hood's army was back south of the Tennessee River, General Smith gave Beauregard his answer. No, he said, conditions wouldn't permit the movement.[29]

Meantime Hood had decided to push on to Nashville even though, as General French expressed it, there was written in bold letters on the walls of Hood's tent: "An army that can obtain no recruits must eventually surrender."[30] The reasons given by Hood for his decision are almost pathetic. He realized, he said, that with his limited forces he could not successfully attack Thomas at Nashville. He also realized that in the absence of the prestige of victory he could not push into Kentucky with any hope at all that Tennesseans and Kentuckians would flock to his colors. But he could not turn south with any hope of victory over Sherman unless Kirby Smith should send the divisions which had been requested. The situation being hopeless, therefore, he decided to advance. "Our army was in that condition which rendered it more judicious the men should face a decisive issue rather than retreat . . . ," he wrote. "I therefore determined to move upon Nashville, to entrench, to accept the chances of reinforcements from Texas, and, even at the risk of an attack in the meantime by overwhelming numbers, to adopt the only feasible means of defeating the enemy with my reduced numbers, viz., to await his attack, and if favored by success, to follow him into his works."[31]

Lee's corps marched in advance this time, followed by Stewart's and Cheatham's, and on the morning of the second of December their pitifully thin line of battle was formed. Forrest was on the extreme right nearest the Cumberland River. Next to him on the left was Cheatham, then Lee, and on the extreme left Stewart. The line extended from the Nashville and Chattanooga Railroad on the right to the Hillsboro Pike on the left, a distance of nearly four miles. Facing them were two Federal lines. The exterior extended from river to river in the loop of the Cumberland very much as the lines had run at Franklin. The interior and shorter line ran from the Cumberland on the west in a southeasterly direction to the Franklin Pike, where it joined the exterior line.

But these lines had not appeared overnight. Since his arrival in Nashville early in October, Thomas had been working hard to build and man them. Originally sent from Sherman's army to organize middle Tennessee defenses against Forrest, he found his task increased enormously when it became evident in November that Hood would strike at Nashville. Hood's delay at Tuscumbia had given him additional precious time, but none too much, for there was much to be done. The entrenchments around the city had to be completed, horses secured for the cavalry, arms and supplies collected and, above all, an army assembled.[32]

This latter problem gave him particular concern. The two largest units of his proposed army were those of Schofield moving from Pulaski and A. J. Smith's forces from Missouri. If either or both these should be delayed his chances of whipping Hood would be greatly reduced. How close Schofield came to missing the rendezvous has just been related, but Smith's expedition caused Thomas equal anxiety—not because a hostile army was threatening it but because Smith couldn't seem to get his men and supplies loaded on transports at St. Louis and get under way. Finally he did sail, however, and on the night of December 1 his steamers tied up at the wharves along Nashville's river front.[33] Schofield and Smith with a total of some 40,000 troops had arrived within a few hours of each other.

Now there remained but one major problem—getting General James H. Wilson's cavalry mounted and equipped. "If Hood attacks me here, he will be more seriously damaged than he was yesterday; if he remains until Wilson gets equipped, I can whip him and will move against him at once," Thomas confidently wired General Halleck in Washington.[34]

Meantime Hood was constructing and securing his own lines and attempting to deal with the Federal cavalry now rapidly being supplied with horses and arms. In addition to the front-line intrenchments secondary positions were prepared in the rear and extra precautions taken to strengthen the flanks with artillery works to prevent a possible turning movement.[35] General Bate with his division and two extra brigades was sent to Murfreesboro to assist Forrest in coping with the enemy cavalry, but he was withdrawn on the eighth when it appeared Thomas might be ready to attack. Indeed, Thomas, after considerable prodding by his superiors, was ready to attack—and then the ice came. The rain fell, freezing as it came down. Then snow and sleet covered the icy sheath and Nashville became a frozen ghost city out of some lost world. Men could not walk on level ground, much less charge up slopes; and so the attack was delayed. Firewood became a problem in the city, but "sans tents, sans overcoats, sans shoes and in many instances almost sans clothing, the Confederates were in but sorry plight to endure such exposures."[36] Moreover it interfered with their intrenching operations.

By December 13, however, the ice began to melt and the next evening Thomas explained his plans for the battle, just in time, it might be added, to prevent Grant removing him from command.[37] General James B. Steedman was to move at daylight on the fifteenth against Cheatham on the Confederate right. The cavalry and A. J. Smith's corps were to attack simultaneously the Confederate left under Stewart and roll it back. General T. J. Wood would act as the pivot for the turning movement. Schofield was to be held in reserve in the left center for use wherever needed.[38]

By six o'clock in the morning the Federals were ready. A heavy fog clung to the valleys, but soon a warm winter sun dispelled it. Steedman moved out with his mixed white and Negro brigades to pin down Cheatham. On the right Smith's division and Wilson's cavalry moved in and felt out Stewart's positions near the Hillsboro Pike. One brigade of Wood's division crept forward toward Montgomery Hill, a fortified point in Stewart's front. Everything was going according to schedule. The Federals were maneuvering into position. Hood's cannoneers stood by their guns and the infantry peeped over their breastworks with rifles ready. It was the tense few minutes before a battle when men's hearts are in their throats and pulses pound furiously.

In front of Montgomery Hill Wood's men looked up at the artillery-crowned brow. Why not take it? They charged into a hail of musket fire and canister, but they took it and its garrison. Almost at the same moment from farther to the right came the sound of heavy firing. Smith's and Wilson's divisions were engaged. The turning movement was on. Here on the Confederate left the assaults were so fierce that Hood pulled two brigades of Lee's corps out of the center and brought them to Stewart's assistance. Then Wood's entire division moved up and successfully assaulted the whole fortified salient on Lee's left. This was the story of the first day's battle: Steedman pinned down Cheatham. Wood pinned down Lee. On the left Stewart caught hell—so much hell that his thin lines could not hold on. Slowly, grudgingly they bent and then broke to re-form on the Granny White Pike more than a mile in their rear.

During the night Hood desperately strengthened his new positions. Cheatham was moved from his position on the right to the left, Stewart now becoming the center and Lee the right.[39] The new line was only about half as long as the one of the previous day. New works were thrown up and the hills on their flanks were studded with artillery. On this shortened line Hood proposed to fight it out to the death. Actually it was a stronger position than he had occupied the previous day. His right was anchored on Overton's Hill, a well-fortified eminence. The rest of his line from east to west was well protected by hills furrowed by infantry barricades and entrenchments and crowned by artillery. Confederate engineers had done an excellent job.

At dawn the battle was renewed, the Federals resorting to the same general plan they had used the day before—pin down Hood's right and center and hammer the left. Schofield had now been added to Smith's and Wilson's divisions to help do the job. Steedman hurried forward. Wood moved up on his right. To his right Schofield and Andrew J. Smith shifted their brigades into line. Wilson swung far around the Confederate left and took possession of the Granny White Pike in Hood's rear. By noon the two opposing lines were not more than 600 yards apart and except for preliminary skirmishing there had been no fighting.

Then as if by signal the battle began. Colonel Sidney Post's brigade of Wood's division which had the day before stormed Montgomery Hill attempted to repeat its previous performance by assaulting Overton's Hill. In a fierce charge it was hurled back with heavy loss. Then Steedman threw in a brigade of his Negro troops and it was cut to pieces. Hood's right was holding firm and there was no reason for anyone to suspect what was about to happen.

When Hood saw the determined nature of the attack on Overton's Hill he hastily snatched Cleburne's division (now commanded by Brigadier General J. A. Smith) from the left and sent it to Lee's succor on the right. This left Bate's division on the extreme left; and it was here that the end came to the Army of Tennessee. Brigadier General John MacArthur commanding the First Division of A. J. Smith's troops touched off the explosion. Receiving permission from Thomas, he took his first brigade commanded by Colonel William L. McMillen, moved with them across the intervening space and with fixed bayonets charged Bate's position with wild fury. At the same time General Edward Hatch with his division of dismounted cavalry gained Bate's rear and began to pour in a deadly fire from rifles and two pieces of artillery. Thus attacked from front and rear, Bate's men broke and ran wildly toward the Franklin Pike. As Bate's men ran their hysteria was quickly transmitted to the other brigades in the lines. Nobody knows who followed whom to the rear. All were mingled in inextricable confusion—the Army of Tennessee had degenerated into a mob clawing its way down the Franklin Pike toward safety.

"I was seated upon my horse not far in the rear when the breach was effected," Hood wrote, "and soon discovered that all hope to rally the troops was vain."[40]

Of all the decisions made by Hood during the entire Atlanta and Tennessee campaigns this is the only one the author has discovered which has not been subject to attack by at least one critic. For once Hood was clearly and unmistakably right. There was no need to try to rally these men. They had had enough. They were through; and that night as he listened to the rain on his canvas roof he wept his heart out.

A rear guard was hastily organized and the next day some semblance of order was restored. To Lee's corps was assigned the all-important rear-guard actions, most of the initial phases of which were conducted by a portion of Clayton's and Stevenson's divisions. By ten o'clock on the night of the sixteenth they had reached a point seven miles north of Franklin and had deployed to receive the impact of the Federal pursuit; and on the morning of the seventeenth it came. Wilson's cavalry with infantry support attacked and for a few minutes it seemed that it would break through. But the stubborn defense put up by Gibson's brigade of Louisianians staved off disaster and Hood's fleeing columns escaped.[41] Years later one of the survivors of this stand *in extremis* gave his version of his and his fellow soldiers' reactions. They didn't hope, he said. They merely held on as long as they could expecting any minute that the whole Federal Army would come crashing through. Above all they wished for Forrest. The whole Yankee army was afraid of Forrest.[42]

Falling back to Franklin they found the town "filled with bewilderment and confusion. The turnpike far to the south was crowded with army wagons and such artillery as we had, while the columns of infantry marched over the fields and by any way practicable."[43] Lee burned the bridge at Franklin and that afternoon made another stand four miles south of the town. The next day, December 19, Hood's scattered columns were concentrated near Columbia and there a portion of Forrest's cavalry arrived from Murfreesboro. Never had they been more welcome or appreciated than they were now. Although Old Bedford himself had gone on with most of his command to meet Hood at Duck River, the very fact that "Forrest's men" were now in the rear guard acted as a deterrent to Wilson's boldness.[44]

It had been Hood's hope that he could remain in Tennessee on the line of Duck River for the winter, but when he got there it did not take him long to decide that the condition of his troops and the steady pressure from the enemy made it necessary for him to continue his retreat southward.[45] In view of this continuation of the retirement he organized a permanent rear guard of Forrest's corps and a few scattered infantry regiments—a force that fought and fell back over and over again for the next six days. The Federal pursuit was about six or seven hours behind Hood all the way, but Forrest was engaged almost constantly. His artillery teams gave out, but he impressed oxen from the countryside and kept his guns rolling. His infantry was barefoot and the icy roads made mincemeat of their feet, but he solved this difficulty by letting as many as possible ride in the wagons until it came time to fight. They would leap from the wagons, form in line of battle and then jump back onto the wagons. But they fought—and they held.[46]

The capricious weather now began acting up again. Rain fell in torrents and then froze in a layer of ice over the mud beneath. Wagons and artillery bogged down and infantry found the footing almost impossible. "Heavy rains alternating with snow and ice now set in," a participant wrote. "To add to our suffering our clothing was worn threadbare and many were actually without shoes. These constituted the barefoot brigade, and were compelled to cover their feet with raw hide that being the only material at hand. . . . As we neared Pulaski the weather grew more and more inclement and added to the severity of the hardships we underwent. An exhausting day's march, prolonged far into the night, a halt in the forest, where not only the ground was frozen hard, but the very trees were coated with ice, so that we could neither build fires to warm ourselves and dry our clothing, nor obtain the benefits of a little sleep, while our rations of the plainest food were extremely scanty. . . ."[47]

Slowly as in a nightmare the cavalcade of ragged shivering men crawled toward the Tennessee. On Christmas Day they were splashing through creeks near the river and their spirits revived. Just across the river were safety and food and warmth—so they gleefully called to each other "Hood's Christmas present."[48] They crossed the river on pontoon bridges and went into camp on the opposite shore. The remnants were safe, but the Army of Tennessee had died in front of the gap at Franklin and on the hillsides at Nashville. In Louisiana an unknown poet gave expression to the anguish which the South felt:

> Weep! Weep for a fallen land,
> For a standard-sheet laid low.
> Freedom is lost! Let every heart
> Echo the note of woe;
> Yea weep, ye soldiers, weep!
> 'Twill not your manhood stain,
> To mourn with grievous bitterness
> Honor and Valor slain.[49]

CHAPTER XIV

Years of Peace

Hood led the battered remnants of his army numbering some 15,000 men to Tupelo, Mississippi. It was to this town that the Army of Tennessee had retreated after Shiloh in April 1862. Now after two years of campaigning it was back where it started, a mere skeleton of its former proud self. Hood, of course, would not remain in command. He was finished along with the army. But he did not wait to be relieved. On January 23 he resigned and his resignation was promptly accepted by Beauregard, who at the same time announced the appointment of General Richard Taylor to command.[1]

But, in his own mind at least, he was not through with the war. On the same day that his resignation became effective he wired the President:

I wish to cross the Mississippi River to bring to your aid 25,000 troops. I know this can be accomplished, and earnestly desire this chance to do you so much good service. Will explain my plan on arrival. I leave today for Richmond.[2]

He was battered, beaten, discredited and a hopeless cripple. One would think he might crave retirement and peace. But not Hood! He had a fierce loyalty to the Confederacy and an indomitable fighting spirit. So he was dreaming up new ways of aiding the cause—new ways to get back into the fight. It was the same urge which made him forsake an easy life in Richmond and go back to the army after he had lost his leg at Chickamauga.

On his way to Richmond he stopped in Columbia, South Carolina, for a visit with the Prestons and a reunion with Sally. "Hood came yesterday," Mrs. Chesnut reported. "He is staying at the Prestons, and they sent for us. What a heartfelt greeting he gave us. He can stand well enough without his crutch, but he does very slow walking. How plainly he spoke out these dreadful words. 'My defeat and discomfiture! My army is destroyed. My losses.' He said he had no one to blame but himself."[3] His melancholia was virulent and consuming, even though he was back in pleasant surroundings again. He sat and stared into the fire, paying little attention to the prattle of conversation around him. Livid spots came out on his face and huge drops of perspiration rolled from his forehead. "He is going over some bitter hours," Sally's younger brother Jack thought. "He sees Willie Preston with his heart shot away. He feels the panic at Nashville and its shame . . . and the dead on the battlefield at Franklin. And that agony in his face comes again and again. . . . He looks in the fire and forgets me and seems going through in his own mind the torture of the damned. . . ."[4]

Undoubtedly he was reliving the hell of Franklin and Nashville, but there is every reason to believe that he was also oppressed by the doubt of whether Sally would actually go through with the marriage. There apparently was no quarreling between them, but obviously there was a coolness on her part which worried him. But Johnny Chesnut in a strangely prophetic way had it all figured out. "If he will not when he may, when he will, he shall have nay," he quipped. "There will be no wedding! You will see. He lost his chance last winter! He made his siege too long! He grew tedious. . . ."[5]

When he arrived in Richmond he found himself and the President the objects of bitter attacks by the people, the press and the politicians. Perhaps for the first time Hood fully realized the political implications of his appointment and subsequent failure.

The Richmond newspapers were hurling imprecations at him and Davis. "He has been tried and found palpably wanting." "The army has no confidence in Hood—they had none at first." "The campaign was above Hood's capacity to manage." "The evil spirit which had haunted Bragg returned into the army when Hood took command." "Hood stepped out of the way, hat in hand, and asked Sherman to walk through Georgia."[6] These were typical newspaper comments. Hood's old friend Wigfall commented: "That young man Hood had a fine career before him until Davis undertook to make of him what the good Lord had not done—to make a great general of him. He has thus ruined Hood and destroyed the last hope of the Southern Confederacy."[7]

In Congress the feeling was intense and for a time Davis' friends felt that an attempt might be made to impeach him. On every hand there were demands that Johnston be restored, and the general himself was always ready to plead his own case before Congress.[8] Although the House did invite Hood to "a privileged seat on the floor"[9] the invitation was an empty gesture. They were after Hood because he was the Achilles' heel of Jefferson Davis. Only a few days before, this same House had called on the President to give it "all the correspondence between himself and General Joseph E. Johnston, touching the command and movements of the Army of Tennessee, and all the correspondence between himself and Generals Beauregard and Hood touching the command and movements of the same army since the removal of General Johnston from the command of it, and up to the retreat of it to the south side of the Tennessee River."[10] Furthermore they proposed to find more ammunition in Hood's own report which had not yet been made public; so they requested Davis to send along a copy of it.[11]

The President complied with this second request and furnished Congress and the newspapers with a copy of Hood's report, which he had been compiling during the early part of February. Obviously the report was done in a period of anger and without full reports from his subordinates, for it is not an objective account of campaigns and battles. Rather it is a pointed and at times almost heated attack on Johnston for his conduct of the Atlanta campaign and an arraignment of Hardee and other subordinate officers who were held responsible for the defeat.[12] Although he had already resumed command of the Army of Tennessee, Johnston proposed to bring the whole question before the public by angrily announcing that he would prefer charges against Hood "as soon as I can find leisure."[13] Hood retorted by requesting that a court of inquiry be called,[14] but wise old General Cooper shut them both off by advising Hood: "A court of inquiry cannot be convened in your case at present. Proceed to Texas as ordered."[15]

Hood was already on his way to Texas when he received General Cooper's message. Obviously it had not been difficult to convince the President that fresh troops could be brought out of the West, for he entertained till the very last the notion that the war could be continued in the Trans-Mississippi area. But though Hood was on his way, he had made a detour via Chester, South Carolina, for another visit to the Prestons. He had left Richmond in mid-March and now he seemed unable to tear himself away, even though Mrs. Chesnut recorded: "The Hood melodrama is over, though the curtain has not fallen on the last scene. Hood stock is going down. When that style of enthusiasm is on the wane, the rapidity of its extinction is miraculous, like the snuffing out of a candle; one moment here, then gone forever."[16]

As he dallied in Chester the tidal wave of catastrophe swept over them all. On April 2 Jefferson Davis learned that Richmond could not be held and the next day a long train of cars loaded with official records, anxious officials, a half million dollars in Treasury funds and the Davis family slowly rolled southward, toward Danville. Here the disintegrating fragments of the government received the news of Lee's surrender. Mournfully the journey was resumed. On the tenth they were in Greensboro. Nine days later the cortege reached Charlotte to find that Joe Johnston had surrendered to Sherman. They were all surrounded now, hemmed in on every side by hostile armies. A world was coming to its end.

At Charlotte Mrs. Davis and the children left the main party and went by rail to Chester, South Carolina, expecting to join her husband later at Abbeville. At Chester she was met by Generals Preston, Chesnut and Hood. Mrs. Chesnut did what she could to make the fleeing First Lady comfortable, but the men had little of a hopeful nature to offer. "If I have lost my leg and also lost my freedom, I am miserable indeed," Hood moaned. "Let me help you if I can," General Chesnut offered, "it is probably the last service I can render."[17]

But for Hood another world, his own private world which contained only himself and Sally, had come to an end. No one can say precisely how and why it ended, but as he mounted his horse and rode away toward Texas he was riding out of Buck's life forever. There apparently had been no dramatics, no spectacular quarrel. The romance just played out. Hood's strategy and tactics both had been poor. With her head on Mrs. Chesnut's knee Buck sobbed out her story, or at least a part of the story. "A sickening, almost insane longing comes over one just to see him once more, and I know I never will. He is gone forever. If he had been persistent, if he had not given way under Mamma's violent refusal to listen to us, if he had asked *me*. When you refused to let anybody be married in your house, well I would have gone down on the sidewalk, I would have married him on the pavement, if the parson could be found to do it. I was ready to leave all the world for him, to tie my clothes in a bundle and, like a soldier's wife trudge after him to the ends of the earth. Does that sound like me? Well it was true that day!"[18]

How much of this was actually true and how much was the product of Buck's vivid sense of the dramatic is difficult to say.

If she had told everything she might well have added that she had never known whether she really loved her general or not; and Rollins Lowndes was coming home from the war, and Rolly was rich, handsome and in love with her.[19] At least she had that to think about on the boat going over, for in a few weeks the whole Preston family—Mary and Dr. Darby, Jack, Buck, Tudy, Mrs. Preston and the General—were on their way to Paris.

Meantime Hood and two aides had been making their way southward toward Texas, their progress slowed by the necessity of dodging Federal patrols. When they reached the Mississippi they found every possible passage across the river closed. On the night of May 30 a patrol surrounded and captured the party and the next day they were paroled.[20] The life of a soldier was behind him and civilian life lay ahead—a life for which he had the poorest sort of training. He was virtually broke, he was crippled—but he was free, only thirty-five years of age and a lot of burdens had been lifted from his shoulders during the past few months. Perhaps now his great sad eyes could laugh occasionally.

With his parole as a passport in the pocket of his uniform he went down the river to New Orleans. He was going to Texas anyway—not looking for troops but for a job and for his old friends not only of the Texas brigade but of pre-war days in the old army. On June 24 he was in Houston and the next week in San Antonio.[21] In both cities he was generously welcomed, a fact which must have warmed his heart. He was in Texas now among old comrades to whom Atlanta, Franklin and Nashville were mere names. He was their old Hood—the Hood of Gaines's Mill, Fredericksburg and Chickamauga. "Though the cause for which General Hood has battled so nobly and suffered so manfully has failed, still he has a home in the hearts and under the roof of every brave and generous Texan," one newspaper declared. "He returns to his home in our State poor in purse but rich in the rewards coveted by a brave and chivalrous soldier. He shall never

want for the comforts of life. Long may he live to enjoy the
gratitude of his countrymen."[22]

Apparently his recent defeat and the subsequent attacks on him
still rankled in his soul, however, and in October he left San
Antonio for Washington. The purpose of the trip according to
the newspapers was to visit Jefferson Davis in prison and to get
from him certain information about the last days of the Confederacy and the collapse of the armies.[23] But it is quite unlikely
that he saw Davis, because the stricken ex-President was being
held incommunicado. It appears that the purpose of the trip was
more to determine the status of his own case with respect to a full
pardon—this and a visit to his mother in Kentucky.

As his ship left Galveston for New Orleans he gave out an
interview. The reporter found him neatly dressed in a blue
flannel suit and black hat, a glove on his injured left hand. He
was "quiet, cool and considerate," the journalist reported, and his
appearance, in spite of his youth, was almost patriarchal. He also
found Hood willing to talk, but he limited his remarks to one
subject almost exclusively—a defense of himself and of his conduct
of the Atlanta and Tennessee campaigns. It was virtually a repeti-
tion of what he had said in his final report—the men were dispirited and his officers failed him at crucial points. It was the
account he was to give over and over again in the next few years
and which finally became the substance of his *Advance and Retreat*. As a matter of fact, he informed the reporter, he was already
thinking of writing his memoirs so that everyone might know
the true story of his failure.[24]

A stray letter here and there indicates he spent the month of
December in and around his old home in Kentucky. His mother
was living in Mt. Sterling at the time and the hills were full of
friends of the family and relatives. Whether he had made up his
mind at this time that New Orleans offered a better opportunity
than Texas cannot be determined, but it appears that he had.

While he was in Kentucky he borrowed $10,000 from friends (forty friends put up $250.00 apiece) and returned to New Orleans in January of 1866.[25] There were numerous rumors as to what he proposed to do in New Orleans. One was that he would become a part of an organization which would build a factory for the manufacturing of cotton rope. Another was that he would head a company with a capital of $200,000 for the purpose of draining and sweeping the muddy, dusty, dirty streets of the city by machinery.[26]

But he did neither. Instead, he went in business for himself. In February 1866 he, with John C. Barelli and Fred N. Thayer, established the firm of "J. B. Hood and Co., Cotton Factors and Commission Merchants," with offices and warehouse at 100 Common Street.[27] While he had been away in Kentucky his San Antonio friends had started a state-wide drive for funds to provide him with "a suitable homestead and competency" as a "debt of gratitude." Now that he had decided to settle permanently in New Orleans he politely declined the proposed gift.[28]

Number 100 Common Street is at the point where Canal and Common meet at the river. From his desk Hood could look out on the levee and the bustling revival of trade evidenced by the river steamers and ocean vessels tied up along the wharves.[29] The city had suffered little destruction during the war and now her people looked forward with optimism to the future, to the time when New Orleans would again be the queen city by the river. Some things had changed with the war, of course. Gone were the octoroon balls and *café au lait* mistresses kept in grand style; and their going was symbolic of the passing of an era. But the city managed to retain many of its strangely contradictory moods— partly European, partly American, without too much mixture to water down the flavor of either. Business directories showed a polyglot salmagundi of names—Fitzpatrick, de la Houssaye, Donnier, Brocato, McPherson, Hernandez, Fineburg and plain Smith.

Along the water front the dives were still as dangerous as in Marseilles, and on Basin Street the gambling houses, bars and whore houses did a thriving business. On Royal and Bourbon streets upper-class Creoles gathered in the evenings in their cool patios, conversing politely in soft fluid French and sipping their drinks. In the Garden District well-to-do American and English families entertained in vast chandeliered drawing rooms. On Congo Square the Negroes wore the grass thin with their ritualistic voodoo dances.

To this brazen, brawling, lusty city with its tradition of good food, charming manners and a wickedness which would put Sodom and Gomorrah to shame came many ex-Confederate officers of high rank. Beauregard was back home and president of a railroad. Soon he and Jubal Early would head the fantastic octopus known as the Louisiana lottery. Buckner, Hood's friend and fellow Kentuckian, was there in the brokerage and real-estate business. Only a stone's throw from Hood at 189 Gravier Street fiery little "Fightin' Joe" Wheeler was running a hardware and carriage business. Longstreet also had come to the city to engage in the brokerage business and at the same time to accept the presidency of the Life Association of America.[30] They had all come with one purpose—to pick up the thread of their lives and to earn a livelihood.

Hardly had they hung up their hats before "Radical" reconstruction descended on New Orleans and the South. On March 2, 1867, Congress passed the first of a series of acts affecting the conquered states. The South was divided into five military districts and a major general placed in control of each. Whenever the people came to their senses and drew up constitutions enfranchising the Negroes, disenfranchising most of the "rebels" and providing for the ratification of the 14th amendment the state might seek readmission. What would these men to whom the South had looked for military leadership do?

Hood's good friend from the old army days, General Phil Sheridan, was put in charge of the district of Louisiana and Texas. Hardly had he begun his duties when the New Orleans *Times* put the question squarely up to these men. Calling them by name—Beauregard, Hood, Longstreet and others—the *Times* urged them to give their views. "A great city like New Orleans," the editorial ran, "will be looked to all through the South, as both entitled and bound by the highest obligations of honor and duty to assume her just share of the duty and responsibility of indicating the line and wise course for our southern people to adopt in our present situation."[31]

The first and only one of the group to answer in print was Longstreet. Immediately following the challenge of the *Times* he sent in his letter of opinion. "The striking feature, and one that our people should keep in view," he wrote, "is that we are a conquered people. Recognizing this fairly and squarely there is but one course left for wise men to pursue. Accept the terms that are offered us by the conquerers! . . . Our people earnestly desire that the constitutional government shall be reestablished, and the only means to accomplish this is to comply with the requirements of the recent congressional legislation. . . . Let us accept the terms as we are duty-bound to do, and if there is any lack of good faith let it be upon others."[32]

And that was the beginning of the end for "old Pete" as a rebel. In New Orleans, as elsewhere in the South, he was denounced as a traitor and a Black Republican. It was rumored that he had called a meeting of the "New Orleans Generals" before he sent the letter and that they had agreed to support him in his stand, but in later years he denied this. "There never was such a meeting held," he stated. "General Hood met me and we talked about the editorial. He said in effect that it aimed at a condition that we all devoutly hoped for, but he added, 'If you declare yourself on those lines the Southern press and the Southern people will vilify and abuse you. It may be very patriotic and all that, but it will be very foolish.' . . . That evening I wrote my letter on Reconstruction to the *Times*. It was first published in its columns and first read by General Hood when it appeared in print. However much General Hood may have shared my sentiments he never trusted himself to public expression of them. . . . There never was an arrangement under which my letter was to be followed. . . . If I did tread the wine press alone, I did so on my own motion."[33] Actually it appears that Hood's ideas were somewhat in line with those of Longstreet with this difference—Hood's views were expressed before the passage of the radical reconstruction legislation.[34] After it was passed he maintained silence.

Perhaps the first tangible results of Longstreet's stand were felt in his business. As pressure and indignation against him increased he found it necessary to get out of business. "The day after the announcement old comrades passed me on the streets without speaking," he wrote. "Business began to grow dull. General Hood (the only one of my old comrades who occasionally visited me) thought that he could save the insurance business, and in a few weeks I found myself at leisure."[35] The insurance business was turned over to Hood early in 1869, and undoubtedly he was glad to get it for it is evident that his brokerage and commission business was doing none too well. The salary of $5,000 as president of the company was more money than he had ever made even in Confederate money as a full general.[36]

But purely business matters were not the only concern of Hood during these early years in New Orleans, for he had fallen in love again. Sally Preston had returned from Paris in 1867 and married Rollins Lowndes. Whether Hood had been "carrying a torch" for her can only be a matter of conjecture. Whatever memories he may have cherished, he had met a young lady in New Orleans equally as charming and talented as Sally, and on April 30, 1868, with Simon Bolivar Buckner as his best man and a special dispensation for mixed religion he married her.[37] She was Anna Maria Hennen, daughter of Duncan N. Hennen, a prominent New Orleans attorney, and granddaughter of Alfred Hennen, a justice of the Supreme Court of Louisiana.[38] Portraits and descriptions indicate she was a young woman of considerable beauty, charm and talent. The Hennen family did not possess what is usually termed a great fortune but, in the colloquial, Mr. Hennen left his wife and daughter "well fixed." They were able to afford an apartment at the exclusive Pontalba Apartments and to maintain the family plantation "The Retreat" near Hammond, Louisiana. They were also able to give Anna the benefit of a Parisian education.[39] Although the war had depleted her inheritance, Hood indeed had "married well."

The years from 1866 to 1877 were the Reconstruction years in Louisiana—a period of storm, stress and corruption in public affairs. For Hood, however, they brought the most peaceful period of his life. He and his wife together with her mother moved to a great high-ceilinged house in the Garden District at the uptown, lake side of Third and Camp streets, a house ordinarily referred to as "The Hood Mansion."[40] Here for ten years he lived in comparative comfort and security with his growing family—and grow it did! The first year it was a girl, Lydia Marie. The next year it was twins, Anna Bell and Ethel. Then came singles, John Bell II and Duncan Norbert. Twins came the next year and the next, Marion and Lillian, Odile and Ida. Then singles again, Oswald and Anna. In all there were eleven children in ten years—three sets of twins and five singles.[41] It is said that when Hood took his family north for the summers together with Mrs. Hennen and a nurse or two, the hotel employees would laugh and say to each other: "Here comes Hood's brigade."[42]

During the period 1870-1878 it appears that Hood prospered. The newspapers report that "he engaged in various enterprises that at one time enriched him,"[43] but he might have made even more money had he been willing to associate himself with the lottery. This powerful and corrupt organization chartered by the carpetbag state legislature in 1868 continued uninterrupted into the nineties, milking the public of millions of dollars. So insidious was its influence that friend was set against friend and families were divided into pro and anti factions. Everywhere one turned in the city he was confronted by lottery tickets selling generally at $1.00 each. Drawings were held monthly and semi-annually and then a grand annual whirl of the wheel for prizes totaling $1,000,-000 (for which $2,000,000 had been paid in). It is estimated that the annual "take" of the lottery was approximately $28,000,000 of which not more than 52 per cent went for prizes and charitable donations.[44] Do you want a lucky number? Buy a ticket numbered 6 if you have seen a stray dog—or 14 for a drunk—or 11 for an exposed feminine leg. Or even better than that, for five cents strolling vendors would have their pet parakeets draw a lucky ticket for you.[45]

On the day of the drawing the city was in a ferment, as though it were Mardi Gras. Crowds gathered and vendors cried their last-minute ticket sales. Inside the theater where the great wheel sat on the stage ladies occupied the boxes, enduring the miasmic stench caused by the mingled odors of whisky, tobacco and un-bathed bodies. Then from the wings stepped a "commissioner." It was the handsome swarthy Beauregard. (The next drawing would be presided over by bearded, patriarchal Jubal A. Early.) The wheel was spun, and a blindfolded boy reached in and pulled out a gutta-percha tube with a slip inside bearing a number. Solemnly the commissioner opened the tube and read the number. Someone had won first prize and the crowd shouted. Then another tube was drawn and then another until the allotted number of prizes was awarded.[46]

For their few minutes work each month Beauregard and Early were paid handsome annual salaries variously estimated at from

$12,000 to $30,000—but they were worth it. These Confederate heroes gave the game a semblance of respectability. It was this position of commissioner, good authority has it, which was offered to Hood and which he declined. It is related that his declining the offer caused some coolness between him and some of his friends and even with some of Mrs. Hood's relatives who were involved in the scheme.[47] Apparently Hood shared the shame which thousands of persons throughout the South felt at the sight of their former leaders presiding over a lottery. He preferred to carry on his insurance business and to buy and sell on the cotton exchange.

These indeed must have been peaceful years for Hood. A good home handsomely furnished,[48] a charming wife and happy children, a position of dignity in the community and what he believed to be reasonable financial security—these were his. But there were bitter memories of Atlanta, Franklin and Nashville. He was steadily working on his memoirs to show that Joe Johnston and Hardee were to blame. The fact that these two were now teamed up in promoting the Meridian and Selma Railroad and were frequent visitors to New Orleans only reminded him of the old days. He was nearing the conclusion of these memoirs when calamity struck.

It is impossible to describe in exact detail just what happened in the winter of 1878-1879, but when the whirlwind had passed Hood was cleaned out, broke. His insurance company folded up along with all the others in New Orleans except two.[49] The great yellow-fever epidemic of the summer of 1878 virtually isolated New Orleans and closed the cotton exchange. Hood apparently was caught in the market and wiped out.[50] Whatever may have been the cause, the fact remains that by the summer of 1879 the Hood family was in dire straits. Each previous summer he had been able to take the family out of the city, but this summer they had to remain in New Orleans—and this fact completed the destruction of the Hood family.

The summer of 1878 had been the period of terror in New Orleans. During that time more than 3,000 persons died of the dread yellow fever. During 1879, however, there were only seventeen cases and six deaths—three of them in the Hood household.[51] On July 24 the *Times* called attention to the fact that "there is not a case of yellow fever in the city."[52] On August 20, however, a case developed in the house diagonally across the street from the Hood home and Dr. T. G. Richardson, the family physician, advised Hood to take his family out of the city.[53] He had been very close to Dr. Richardson since Chickamauga, where the kindly doctor had performed the amputation, but this summer he couldn't afford to leave. So he and the family stayed on, and on August 21 Bronze John paid a call.[54] Mrs. Hood was the first victim, and on Sunday, August 24, 1879, at 9:25 in the evening she died.[55] On the twenty-sixth ten-year-old Lydia came down, and on Thursday the twenty-seventh, Hood himself was stricken.

From the very first his physicians were concerned about him. For months he had worried himself sick over finances, and the death of Mrs. Hood had almost taken away the desire to live. On Friday it seemed as if he might have a chance, but by Saturday it was becoming obvious that he would not recover. That day at noon Lydia died and that afternoon a minister was called to administer the last rites of the Episcopal Church. Shortly after this Hood became delirious. Once or twice he attempted to raise himself in bed, but he was easily controlled. "Only once," it is reported, "did his mind seem to revert to those grand old heroic days when his name was a rallying cry, and he battled with all the energy of his great and fearless soul for his native South. In a tone of command he exclaimed, 'I want those stores taken from my own commissary.' "[56] Then he lifted himself up, threw his head around and seemed to be gazing into the distance with flashing eyes and such an expression as he wore when in the heat of battle he looked back for his old brigade. Shortly after eleven o'clock he regained consciousness. For a few minutes he talked with his friends around the bed about the children. Ten of them were left and they would have no home. But, he murmured as he slipped back into unconsciousness, the Texas brigade would care for them—that is what he wished. Then as he ceased speaking he was shaken by violent hiccuping—and then came the black vomit, dread sign of death. Suddenly his face stiffened. Its lines were sharply defined. John Bell Hood was dead.[57] He was forty-eight years of age.

The problem of the children was indeed a pressing one. Left with an aging grandmother and without money, they became wards of the South. Immediately friends began to raise a fund for them. Subscriptions were received, a memorial edition of Hood's *Advance and Retreat* was brought out by Beauregard, souvenir pictures of the family were sold and other methods resorted to for raising money.[58] Mrs. Hennen made a trip to Texas to confer with officials of the newly organized Hood's Texas Brigade Association who were prepared to buy a house and hire a housemother to care for them. But in the end it was decided that perhaps it would be best if each child had an individual home. When this decision was announced, offers to adopt flooded in from all parts of the country. One by one the children were placed in good homes.[59]

It has often been said that Hood was a failure as a soldier and as a businessman; and, measured by most standards of success, this was true. At Nashville his military reputation was shattered, and at New Orleans he came to the close of his life with a business disaster. It seemed almost as if he were predestined to fail—as if there were in the background of his life the doleful chanting chorus of a Greek tragedy always reminding him of impending doom. Struggle as he might, he could not shake off the fate that pursued him. (Or it might be less obscure to drop all talk of fates and Greek drama and simply say that he got a lot of bad breaks.)

To a degree, of course, he himself was to blame for his mis-

fortunes, but there were many instances when tragic results were
due to the breaks alone. There was, for example, the day Dodge's
corps at Atlanta blundered into a position never intended for it
and thus prevented Hardee from rolling back the Federal left. Had
he not encountered this situation Franklin and Nashville probably
would not have been necessary. Spring Hill was another such
tragedy for him. And, as if he had not had his share of misfortune
as a soldier, the *aedes aegypti* descended on New Orleans in the
summer of 1878 with their bite of death, closing the port, isolating
the city and driving Hood's and scores of other business firms into
bankruptcy. The next summer the mosquitoes virtually singled
out the Hood home and destroyed it. Indeed there were reasons
other than heredity why his face wore a look of perpetual sorrow.

Most of his worst mistakes seem to have grown out of the nature
of his personality. He was essentially a man of emotion rather
than of intellect. He was never a reasoning and analytical man
who carefully weighed all possible factors in a given problem or
situation. Rather he was much inclined to be impetuous in his decisions, trusting his intuition and his blind optimism to see him
through.

As a man of emotion he was given to fierce loyalties and equally
fierce enmities. To Robert E. Lee and Jefferson Davis he gave a
blind allegiance which made it impossible for him to see any faults
they might have had. For Joseph E. Johnston he had a searing
hatred which steadily grew more consuming in the years after
the war and made it impossible for him to see any virtue in this
officer. To Hood the Confederate cause was a great ideal—almost
a religion—and he fought for this abstraction with complete abandon. At times his zeal tended to overrun itself, however, and it
was unfortunate that he was not sufficiently introspective to detect
his own errors and correct them.

He was happiest and most successful when personally leading
his troops in battle, for it was here that he could best satisfy the

necessity for an emotional outlet. In battle his great sorrowful eyes blazed with a terrific fury. He was transformed from a shy, awkward young general perplexed by the minutiae of paper work, tactical details and camp routine into a fearless and almost terrible leader who inspired his men to heroic feats. This quality of leadership so necessary in a combat officer became one of his greatest liabilities as a commanding general. He never was, as an independent commander, able to think of battle except in terms of long lines of men charging to glory across an open field. Planning the details of a campaign and personally supervising every feature of it was always distasteful to him.

Off the battlefield he was reserved and reticent. Even when he was convivial he was not loquacious, and one finds it difficult to imagine his giving forth with a deep, satisfying belly laugh. At most his eyes twinkled and he smiled broadly when amused. This natural reticence and dignity increased in civilian life after the war. He also grew more religious after his conversion and baptism by Bishop Polk during the Atlanta campaign. In religion he seemed to find a release from his problems and more and more one finds the expression "It is God's will" creeping into his conversation. Lacking the excitement of battle after the war and faced with the necessity of caring for his growing family, he became even more subdued. Gone was the old impetuous, gambling Hood; he had become at forty-five a patient, bearded, benevolent patriarch—a man of great integrity and great sorrows.

It is quite possible that of all the tributes paid him after his death he, being an emotional man and a religious man, would have appreciated most the one that came from a former chaplain of the Army of Tennessee: "I never looked into the face of General Hood, but felt an inspiration coming from him upon me always to act out the true, the brave, the right thing."[60]

NOTES, ACKNOWLEDGMENTS AND INDEX

NOTES

CHAPTER I

[1] Stanley F. Horn, *The Army of Tennessee* (Indianapolis, 1941), 418.

[2] Otto Eisenschiml and Ralph Newman, *The American Iliad* (Indianapolis, 1947), 643.

[3] *Ibid.*, 645.

[4] Douglas Southall Freeman, *R. E. Lee, A Biography*, 4 vols. (New York, 1935), I, 329. Cited hereafter as Freeman, *R. E. Lee.*

[5] Quoted in Horn, *The Army of Tennessee*, 417. The statement is attributed to Schofield.

[6] Bell Irvin Wiley, *The Life of Johnny Reb* (Indianapolis, 1943), 121. Horn in *The Army of Tennessee*, 418, gives a slightly different version of the words.

[7] The Dallas *Herald* of July 22, 1865, reflected this admiration for Hood when it stated that "he has a home in the heart and under the roof of every brave and generous Texan."

[8] Certified copy of will taken from Will Book IV, 82, Records of Frederick County, Virginia. Copy in possession of Dr. George F. Doyle, Winchester, Kentucky, who has made an extensive collection of data concerning Kentucky's early doctors. Cited hereafter as Doyle Collection.

[9] John H. Gwathmey, *Historical Register of Virginians in the Revolution* (Richmond, 1938), 289. Luke Hood's service record has not been located.

[10] Cemetery records in Doyle Collection.

[11] Thomas Speed, *The Wilderness Road, A Description of the Routes of Travel by Which the Pioneers and Early Settlers Came to Kentucky* (Louisville, 1886), 42-43.

[12] MSS. of family records of Hood, Callaway and French families. In possession of James H. French of Winchester, Kentucky. Many of the items are excerpts from the Draper Collection. Cited hereafter as French Collection.

[13] Willard Rouse Jillson, *Old Kentucky Entries and Deeds* (Louisville, 1926), 421. Filson Club Publication No. 34.

[14] Cemetery records, Doyle Collection.

[15] Unidentified clipping in Doyle Collection.

[16] Related to the author by Fanny Hood Hampton, Winchester, Kentucky.

[17] Birth date from tombstone in family cemetery.

[18] Charles W. Bryan, Jr., "Richard Callaway, Kentucky Pioneer," *Filson Club Historical Quarterly*, IX, 48-49. The marble marker at the site of Fort Boonesborough lists the following adults in the fort at the time of its founding: Daniel Boone; Rebecca Boone; Jemima Boone; Squire Boone; William Bentley; Colonel Richard Callaway; Betsy Callaway; Frances Callaway; Adam Caperton; General Green Clay; Captain John Holder; Daniel Crews; William Cradlebauch; William Chenault; Elizabeth Mullhis Chenault; Captain James Estill; Samuel Estill; Colonel Ezekiel Field; Colonel Nathaniel Hart; Colonel Richard Henderson; Dr. Hinds; Richard Hogan. Evidently the younger children of Colonel Callaway arrived later.

[19] *Ibid.*

[20] Original commission in French Collection.

[21] Original deeds in French Collection.

[22] Tax records, Bath County, Kentucky, 1823. The three Hoods apparently were "reading" medicine at the time.

[23] Records of Bath County, Kentucky. Deed Book E, 119, 266. Deed Book F, 227.

[24] *Ibid.*, Book F, 90.

[25] Matriculation records, University of Pennsylvania School of Medicine, 1829-1830. In Medical School Library.

[26] *Ibid.*, 1834-1835. Dr. Hood later related that as a young man he was subject to hemorrhage of the lungs with a "weak or inefficient digestive apparatus and a morbid sensibility to the effect of heat, cold and moisture." Apparently he displayed some of the symptoms of tuberculosis for he further relates: "Frequently when in health I was suddenly reduced by a flow of blood from the lungs. . . ." John W. Hood, *The Principles and Practice of Medicine* (Philadelphia, 1843), ix, xi.

[27] Registration Book, Jefferson Medical College, 1829-1837. In alumni office of the college.

[28] Tax records for Bath County do not show John W. Hood as a taxpayer after 1834. Tax records of Montgomery County were destroyed by fire, so it is impossible to give the exact date of the move to Montgomery County.

[29] Jillson, *Old Kentucky Entries and Deeds*, 421.

[30] Records of Montgomery County, Kentucky. Will Book D, 515-516.

[31] James H. French to the author.

[32] Destruction of the Montgomery County tax records makes it impossible to determine how many slaves Dr. Hood owned. In the first disposition of his estate found in Deed Book XXVI, 86, Records of Montgomery County, Kentucky, it appears that he owned several—perhaps as many as thirty.

[33] The records of his land purchases are found in Deed Book XX, 310, 404; Book XXI, 132; Book XXII, 274, 407; Book XXIII, 85; Book XXIV, 123, 396, 578. Records of Montgomery County, Kentucky.

⁸⁴ Miss Julia Graves, Winchester, Kentucky, to the author; Mary Boykin Chesnut, *A Diary from Dixie* (New York, 1929), xxi.

³⁵ S. J. Conkwright, *History of the Churches of Boone's Creek Baptist Association* (Winchester, Kentucky, 1923), 137.

³⁶ During the Atlanta campaign Hood was baptized into the Episcopal faith by Bishop General Leonidas Polk.

³⁷ Related to the author by Fanny Hood Hampton, Winchester, Kentucky. For an account of the legendary silver mine which absorbed the lifelong interest of James Hood and many other Kentuckians see Thomas D. Clark, *The Kentucky* (New York, 1942), 28-31.

³⁸ Miss Julia Graves, Winchester, Kentucky, to the author.

³⁹ The people with whom the author discussed the story prefer to remain anonymous since they fear they might become involved in a pending suit against Richard O'Connor and the publishers of *Life,* brought by Sydney Hart Anderson, a descendant of Anne Mitchell, over a story appearing in the October 25, 1948, issue of the magazine. Details of the suit are given in the Lexington (Ky.) *Herald,* January 25, 1949.

⁴⁰ A member of the Hood family who wishes to remain anonymous says General Hood always seemed to attract women because of his deference, shyness and physical good looks. His life bears abundant proof of this.

⁴¹ In the final disposition of his estate Dr. Hood required that each child should "account for what I have charged them with in my book. . . ." Deed Book XXV, 369-370, Records of Montgomery County, Kentucky.

⁴² There were five medical colleges in Philadelphia before 1860: Philadelphia College of Medicine; Franklin Medical College; Pennsylvania Medical College; Jefferson Medical College; and the University of Pennsylvania School of Medicine. Records and bulletins of all are preserved. The latter two schools are, of course, still in existence and have their own records. Records of the other three are in the archives of the College of Physicians Library in Philadelphia.

⁴³ These trusses and supporters are described and pictured in *Principles and Practice of Medicine,* Chap. 5.

⁴⁴ Philadelphia, 1848.

⁴⁵ Philadelphia, 1848.

⁴⁶ Review of Hood's *Principles and Practice of Medicine* in *The American Journal of the Medical Sciences,* XVII (January, 1849), 157.

⁴⁷ *Ibid.*

⁴⁸ Mrs. Julia Prewitt Chenault of Mt. Sterling, Kentucky, has preserved several stories about Dr. Hood's medical school and the cadavers in the orchard. One of the students, George Graves, fell in love with and married Dr. Hood's youngest daughter, Keziah.

⁴⁹ *Clark County Democrat,* September 3, 1879.

⁵⁰ J. B. Hood, *Advance and Retreat—Personal Experiences in the United*

States and Confederate States Armies (New Orleans, 1880), 5. Cited here-after as *Advance and Retreat*.

[51] Original appointment papers in War Records Division, National Archives.

[52] James H. French to the author.

CHAPTER II

[1] Many of these conditions were improved under Lee's superintendency, 1852-1855. See Freeman, *R. E. Lee*, I, Chap. XIX.

[2] *Regulations Established for the Organization and Government of the Military Academy at West Point, New York* (New York, 1839), 25-26. Cited hereafter as *Regulations*.

[3] MSS. of history of student life at West Point before 1860 by Sidney Forman, 149. The author is indebted to Dr. Forman, archivist at the Military Academy Library, for permission to quote from his manuscript. Cited hereafter as Forman MSS.

[4] *Ibid.* Benny Havens maintained his tavern at Buttermilk Falls, now Highland Falls, just outside the post, until 1859.

[5] *Regulations*, 28-36.

[6] *Ibid.*, 10.

[7] *Official Register of the Officers and Cadets of the U. S. Military Academy, 1850*. Cited hereafter as *Official Register*.

[8] Southern cadets usually did not make grades equal to those of Northern. Entrance requirements at the academy were kept low so that cadets from the South could enter.

[9] *Regulations*, 11.

[10] *Official Register, 1851*.

[11] U. S. Military Academy Library Circulation Records, 1847-1853.

[12] *Ibid.*

[13] *Official Register, 1852*.

[14] Lieutenant General John M. Schofield, *Forty-Six Years in the Army* (New York, 1897), 14.

[15] *Post Orders*, Book III, 673.

[16] U. S. Military Academy Register of Delinquencies, VI, 712; VII, 46.

[17] *Official Register, 1853*.

[18] *Post Orders*, Book III, 731.

[19] See Freeman, *R. E. Lee*, I, 325.

[20] *Orders U. S. Corps of Cadets, January 25, 1849-December 28, 1859.* Special Orders No. 117, December 21, 1852.

[21] Special Orders No. 200, December 28, 1852. *Post Orders*, Book IV, 15. Cadet Rich was confined to his room for five consecutive Saturdays

from 2:00 P.M. until tattoo and required to perform five extra tours of Sunday guard duty.

22 Lee's report for December 1852 is on file in the War Records Division, National Archives. Schofield's reference to Hood's "unauthorized festivities of Christmas" supports the theory that the crime was an evening at Benny Havens'. See Schofield, *Forty-Six Years in the Army,* 138.

23 Special Orders No. 200, *Post Orders,* Book IV, 15.

24 Schofield, *Forty-Six Years in the Army,* 138.

25 *Ibid.*

26 Forman MSS., 184-196.

27 *Official Register, 1853.*

28 Original letter in Old Records Division, Adjutant General's Office.

29 Hood, *Advance and Retreat,* 6.

30 *Ibid.*

31 Robert Glass Cleland, *From Wilderness to Empire, A History of California* (New York, 1944), 269-270. See also Rupert Norval Richardson and Carl Coke Rister, *The Greater Southwest* (Glendale, 1934), Chap. XI-XIV.

32 Orders, January 26, 1854. Old Records Division, Adjutant General's Office.

33 Hood, *Advance and Retreat,* 6.

34 Joseph Ellison, *California and the Nation,* University of California Publications in History, XVI (Berkeley, 1927), 93, 102.

35 Hood, *Advance and Retreat,* 6.

36 Rupert Norval Richardson, *Texas: the Lone Star State* (New York, 1943), 202.

37 Carl Coke Rister, *Robert E. Lee in Texas* (Norman, 1946), 13.

38 Richardson, *Texas: the Lone Star State,* 203.

39 The appointment was made May 25, 1855, to rank from March 3, 1855. Returns, 2nd Cavalry, October 15, 1855. War Records Division, National Archives.

40 Hood, *Advance and Retreat,* 7.

41 *Ibid.*

42 Rister, *Robert E. Lee in Texas,* 16. Perhaps the best way to locate the area in which the 2nd Cavalry operated is to draw on a map of Texas a line connecting the present cities of Sherman, Fort Worth, Waco and Austin. Then to the west draw another line from Wichita Falls through Abilene to the Pecos River. The vast territory in between known as the North Central Plains is the country patrolled by Hood's regiment.

43 *Ibid.*

44 Returns, 2nd Cavalry, January, 1856; March, 1856. War Records Division, National Archives.

[45] Miss Julia Graves to the author.

[46] Records of Montgomery County, Kentucky, Book XXVI, 86.

[47] *Ibid.*, 85. October 8, 1856.

[48] Returns, 2nd Cavalry, December 1856. War Records Division, National Archives.

[49] Returns of the 2nd Cavalry for the years 1857-1860 show these various assignments.

[50] Hood, *Advance and Retreat*, 8.

[51] R. H. Williams, *With the Border Ruffians, Memoirs of the Far West 1852-1863* (London, 1907), 213.

[52] Hood, *Advance and Retreat*, 8.

[53] Richardson, *Texas: the Lone Star State*, 203. See also Rupert Norval Richardson, *The Comanche Barrier to South Plains Settlement* (Glendale, 1933), 211-233.

[54] Freeman, *R. E. Lee*, I, 365-367.

[55] The narrative of the expedition is taken from Hood's *Advance and Retreat*, 8-14, and *The National Intelligencer*, August 29, 1857.

[56] *The National Intelligencer*, August 29, 1857. Most of the action took place in what is now the area in Sutton, Crockett, Valverde and Edwards counties, Texas. Devil's River rises in the northern part of Crockett County and flows southward across Valverde County to the Rio Grande.

[57] Chesnut, *A Diary from Dixie*, 230.

[58] Regimental Returns for the years indicated in War Records Division, National Archives.

[59] Hood, *Advance and Retreat*, 15; New York *Times*, August 7, 1864, quoting Mobile *Telegraph*.

[60] Hood file, Old Records Division, Adjutant General's Office, contains the pertinent facts of the case.

CHAPTER III

[1] Original letter in Hood file, Old Records Division, Adjutant General's Office.

[2] Hood, *Advance and Retreat*, 16.

[3] It was this incident plus his later assignment as commander of the Texas brigade which gave rise to the generally accepted idea that Hood was a native Texan.

[4] Special Orders No. 51, May 16, 1861. Special Orders of the Adjutant and Inspector General's Office, Confederate States, 1861, 21. Hood states in *Advance and Retreat*, 16, that he arrived in Richmond "about the 5th of May." From his orders it would appear he arrived in Richmond a few days later than this date, however.

[5] Ellsworth Eliot, Jr., *West Point in the Confederacy* (New York, 1941), xvii-xix, 31-32.

[6] Hood, *Advance and Retreat*, 16.

[7] *Ibid.*, 17.

[8] Lee to Magruder, May 27, 1861, *War of the Rebellion: Official Records of the Union and Confederate Armies* (Washington, 1880-1901), Series I, II, 883. Cited hereafter as *Official Records*. Strangely enough Lee refers to Hood as "Captain" although this letter antedated Magruder's action in elevating Hood to that rank.

[9] Apparently commissions were never issued to Hood as captain and major. However, he was accepted as such by all his superiors up the line to Richmond. The same may be said for Hood's rank as lieutenant colonel, which came a few days later. See Hood, *Advance and Retreat*, 18; Magruder to Lee, July 13, 1861, *Official Records*, Series I, II, 576; Lee to Magruder, July 15, 1861, *ibid.*, 298; Colonel R. O. Johnston to Major G. B. Cosby, July 25, 1861, *ibid.*, 576.

[10] Brevet Major General Joseph B. Carr, "Operations of 1861 About Fort Monroe," Robert V. Johnson and Clarence C. Bull (eds.), *Battles and Leaders of the Civil War*, 4 vols. (New York, 1884-1887), II, 148-150.

[11] Confederate casualties were 11 out of approximately 1,400 troops. Federal casualties were 76 out of approximately 4,400 troops. *Official Records*, Series I, II, 82, 84, 95-96, 97.

[12] Hood's report, July 13, 1861, *Official Records*, Series I, II, 297.

[13] July 13, 1861, *ibid.*

[14] July 15, 1861, *ibid.*, 298.

[15] Douglas Southall Freeman, *Lee's Lieutenants, A Study in Command*, 3 vols. (New York, 1942), I, 198. Cited hereafter as *Lee's Lieutenants*.

[16] Richardson, *Texas: the Lone Star State*, 250-256.

[17] J. B. Polley, *Hood's Texas Brigade, Its Marches, Its Battles, Its Achievements* (New York, 1910), 13. Cited hereafter as *Hood's Texas Brigade*.

[18] Richardson, *Texas: the Lone Star State*, 254.

[19] Polley, *Hood's Texas Brigade*, 14.

[20] *Ibid.* Hood's commission as colonel was dated September 30, 1861. Hood file, Old Records Division, Adjutant General's Office.

[21] New York *Times*, August 7, 1864. Quoting Mobile *Telegraph*.

[22] Freeman, *Lee's Lieutenants*, I, 297.

[23] Muster rolls of brigade as recorded in Polley, *Hood's Texas Brigade*, 296-347.

[24] Reprinted from William Ransom Hogan, *The Texas Republic: A Social and Economic History*, copyright 1946, by the University of Oklahoma Press. Reprinted by kind permission of the publisher.

[25] There never were at any one time enough Texans in Virginia to make up a full brigade. They were brigaded first with the 18th Georgia and later with Hampton's Legion.

[26] Polley, *Hood's Texas Brigade,* 13-14, 18.

[27] Hood, *Advance and Retreat,* 19.

[28] *Ibid.,* 19-20.

[29] Polley, *Hood's Texas Brigade,* 16.

[30] *Ibid.*

[31] *Ibid.,* 17.

[32] For McClellan's own account of the campaign see *Battles and Leaders,* II, 160-187.

[33] President Davis, Lee his military adviser and Joseph E. Johnston, field commander.

[34] The commission was dated March 3, 1862. Hood file, Old Records Division, Adjutant General's Office.

[35] Hood, *Advance and Retreat,* 20.

[36] *Official Records,* Series I, XI, 50.

[37] Polley, *Hood's Texas Brigade,* 22.

[38] See Warren Lee Goss, "Yorktown and Williamsburg," *Battles and Leaders,* II, 189-199.

[39] George B. McClellan, "The Peninsular Campaign," *ibid.,* 170.

[40] Misroon to McClellan, April 5, 1862, *Official Records,* Series I, XVI, part 3, 80.

[41] McClellan to Lincoln, April 5, 1862, *ibid.,* 71.

[42] McClellan to Lincoln, April 6, 1862, *ibid.,* 73.

[43] McClellan to Stanton, April 10, 1862, *ibid.,* 86.

[44] Stanton to McClellan, April 11, 1862, *ibid.,* 90.

[45] Stanton to McClellan, April 13, 1862, *ibid.,* 94. McClellan to Stanton, May 4, 1862, *ibid.,* 134.

[46] H. J. Eckenrode and Bryan Conrad, *James Longstreet, Lee's War Horse* (Chapel Hill, 1936), 34-38.

[47] Report of Major General Gustavus W. Smith, May 12, 1862, *Official Records,* Series I, XI, part 1, 627.

[48] It was not unusual for troops in both armies to march with unloaded guns. This prevented them from taking pot shots at birds or stray bottles. See McClellan's orders on the subject in *Official Records,* Series I, XI, part 3, 82.

[49] Hood, *Advance and Retreat,* 21.

[50] Hood's report, May 7, 1862, *Official Records,* Series I, XI, part 1, 630-632.

[51] Whiting's report, November 14, 1862, *ibid.,* 629-630.

[52] *Ibid.;* Smith's report, *ibid.,* 628; Hill's report, *ibid.,* 605.

[53] "Anecdotes of the Peninsular Campaign," *Battles and Leaders,* II, 276.

CHAPTER IV

[1] Polley, *Hood's Texas Brigade*, 29.

[2] Freeman, *Lee's Lieutenants*, I, 203.

[3] *Ibid.*, 211.

[4] Eliot, *West Point in the Confederacy*, 458.

[5] Davis to Johnston, May 26, 1862, *Official Records*, Series I, XI, part 3, 547.

[6] Freeman, *Lee's Lieutenants*, I, 220.

[7] See G. F. R. Henderson, *Stonewall Jackson and the American Civil War* (New York, 1949), Chapter X.

[8] Eckenrode and Conrad, *James Longstreet*, 42.

[9] Hill's report, undated, 1862, *Official Records*, Series I, XI, part 1, 943.

[10] None of these plans was revealed to Davis. In the Johnston manner he was keeping everything to himself.

[11] On May 28, Hatton's and Pettigrew's brigades had been added to Whiting's division. His division now consisted of Hood's, Hampton's, Whiting's own, Hatton's and Pettigrew's. Total strength was 10,592. *Official Records*, Series I, XI, part 3, 530, 558.

[12] Hill's report, *ibid.*, part 1, 943.

[13] Smith's report, June 23, 1862, *ibid.*, 990. Johnston's report, June 24, 1862, *ibid.*, 934. Johnston states that he ordered Hood to keep moving.

[14] *Ibid.*, 992.

[15] *Ibid.*, 991.

[16] Thomas L. Livermore, *Numbers and Losses in the Civil War in America 1861-1865* (New York, 1901), 81.

[17] Freeman, *R. E. Lee*, II, 74.

[18] *Ibid.*, 81-82.

[19] Wade Hampton was then on leave convalescing from the wound received. However, his "Legion" was still a part of Hood's brigade. So was the 18th Georgia.

[20] Polley, *Hood's Texas Brigade*, 33.

[21] Henderson, *Stonewall Jackson*, 298-299.

[22] J. B. Jones, *A Rebel War Clerk's Diary at the Confederate States Capitol* (New York, 1935), II, 37. (New edition edited by Howard Swiggett.)

[23] Polley, *Hood's Texas Brigade*, 34.

[24] Henderson, *Stonewall Jackson*, 300.

[25] Polley, *Hood's Texas Brigade*, 35. Hood states in *Advance and Retreat*, 24, that both he and Whiting knew before they left Richmond what the general plan was.

[26] *Ibid.*, 36.

[27] Freeman, *R. E. Lee*, II, 110-111; Henderson, *Stonewall Jackson*, 347-350; Eckenrode and Conrad, *Longstreet*, 63-64.

[28] Branch's report, undated, 1862, *Official Records*, Series I, XI, part 2, 881.

[29] *Ibid.*, 882.

[30] A. P. Hill's report, February 28, 1863, *ibid.*, 835.

[31] D. H. Hill's report, July 3, 1863, *ibid.*, 623.

[32] Longstreet's report, July 29, 1862, *ibid.*, 756.

[33] Jackson's report, February 20, 1863, *ibid.*, 552-553.

[34] Apparently Jackson never explained his tardiness and Lee never asked for such. The evidence indicates that the delay was due to: (1) unexpected opposition from Federal troops, (2) fatigue among his troops. See Freeman, *R. E. Lee*, II, 139-140; Henderson, *Stonewall Jackson*, 351.

[35] See reports of A. P. Hill, D. H. Hill, in *Official Records*, Series I, XI, part, 2, 835, 623.

[36] Lee's report, March 6, 1863, *ibid.*, 491.

[37] Livermore, *Numbers and Losses*, 82.

[38] Fitz John Porter's report, July 8, 1865, *Official Records*, Series I, XI, part 2, 221.

[39] W. H. C. Whiting's report, July ?, 1862, *ibid.*, 563.

[40] Longstreet's report, July 29, 1862, *ibid.*, 757.

[41] D. H. Hill's report, July 3, 1863, *ibid.*, 624-625.

[42] A. P. Hill's report, February 28, 1863, *ibid.*, 837.

[43] Lee's report, March 6, 1863, *ibid.*, 493.

[44] Hood, *Advance and Retreat*, 25.

[45] Polley, *Hood's Texas Brigade*, 57.

[46] Hood's report, July 10, 1862, *Official Records*, Series I, XI, part 2, 569; Whiting's report, undated, 1862, *ibid.*, 565.

[47] Polley, *Hood's Texas Brigade*, 64-65.

[48] *Ibid.*, 57.

[49] Whiting's report, July ?, 1862, *Official Records*, Series I, XI, part 2, 563.

[50] Freeman, *R. E. Lee*, II, 155.

[51] Major General E. M. Law, "On the Confederate Right at Gaines's Mill," *Battles and Leaders*, II, 364.

[52] Rev. W. H. Hitchcock, "Recollections of a Participant in the Charge," *ibid.*, 346.

[53] Major General Philip St. George Cooke, "The Charge of Cooke's Cavalry at Gaines's Mill," *ibid.*, 344.

[54] Hood, *Advance and Retreat*, 29.

[55] Jackson's report, February 20, 1863, *Official Records*, Series I, XI, part 2, 559.

[56] Freeman, *R. E. Lee*, II, 155.

[57] Whiting's report, *Official Records*, Series I, XI, part 2, 565. Colonel Archer, former commander of the 5th Texas had been promoted and was at the time of the battle commanding a brigade in A. P. Hill's division.

[58] Polley, *Hood's Texas Brigade*, 68.

[59] *Ibid.*, 48-49.

[60] Hood, *Advance and Retreat*, 29.

[61] Freeman, *R. E. Lee*, II, 159.

[62] *Ibid.*, 161.

[63] *Ibid.*, 162.

[64] Hood, *Advance and Retreat*, 28.

[65] Freeman, *Lee's Lieutenants*, I, 620-632.

[66] McClellan's report, *Official Records*, Series I, XI, part 2, 19, 21. The event which had alarmed McClellan and which had made him "provide for this contingency" was Stuart's raid on his base at White House about the middle of June.

[67] Freeman, *R. E. Lee*, II, 165.

[68] Ewell's report, August 4, 1862, *Official Records*, Series I, XI, part 2, 607; Stuart's report, July 14, 1862, *ibid.*, 517; Jackson's report, February 20, 1863, *ibid.*, 556; Longstreet's report, July 29, 1862, *ibid.*, 759.

[69] James Longstreet, "The Seven Days, Including Frayser's Farm," *Battles and Leaders*, II, 400-401; Longstreet's report, *Official Records*, Series I, XI, part 2, 759.

[70] Huger's report, July 21, 1862, *ibid.*, 789.

[71] Henderson, *Stonewall Jackson*, 376-383.

[72] Jackson's report, February 20, 1863, *Official Records*, Series I, XI, part 2, 556-557.

[73] *Ibid.*

[74] Whiting's report, July ?, 1862, *ibid.*, 566.

[75] Lee's report, March 6, 1863, *ibid.*, 496.

[76] *Ibid.*, 496-497.

[77] See Fitz John Porter, "The Battle of Malvern Hill," *Battles and Leaders*, II, 417.

[78] Hood, *Advance and Retreat*, 30-31.

[79] Lee's report, March 6, 1863, *Official Records*, Series I, XI, part 2, 497.

[80] Livermore, *Numbers and Losses*, 86.

[81] Richmond *Whig*, July 5, 1862.

[82] McClellan to Lincoln, July 3, 1862, *Official Records*, Series I, XI, part 3, 291-292.

[83] Lee to George W. Randolph, July 7, 1862, *ibid.*, 635.

[84] Special Orders, July 8, 1862, *ibid.*, 636-637.

[85] Polley, *Hood's Texas Brigade*, 72.

[86] *Daily Richmond Enquirer,* July 17, 1862.

[87] Hood, *Advance and Retreat,* 30.

[88] Richmond *Whig,* July 12, 1862.

[89] *Official Records,* Series I, XI, part 3, 530.

[90] This is an estimate based on original strength less casualties. Exact strength cannot be determined. Lee estimated it would take 1,336 recruits to bring the brigade up to full strength. See Lee to Wigfall, July 26, 1862, *ibid.,* 655.

[91] *Ibid.*

[92] See Chesnut, *A Diary from Dixie,* 266.

[93] Lee to Preston, August 12, 1862. *Official Records,* Series I, XI, part 3, 672.

[94] July 11, 1862, *ibid.,* 639.

[95] Freeman, *Lee's Lieutenants,* I, 607, 613.

[96] *Ibid.,* 620-621; II, 64, 259.

CHAPTER V

[1] McClellan to Lincoln, July 11, 1862, *Official Records,* Series I, XI, part 3, 315.

[2] Livermore, *Numbers and Losses,* 86.

[3] Lincoln to McClellan, July 13, 1862, *Official Records,* Series I, XI, part 3, 319. Actually Lincoln greatly overestimated the numbers involved and the number of stragglers.

[4] Halleck's report, November 25, 1862, *ibid.,* XII, part 2, 5.

[5] Henderson, *Stonewall Jackson,* 397-398.

[6] *Ibid.,* 398-399.

[7] *Official Records,* Series I, XII, part 3, 473-474.

[8] General Orders No. 5, July 18, 1862, *ibid.,* part 2, 50.

[9] General Orders No. 7, July 10,   ?   , 1862, *ibid.,* 51.

[10] General Orders No. 11, July 23, 1862, *ibid.,* 52.

[11] G. J. Fiebeger, *Campaigns of the American Civil War* (West Point, 1914), 55.

[12] *Ibid.*

[13] *Ibid.,* 56.

[14] Halleck's report, November 25, 1862, *Official Records,* Series I, XII, part 2, 5; Henderson, *Stonewall Jackson,* 402.

[15] *Ibid.*

[16] Lee to Jackson, August 8, 1862, *ibid.,* part 3, 926.

[17] Henderson, *Stonewall Jackson,* 404.

[18] Lee to Jackson, August 12, 1862, *Official Records,* Series I, XII, part 2, 185.

[19] Lee to Longstreet, August 13, 1862, *ibid.*, XI, part 3, 675.

[20] Lee to Hood, August 13, 1862, *ibid.*, 928.

[21] James Longstreet, *From Manassas to Appomattox* (Philadelphia, 1896), 158. For approximate strength see *Official Records*, Series I, XIX, part 2, 621.

[22] Special Orders No. 231, October 27, 1862, *ibid.*, 684.

[23] Hood, *Advance and Retreat*, 31.

[24] *Battles and Leaders*, II, 499.

[25] Polley, *Hood's Texas Brigade*, 73.

[26] Freeman, *R. E. Lee*, II, 277.

[27] *Ibid.*, 280.

[28] Stuart's report, February 5, 1863, *Official Records*, Series I, XII, part 2, 726.

[29] Longstreet, *From Manassas to Appomattox*, 162.

[30] Pope's report, September 3, 1862, *Official Records*, Series I, XII, part 2, 13.

[31] Polley, *Hood's Texas Brigade*, 73-74.

[32] Hood's report, September 27, 1862, *Official Records*, Series I, XII, part 2, 605.

[33] Polley, *Hood's Texas Brigade*, 74.

[34] Stuart's report, February 5, 1862, *Official Records*, Series I, XII, part 2, 731.

[35] Major General W. B. Taliaferro, "Jackson's Raid Around Pope," *Battles and Leaders*, II, 501-511; Henderson, *Stonewall Jackson*, 433-437.

[36] Polley, *Hood's Texas Brigade*, 76.

[37] Hood, *Advance and Retreat*, 32.

[38] *Ibid.*, 33.

[39] Longstreet, *From Manassas to Appomattox*, 175.

[40] Freeman, *R. E. Lee*, II, 316.

[41] Hood, *Advance and Retreat*, 33.

[42] Longstreet, *From Manassas to Appomattox*, 180-181.

[43] Henderson, *Stonewall Jackson*, 450-452.

[44] Lee's report, June 8, 1863, *Official Records*, Series I, XII, part 2, 556. General Evans and his brigade of South Carolinians had joined the Army of Northern Virginia late in July. The brigade was now attached to Hood's division and, since Evans' commission was issued before Hood's, Evans was the senior brigadier and thus technically, to the annoyance of Hood and Law, commanded the division.

[45] Livermore, *Numbers and Losses*, 89.

[46] Major General John Pope, "The Second Battle of Bull Run," *Battles and Leaders*, II, 473.

[47] Livermore, *Numbers and Losses*, 88.

[48] Henderson, *Stonewall Jackson*, 460-463.

[49] Longstreet, *From Manassas to Appomattox*, 183-184.

[50] *Ibid.*

[51] Law's report, September 10, 1862, *Official Records*, Series I, XII, part 2, 623.

[52] Work's report, September 9, 1862, *ibid.*, 611-612.

[53] Carter's report, September 8, 1862, *ibid.*, 614-615.

[54] Wofford's report, September 4, 1862, *ibid.*, 608.

[55] Longstreet, *From Manassas to Appomattox*, 184.

[56] Freeman, *R. E. Lee*, II, 328.

[57] James Longstreet, "Our March Against Pope," *Battles and Leaders*, II, 520.

[58] Pope to Halleck, August 30, 1862, *Official Records*, Series I, XII, part 3, 741.

[59] *Ibid.*

[60] Longstreet, *From Manassas to Appomattox*, 186.

[61] Freeman, *R. E. Lee*, II, 331.

[62] Hood, *Advance and Retreat*, 36.

[63] T. C. DeLeon, *Four Years in Rebel Capitals* (New York, 1890), 242-243.

[64] Hood, *Advance and Retreat*, 36.

[65] Lee's report, June 8, 1863, *Official Records*, Series I, XII, part 2, 556.

[66] Law's report, September 10, 1862, *ibid.*, 623-624.

[67] Work's report, September 9, 1862, *ibid.*, 613-615.

[68] Wofford's report, September 9, 1862, *ibid.*, 609.

[69] *Ibid.;* Robertson's report, September 10, 1862, *ibid.*, 617; Gary's report, September 9, 1862, *ibid.*, 610.

[70] Syke's report, September 6, 1862, *ibid.*, 482.

[71] Hood, *Advance and Retreat*, 37.

[72] Lee's report, June 8, 1863, *Official Records*, Series I, XII, part 2, 557.

[73] Hood, *Advance and Retreat*, 36.

[74] Lee's report, June 8, 1863, *Official Records*, Series I, XII, part 2, 557.

[75] Hood, *Advance and Retreat*, 37.

[76] *Ibid.*

[77] Livermore, *Numbers and Losses*, 88-89.

[78] Hood's report, September 27, 1862, *Official Records*, Series I, XII, part 2, 606.

[79] Polley, *Hood's Texas Brigade*, 89.

[80] Livermore, *Numbers and Losses*, 88.

[81] Lee's report, *Official Records*, Series I, XII, part 2, 558.

[82] Hood, *Advance and Retreat*, 38-39. General Evans, a West Pointer, Class of '48, was unfortunate in achieving a good reputation at the begin-

ning of the war only to lose afterwards the confidence of his superior officers. He had fought bravely in the first battle of Bull Run, and in October 1861 the state of South Carolina presented him a medal in recognition of his services. After his service with Lee he served under Joseph E. Johnston. Subsequently Beauregard removed him from command as incompetent. See Eliot, *West Point in the Confederacy*, 331. Colonel Sorrel, Longstreet's chief of staff, says it was a problem what to do with Evans. See G. Moxley Sorrel, *Recollections of a Confederate Staff Officer* (New York, 1917), 94.

[83] *Ibid.*

[84] See Freeman, *Lee's Lieutenants*, I, Chap. XXXIX.

CHAPTER VI

[1] Livermore, *Numbers and Losses*, 92.

[2] Fiebeger, *Campaigns of the American Civil War*, 68.

[3] Longstreet's report, October 10, 1862. *Official Records*, Series I, XIX, part 1, 839; Lee's report, September 15, 1862, *ibid.*, 140.

[4] *Ibid.*

[5] Hood, *Advance and Retreat*, 39.

[6] Polley, *Hood's Texas Brigade*, 114.

[7] Hood, *Advance and Retreat*, 40. Lee's order dated September 14, 1862, releasing Hood from arrest is found in *Official Records*, Series I, XIX, part 2, 609. See also Freeman, *R. E. Lee*, II, 370.

[8] Polley, *Hood's Texas Brigade*, 114.

[9] Hill's report, undated (1862), *Official Records*, Series I, XIX, part 1, 1,020.

[10] Lieutenant General Daniel H. Hill, "The Battle of South Mountain, Or Boonsboro," *Battles and Leaders*, II, 566.

[11] Hill's report, undated (1862), *Official Records*, Series I, XIX, part 1, 1,020.

[12] Longstreet's report, October 10, 1862, *ibid.*, 839.

[13] Hill's report, undated (1862), *ibid.*, 1,021.

[14] Hill's reports are usually written in most unorthodox military language. For example in reporting the death of General Jesse L. Reno at South Mountain he says: "The Yankees on their side lost General Reno, a renegade Virginian, who was killed by a happy shot from the Twenty-Third North Carolina." *Ibid.*, 1,020.

[15] Hood's report, September 27, 1862, *ibid.*, 923.

[16] Longstreet's report, October 10, 1862, *ibid.*, 839.

[17] Jones's report, December 8, 1862, *ibid.*, 886.

[18] Hill's report, undated (1862), *ibid.*, 1,021.

[19] Hood, *Advance and Retreat*, 41.

[20] See Eckenrode and Conrad, *James Longstreet*, 121-123.

[21] Hill, "The Battle of South Mountain, Or Boonsboro," *Battles and Leaders*, II, 580.

[22] Hood, *Advance and Retreat*, 41.

[23] Hood's report, September 27, 1862, *Official Records*, Series I, XIX, part 1, 922-923.

[24] Frobel's report, October 1, 1862, *ibid.*, 925.

[25] Major General Jacob D. Cox, "The Battle of Antietam," *Battles and Leaders*, II, 630-631; Hood's report, *Official Records*, Series I, XIX, part 1, 923.

[26] Hooker's report, November 8, 1862, *ibid.*, 217.

[27] *Ibid.*, 218.

[28] Hood, *Advance and Retreat*, 42.

[29] Hood's report, *Official Records*, Series I, XIX, part 1, 922-923.

[30] Hooker's report, November 8, 1862, *ibid.*, 217.

[31] Jackson's report, April 23, 1863, *ibid.*, 956.

[32] Hooker's report, November 8, 1862, *ibid.*, 218.

[33] Jones's report, January 21, 1863, *ibid.*, 1,008.

[34] *Ibid.*

[35] Jackson's report, April 23, 1863, *ibid.*, 956.

[36] Gary's report, September 23, 1862, *ibid.*, 931.

[37] Work's report, September 23, 1862, *ibid.*, 932-933. Out of 226 men in the regiment 186 were killed or wounded. See *Ibid.*, 811.

[38] Ruff's report, September 23, 1862, *ibid.*, 930. Colonel W. T. Wofford of the 18th Georgia was now commanding the Texas brigade.

[39] Turner's report, September 24, 1862, *ibid.*, 936.

[40] Law's report, October 2, 1862, *ibid.*, 938.

[41] Freeman, *R. E. Lee*, II, 389.

[42] *Ibid.*, 390-391.

[43] Hood, *Advance and Retreat*, 44.

[44] Report of casualties, *Official Records*, Series I, XIX, part 1, 811.

[45] Freeman, *R. E. Lee*, II, 393.

[46] Hood's report, September 27, 1862, *Official Records*, Series I, XIX, part 1, 923.

[47] Franklin's report, October 7, 1862, *ibid.*, 377.

[48] Major General John G. Walker, "Sharpsburg," *Battles and Leaders*, II, 681.

[49] Hood, *Advance and Retreat*, 44.

[50] Livermore, *Numbers and Losses*, 92-93.

[51] Polley, *Hood's Texas Brigade*, 134. Polley is here giving Stephen D. Lee's account of the meeting between Lee and his generals. Lee's account

has been discounted by Freeman in *R. E. Lee,* II. 404n. So far as Hood is concerned the account seems probable since it is well known that he was apt to be emotionally unstrung over his losses.

[52] Polley, *Hood's Texas Brigade,* 136.

[53] Lee to Wigfall, September 21, 1862. Quoted in Polley, *Hood's Texas Brigade,* 135.

[54] Jackson to General Samuel Cooper, September 27, 1862. Quoted in Hood, *Advance and Retreat,* 45. Undoubtedly the original of this letter was in General Hood's papers when he died in New Orleans in 1879. None of the family knows what happened to his papers, but it is believed they were carelessly burned as trash.

[55] Lee to Secretary of War George W. Randolph, October 27, 1862, *Official Records,* Series I, XIX, part 2, 683.

[56] Special Orders, No. 234, November 6, 1862, *ibid.,* 699.

[57] Lee to Hood, November 14, 1862, *ibid.,* 718.

[58] *Ibid.,* 719.

[59] *Ibid.*

[60] *Ibid.*

[61] *Ibid.*

[62] For example, there were 2,003 barefoot men in Anderson's division; 2,071 in Pickett's; 1,475 in McLaws'. R. H. Chilton, Assistant Adjutant and Inspector General to War Department C.S.A., November 14, 1862, *Official Records,* Series I, XIX, part 2, 721. On this same day A. C. Myers, Quartermaster General, reported 8,153 pairs of shoes on their way to Lee. *Ibid.,* 718.

[63] Lee to Jefferson Davis, July 2, 1864. Quoted in Douglas Southall Freeman (ed.), *Lee's Dispatches* (New York, 1915), 283.

[64] Freeman, *R. E. Lee,* II, 415. See also Lee to Longstreet and Jackson, September 22, 1862, *Official Records,* Series I, XIX, part 2, 618-619.

[65] Special Orders No. 234, November 6, 1862, *ibid.,* 699.

[66] Freeman, *Lee's Lieutenants,* II, 269. Jones died January 15, 1863. See also Lee to George W. Randolph, Secretary of War, October 27, 1862, *Official Records,* Series I, XIX, part 2, 683.

[67] Field returns, October 10, 1862, *ibid.,* 660.

[68] *Ibid.*

[69] Field returns, November 10, 1862, *ibid.,* 713.

[70] Livermore, *Numbers and Losses,* 93.

[71] Lee to Longstreet and Jackson, September 22, 1862, *Official Records,* Series I, XIX, part 2, 618.

[72] Lee to Davis, September 23, 1862, *ibid.,* 622-623. Italics mine.

[73] Lee to George W. Randolph, Secretary of War, September 29, 1862, *ibid.,* 622.

[74] Lee to Jefferson Davis, October 2, 1862, *ibid.,* 643-644.

[75] Polley, *Hood's Texas Brigade,* 136.

[76] Lee to Longstreet, October 28, 1862, *Official Records,* Series I, XIX, part 2, 686.

[77] Lee to Jefferson Davis, September 28, 1862, *ibid.,* 633.

[78] R. H. Chilton, Assistant Adjutant and Inspector General, to General S. Cooper, Adjutant and Inspector General, November 14, 1862, *ibid.,* 721.

[79] Polley, *Hood's Texas Brigade,* 239.

[80] *Ibid.* The visitor was Colonel Garnet Wolseley, later Field Ma⏤ual Lord Wolseley. See Freeman, *R. E. Lee,* II, 420.

[81] George W. Randolph, Secretary of War, to Lee, November 14, 1862, *Official Records,* Series I, XIX, part 2, 717.

[82] See General Orders No. 127, November 14, 1862, *ibid.,* 722.

[83] *Battles and Leaders,* III, 143-145.

[84] Livermore, *Numbers and Losses,* 96.

[85] This is, of course, an oversimplification from the purely military point of view. For details of the plans see Burnside's report, November 13, 1865, *Official Records,* Series I, XXI, 83-84.

[86] Major General Darius H. Couch, "Sumner's Right Grand Division," *Battles and Leaders,* III, 107.

[87] Longstreet, *From Manassas to Appomattox,* 291.

[88] *Ibid.,* 297-299.

[89] Henderson, *Stonewall Jackson,* 571.

[90] Hood, *Advance and Retreat,* 49.

[91] Freeman, *R. E. Lee,* II, 434-435.

[92] Longstreet, *From Manassas to Appomattox,* 300-301.

[93] Freeman, *R. E. Lee,* II, 443.

[94] Lee's report, December 14, 1862, *Official Records,* Series I, XXI, 546.

[95] Longstreet, *From Manassas to Appomattox,* 306.

[96] Longstreet's report, December 20, 1862, *Official Records,* Series I, XXI, 569.

[97] *Ibid.,* 570; Hood, *Advance and Retreat,* 50.

[98] Freeman, *R. E. Lee,* II, 451.

[99] *Ibid.*

[100] James Longstreet, "The Battle of Fredericksburg," *Battles and Leaders,* III, 76-77.

[101] Jackson's report, January 31, 1863, *Official Records,* Series I, XXI, 632.

[102] Hood's report (not dated), 1862, *ibid.,* 622.

[103] Polley, *Hood's Texas Brigade,* 139.

[104] *Ibid.*

[105] Lafayette McLaws, "The Confederate Left at Fredericksburg," *Battles and Leaders,* III, 91.

[106] Darius N. Couch, "Sumner's Right Grand Division," *ibid.*, 113.

[107] *Ibid.*, 116.

[108] *Ibid.*, 117.

[109] Hood, *Advance and Retreat*, 50; Freeman, *R. E. Lee*, II, 466.

[110] Hood, *Advance and Retreat*, 50.

[111] Livermore, *Numbers and Losses*, 96.

CHAPTER VII

[1] Longstreet's report, December 20, 1862, *Official Records*, Series I, XXI, 570. Italics mine.

[2] Longstreet, *From Manassas to Appomattox*, 317.

[3] Longstreet, "The Battle of Fredericksburg," *Battles and Leaders*, III, 84.

[4] Freeman, *Lee's Lieutenants*, II, 257.

[5] Longstreet, *From Manassas to Appomattox*, 317.

[6] *From Manassas to Appomattox* was published in 1896. His article on Fredericksburg in *Battles and Leaders* was published in 1888. Hood died in 1879.

[7] Burnside's report, January 23, 1863, *Official Records*, Series I, XXI, 68-69.

[8] Freeman, *R. E. Lee*, II, 481.

[9] Polley, *Hood's Texas Brigade*, 139-140.

[10] Second Lieutenant Halsey Wigfall to his father and mother (General and Mrs. Lovis T. Wigfall), December ?, 1862. Quoted in Mrs. D. Giraud Wright, *A Southern Girl in '61* (New York, 1905), 116.

[11] *Ibid.*, 115.

[12] *Ibid.*, 114.

[13] Hood, *Advance and Retreat*, 51.

[14] *Ibid.*

[15] Freeman, *R. E. Lee*, II, 486.

[16] Eckenrode and Conrad, *James Longstreet*, 153.

[17] Polley, *Hood's Texas Brigade*, 140.

[18] *Ibid.*, 141.

[19] *Daily Richmond Enquirer*, January 8, 1863.

[20] *Daily Richmond Examiner*, February 6, 1863.

[21] Alfred Hoyt Bill, *The Beleaguered City* (New York, 1946), 162-164.

[22] T. C. DeLeon, *Four Years in Rebel Capitals* (New York, 1890), Chap. XVIII, *passim;* Rembert W. Patrick, *Jefferson Davis and His Cabinet* (Baton Rouge, 1944), Chap. X, *passim; Daily Richmond Enquirer*, January 17, 1863.

[23] Jones, *A Rebel War Clerk's Diary*, II, 173.

[24] Mrs. Burton N. Harrison, "Recollections, Grave and Gay," *Scribner's*, XLIX (May, 1911), 562.

[25] Virginia Clay-Clopton, *A Belle of the Fifties* (New York, 1905), 173-177; see also Patrick, *Jefferson Davis and His Cabinet*, 332.

[26] DeLeon, *Four Years in Rebel Capitals*, 154-155.

[27] Freeman, *R. E. Lee*, II, appendix (Pulitzer Prize edition).

[28] Dumas Malone (ed.), *Dictionary of American Biography*, 21 vols. (New York, 1928-1944), XV, 202-203.

[29] Preston to Beauregard, September 27, 1862, Preston file, Old Records Division, Adjutant General's Office.

[30] *Ibid.*

[31] *Dictionary of American Biography*, XV, 203. He was nominated a brigadier general on June 9, 1864. James A. Seddon to the Adjutant General, June 9, 1864, Old Records Division, Adjutant General's Office.

[32] *Dictionary of American Biography*, IV, 57-58. He was also made a brigadier general in 1864 and given line duty.

[33] Mrs. Burton Harrison, *Recollections, Grave and Gay* (New York, 1911), 148, 154.

[34] Chesnut, *A Diary from Dixie*, 69-76.

[35] Patrick, *Jefferson Davis and His Cabinet*, 333-336.

[36] Harrison, *Recollections, Grave and Gay*, Chapter VI, *passim*.

[37] *R. E. Lee* (Pulitzer Prize edition), II, appendix, photographic section.

[38] Chesnut, *A Diary from Dixie*, 230. Mrs. Chesnut places the formal introduction between August 10 and September 7, 1863. This date, however, is obviously incorrect. The time was about May 10-15.

[39] Polley, *Hood's Texas Brigade*, 141-142. See also Lee to Longstreet, March 19, 1863, in *Official Records*, Series I, XVIII, 927.

[40] Jones, *A Rebel War Clerk's Diary*, II, 277.

[41] Lee to Longstreet, February 18, 1863, *Official Records*, Series I, XVIII, 883-884.

[42] *Ibid.*, 884.

[43] Longstreet's proclamation, February 26, 1863, *ibid.*, 896.

[44] Eckenrode and Conrad, *James Longstreet*, 160.

[45] See Freeman, *Lee's Lieutenants*, II, 469-473.

[46] Neither did he make a full report after the campaign was over.

[47] Longstreet to Hill, March 1, 1863, *Official Records*, Series I, XVIII, 903.

[48] *Ibid.* See also Longstreet to Hill, March 18, 1863, *ibid.*, 920-921.

[49] Whiting to Longstreet, March 4, 1863, *ibid.*, 908.

[50] Whiting to Hill, March 6, 1863, *ibid.*, 911.

[51] Hill's report, March 16, 1863, *ibid.*, 188.

[52] Longstreet to James A. Seddon, Secretary of War, April 7, 1863, *ibid.*, 970.

[53] Whiting to Longstreet, March 25, 1863, *ibid.*, 943.

[54] Ransom to Longstreet, April 4, 1863, *ibid.*, 960.

[55] Vance to Seddon, March 21, 1863, *ibid.*, 934-935.

[56] Longstreet to Hill, April 7, 1863, *ibid.*, 969; Longstreet to Seddon, April 7, 1863, *ibid.*, 970.

[57] Samuel G. French, *Two Wars: An Autobiography of General Samuel G. French* (Nashville, 1901), 160. Cited hereafter as *Two Wars*.

[58] *Ibid.*

[59] Special Orders, April 14, 1863, *Official Records*, Series I, XVIII, 988. See also Freeman, *Lee's Lieutenants*, II, 483.

[60] French, *Two Wars*, 161-162. French wrote: "I told him [Longstreet] I did not intend to give up the command of my division to anyone. . . ."

[61] *Ibid.*, 159.

[62] *Ibid.*, 160.

[63] See map.

[64] Longstreet to Seddon, April 6, 1863, *Official Records*, Series I, XVIII, 910; Seddon to Longstreet, April 7, 1863, *ibid.*, 968.

[65] Stribling's report, May 6, 1863, *ibid.*, 336.

[66] Connally's report, April 22, 1863, *ibid.*, 338.

[67] Longstreet's endorsement of French's report of April 22, 1863, *ibid.*, 326.

[68] French's report, April 22, 1863, *ibid.*

[69] French, *Two Wars*, 163; Stribling's report, May 6, 1863, *Official Records*, Series I, XVIII, 336.

[70] Connally's report, April 22, 1863, *ibid.*, 338-339.

[71] French, *Two Wars*, 162.

[72] *Ibid.*, 163.

[73] *Ibid.*

[74] French's report, April 22, 1863, *Official Records*, Series I, XVIII, 324-326.

[75] Longstreet's endorsement of French's report, April 25, 1863, *ibid.*, 326-327.

[76] Freeman, *Lee's Lieutenants*, II, 488-489.

[77] Hood to Lee, April 29, 1863, *Official Records*, Series I, XI, part 2, 697. Italics mine.

[78] Garnett to Hill, April 15, 1863, *ibid.*, XVIII, 988.

[79] Seddon to Longstreet, April 18, 1863, *ibid.*, 999.

[80] Longstreet to Seddon, April 17, 1863, *ibid.*, 997.

[81] March 16, 1863, *ibid.*, 922.

[82] March 17, 1863, *ibid.*, 923.

[83] March 18, 1863, *ibid.*, 925.

[84] March 27, 1863, *ibid.*, 944.

[85] March 30, 1863, *ibid.*, 950.

[86] May 7, 1863, *ibid.*, 1,049.

[87] Henderson, *Stonewall Jackson*, 678, 693.

[88] Hood, *Advance and Retreat*, 52.

[89] *Ibid.*

[90] May 21, 1863, quoted in *ibid.*, 52-53.

[91] Longstreet to James A. Seddon, May 4, 1863, *Official Records*, Series I, XVIII, 1,042.

[92] Chesnut, *A Diary from Dixie*, 230. Dr. Darby, a native of South Carolina, entered the Confederate Army at the outbreak of the war as surgeon of Hampton's Legion. After the Legion became a part of Hood's brigade, Darby became chief surgeon of the brigade. When Hood assumed command of a division, Darby became chief surgeon of the division and a warm friendship developed between him and Hood. Dr. Darby married Mary Preston and after the war became one of South Carolina's famous doctors. A brief but factual summary of his career is found in the Charleston *News and Courier*, June 10, 1879.

[93] Chesnut, *A Diary from Dixie*, 288.

[94] *Ibid.*, 303.

[95] *Ibid.*, 288.

[96] From photographs.

[97] Chesnut, *A Diary from Dixie*, 230.

[98] *Ibid.*, 231-232.

CHAPTER VIII

[1] Livermore, *Numbers and Losses*, 98-99.

[2] Freeman, *R. E. Lee*, III, 18-20.

[3] See Lee to Davis, June 2, 1863, *Official Records*, Series I, XXV, part 2, 848-849; Lee to Seddon, June 2, 1863, *ibid.*, 849.

[4] Livermore, *Numbers and Losses*, 103, places the number at approximately 75,000. *Battles and Leaders*, III, 440, lists Lee's strength as "at least 70,000 men."

[5] Longstreet to Hood, May 31, 1863, *Official Records*, Series I, XXV, part 2, 844.

[6] Longstreet, *From Manassas to Appomattox*, 337.

[7] John Esten Cook, *Wearing of the Gray; Being Personal Portraits, Scenes and Adventures of the War* (New York, 1867), 317.

[8] Pleasanton's report, June 10, 1863, *Official Records*, Series I, XXVII, part 1, 904.

[9] Hooker to E. M. Stanton, June 14, 1863, *ibid.*, 38.

[10] James Longstreet, "Lee's Invasion of Pennsylvania," *Battles and Leaders*, III, 249.

[11] Longstreet, *From Manassas to Appomattox*, 340-341.

[12] *Ibid.*, 341.

[13] *Ibid.*, 342, 344.

[14] Polley, *Hood's Texas Brigade*, 146-147.

[15] Lee to Jefferson Davis, June 23, 1863, *Official Records*, Series I, XXVII, part 2, 298.

[16] Polley, *Hood's Texas Brigade*, 147.

[17] *Ibid.*, 148.

[18] General Henry J. Hunt, U.S.A., "The First Day at Gettysburg," *Battles and Leaders*, III, 269.

[19] Halleck to Hooker, June 27, 1863, *Official Records*, Series I, XXVII, part 1, 59; Hooker to Halleck, June 27, 1863, *ibid.*, 60.

[20] For a vivid account of the raid see John W. Thomason, Jr., *Jeb Stuart* (New York, 1934), Chap. XVIII.

[21] Freeman, *R. E. Lee*, III, 63.

[22] Hood, *Advance and Retreat*, 55.

[23] Longstreet, *From Manassas to Appomattox*, 347.

[24] Lee to President Davis, July 4, 1863, *Official Records*, Series I, XXVII, part 2, 398.

[25] Heth's report, September 13, 1863, *ibid.*, 637.

[26] Freeman, *R. E. Lee*, III, 68.

[27] Heth's report, September 13, 1863, *Official Records*, Series I, XXVII, part 2, 298.

[28] Rodes's report, undated (1863), *ibid.*, 552.

[29] Freeman, *R. E. Lee*, III, 70.

[30] Early's report, August 22, 1863, *Official Records*, Series I, XXVII, part 2, 468.

[31] *Ibid.*, 470.

[32] Lee's report, January 1864, *ibid.*, 318.

[33] James Longstreet, "Lee's Right Wing at Gettysburg," *Battles and Leaders*, III, 339.

[34] *Ibid.*, 340. This was written in 1884. In 1896 he reported that Lee struck the air with his closed fist and said: "If he is there tomorrow I will attack him." Longstreet, *From Manassas to Appomattox*, 358.

[35] Freeman, *R. E. Lee*, III, 76.

[36] Lee's report, January ?, 1864, *Official Records*, Series I, XXVII, part 2, 318.

[37] Polley, *Hood's Texas Brigade*, 154.

[38] Hood, *Advance and Retreat*, 57.

[39] Freeman, *R. E. Lee*, III, 92.

[40] Longstreet, *From Manassas to Appomattox*, 365.

[41] General E. M. Law, "The Struggle for Round Top," *Battles and Leaders*, III, 319.

[42] *Ibid.*, 320.

[43] Longstreet's report, July 27, 1863, *Official Records*, Series I, XXVII, part 2, 358.

[44] Law, "The Struggle for Round Top," *Battles and Leaders*, III, 319.

[45] *Ibid.*, 321-322.

[46] Hood to Longstreet, June 28, 1875. Quoted in Hood, *Advance and Retreat*, 58-59.

[47] Longstreet obviously recognized the merit of the plan submitted by Hood, for on the next day he planned to do the same thing himself. The plan, he said, would have been a slow process but not very difficult. See Longstreet's report, *Official Records*, Series I, XXVII, part 2, 359.

[48] See Hood, *Advance and Retreat*, 64.

[49] Polley, *Hood's Texas Brigade*, 169.

[50] General J. B. Robertson's report, July 17, 1863, *Official Records*, Series I, XXVII, part 2, 404-406.

[51] General Henry L. Benning's report, August 3, 1863, *ibid.*, 415.

[52] Polley, *Hood's Texas Brigade*, 172.

[53] *Ibid.*, 171.

[54] *Ibid.*, 175.

[55] Law, "The Struggle for Round Top," *Battles and Leaders*, III, 324.

[56] General J. B. Kershaw, "Kershaw's Brigade at Gettysburg," *ibid.*, 336.

[57] General Kershaw's report, October 1, 1863, *Official Records*, Series I, XXVII, part 2, 365-369.

[58] Early's report, August 22, 1863, *ibid.*, 470.

[59] Johnson's report, September 30, 1863, *ibid.*, 504.

[60] Related to the author by a member of the Hood family who prefers to remain anonymous.

[61] Freeman, *R. E. Lee*, III, 135.

[62] General Orders No. 74, July 4, 1863, *Official Records*, Series I, XXVII, part 2, 311.

[63] Livermore, *Numbers and Losses*, 103. 3,903 killed, 18,735 wounded, 5,425 missing.

[64] Hood, *Advance and Retreat*, 60.

[35] *Ibid.*

[66] Hampton to Wigfall, July 15, 1863. Quoted in Wright, *A Southern Girl in '61*, 142. The letter was written from Charlottesville. Mrs. Wright cited above was Louise "Louly" Wigfall.

[67] He took a suite for which the Confederate Treasury paid $10 per day. Voucher No. 21, Confederate States, in Old Records Division, Adjutant General's Office.

[68] Wright, *A Southern Girl in '61*, 230. Miss Wigfall was not quite eighteen in 1863.

[69] Polley, *Hood's Texas Brigade*, 197.

70 Freeman, *R. E. Lee*, III, 165.

71 *Official Records*, Series I, XXIX, part 2, 713; *ibid.*, XXVIII, part 1, 131.

72 Freeman, *Lee's Lieutenants*, III, 225.

73 Hood, *Advance and Retreat*, 55.

74 Freeman, *Lee's Lieutenants*, III, 226.

75 Ben Ames Williams (ed.), Mary Boykin Chesnut, *A Diary from Dixie* (New York, 1949), 341-342.

76 *Ibid.*

77 Polley, *Hood's Texas Brigade*, 198-199.

78 Colonel M. H. Wright to General W. W. Mackall, Chief of Staff, September 12, 1863, *Official Records*, Series I, XXX, part 4, 643.

79 *Id.* to Colonel George W. Brent, Assistant Adjutant General, September 15, 1863, *ibid.*, 652.

80 Brigadier General J. B. Kershaw's report, October 15, 1863, *ibid.*, part 2, 503.

81 Hood, *Advance and Retreat*, 61.

82 Polley, *Hood's Texas Brigade*, 199.

83 For an adequate account of the entire campaign see Stanley Horn, *The Army of Tennessee*, 222-274.

84 Livermore, *Numbers and Losses*, 106, gives the Confederate strength as 66,326 and Federal as 58,222.

85 Hood, *Advance and Retreat*, 61; Forrest's report, October 22, 1863, *Official Records*, Series I, XXX, part 2, 524.

86 Bragg's orders contemplated having all divisions in position on the eighteenth, but "the resistance offered by the enemy's cavalry and the difficulties arising from the bad and narrow country roads caused unexpected delays. . . ." See Bragg's report, December 28, 1863, *Official Records*, Series I, XXX, part 2, 31.

87 Horn, *The Army of Tennessee*, 258.

88 Robertson's report, October 4, 1863, *Official Records*, Series I, XXX, part 2, 510-511.

89 Benning's report, October 8, 1863, *ibid.*, 518.

90 Hood, *Advance and Retreat*, 62.

91 Longstreet arrived about 11:00 P.M. See Longstreet's report, October ?, 1863, *Official Records*, Series I, XXX, part 2, 287.

92 Hood, *Advance and Retreat*, 63.

93 Bragg's report, December 28, 1863, *Official Records*, Series I, XXX, part 2, 33.

94 Freeman Cleaves, *Rock of Chickamauga: The Life of General George H. Thomas* (Norman, 1949), 163.

95 D. H. Hill, "Chickamauga—The Great Battle of the West," *Battles and Leaders*, III, 648.

[96] *Ibid.,* 653.

[97] Bragg's report, December 28, 1863, *Official Records,* Series I, XXX, part 2, 33.

[98] Hill, "Chickamauga—The Great Battle of the West," *Battles and Leaders,* III, 650.

[99] Cleaves, *Rock of Chickamauga,* 167.

[100] *Ibid.,* 168.

[101] Gates P. Thruston, "The Crisis at Chickamauga," *Battles and Leaders,* III, 663-664.

[102] Robertson's report, October 4, 1863, *Official Records,* Series I, XXX, part 2, 512; Hood, *Advance and Retreat,* 64.

[103] Polley, *Hood's Texas Brigade,* 204.

CHAPTER IX

[1] Richmond *Enquirer,* September 23, 1863.

[2] Hood, *Advance and Retreat,* 64.

[3] *Ibid.,* 64. Hood describes the wound as being in "the upper third of the right leg." A relative says that he had barely enough stump left to accommodate an artificial limb.

[4] *Ibid.,* 65.

[5] Little was colonel of the 11th Georgia of G. T. Anderson's brigade, Hood's division. Armuchee Valley lies behind Taylor's Ridge almost due south of LaFayette in Chattooga County.

[6] Hood, *Advance and Retreat,* 65.

[7] Freeman, *Lee's Lieutenants,* III, 231.

[8] Longstreet to General S. Cooper, September 24, 1863, Old Records Division, Adjutant General's Office. Commission issued February 1864 to date from September 20, 1863.

[9] Wright, *A Southern Girl in '61,* 149.

[10] Hood, *Advance and Retreat,* 65.

[11] Williams (ed.), Chesnut, *A Diary from Dixie,* 326.

[12] *Ibid.,* 332.

[13] *Ibid.*

[14] Bill, *The Beleaguered City,* 188.

[15] Williams (ed.), Chesnut, *A Diary from Dixie,* 333.

[16] *Ibid.,* 336. Henry Persy Brewster was a native South Carolinian who moved to Texas in 1836. He served as secretary to Sam Houston and then as Attorney General in the Republic of Texas. In 1855 he moved to Washington and engaged in the practice of law. Under Postmaster General Reagan he helped organize the Confederate postal service. He was now (1863) ~ wisecracking, ubiquitous aide on Hood's staff. See Amelia W. Williams and Eugene C. Barker (eds.), *The Writings of Sam Houston,*

3 vols. (Austin, 1938), I, 428; Patrick, *Jefferson Davis and His Cabinet*, 276-277.

17 Williams (ed.), Chesnut, *A Diary from Dixie*, 336-337.

18 *Ibid.*, 339.

19 *Ibid.*, 337. Hood earned the nickname at West Point and it followed him to Richmond.

20 For Bragg's letter see *Official Records*, Series I, XXX, part 4, 705-706.

21 October 4, 1863, *ibid.*, part 2, 65-66.

22 October 6, 1863, *ibid.*, 67-68.

23 See John P. Dyer, *Fightin' Joe Wheeler* (Baton Rouge, 1941), 140-141.

24 Longstreet's report, March 25, 1864, *Official Records*, Series I, XXXI, part 1, 218.

25 See specifications in *ibid.*, 470.

26 Special Orders No. 290, November 8, 1863, *ibid.*, 467.

27 For specifications see *ibid.*, 503-504.

28 Williams (ed.), Chesnut, *A Diary from Dixie*, 341.

29 MSS. Journal of the House of Representatives, C. S. A., Fourth Session, 17th day, Monday, December 28, 1863. War Records Division, National Archives.

30 Longstreet's charges, March 22, 1864, *Official Records*, Series I, XXXI, part 1, 471.

31 Freeman, *Lee's Lieutenants*, III, 305.

32 Cooper to Longstreet, April 27, 1864, *Official Records*, Series I, XXXI, part 1, 473.

33 Jones, *A Rebel War Clerk's Diary*, II, 136.

34 Hood, *Advance and Retreat*, 67.

35 Harrison, *Recollections, Grave and Gay*, 173.

36 *Ibid.*, 172-179.

37 *Ibid.*, 172.

38 *Ibid.*, 174.

39 Williams (ed.), Chesnut, *A Diary from Dixie*, 367.

40 *Ibid.*, 334.

41 *Ibid.*, 372.

42 Bill, *The Beleaguered City*, 223.

43 *Ibid.*, 189. See also Harrison, *Recollections, Grave and Gay*, 177.

44 Williams (ed.), Chesnut, *A Diary from Dixie*, 382.

45 *Ibid.*, 370.

46 *Ibid.*

47 Sorrel, *Recollections of a Confederate Staff Officer*, 134.

48 Williams (ed.), Chesnut, *A Diary from Dixie*, 368.

49 Hood, *Advance and Retreat*, 67.

50 Williams (ed.), Chesnut, *A Diary from Dixie*, 349.

[51] *Ibid.*, 375.

[52] *Ibid.*, 380.

[53] *Ibid.*, 373.

[54] Hood, *Advance and Retreat*, 67. Italics mine.

[55] See Eckenrode and Conrad, *James Longstreet*, 267-268. Although Longstreet was not in the good graces of Davis his chief opposition was directed against Bragg.

[56] Confirmed February 4, 1864, to rank from September 20, 1863. See *Journal of the Confederate States Congress*, III, 675.

[57] Williams (ed.), Chesnut, *A Diary from Dixie*, 376.

[58] *Ibid.*

[59] *Ibid.*, 377.

[60] *Ibid.*, 367.

[61] Hood to Jefferson Davis, March 7, 1864, *Official Records*, Series I, XXXII, part 3, 607.

[62] Williams (ed.), Chesnut, *A Diary from Dixie*, 378-379.

[63] Fiebeger, *Campaigns of the American Civil War*, 246; Freeman, *R. E. Lee*, III, 259-268.

[64] Special Orders No. 33, February 9, 1864, *Official Records*, Series I, XXXII, part 2, 699.

[65] Johnston to General S. Cooper, February 18, 1864, *ibid.*, 763. See also Thomas Robson Hay, "The Davis-Hood-Johnston Controversy," *Mississippi Valley Historical Review*, XI (1924), 59.

[66] General Orders No. 26, February 25, 1864, *Official Records*, Series I, XXXII, part 2, 804.

[67] Williams (ed.), Chesnut, *A Diary from Dixie*, 367.

CHAPTER X

[1] Special Orders No. 57, February 28, 1864, *Official Records*, Series I, XXXII, part 2, 812.

[2] Malone (ed.), *Dictionary of American Biography*, XVII, 631.

[3] *Ibid.*, XVIII, 3. After the war he served as chancellor of the University of Mississippi.

[4] *Ibid.*, IX, 61-62. See also Horn, *The Army of Tennessee*, 250-257.

[5] Returns of the Army of Tennessee, March 10, 1864, *Official Records*, Series I, XXXII, part 3, 603, 869. In Hood's corps were 5 Alabama brigades, 2 Georgia, 1 Louisiana, 2 Mississippi, 1 Tennessee, 1 mixed Virginia and North Carolina.

[6] Johnston to Jefferson Davis, February 1, 1864, *ibid.*, part 2, 644-645.

[7] Hood, *Advance and Retreat*, 91. Wherever possible original sources are cited rather than the obviously biased memoirs of Johnston, Hood and Davis.

[8] *Ibid.,* 91-92.

[9] Hood to Davis, March 7, 1864, *Official Records,* Series I, XXXII, part 3, 606-607. Hood's statement that the army was in good condition is at variance with Johnston's report a month earlier. Undoubtedly Johnston had in the month of February made vast improvements. It is also possible that both generals exaggerated the strength and weakness of the army in order to carry their points.

[10] *Ibid.,* 607.

[11] *Ibid.,* 606, 607.

[12] Bragg to Johnston, March 12, 1864, *ibid.,* 614.

[13] *Ibid.,* 615.

[14] Johnston to Bragg, March 18, 1864, *ibid.,* 649.

[15] *Id.* to *id.,* March 22, 1864, *ibid.,* 666.

[16] Johnston to Longstreet, March 13, 1864, *ibid.,* 618.

[17] Hood to Bragg, April 13, 1864, *ibid.,* 781.

[18] Williams (ed.), Chesnut, *A Diary from Dixie,* 386. The "R. L." is apparently Rollins Lowndes.

[19] William T. Sherman, "The Grand Strategy of the Last Year of the War," *Battles and Leaders,* IV, 247.

[20] Not all these were present when the campaign began on May 4, but all were in action soon thereafter.

[21] William M. Polk, *Leonidas Polk, Bishop and General* (New York, 1894), II, 324-325; William T. Sherman, *Memoirs of General William T. Sherman* (New York, 1887), II, 34.

[22] Polk, *Leonidas Polk,* II, 329.

[23] *Ibid.,* 330.

[24] The Federal troops which Hood encountered were from the Third Brigade, Third Division, Hooker's Corps. They had strayed several miles from the Federal left and were out of their normal position. See report of Colonel James Wood, Jr., September 23, 1864, *Official Records,* Series I, XXXVIII, part 2, 437.

[25] Johnston, *Narrative,* 323; French, *Two Wars,* 381.

[26] Hood, *Advance and Retreat,* 106.

[27] Polk, *Leonidas Polk,* 355.

[28] Johnston, *Narrative,* 324.

[29] French, *Two Wars,* 370-382. Polk, of course, was killed before he had made any report of the affair.

[30] See Thomas R. Hay, "The Atlanta Campaign," *Georgia Historical Quarterly,* VII (1923), 24.

[31] Williams (ed.), Chesnut, *A Diary from Dixie,* 395.

[32] *Ibid.,* 410.

[33] Oliver O. Howard, "The Struggle for Atlanta," *Battles and Leaders,* IV, 306-307.

[34] Davis to Johnston, May 18, 1864, *Official Records*, Series I, XXXVIII, part 4, 725.

[35] Johnston to Davis, May 20, 1864, *ibid.*

[36] Elizabeth B. Custer, *Tenting on the Plains* (New York, 1887), 57-58. While Mrs. Custer was on a visit to New Orleans, Hood told her about his difficulties with his artificial limb during the campaign.

[37] Johnston, *Narrative*, 333-334; Hood, *Advance and Retreat*, 121-122.

[38] Lieutenant T. B. Makall, "Journal of Operations of the Army of Tennessee May 14, June 4," *Official Records*, Series I, XXXVIII, part 3, 991. Lieutenant Makall was aide-de-camp to Brigadier General W. W. Makall, Johnston's chief of staff.

[39] Johnston's report, October 20, 1864, *ibid.*, 616-617.

[40] Polk, *Leonidas Polk*, II, 372.

[41] Johnston's report, October 20, 1864, *Official Records*, Series I, XXXVIII, part 3, 617.

[42] Hooker's report, June 22, 1864, *ibid.*, part 2, 14-15.

[43] Johnston, *Narrative*, 340.

[44] Sherman, *Memoirs*, II, 58-59.

[45] See Horn, *The Army of Tennessee*, 335-337.

[46] Sherman, *Memoirs*, II, 62.

[47] Hood to division commanders, June 26, 1864, *Official Records*, Series I, XXXVIII, part 4, 795.

[48] Horn, *The Army of Tennessee*, 338.

[49] Sherman, *Memoirs*, II, 70.

[50] Johnston to Bragg, June 27, 1864, *Official Records*, Series I, XXXVIII, part 4, 796.

[51] Bragg to Johnston, June 27, 1864, *ibid.*

[52] Davis to Johnston, July 7, 1864, *ibid.*, part 5, 867.

[53] Johnston to Davis, July 8, 1864, *ibid.*, 868-869.

[54] William E. Dodd, *Jefferson Davis* (Philadelphia, 1907), 332.

[55] Judah P. Benjamin to Jefferson Davis, February 15, 1879, in Dunbar Rowland, "The Private and Official Papers of Jefferson Davis," *Harper's Magazine*, CXXIV (December, 1911), 102.

[56] Horn, *The Army of Tennessee*, 343.

[57] Johnston to Bragg, July 11, 1864, *Official Records*, Series I, XXXVIII, part 5, 876.

[58] Dodd, *Jefferson Davis*, 332.

[59] Lee to Davis, July 12, 1864, quoted in Freeman, *Lee's Dispatches*, 282-283.

[60] Johnston, *Narrative*, 348.

[61] Bragg to Davis, July 15, 1864, *Official Records*, Series I, XXXVIII, part 5, 881.

[62] *Ibid.*

[63] Hood to Bragg, July 14, 1864, *ibid.*, 879-880.

[64] Bragg to Davis, July 15, 1864, *ibid.*, XXXIX, part 2, 713.

[65] Davis to Johnston, July 16, 1864, *ibid.*, XXXVIII, part 5, 882.

[66] Johnston to Davis, July 16, 1864, *ibid.*, 883.

[67] Cooper to Johnston, July 17, 1864, *ibid.*, 885.

[68] Seddon to Hood, July 17, 1864, *ibid.*

[69] Williams (ed.), Chesnut, *A Diary from Dixie*, 420.

CHAPTER XI

[1] Hood, *Advance and Retreat*, 126.

[2] Stewart to Hood, August 7, 1872. Quoted in *ibid.*

[3] Hood to Davis, July 18, 1864, *Official Records*, Series I, XXXVIII, part 5, 888.

[4] Davis to Hood, Hardee and Stewart, July 18, 1864, *ibid.*

[5] Johnston to Cooper, July 18, 1864, *ibid.*

[6] Joseph E. Johnston, "Opposing Sherman's Advance to Atlanta," *Battles and Leaders*, IV, 275. In later years Hood accused Johnston of deserting him but the accusation does not seem well founded. See Hood, *Advance and Retreat*, 128.

[7] Hay, "The Atlanta Campaign," *Georgia Historical Quarterly*, VII, 29.

[8] Quoted in Horn, *The Army of Tennessee*, 345.

[9] Frank E. Vandiver (ed.), *The Civil War Diary of General Josiah Gorgas* (University of Alabama, 1947), 140.

[10] Hardee to Davis, August 6, 1864, *Official Records*, Series I, XXXVIII, part 5, 988.

[11] Williams (ed.), Chesnut, *A Diary from Dixie*, 430.

[12] See Hood, *Advance and Retreat*, 621.

[13] Jones, *A Rebel War Clerk's Diary*, II, 283.

[14] John B. Gordon, *Reminiscences of the Civil War* (New York, 1903), 127-128.

[15] See Freeman, *R. E. Lee*, II, 79.

[16] For evidence of this see Samual R. Watkins, *Co. "Aytch"—First Tennessee Regiment* (Nashville, 1882); Dr. W. J. Worsham, *The Old Nineteenth Tennessee* (Knoxville, 1902); W. J. McMurray, *History of the Twentieth Tennessee Regiment* (Nashville, 1904).

[17] Richmond *Enquirer*, July 19, 1864.

[18] Richmond *Whig*, July 19, 1864.

[19] Among those suspending judgment or taking a negative attitude were: the Atlanta *Appeal;* Augusta *Daily Constitutionalist;* Macon *Confederate;* Charlottesville *Chronicle.* See also Hay, "The Davis-Hood-Johnston Controversy of 1864," in *Mississippi Valley Historical Review*, XI, 71-72.

20 Sherman, *Memoirs*, II, 72.

21 O. O. Howard, "The Struggle for Atlanta," *Battles and Leaders*, IV, 313.

22 New York *Times*, October 31, 1864.

23 See Hood, *Advance and Retreat*, 157-158.

24 Sherman's report, September 15, 1864, *Official Records*, Series I, XXXVIII, part 1, 71.

25 *Ibid.*

26 Hood's report, February 15, 1865, *ibid.*, part 3, 630.

27 *Ibid.*

28 Hardee's report, April 5, 1865, *ibid.*, 698. This movement became a topic of heated controversy between Hood and Hardee after the war.

29 Sherman's report, September 15, 1864, *ibid.*, part 1, 71. See also Hay, "The Atlanta Campaign," *Georgia Historical Quarterly*, VII, 36.

30 Hardee's report, April 5, 1865, *Official Records*, Series I, XXXVIII, part 3, 698.

31 Stewart's report, January 12, 1865, *ibid.*, 871.

32 Livermore, *Numbers and Losses*, 122.

33 Sherman, *Memoirs*, II, 75.

34 Dyer, *Fightin' Joe Wheeler*, 177-178.

35 Irving A. Buck, *Cleburne and His Command* (New York, 1908), 272. Cleburne's official report of the battle is missing.

36 See Horn, *The Army of Tennessee*, 354.

37 Hood's report, February 15, 1864, *Official Records*, Series I, XXXVIII, part 3, 631.

38 Hay, "The Atlanta Campaign," *Georgia Historical Quarterly*, VII, 40.

39 Dodge's report, November 25, 1864, *Official Records*, Series I, XXXVIII, part 3, 384.

40 Sherman, *Memoirs*, II, 76.

41 W. H. Chamberlain, "Hood's Second Sortie at Atlanta," *Battles and Leaders*, IV, 326.

42 *Ibid.*

43 Livermore, *Numbers and Losses*, 122-123.

44 Blair's report, (?) 3, 1864, *Official Records*, Series I, XXXVIII, part 3, 545.

45 Quoted in Hood, *Advance and Retreat*, 190.

46 Hood's report, February 15, 1865, *Official Records*, Series I, XXXVIII, part 3, 631.

47 Howard, "The Struggle for Atlanta," *Battles and Leaders*, IV, 317.

48 *Official Register of the Officers and Cadets of the U. S. Military Academy, 1852, 1853, passim.*

49 Hood, *Advance and Retreat*, 182.

50 *Ibid.*

[51] Joel Chandler Harris and others, *Memoirs of Georgia*, 2 vols. (Atlanta, 1895), I, 1,031.

[52] Livermore, *Numbers and Losses*, 122-123.

[53] "Journal of Brig. Gen. Francis A. Shoup, C. S. Army, Chief of Staff, of Operations July 25-September 7," in *Official Records*, Series I, XXXVIII, part 3, 688-690. Cited hereafter as Shoup's Journal.

[54] New York *Times*, August 7, 1864. Quoting Mobile *News*.

[55] Sherman's report, September 15, 1864, *Official Records*, Series I, XXXVIII, part 1, 75.

[56] Dyer, *Fightin' Joe Wheeler*, 182, 185.

[57] *Ibid.*, 184.

[58] Sherman, *Memoirs*, II, 98.

[59] Howard, "The Struggle for Atlanta," *Battles and Leaders*, IV, 319.

[60] *Ibid.*

[61] See Jacob D. Cox, *Atlanta* (New York, 1909), 180-186.

[62] Confederate losses were 4,100 killed and wounded. Federal losses were 559 killed and wounded. See Livermore, *Numbers and Losses*, 124.

[63] See Hood, *Advance and Retreat*, 194-195.

[64] Dyer, *Fightin' Joe Wheeler*, 188-196.

[65] Shoup's Journal, *Official Records*, Series I, XXXVIII, part 3, 691.

[66] *Ibid.*, 693.

[67] Colonel T. B. Ray, "General Hardee and the Operations Around Atlanta," *Southern Historical Society Papers* (Richmond), VIII (August and September 1880), 341. Hood's ignorance of Sherman's movements is confirmed in a hitherto unknown letter to Bragg in which he states: "On the 29th I found that the enemy had detached *what I thought to be two or three of his smaller corps* in a movement against Jonesboro." Hood to General Braxton Bragg, September 4, 1864, Jefferson Davis Papers, Duke University Library.

[68] *Ibid.*, 342.

[69] Hood, *Advance and Retreat*, 205.

[70] Ray, "General Hardee and the Operations Around Atlanta," *Southern Historical Society Papers*, VIII, 344. Hood wrote Bragg: "I am officially informed that there is a tacit if not expressed determination among the men of this army, extending to officers as high, in some instances, as colonel, that they will not attack breastworks." Hood to General Braxton Bragg, September 4, 1864, Jefferson Davis Papers, Duke University Library.

[71] This Sherman strongly intimated. See Sherman, *Memoirs*, II, 106-107.

[72] *Ibid.*, 108.

[73] Shoup's Journal, *Official Records*, Series I, XXXVIII, part 3, 695.

[74] *Findings of the Court of Inquiry upon the Loss of Confederate Stores at Atlanta.* Special Orders No. 51, March 2, 1865, *ibid.*, 992.

CHAPTER XII

[1] Shoup's Journal, *Official Records,* Series I, XXXVIII, part 3, 695.

[2] Sherman, *Memoirs,* II, 110.

[3] *Ibid.,* 135.

[4] The figure is Hood's. See *Advance and Retreat,* 218.

[5] Hood to Davis, September 6, 1864, *Official Records,* Series I, XXXVIII, part 5, 1,023.

[6] Hood to Bragg, September 7, 1864, *ibid.,* 1,027.

[7] Hood, *Advance and Retreat,* 245.

[8] Davis to Hardee, September 5, 1864, *Official Records,* Series I, XXXVIII, part 5, 1,021.

[9] For an account of Brown's defection see Louise Biles Hill, *Joseph E. Brown and the Confederacy* (Chapel Hill, 1939), Chapter IX.

[10] Sherman to Hood, September 7, 1864, *Official Records,* Series I, XXXVIII, part 5, 822.

[11] For this correspondence see *ibid.,* XXXIX, part 2.

[12] See Horn, *The Army of Tennessee,* 371-372, for examples of the lack of confidence among Hood's subordinates.

[13] See Davis to Colonel T. B. Ray, February 29, 1880, in *Southern Historical Society Papers,* VIII, 377.

[14] See Robert McElroy, *Jefferson Davis: The Unreal and the Real,* 2 vols. (New York, 1937), II, 420. The date of September 28 given in this work obviously is incorrect.

[15] Hood, *Advance and Retreat,* 253.

[16] Quoted in Thomas Robson Hay, *Hood's Tennessee Campaign* (New York, 1929), 23. Just what Davis had reference to here is not clear, for Hood's Tennessee campaign as it later developed had not been planned at this time. Perhaps he had in mind the possibility that Hood could draw Sherman out of Georgia into Tennessee.

[17] Davis to Ray, February 29, 1880, quoted in *Southern Historical Society Papers,* VIII, 377.

[18] Hood, *Advance and Retreat,* 254.

[19] *Ibid.,* 254, 255.

[20] Hay in *Hood's Tennessee Campaign,* x, takes the position that Hood should have been removed.

[21] Augusta *Constitutionalist,* October 4, 1864.

[22] New York *Times,* October 8, 21, 1864.

[23] Sherman, *Memoirs,* II, 141.

[24] Williams (ed.), Chesnut, *A Diary from Dixie,* 439.

[25] *Ibid.,* 439-440.

26 Manly Wade Wellman, *Giant in Gray: A Biography of Wade Hampton of South Carolina* (New York, 1949), 161.

27 Williams (ed.), Chesnut, *A Diary from Dixie*, 436.

28 *Ibid.*, 437.

29 Wellman, *Giant in Gray*, 161, 181.

30 This is Hood's estimate. See *Advance and Retreat*, 325.

31 Shoup's Journal, *Official Records*, Series I, XXXIX, part 1, 806.

32 See French, *Two Wars*, 241-258.

33 New York *Times*, October 8, 1864.

34 Sherman, *Memoirs*, II, 146.

35 Cleave, *Rock of Chickamauga*, 242.

36 Hood, *Advance and Retreat*, 264.

37 Colonel Henry Stone, "Repelling Hood's Invasion of Tennessee," *Battles and Leaders*, IV, 441.

38 New York *Times*, November 16, 1864, quoting Cincinnati *Commercial*.

39 Hood, *Advance and Retreat*, 264.

40 Alfred Roman, *The Military Operations of General Beauregard*, 2 vols. (New York, 1884), II, 288. Cited hereafter as *Military Operations*.

41 Jefferson Davis, *The Rise and Fall of the Confederate Government*, 2 vols. (New York, 1881), II, 569.

42 See Hay, *Hood's Tennessee Campaign*, Chap. VII.

43 Roman, *Military Operations*, II, 300.

44 New York *Times*, November 16, 1864, quoting Cincinnati *Commercial*.

45 Roman, *Military Operations*, II, 293.

46 Stone, "Repelling Hood's Invasion of Tennessee," *Battles and Leaders*, IV, 441.

47 Hood, *Advance and Retreat*, 271-272; New York *Times*, November 29, 1864; Hood to Jefferson Davis, November 13, 1864, in *Official Records*, Series I, XXXIX, part 3, 913.

48 Hood to Beauregard, November 4, 1864, *ibid.*, 887-888.

49 Sherman, *Memoirs*, II, 178-179.

50 A clear and judicious account of the Spring Hill fiasco is given in Hay, *Hood's Tennessee Campaign*, 83-102. See also Horn, *The Army of Tennessee*, 384-393. General Cheatham's version is given in an article entitled "The Lost Opportunity at Spring Hill, Tenn.—General Cheatham's Reply to General Hood" in *Southern Historical Society Papers*, IX, 524-541. Cleburne was killed the next day at Franklin and made no report. Reports of other Confederate officers and the Union commanders are found in *Official Records*, Series I, XLV, part 1.

51 Cheatham apparently felt that Cleburne's command was badly demoralized. See J. P. Young, "Hood's Failure at Spring Hill," in *Confed-*

erate Veteran (Nashville), XVI (January, 1908), 32. See also John K. Shellenberger, "The Fighting at Spring Hill, Tenn.," *ibid.,* XXXVI, 102.

[52] Bate's report, January 25, 1865, *Official Records,* Series I, XLV, part 1, 742.

[53] Bate to Cheatham, November 29, 1881. *Southern Historical Society Papers,* IX, 541.

[54] Cheatham, "The Lost Opportunity at Spring Hill," *Southern Historical Society Papers,* IX, 527.

[55] Ex-Governor Isham G. Harris to Governor James D. Porter, May 20, 1877, quoted in *ibid.,* 532.

CHAPTER XIII

[1] Young, "Hood's Failure at Spring Hill," *Confederate Veteran,* XVI, 36.

[2] Horn, *The Army of Tennessee,* 394.

[3] W. O. Dodd, "Reminiscences of Hood's Tennessee Campaign," *Southern Historical Society Papers,* IX, 522.

[4] *Ibid.*

[5] A. J. Lewis, "Into Tennessee," New Orleans *Times-Democrat,* March 5, 1893.

[6] *Ibid.*

[7] Hood, *Advance and Retreat,* 297.

[8] Schofield's report, December 31, 1864, *Official Records,* Series I, XLV, part 1, 342.

[9] Stone, "Repelling Hood's Invasion of Tennessee," *Battles and Leaders,* IV, 449.

[10] Hood's report, February 15, 1865, *Official Records,* Series I, XLV, part 1, 653.

[11] Schofield's report, December 31, 1864, *ibid.,* 342.

[12] Robert Selph Henry, *"First With the Most" Forrest* (Indianapolis, 1944), 397.

[13] Quoted in Hay, *Hood's Tennessee Campaign,* 120.

[14] Buck, *Cleburne and His Command,* 327.

[15] Hood's report, February 15, 1865, *Official Records,* Series I, XLV, part 1, 653.

[16] Hood, *Advance and Retreat,* 293.

[17] Stone, "Repelling Hood's Invasion of Tennessee," *Battles and Leaders,* IV, 451.

[18] *Ibid.* See also Wagner's report, December 15, 1864, *Official Records,* Series I, XLV, part 1, 231.

[19] *Ibid.* See also Buck, *Cleburne and His Command,* 330-331.

[20] Hay, *Hood's Tennessee Campaign,* 124-125; Horn, *The Army of Tennessee,* 403.

21 Stewart's report, January 20, 1865, *Official Records,* Series I, XLV, part 1, 708.

22 Lytle, *Bedford Forrest and His Critter Company,* 359.

23 Livermore, *Numbers and Losses,* 131-132, gives the Confederate losses as 1,750 killed, 3,800 wounded, 702 missing—a total of 6,252. Federal losses are listed as: 189 killed, 1,033 wounded, 1,104 missing—a total of 2,326.

24 A. J. Lewis, "Into Tennessee," New Orleans *Times-Democrat,* March 5, 1893.

25 Beauregard to Davis, December 2, 1864, *Official Records,* Series I, XLV, part 2, 636.

26 Davis to Beauregard, December 4, 1864, *ibid.*

27 Smith to Buckner, January 3, 1865, *ibid.,* 765.

28 Buckner to Smith, January 5, 1865, *ibid.*

29 Smith to Beauregard, January 6, 1865, *ibid.,* 766.

30 French, *Two Wars,* 304.

31 Hood, *Advance and Retreat,* 299-300.

32 For a description of Thomas' work see Cleaves, *Rock of Chickamauga,* 249-259.

33 *Ibid.,* 254.

34 Thomas to Halleck, December 1, 1864, *Official Records,* Series I, XLV, part 2, 3.

35 Hood, *Advance and Retreat,* 302.

36 A. J. Lewis, "From Nashville to Tupelo," New Orleans *Times-Democrat,* March 12, 1893.

37 On December 7, Grant advised Secretary Stanton that if Thomas did not attack immediately he would recommend superseding him by Schofield. See *Official Records,* Series I, XLV, part 2, 84. From that time on Grant constantly urged speed and continued to threaten Thomas' removal.

38 Thomas' report, January 20, 1865, *ibid.,* part 1, 38.

39 The author has made no attempt to cite authority for each of the detailed movements of either army. Good accounts of the battle may found in Horn, *The Army of Tennessee,* 404-416; Hay, *Hood's Tennessee Campaign,* 148-170; Stone, "Repelling Hood's Invasion of Tennessee," *Battles and Leaders,* IV, 456-464. Reports of most of the officers on both sides may be found in *Official Records,* Series I, XLV, part 1.

40 Hood, *Advance and Retreat,* 303.

41 Lee's report, January 30, 1865, *Official Records,* Series I, XLV, part 1, 689.

42 Lewis, "From Nashville to Tupelo," New Orleans *Times-Democrat,* March 12, 1893.

43 *Ibid.*

44 Henry, *"First With the Most"* Forrest, 410.

[45] Hood's report, February 15, 1865, *Official Records*, Series I, XLV, part 1, 654.

[46] Lytle, *Bedford Forrest and His Critter Company*, 364-368.

[47] Lewis, "From Nashville to Tupelo," New Orleans *Times-Democrat*, March 12, 1893.

[48] *Ibid.*

[49] MS of unidentified poem written shortly after Nashville. In collection of miscellaneous Confederate papers owned by Miss Mary Elizabeth Singletary of New Orleans.

CHAPTER XIV

[1] Special Field Orders No. ?, January 23, 1865, *Official Records*, Series I, XLV, part 2, 805.

[2] Hood to Davis, January 23, 1865, *ibid.*, 804.

[3] Williams (ed.), Chesnut, *A Diary from Dixie*, 473-474.

[4] *Ibid.*, 474.

[5] *Ibid.*

[6] Richmond *Whig*, December 21, 1864; Richmond *Examiner*, January 5, 1865.

[7] Quoted in Eliot, *West Point in the Confederacy*, 106.

[8] Dodd, *Jefferson Davis*, 340.

[9] Journal of the House of Representatives, C.S.A. Second Congress, Second Session (February 9, 1865), 6. Original in Old Records Division, National Archives.

[10] *Ibid.*, January 20, 1865, 23-24.

[11] *Ibid.*, February 23, 1865, 640.

[12] The report is found in *Official Records*, Series I, XXXVIII, part 3, 628-636.

[13] Johnston to General Samuel Cooper, April 1, 1865, *ibid.*, part 3, 637.

[14] Hood to Cooper, April 5, 1865, *ibid.*

[15] Cooper to Hood, April 7, 1865, *ibid.*, 638.

[16] Williams (ed.), Chesnut, *A Diary from Dixie*, 510.

[17] Varina Jefferson Davis, *Jefferson Davis, Ex-President of the Confederate States of America: A Memoir by His Wife*, 2 vols. (New York, 1890), II, 611.

[18] Williams (ed.), Chesnut, *A Diary from Dixie*, 530.

[19] At the outbreak of the war the Lowndes family had converted its fortune into English securities. At the close of the war, therefore, the fortune was intact. John T. Darby, Arlington, Virginia, to the author, December 8, 1949.

[20] Major General J. W. Davidson to Major General James M. Warren, May 31, 1865, Old Records Division, Adjutant General's Office.

21 Dallas *Herald*, June 24, 1865; *ibid.*, July 22, 1865.

22 *Ibid.*, July 22, 1865.

23 New York *Herald*, October 15, 1865.

24 New York *Times*, November 2, 1865.

25 *Clark County Democrat*, September 7, 1879; New York *Herald*, January 20, 1865.

26 New York *Times*, May 28, 1866.

27 Announcement in New Orleans *Price Current*, February 21, 1866.

28 Dallas *Herald*, June 16, 1866.

29 Travelers in the city shortly after the war noted with amazement its rapid recovery and were astonished to see the countless river boats and ocean steamers moored along the wharves. See Giulio Adamoli, "New Orleans in 1867," *Louisiana Historical Quarterly* (Baton Rouge), VI (April 1923), 272.

30 *Gardner's New Orleans Directory for 1868* (New Orleans, 1868); E. Merton Coulter, *The South During Reconstruction, 1865-1877* (Baton Rouge, 1947), 196; Dyer, *Fightin' Joe Wheeler*, 244.

31 New Orleans *Times*, March 17, 1867.

32 *Ibid.*, March 19, 1867.

33 New York *Times*, June 8, 1890.

34 Hood counseled "submission with dignity," Dallas *Herald*, July 22, 1865; New York *Times*, October 15, 1866; *ibid.*, November 2, 1865.

35 Longstreet, *From Manassas to Appomattox*, 637.

36 Eckenrode and Conrad, *James Longstreet*, 372. According to the announcement in the New Orleans *Times* of April 18, 1869, the Life Association of America was a St. Louis corporation chartered in 1868. It is described as being "a purely mutual company, and the Louisiana department having the privilege of investing its premium receipts within the state, it combines the advantages of a home institution with the security of risks being extended over a large area of country."

37 Marriage records, Church of the Immaculate Conception, New Orleans, XVIII, 449. Hood was an Episcopalian. Mrs. Hood was Roman Catholic.

38 Miscellaneous family papers in possession of Miss Ida Hood of New Orleans. Cited hereafter as *Miscellaneous Papers*.

39 *Ibid.*

40 New Orleanians will recognize immediately the designation "uptown, lake side of Third and Camp." For others it may be explained that in New Orleans the directions east, west, north and south are rarely used. With the river on one side of the city and Lake Pontchartrain on the other it is much easier to designate a point as being on the lake side or river side of town, either toward uptown or downtown.

41 *Miscellaneous Papers*.

[42] Related to the author by Miss Julia Graves, Winchester, Kentucky.

[43] New Orleans *Picayune,* August 31, 1879.

[44] C. C. Buel, "The Degradation of a State," *Century Magazine* (New York), XLIII (February 1892), 618-632.

[45] *Ibid.,* 620.

[46] *Ibid.*

[47] Related to the author by a member of the Hood family who wishes to remain anonymous. John A. Morris, who married Mrs. Hood's half aunt, Cora Hennen, was one of the chief promoters of the lottery.

[48] A letter written by Mrs. Hennen from Niagara Falls to the Hood housekeeper, August 8, 1874, describes nearly every article of furniture in the house and gives directions for its care. Letter in *Miscellaneous Papers.*

[49] *Soard's New Orleans City Directory for 1880.*

[50] A member of the Hood family related to the author: "General Hood made most of his money in the cotton market and lost it the same way."

[51] New Orleans *Times,* August 31, 1879.

[52] *Ibid.,* July 24, 1879.

[53] New Orleans *Democrat,* September 9, 1879.

[54] "Bronze John" and not "Yellow Jack" was the name used most commonly in New Orleans for yellow fever.

[55] New Orleans *Times,* August 31, 1879.

[56] New Orleans *Democrat,* September 9, 1879.

[57] New Orleans *Times,* August 31, 1879.

[58] In all some $30,000 was raised. This was divided among the children as they reached twenty-one years of age. See *Confederate Veteran,* XX (March 1912), 123.

[59] The following is a record of the children:

Lydia, born May 29, 1869. Died August 30, 1879.

Annabel and Ethel, born June 27, 1870. Not adopted. Reared by Mr. and Mrs. John A. Morris, their uncle, in New Orleans.

John B. II, born September 19, 1871. Adopted by Mr. and Mrs. David M. Russell of Jonestown, Mississippi.

Duncan N., born January 25, 1873. Adopted by Miss Clementina Furness of New York.

Marion and Lillian, born March 6, 1874. Adopted by Mr. and Mrs. Thatcher McAdams of New York.

Odile and Ida, born October 19, 1876. Adopted by Mr. and Mrs. George Thomas McGehee, Woodville, Mississippi.

Oswald, born July 13, 1878. Adopted by Mr. and Mrs. Charles Harrison Harvey, Lexington, Kentucky.

Anna, born April 12, 1879. Adopted by Mrs. M. E. Joseph, Columbus, Georgia.

[60] New Orleans *Times,* September 2, 1879.

ACKNOWLEDGMENTS

THE author wishes to make acknowledgments to the following:

James H. French, Miss Julia Graves, Dr. George F. Doyle and Fanny Hood Hampton of Winchester, Kentucky, for hospitality and assistance.

Lieutenant Colonel W. J. Morton, librarian, and Dr. Sidney Forman, archivist, of the United States Military Academy Library, for making the author's visit there a pleasant and profitable one.

The New York Public Library; the library of the College of Physicians and Surgeons, Philadelphia; the Library of Congress, including the National Archives; the Howard-Tilton Memorial Library of Tulane University; the Duke University Library; the New Orleans Public Library; the Department of Archives of Louisiana State University.

Thomas R. Hay of Locust Valley, New York, generously supplied the author with considerable material and critically read the manuscript. Professors Wendell H. Stephenson and Fred Cole of Tulane University also read portions of the manuscript.

Ida R. Hood of New Orleans kindly gave the author access to such family papers as exist. Mrs. S. P. Walmsley of New Orleans also supplied certain information, as did John T. Darby of Arlington, Virginia.

The Tulane University Council on Research, composed of Dean Roger P. McCutcheon, chairman, and Professors Fred R. Cagle, Harold Cummins, Leon Hubert, John K. Mayer, Rose L. Mooney, Panos P. Morphos, Wendell H. Stephenson, Florence Sytz and Gerald E. Warren, made possible much of the research for this book through a grant in aid.

Frances T. Dyer, the author's wife, assisted with research and with details incident to publication.

The following publishers have given the author permission to quote:
Houghton Mifflin Co., Boston.
  Ben Ames Williams (ed.), Mary Boykin Chesnut, *A Diary from Dixie,* 1949.
Charles Scribner's Sons, New York.
  Douglas S. Freeman, *R. E. Lee, A Biography,* 4 vols., 1935
  Mrs. Burton Harrison, *Recollections, Grave and Gay,* 1911.

Alfred A. Knopf, Inc., New York.
  Alfred Hoyt Bill, *The Beleaguered City,* 1946.
University of Oklahoma Press, Norman.
  William R. Hogan, *The Texas Republic: A Social and Economic History,* 1946.
Longmans, Green & Co., Inc., New York.
  G. F. R. Henderson, *Stonewall Jackson and the American Civil War,* 1949.
Doubleday & Company, Inc., New York.
  Mrs. D. Giraud Wright, *A Southern Girl in '61,* 1905.
University of Alabama Press, Tuscaloosa.
  Frank Vandiver (ed.), *The Civil War Diary of General Josiah Gorgas,* 1947.
Appleton-Century-Crofts, Inc., New York.
  John M. Schofield, *Forty-Six Years in the Army,* 1897.
  Photograph from Isabelle D. Martin and Myrta Lockett Avary (eds.), Mary Boykin Chesnut, *A Diary from Dixie,* 1905.

NOTES ON SOURCES

THE author has found no appreciable amount of Hood correspondence other than that contained in the *Official Records*. General Hood had just completed his memoirs shortly before his death. He apparently had accumulated a considerable collection of letters and documents bearing on his career, but most of this was destroyed in the general house cleaning which followed his and Mrs. Hood's tragic deaths. Ida Richardson Hood of New Orleans has in her possession some of her father's family papers and photographs, but these are limited. James H. French of Winchester, Kentucky, has made an extensive collection of papers on the French family, and a few items in this collection shed light on the Hood side of the family. Records of Clark, Montgomery and Bath counties, Kentucky, were of considerable assistance. Scattered miscellaneous documents are found in the Roman Collection of the Manuscript Division, Library of Congress; in the Old Records Division of the Adjutant General's Office; and in the War Records Office of the National Archives. One important letter was located in the Jefferson Davis Correspondence in Duke University Library. However, *War of the Rebellion: A Compilation of the Official Records of the Union and Confederate Armies*, 130 vols. (Washington, 1880-1901), remains the only satisfying source of Hood correspondence.

Contemporary newspapers contain much interesting information, particularly on the Atlanta and Tennessee campaigns and on Hood's life in New Orleans. Newspapers most used were: New York *Times*, 1864-1866; New Orleans *Democrat*, 1879; New Orleans *Times*, 1878-1879; New Orleans *Price Current*, 1870-1878; Dallas *Herald*, 1865-1866; New York *Herald*, 1864; Richmond *Examiner*, 1863-1865; Richmond *Whig*, 1863-1865; Richmond *Enquirer*, 1864. The files of the *Confederate Veteran* and *Southern Historical Society Papers* are replete with anecdotal and other material on Hood's military career. The *Mississippi Valley Historical Review*, XI, and the *Georgia Historical Quarterly*, VII, contain valuable articles on the Atlanta campaign and on the Hood-Davis-Johnston controversy. Used also were the files of *Harper's Magazine* and *Century Magazine*.

In the classification of memoirs and diaries, two works are outstanding: John B. Hood, *Advance and Retreat: Personal Experiences in the United States and Confederate Armies* (privately printed by Hood Orphan Memorial Fund, New Orleans, 1880), and Ben Ames Williams (ed.), Mary Boykin Chesnut, *A Diary from Dixie* (Houghton Mifflin, Boston, 1949). Hood's own book, written largely as a defense of himself, is biased and at times inaccurate, but it also contains valuable material. The sprightly *Diary from Dixie* is invaluable in studying Hood's love affair with Sally Preston.

Other memoirs and diaries include:

Custer, Elizabeth B. *Tenting on the Plains.* C. L. Webster, New York, 1887.

Cooke, John Esten. *Wearing of the Gray: Being Personal Portraits, Scenes and Adventures of the War.* E. B. Treat, New York, 1867.

Davis, Jefferson. *The Rise and Fall of the Confederate Government.* 2 vols. Appleton, New York, 1881.

Davis, Varina. *Jefferson Davis, Ex-President of the Confederate States of America.* New York, 1890.

De Leon, T. C. *Four Years in Rebel Capitals.* New York, 1890.

French, Samuel G. *Two Wars: An Autobiography of General Samuel G. French.* Nashville, 1901.

Gordon, John B. *Reminiscences of the Civil War.* Scribner's, New York, 1903.

Harrison, Mrs. Burton. *Recollections, Grave and Gay.* Scribner's, New York, 1911.

Longstreet, James. *From Manassas to Appomattox.* Lippincott, Philadelphia, 1896.

Martin, Isabelle D. and Myrta L. Avary (eds.). Mary Boykin Chesnut. *A Diary from Dixie.* Appleton, New York, 1905.

Schofield, John M. *Forty-Six Years in the Army.* Century, New York, 1897.

Sherman, W. T. *Personal Memoirs.* 2 vols. Appleton, New York, 1887.

Sorrel, G. Moxley. *Recollections of a Confederate Staff Officer.* Neale, New York, 1905.

Swiggett, Howard (ed.). J. B. Jones. *A Rebel War Clerk's Diary at the Confederate States Capitol.* Old Hickory Bookshop, New York, 1935.

Vandiver, Frank (ed.). *The Civil War Diary of General Josiah Gorgas.* University of Alabama Press, 1947.

Wright, Mrs. Giraud. *A Southern Girl in '61.* Doubleday, New York, 1905.

Williams, R. H. *With the Border Ruffians.* Dutton, New York, 1907.

In the field of biography, Douglas Southall Freeman's monumental *R. E. Lee, A Biography,* 4 vols. (Scribner's, New York, 1935) and *Lee's Lieutenants, A Study in Command,* 3 vols. (Scribner's, New York, 1942) are, of course, necessary for anyone who writes about the Civil War. The outstanding work on one phase of Hood's career is Thomas R. Hay, *Hood's Tennessee Campaign* (Neale, New York, 1929).

Other biographies used include:

Buck, Irving A. *Cleburne and His Command.* Neale, New York, 1908.

Cleaves, Freeman. *Rock of Chickamauga: The Life of General George H. Thomas.* University of Oklahoma Press, 1949.

Dodd, William E. *Jefferson Davis.* Jacobs, New York, 1907.

Dyer, John P. *Fightin' Joe Wheeler.* Louisiana State University Press, 1941.

Eckenrode, H. J., and Conrad Bryan. *James Longstreet, Lee's War Horse.* University of North Carolina Press, 1936.

Eliot, Ellsworth. *West Point in the Confederacy.* Baker, New York, 1941.

Henry, Robert S. *"First with the Most" Forrest.* Bobbs-Merrill, Indianapolis, 1944.

Henderson, G. F. R. *Stonewall Jackson and the American Civil War.* Longmans, Green, New York, 1949.

Lytle, Andrew Nelson. *Bedford Forrest and His Critter Company.* Minton Balch, New York, 1931.

McElroy, Robert. *Jefferson Davis: The Unreal and the Real.* 2 vols. Harper, New York, 1937.

Polk, William M. *Leonidas Polk, Bishop and General.* Longmans, Green, New York, 1893.

Patrick, Rembert W. *Jefferson Davis and His Cabinet.* Louisiana State University Press, 1944.

Rister, Carl Coke. *Robert E. Lee in Texas.* University of Oklahoma Press, 1946.

Roman, Alfred. *The Military Operations of General Beauregard.* 2 vols. Harper, New York, 1884.

Thomason, John W. *Jeb Stuart.* Scribner's, New York, 1934.

Wellman, Manly W. *Giant in Gray: A Biography of Wade Hampton of South Carolina.* Scribner's, New York, 1949.

There are many good general histories of the Civil War. Regimental histories are also numerous. Perhaps the beginning point for the historian of the period is Robert Underwood Johnson and Clarence C. Buel (eds.), *Battles and Leaders of the Civil War,* 4 vols. (Century, New York, 1887). Stanley F. Horn, *The Army of Tennessee* (Bobbs-Merrill, Indianapolis, 1941) is an excellent account of operations in the West. J. B. Polley, *Hood's Texas Brigade* (Neale, New York, 1910) is not always completely accurate and reliable, but it is a colorful account of the famous Texas brigade.

Other works of a general nature are:

Bill, Alfred Hoyt. *The Beleaguered City.* Knopf, New York, 1946.

Clark, Thomas D. *The Kentucky.* Farrar and Rinehart, New York, 1942.

Coulter, E. Merton. *The Confederate States of America, 1861-1865.* Louisiana State University Press, 1950.

Cox, Jacob D. *Atlanta.* Scribner's, New York, 1909.

Eisenschiml, Otto, and Ralph Newman. *The American Iliad.* Bobbs-Merrill, Indianapolis, 1947.

Fiebeger, G. J. *Campaigns of the American Civil War.* U. S. Military Academy Printing Office, 1914.

Hogan, William R. *The Texas Republic.* University of Oklahoma Press, 1946.

Livermore, Thomas L. *Numbers and Losses in the Civil War.* Houghton Mifflin, Boston, 1901.

McMurray, W. J. *History of the Twentieth Tennessee Regiment.* Privately printed, Nashville, 1904.

Richardson, Rupert N. *Texas: the Lone Star State.* Prentice Hall, New York, 1943.

Watkins, Samuel R. *Co. "Aytch," First Tennessee Regiment,* Cumberland Presbyterian Publishing House, Nashville, 1882.

Wiley, Bell Irvin. *The Life of Johnny Reb.* Bobbs-Merrill, Indianapolis, 1943.

Worsham, W. J. *The Old Nineteenth Tennessee.* Press of Paragon Printing Company, Knoxville, 1902.